RENDERING IN MIXED MEDIA

by Joseph Ungar

Watson-Guptill Publications
Whitney Library of Design/New York

First published 1985 in New York by Watson-Guptill Publications,
a division of Billboard Publications, Inc.,
1515 Broadway, New York, N.Y. 10036

Library of Congress Cataloging in Publication Data
Ungar, Joseph, 1948—
Rendering in mixed media.
1. Design, Industrial—Technique. 2. Artists' materials. 3. Artists' tools. I. Title.
TS171.4.U54 1985 745.2 85-11498
ISBN 0-8230-7426-9
ISBN 0-8230-7427-7 (pbk.)

Distributed in the United Kingdom by Phaidon Press Ltd.,
Littlegate House, St. Ebbe's St., Oxford

Manufactured in Singapore

First Printing, 1985

5 6 7 8 9 10/95 94 93 92 91

Original designs and photographs by Joseph Ungar
Edited by Stephen Kliment and Barbara Klinger
Designed by Areta Buk
Graphic production by Hector Campbell
Text set in 9 pt Helvetica regular

ACKNOWLEDGMENTS

The task of creating a manuscript for a book such as this has proven to be a considerable challenge. I owe a great deal of thanks to the Industrial Design Society of America for first whispering to me the suggestion of writing such a book. With equal gratitude, I thank Stephen Kliment, Susan Davis, and Barbara Klinger of Watson-Guptill Publications for doing such a fine job of editing.

My greatest appreciation, however, is towards Rebecca and Jocelyn, to whom this book is dedicated. Their unfailing support and inspiration made the project both enjoyable and worthwhile.

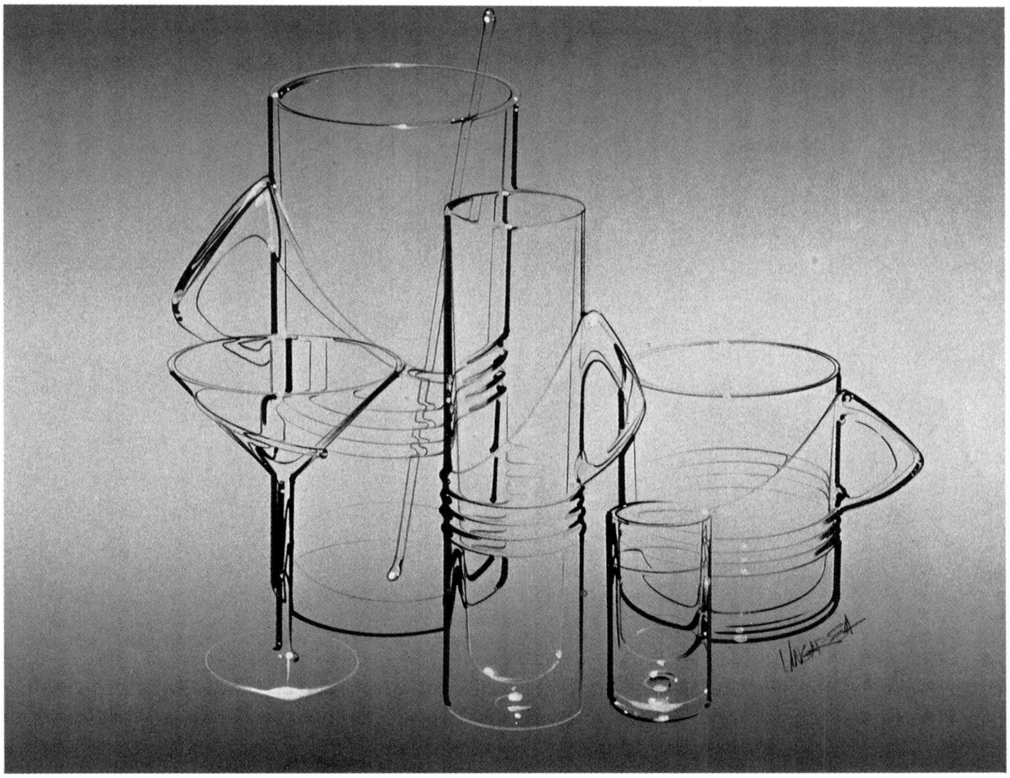

Glassware
Media: white gouache, black pen, black Prismacolor pencil, pastel, on Pantone graduated paper; 50 × 70 cm.

FOREWORD

A designer's mind is an incredible device that will process information, manipulate data and trends, formulate directions, and develop conceptual images of problem analyses and solutions. This internal imagery (our holographic pictorial plane) is one of our greatest assets.

Unfortunately, our ability to convey these images can fall very short of our own expectations. Too often our efforts at pictorial analysis lack the meaning and sensitivity we perceive internally. Somehow the renderings don't show the excitement and creativity of our concepts; the drawings may appear awkward, unclear, even visually confusing and overworked. It seems that our own creative drawing skills are not supporting our most basic design need—communication.

As a practicing industrial designer in both consultant and corporate fields for nineteen years, I realize the importance of visual communication and thought development. I have seen frustrated designers trying to find that one *technique to support their needs. Unfortunately, relying on one technique may limit their real capability because of actual drawing time, application possibilities and conceptual freedom.*

Joseph Ungar's work is the first publication to address the need for creative and visually exciting concept-presentation techniques. It is important both to the practicing designer and to design management. It challenges us to use new methods of rapid, suggestive and exciting visualization and explores techniques that offer design freedom while enhancing the involvement of our design audience. This book is a new design-communication text which will offer many of us control over design skills we've lost—or have never mastered.

LeRoy J. LaCelle, IDSA
Industrial Design Manager
Advanced Technology Laboratories
Western District Vice President, ISDA

PREFACE

Within the world of the professional designer, communication techniques often vary as much as the personalities involved. It is a definite challenge to attempt to embrace the multitudinous possibilities and elucidate those techniques that are most effective. In working toward this goal, I had the rare opportunity to create many of the illustrations without client specifications and hence to express myself as an industrial designer in the origination of new product designs and scenarios. Set in the present and near future, all of my designs reflect either current technology or ongoing technological research. I chose to do the book this way so that it might serve a twofold purpose: first, one of instruction and second, one of inspiration to students as well as professionals.

As technology advances and reshapes our lives, techniques for expressing ideas will change accordingly. Designers must be able to keep up with such developments. I hope that this book will inspire you to constantly re-evaluate your techniques, to experiment with and adapt to new avenues of expression, and above all to continue to change and grow as design professionals.

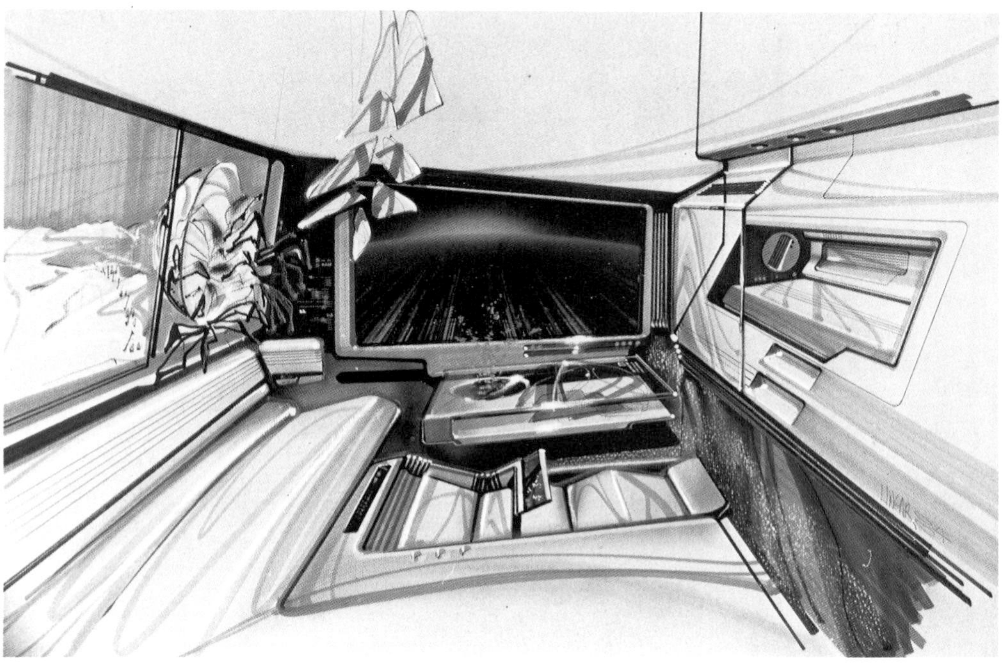

Ski habitat
Media: dry marker, photo montage, gouache, Prismacolor pencil, pastel; 50 × 70 cm.

CONTENTS

INTRODUCTION

Few design disciplines rely upon graphic visualization skills as heavily as industrial design does. Whether images are generated from the controls of a computer work station or are deftly rendered by hand with various media on paper or board, the industrial designer is in the business of communication.

His or her solution-oriented concepts are critical at the inception of a design program and must be developed from there, until the given program parameters are satisfactorily resolved. The ability to express oneself visually with little or no effort is paramount to the designer. Two- and three-dimensional expression is the very essence of the design process.

The design process is, of course, shared across many disciplines, and the need for fast, effective visualization techniques is a common one. Efficient, communicative rendering skills should be the designer's basic tools, to be wielded with pride and professional integrity. Unfortunately, there are far too many talented students and professionals who leave this aspect of their training to an uncertain future date. Perhaps they hope their skills will evolve "on the boards" in the professional environment. This idea assumes, however, that the talented designer will be surrounded and tutored by fellow professionals.

Such a situation would be enviable, but unfortunately, statistics work against this assumption. Design positions are traditionally ultracompetitive, and high caliber professional tools are assumed to be brought into the work environment; they are seldom learned after the fact.

This book bridges the gap between school and professional experience and focuses on techniques for rapid visualization, the one specialized skill that seems most elusive to those not familiar with the principles involved.

Although this book zeroes in on visualization techniques most often used in industrial-design areas, such as product or transportation development, the basic elements and principles are directly applicable to all design fields. The distinctive set of skills required for effective visualization can be readily learned and will bring excitement to what has in the past been a rather dry approach to concept representations.

In the end, it is the drawing content, the functional problem-solving, that must pan out. Corporations and consultant agencies hire designers, not artists. The designer's most valuable business asset is the ability to communicate when called upon at each and every point in the design process. Most often this is as a liaison between marketing and engineering and usually as a member of a design team, which means that several designers show their work simultaneously. These presentations must show strength, graphic confidence, and a consistency of professionalism by the design team. This book will teach you the fast, multi-media techniques you need to be successful.

Optical disc player
Media: lacquer/water, pastel, dry marker; 50 × 70 cm.

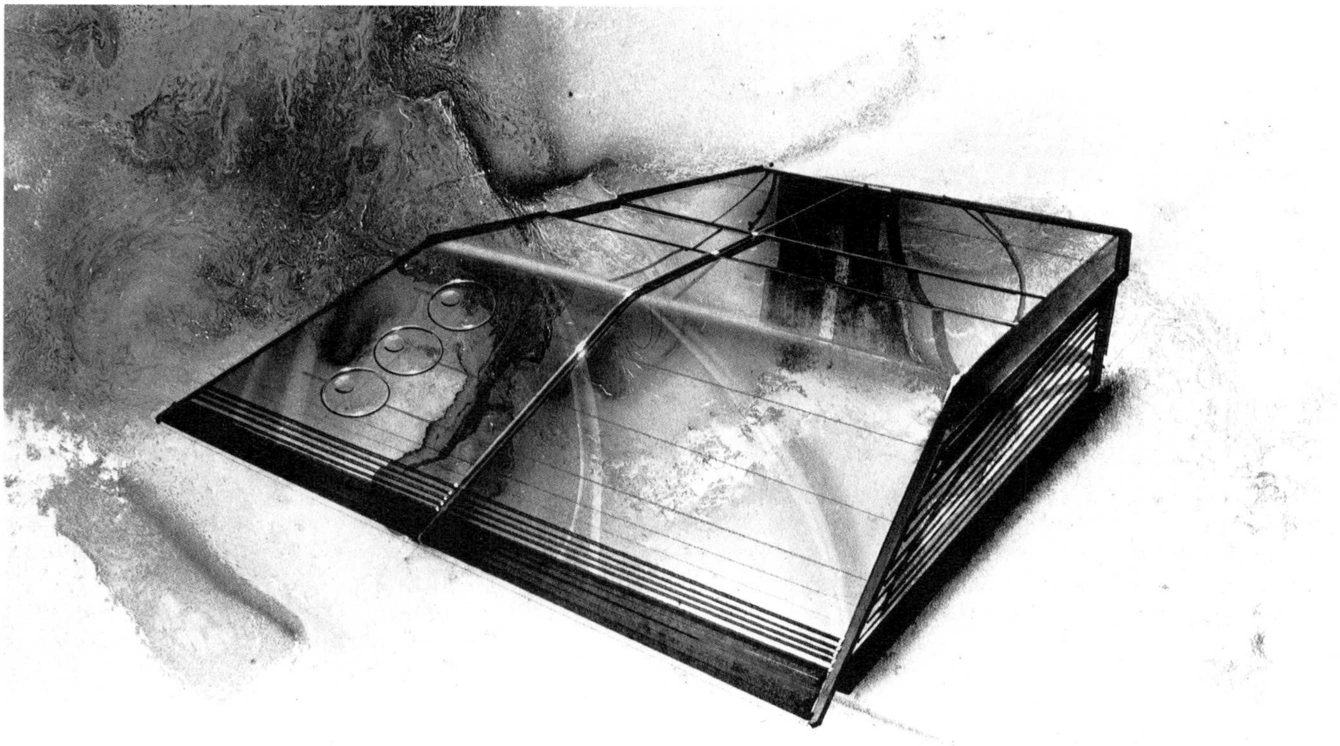

Deep-space habitat
Media: dry marker, photo montage, gouache, pastel, Prismacolor pencil, fluorescent paint; 50 × 70 cm.

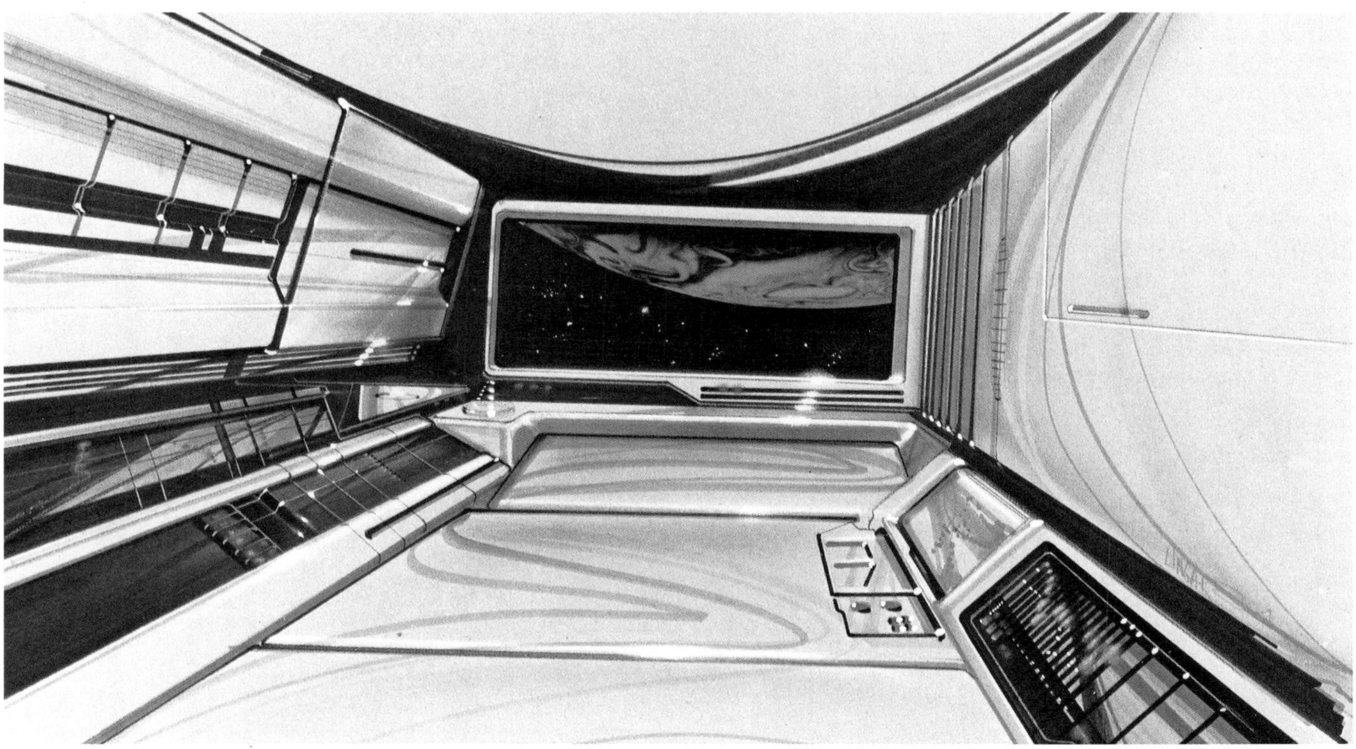

1 MATERIALS: A SURVIVAL KIT

In today's world, the practicing industrial designer, or for that matter any designer, faces a barrage of products in the marketplace. This has not always been the case. As little as ten years ago, when I was an undergraduate, there was but a mere fraction of the design supplies that are pleading for attention today. Traditional design media were charcoals and pastels, or colored pencil and gouache. Dry markers were new, and few people knew how to really use them. Varieties of paper were just as limited, and I usually had to settle for tracing papers that really were not designed for multi-media application. There were few, if any, marker sprays, designer pens, or color concentrates such as we see today.

The well-stocked inventory of today's large art store can be overwhelming, to the point of putting a freshman design student into a state of "techno-shock," a temporary panic condition induced by the sudden introduction to a multitude of high-technology art supplies with their accompanying price tags! How does one make sense of it? How can anyone effectively choose among fourteen kinds of erasers—or among twenty kinds of dry markers, each of which promises to provide shades of color more subtle than the next one?

I found that the best answer was the most obvious and, at the same time, the most evasive. After fifteen years of constantly buying new equipment to support my "design habit," it dawned on me. Why don't I learn how to draw? That is, to communicate the essence of an idea with the least amount of reliance on equipment or design tools.

The correct materials are essential, but these materials really amount to a few, well-selected items. In this book, the message is not *the medium, but rather the fundamental strength of your drawing skills.*

This chapter outlines the essential tools for a professional designer. I have selected both generic and popular-brand items based on my own experience and on the collective observations of other professional colleagues. I urge you to experiment, however, and to try original adaptations of new design tools as they are introduced in the marketplace.

The Essential Ingredients

As a design professional, you will constantly be reminded by advertising of the vast array of design tools available for purchase. Experience will show you that the tools of expression are almost incidental compared with the simplistic power of expressive lines drawn upon the page. Some ingredients, however, can be a catalyst to a very free form of expression, offering creative options to your concept renderings. These materials will be discussed in convenient groupings, such as dry mediums and wet mediums.

I suggest a limited but well-chosen arsenal of design tools. You should try to get acquainted as soon as possible with all the materials discussed here. If you are limited by a budget, I recommend purchasing the following materials:

1. A pad of tracing vellum
2. A pad of dry-marker paper such as Letraset, Strathmore, or Bienfang
3. A box of Prismacolor colored pencils
4. A box of pastel chalks such as Grumbacher Golden Palette or Nu-Pastel
5. A box of Webril Handi-Pads or similar lintless wipes
6. A set of Pantone warm-gray dry markers, #1 through #10
7. A few fine-point pens with smear-proof black ink, such as a Sharpie by Sanford
8. A tube of Winsor & Newton white gouache or a bottle of white Liquid Paper (typewriter correction-fluid) for highlights
9. A few small, sable watercolor brushes
10. A roll of Scotch removable, transparent tape (3M tape #281)

This is a bare minimum, but even these materials can be quite effective as you will see.

Confronted by a vast array of art supplies, the discerning professional designer must find a balance between the product's expense and its proven effectiveness, while at the same time being on the alert for helpful new products.

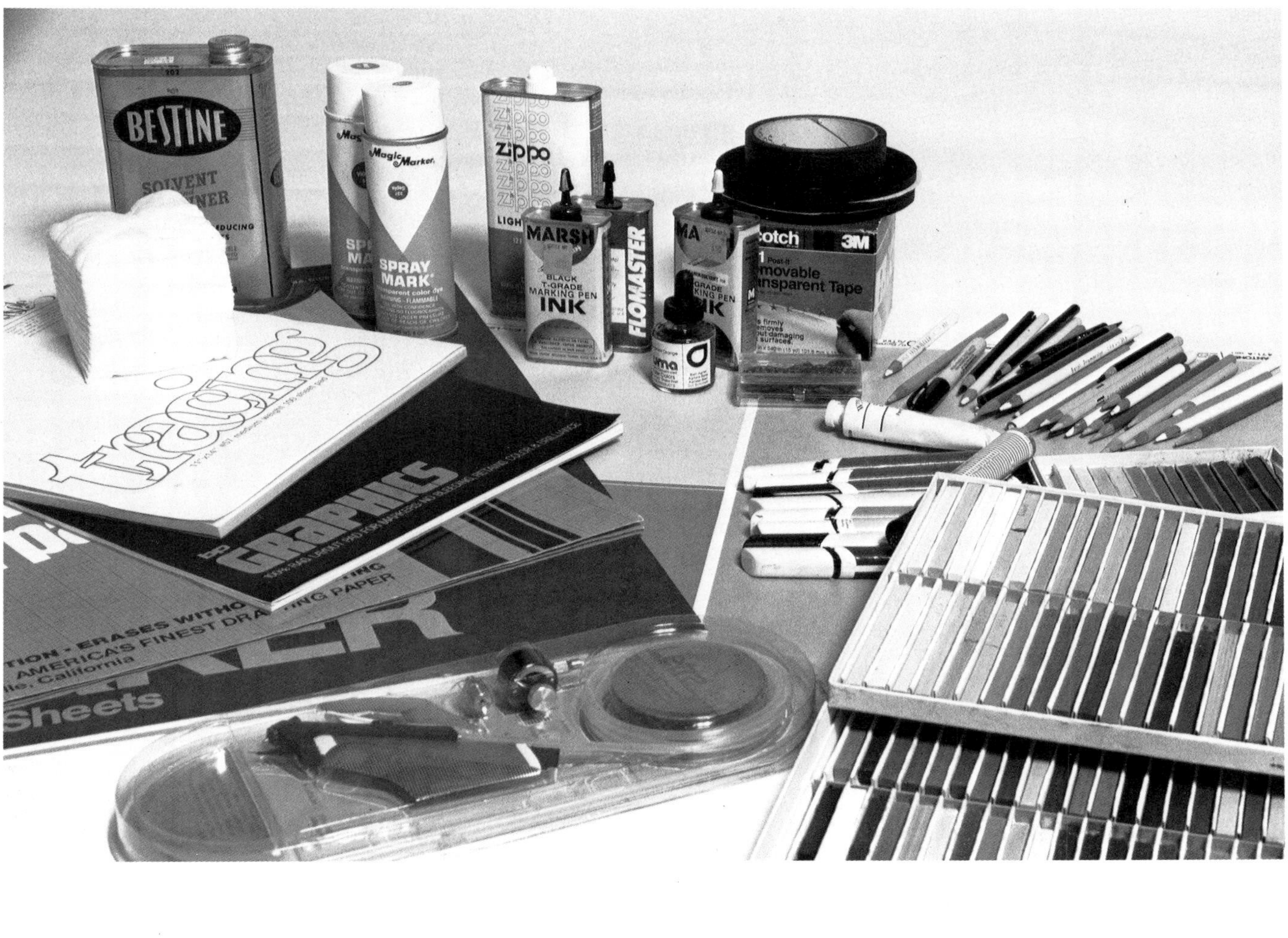

Dry Media

A wide range of products falls within the context of what I call the "dry mediums." These include pencils, pens, pastel chalks, dry markers, marker sprays, drawing tapes, and adhesive films. Using them requires little or no preparation, and they basically interact well together. Dry markers and marker sprays are placed in this group because the coloration they produce dries so rapidly once it is on the page.

Generally, you will find that the dry mediums produce the fastest results. The combination of black Prismacolor definitions and a pastel-chalk background with touches of white-gouache highlights on bond paper, for example, can take a matter of seconds. This particular technique is favored by most design offices today because using the materials requires very little set-up time and the results are more or less predictable and clean.

A variety of effects can be achieved with the combination of different line-weights and dry-marker tones. The background for this living room was created with light and dark dry markers, with simple drafting tape being used to mask the top and bottom edges.

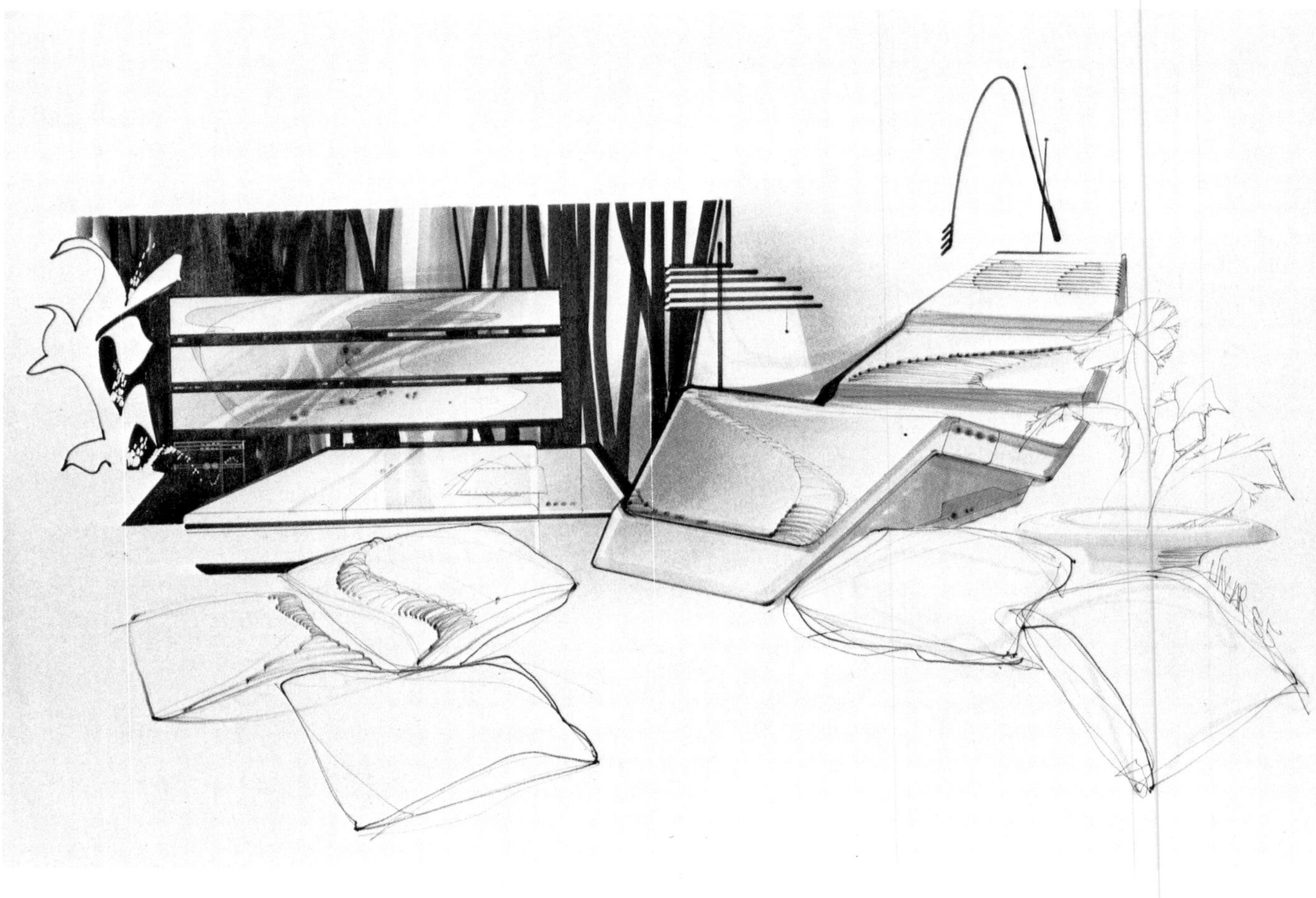

Shadow areas done with black dry marker help define the thin lines of the lawn mower and balance the image on the page.

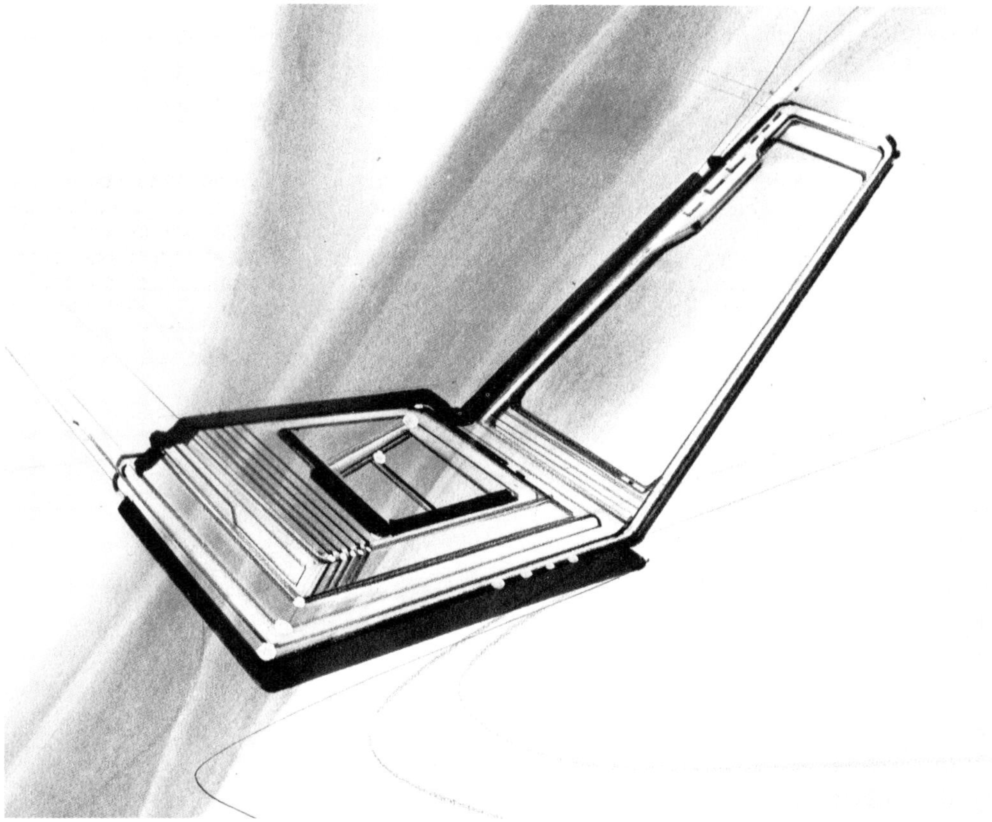

For this camera, I incorporated rub-on texturing technique, using Prismacolor as described in Chapter 8.

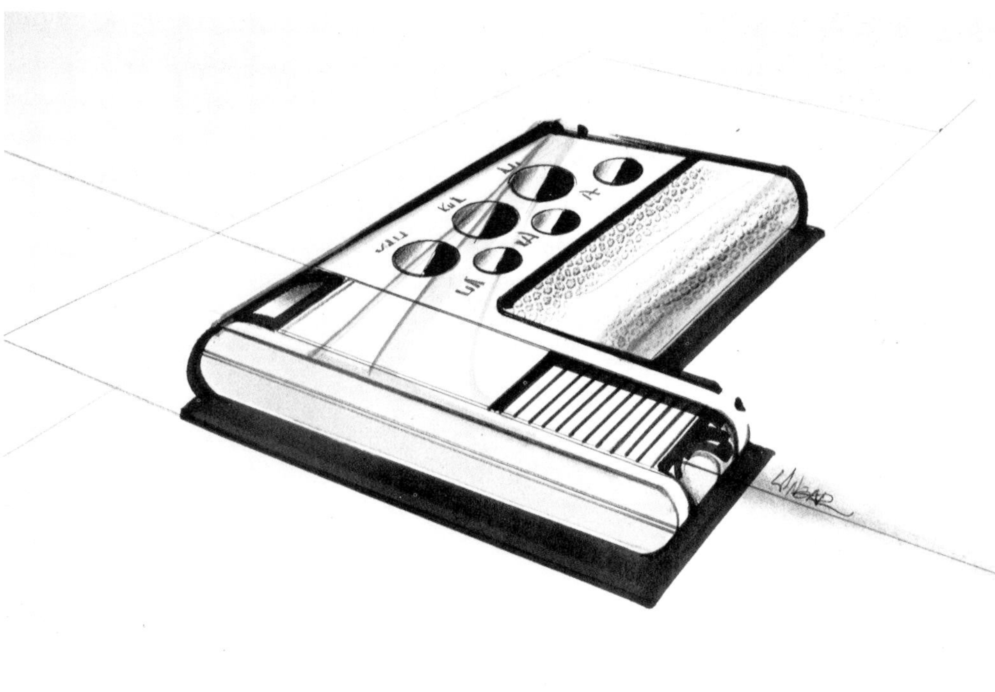

Pencils, Pens, and Pastels

The largest contingent of design products offered is no doubt in the pen-and-pencil area. I find that with colored pencils, Prismacolor brand by Berol is still the best for use on almost any kind of paper medium, including those designed for charcoal and watercolor. The best layout pencils are simply #4H drawing leads, for use with a mechanical pencil holder, or a blue or red Verithin pencil. The charcoal pencils tend to smear with later application of dry marker, so avoid them.

The pens are always fun to experiment with, especially some of the new Outliner pens by Sakura. These precipitate out a second color, such as red, along the ink line, the net effect being a two-tone line. I still use a simple ball-point pen for fast layouts, because the ink will not smear when overlaid with dry marker. For fine and medium black lines, I use a fine-tip Sharpie black by Sanford or a Staedtler Lumocolor 313. In selecting pens, you should attempt to buy ones that not only dry quickly after application to porous paper but also resist smearing if dry markers are passed over them.

Many fine-tipped pens are available in primary colors, as well as in black; but for fine-line details in color, I prefer the intensity of the Prismacolor pencils or the wide range of values found in fine-tipped markers such as those by Pantone.

Chalks play an important role in the creation of fast conceptual sketches as well as in finished presentation renderings. I prefer Grumbacher Golden Palette pastels, with a second best going to NuPastel by Eberhard Faber. The Golden Palettes rub onto paper with a smooth consistency, and each color seems to have an intense chroma value. If possible, you should attempt to purchase as big a set as you can afford—the larger ones, of course, having the biggest range of color values.

The selection of pens and pencils available is often bewildering. You may be tempted to try out all of them—and you should, until you are comfortable with a brand that gives you the results you are seeking. For color work, Pantone fine-tipped markers and Prismacolor pencils are still my favorites. Among the many erasers offered, be sure you buy a soft, kneaded-rubber one and a Pink Pearl for working with pastel chalks.

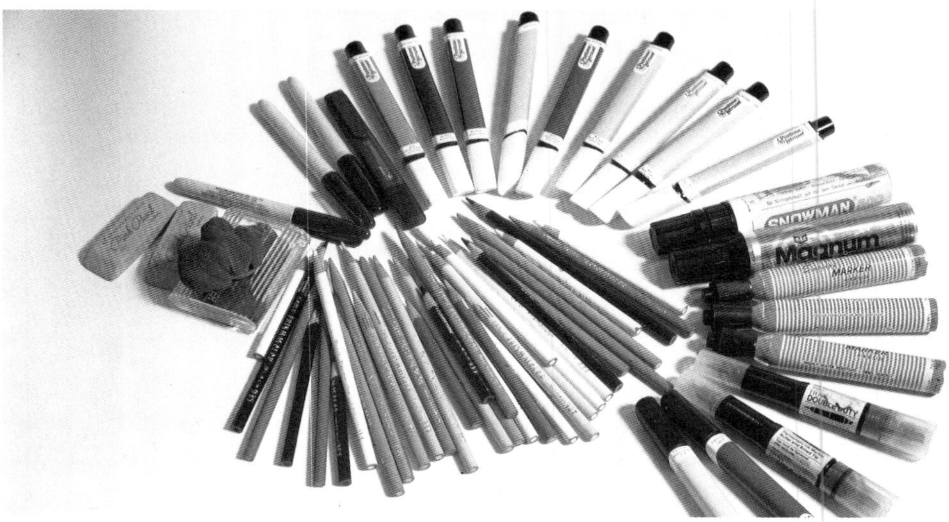

In selecting pastel chalks, look for chroma intensity and the ability of the chalk to blend smoothly on dry-marker pads. Grumbacher Golden Palette pastels are my favorite, although NuPastel by Eberhard Faber and Alphacolor by Weber Costello work almost as well.

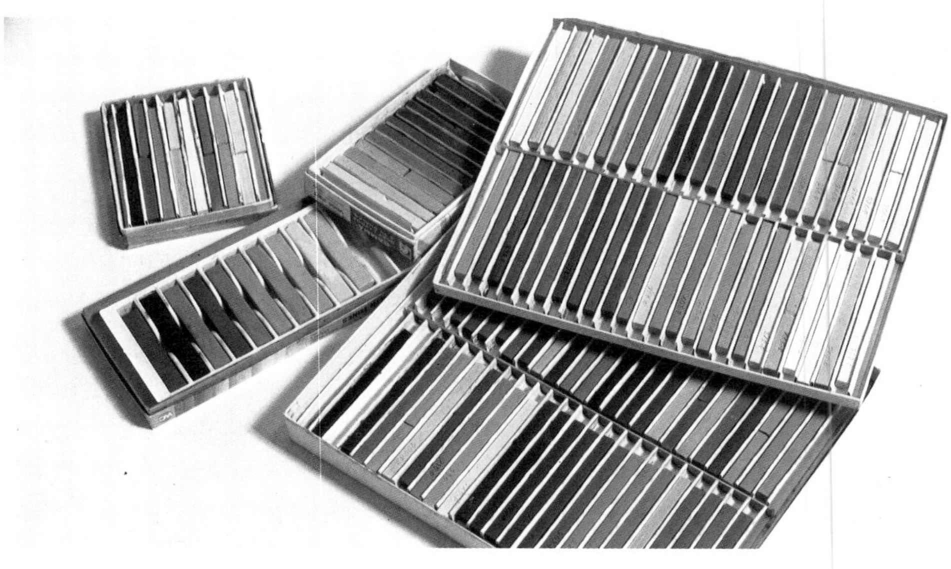

Dense sticks of pastel chalk can have a variety of uses in multimedia renderings. You should first experiment with simple blending exercises such as these to get the feel of the medium.

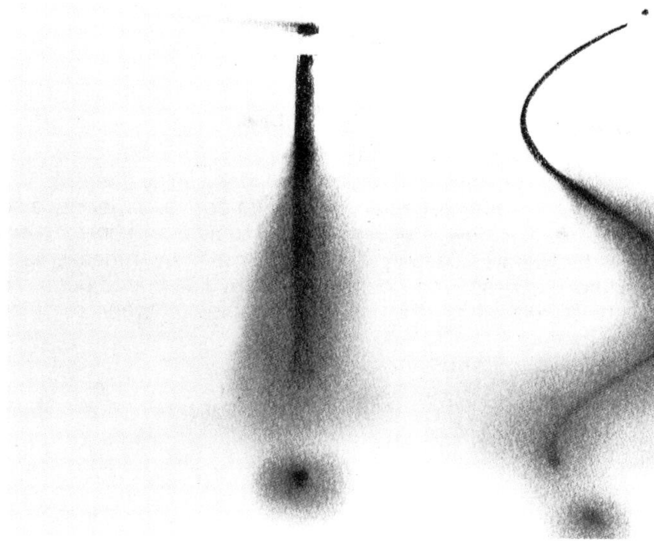

Blend the pastels in a variety of patterns and try masking an area with an edge of paper. The pad on the end of your index finger is a good tool to use if you want to retain intense coloration on small areas. For large areas, it is best to powder the chalk and transfer color to the rendering by using a Webril pad. (See page 64.)

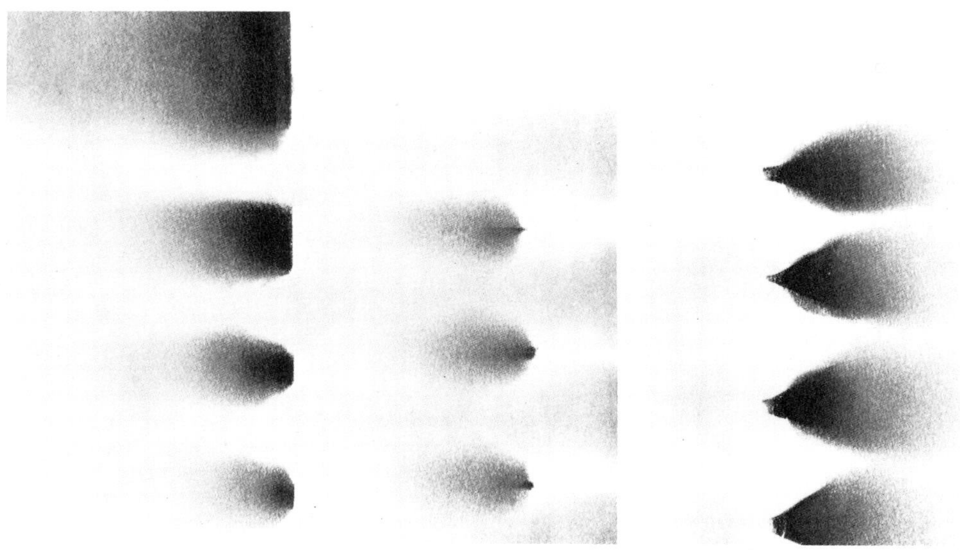

Graphite sticks can be used for simple blends on vellum or bond papers. Graphite is not as clean as pastel, and smudges can be a problem. In general, to prevent smearing when working with graphite or chalks, you should have a separate piece of paper to rest your hand on as you draw.

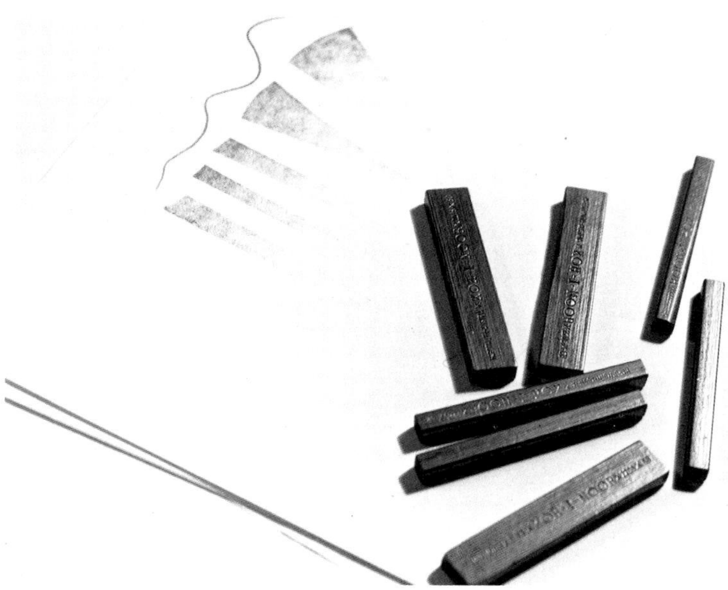

A simple object such as this hair dryer can be rendered with striking results by using only a black dry marker and blended pastel chalk. The reflections follow the sculptural lines of the object, and the solid shadow dramatizes the highlights. (See color picture on page 93.)

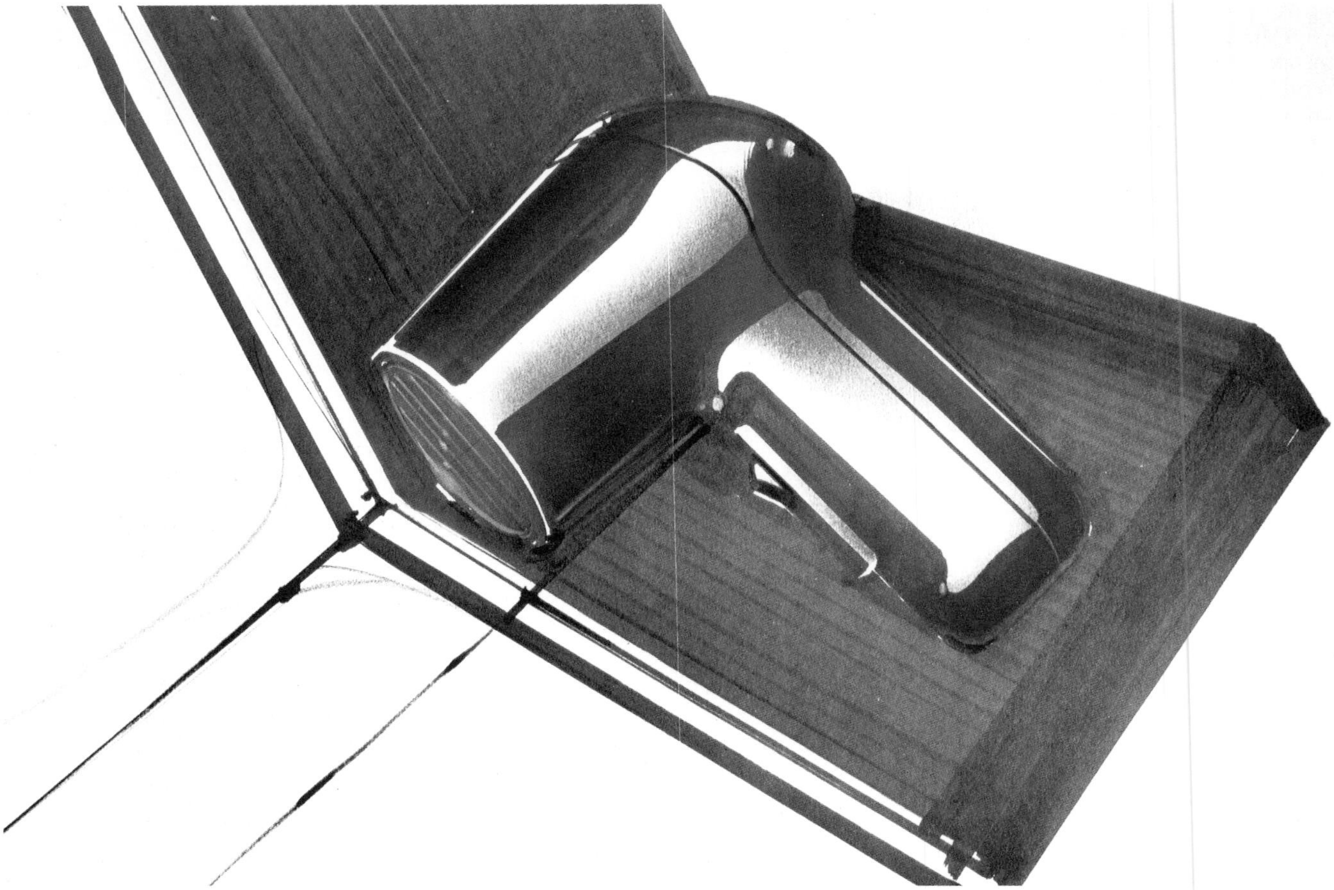

Dry Markers

The dry marker is a versatile tool, but it takes quite a bit of practice to feel comfortable with it. Brands such as Pantone offer a wide range of colors and tonal values, with a complete line of warm and cool grays.

Because initial concepts are usually more successful when rendered without the complications of color, I rely mostly on the various tones of gray markers and seldom use the colored markers. To introduce color after the basic design has been determined, I will usually blend colored chalk over the neutral tones of the gray rendering. I use warm-gray markers for the initial rendering if the overlay or accent colors are warm (reds, yellows, etc.), and I use cool-gray markers if the overlay or accent colors are cool (blues, greens, etc.)

For a basic palette, I suggest the use of Pantone warm grays #1 through #10. The tonal gradations are very consistent, and the drying time of the ink when applied to paper allows for the smoothest blending of strokes without unnecessary streaking.

I suggest testing all new markers before purchasing, to make sure they have a good reservoir of ink. Apply the marker to white paper while you are in the store. The line produced by the marker should be evenly colored and should have crisp edges. If the marker creates a streaked line, it has already dried out and should not be purchased. Make sure you place the cap back on each marker immediately after use—this should become a habit. A marker can sometimes dry out within a half-hour. You can "resuscitate" old markers by soaking the tip briefly in a solvent such as FloMaster cleaner by Faber-Castell. Dry markers that have lost their wetness can be used for effects when streaking is desired, such as in the rendering of textures or heavily grained wood.

Dry markers come in two basic varieties, chisel point or fine tipped. Get both kinds. The fine points can be used for quick-sketch layouts, and the chisels can be used for area work and heavy lines.

Do not try to draw a straight line with a chisel-point marker by running the marker along a straightedge laid flat on the paper. Instead, use a 30°–60° triangle slightly tilted toward the plane you are working on. Simply placing your fingers under the triangle on the far side will give satisfactory results. The tilt prevents the marker ink from "wicking" (bleeding) under the straightedge and ruining what had perhaps been a nice piece of work. The dry marker should be held loosely and not allowed to rest on any one place on the paper for over a second or so. If you hesitate at the end of a line, the marker will apply more ink there and produce a spot effect.

A hesitant effect, however, can be used as a technique in loose concept sketching, to imply a kind of casualness to the rendition. Other effects, such as parallel streaking, can be used as strong background areas. By notching pieces out of a chisel point, you can also create parallel lines to render items like the electrical cords of a product.

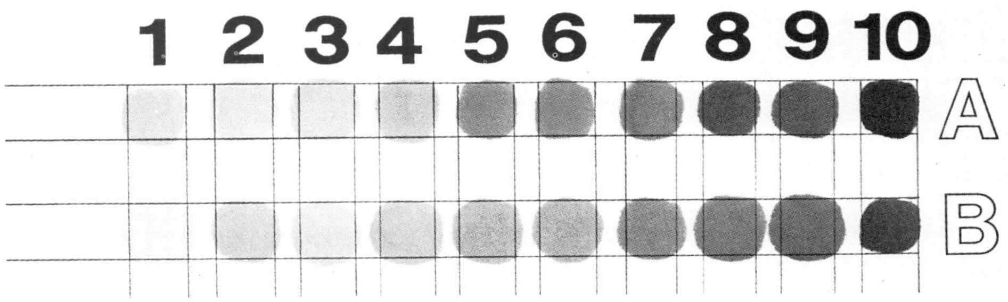

You should always evaluate dry markers before purchasing them. A successful marker, such as Pantone by Letraset, will give a consistent gradation from light tones to dark tones. A minimum set of design supplies should have a full complement (#1 through #10) of both warm and cool grays. (In the photograph, line A shows warm grays; line B, cool grays.)

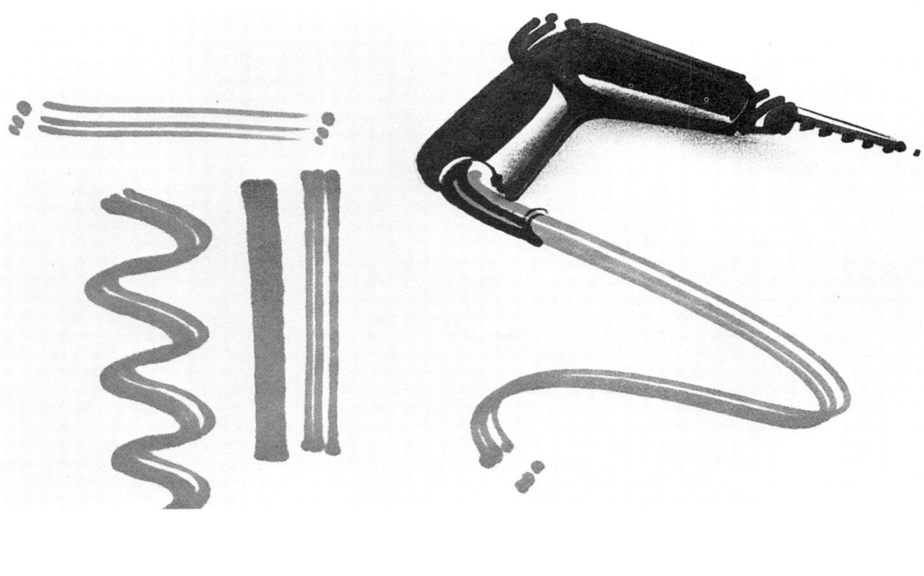

Since most dry markers have a chisel point, many effects can be rendered by changing the angle with which you hold the pen. Notching the end of a marker with an X-Acto blade will enable you to draw parallel lines such as those in this appliance cord.

This tanning-bed illustration uses black dry-marker outlines and shadows to give the concept depth and to highlight the upright panels of the product.

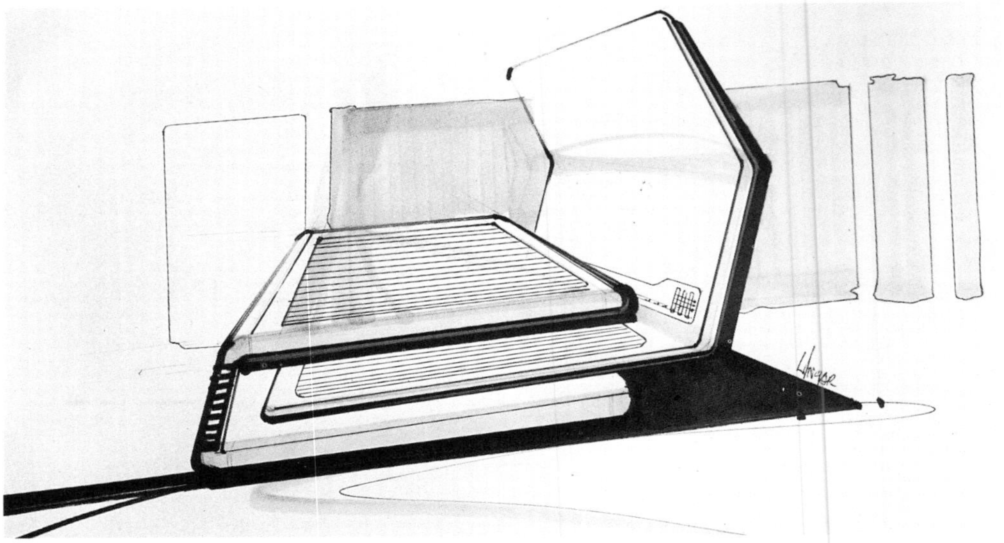

For this three-wheeled vehicle, I used dry markers (Pantone #2 gray and black) and a touch of blended gray pastel. Quickly drawn on copy-machine bond, it combines both mediums as a fast-sketch technique.

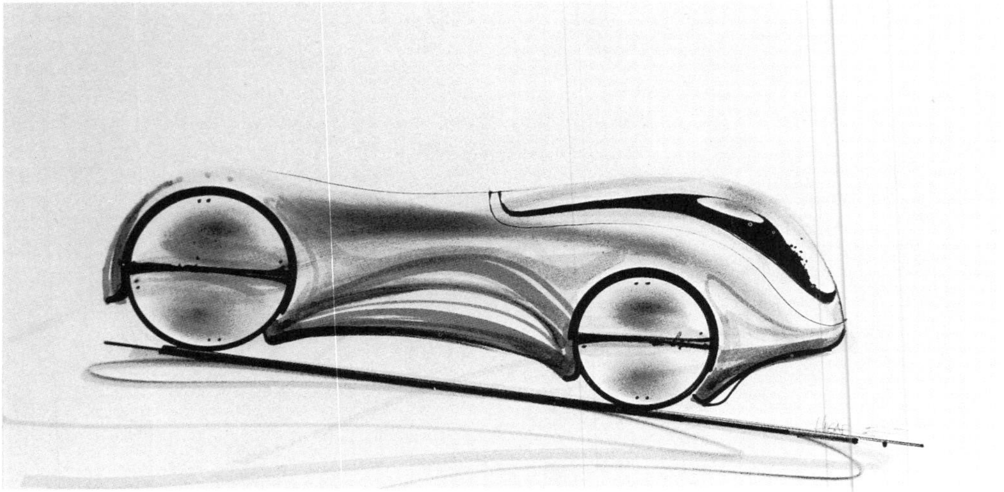

A solid, dark background emphasizes the form of this operating/examining table, drawn with light-gray markers. After the concept was drawn, thin lines were traced around the marker areas with a ball-point pen. Quick sketches like this can be rendered on copy paper (such as Xerox) in less than five minutes. Uniform blocks of color can be created by using parallel marker strokes and allowing the edges to blend together.

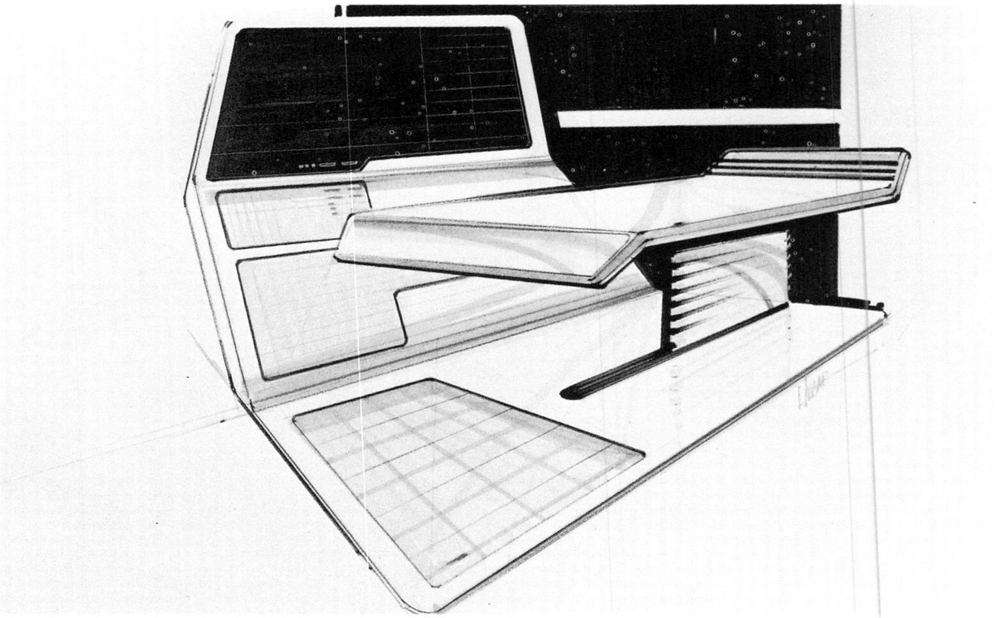

Dry marker has been used in order to create a shiny, reflective effect on the tilework in this interior concept.

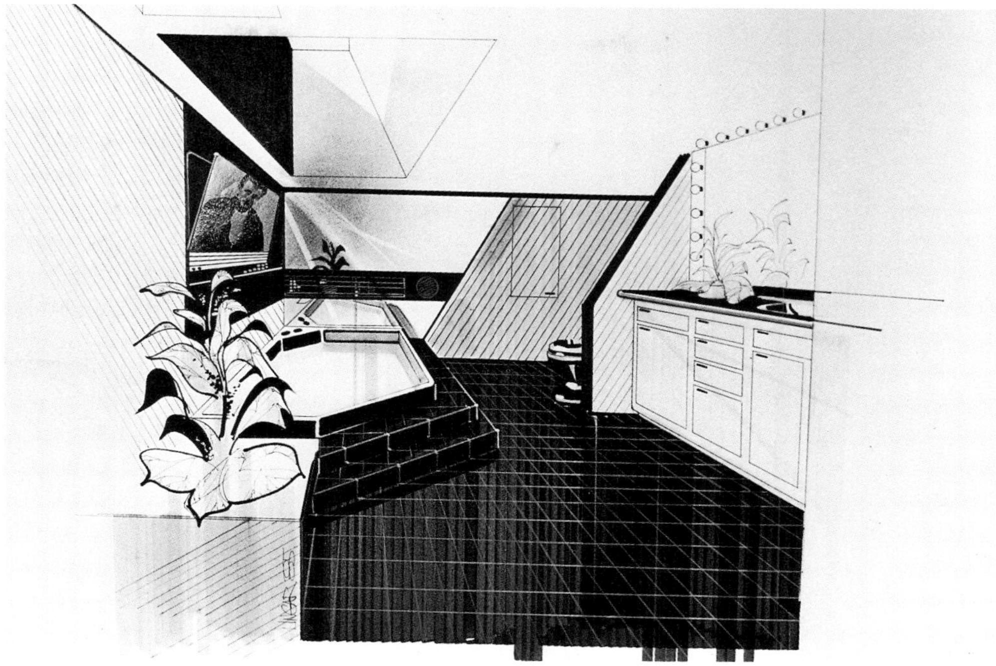

I used a variety of marker strokes to create different textures for the pool float and other items within the one drawing. Blended tones were created by going over the marker strokes with a Webril pad dampened with solvent. Fine details were later added with a Staedtler Lumocolor #313 pen.

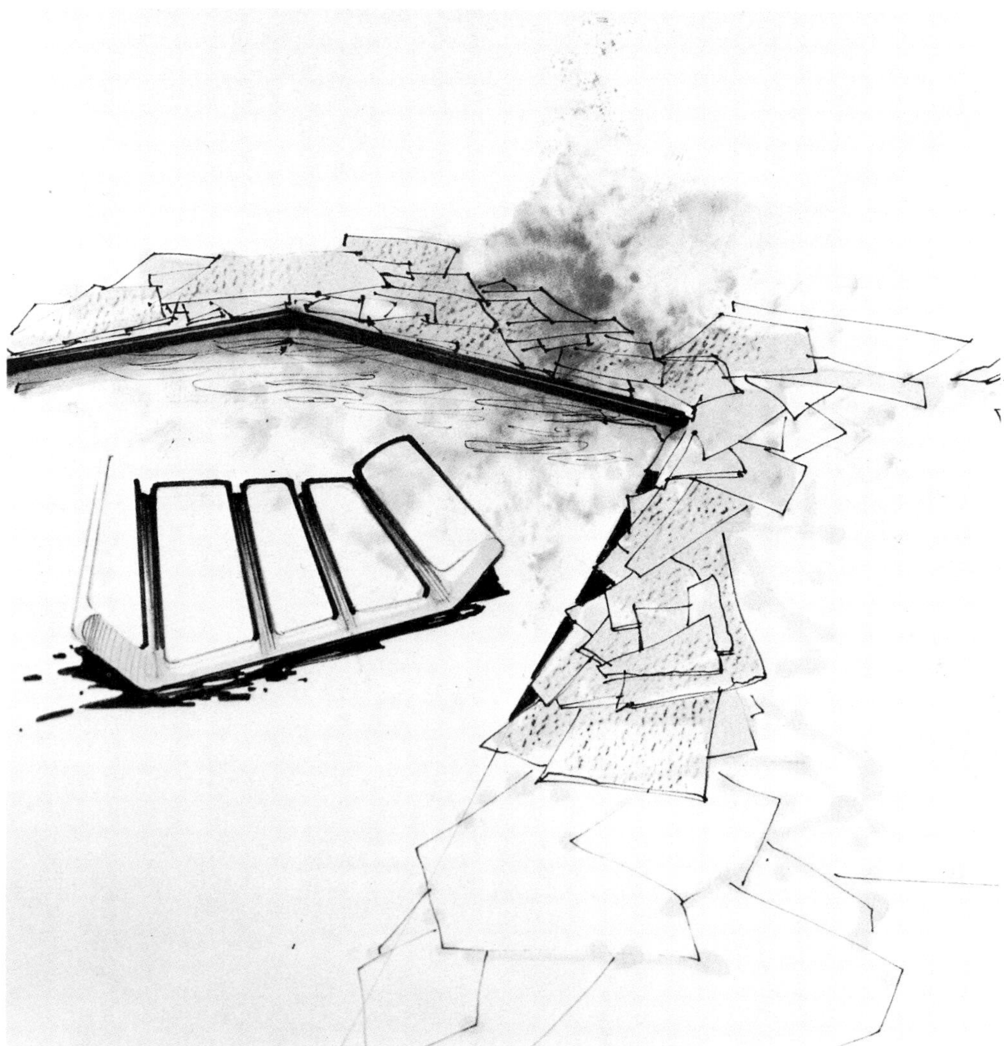

In this fashion watch, fine marker-lines carry the impact of the rendering. Sweeping free-hand curves serve as a counter-point to the tiny, rigid line work within the object and give the design a friendly appeal.

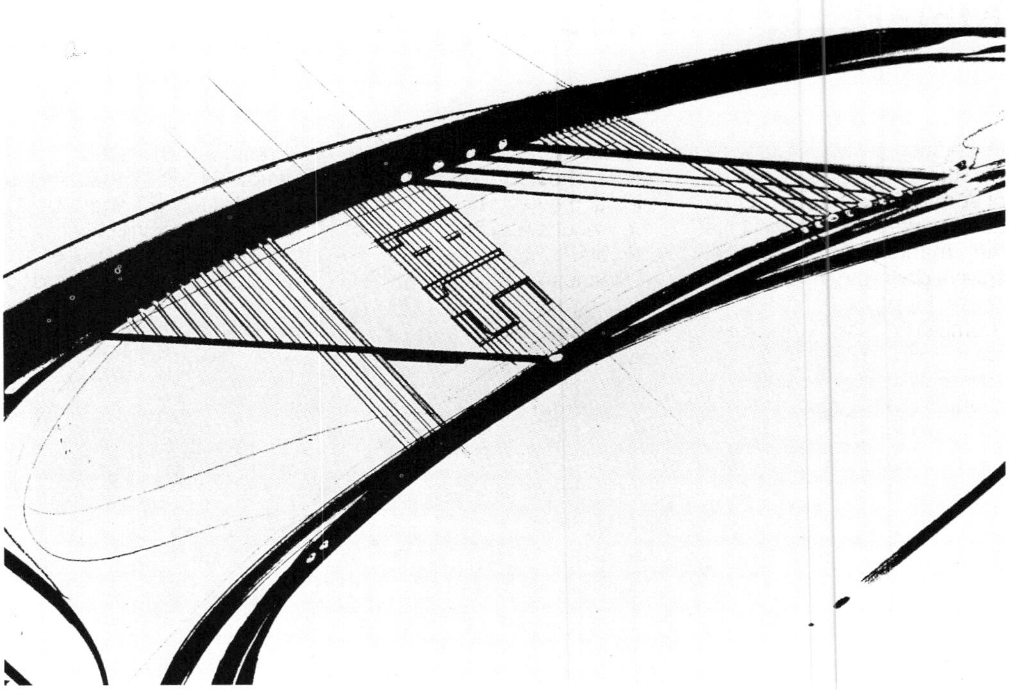

This android illustration uses light grays for the operator and harsh black lines for the machine. The area of solid marker ties the foreground in with the background.

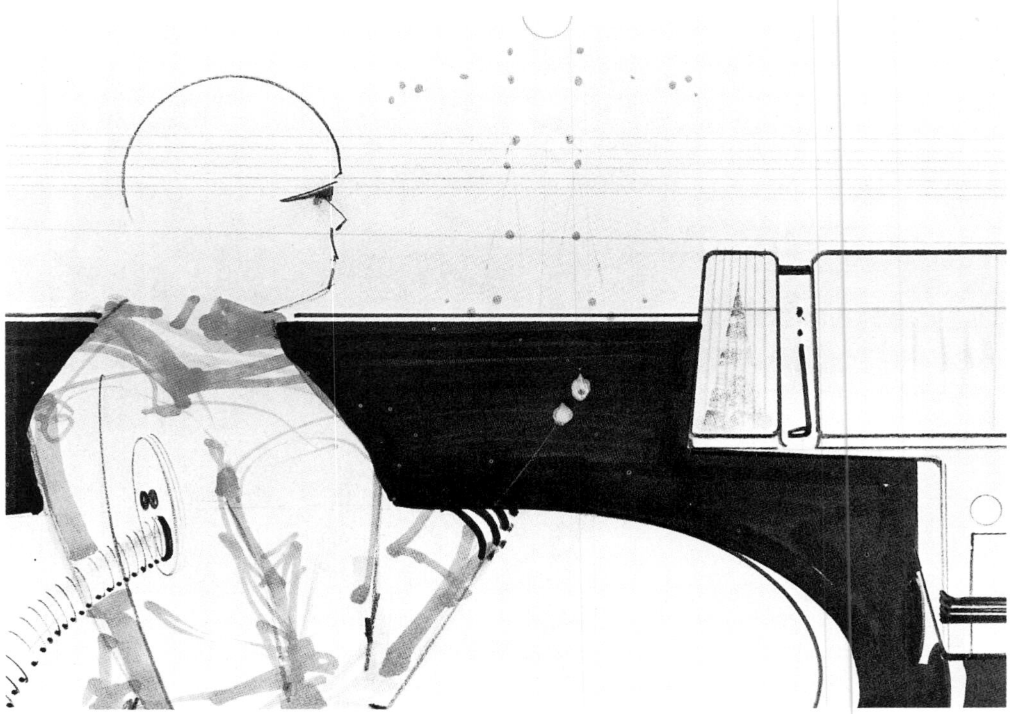

Marker Sprays and LetraJet

In addition to the dry markers, there are various brands of spray markers that can be used on your renderings. Like the markers, the aerosol sprays dry rapidly. The wide-spray format of the typical "bomb can," however, places obvious limitations on control and really can be used only sparingly, as background effects. Handled with care, the sprays can create large areas of color resembling an airbrush technique, although the results are not always reliable.

Because of the careful preparation and masking that is required, airbrush work is usually considered a specialty all its own. A recent product innovation has brought the realm of airbrush work into that of a fast, time-affordable technique. This is the LetraJet by Letraset.

It is not as sophisticated as a professional airbrush, by any means, but you can get a quick, smooth spray of ink with the device. Although it is designed for use with Pantone fine-tip markers, other markers will work with some experimentation. The marker tip must be located near the air nozzle, in a position approximating the Pantone fine-tip location, and then taped in place. The best results will be obtained when you use a new Pantone fine-tip marker in the holder provided on the spray nozzle.

This control station was rendered with dry markers and a fine-point pen after a background vignette had been sprayed on with a marker spray. Later, white gouache highlights were added.

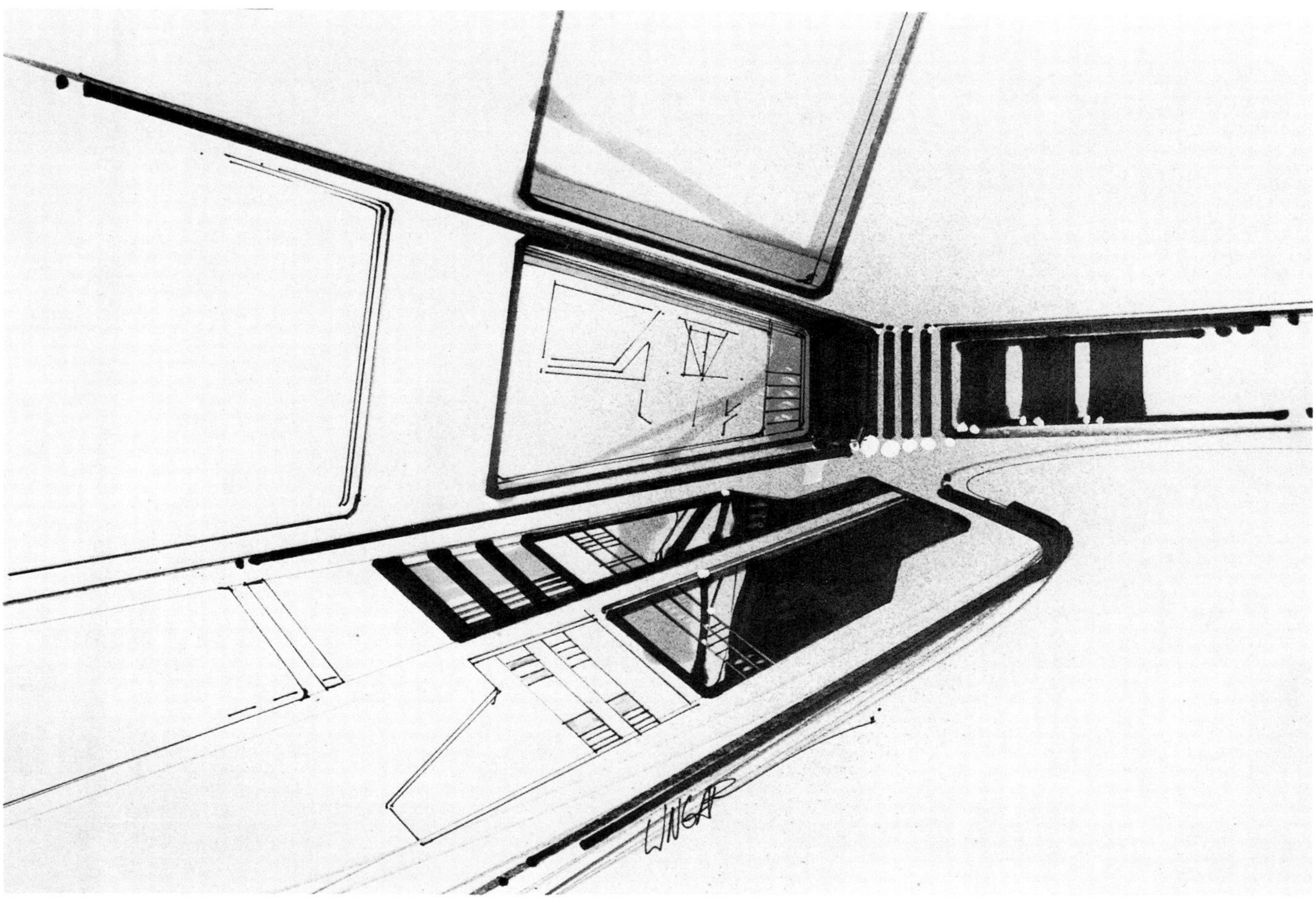

Marker Sprays and LetraJet

The LetraJet air sprayer is a handy companion for fast mixed-media rendering. It requires no clean-up and does not need an air compressor. It is not a replacement for an airbrush but does have a place, particularly for rapid-spray backgrounds and blends.

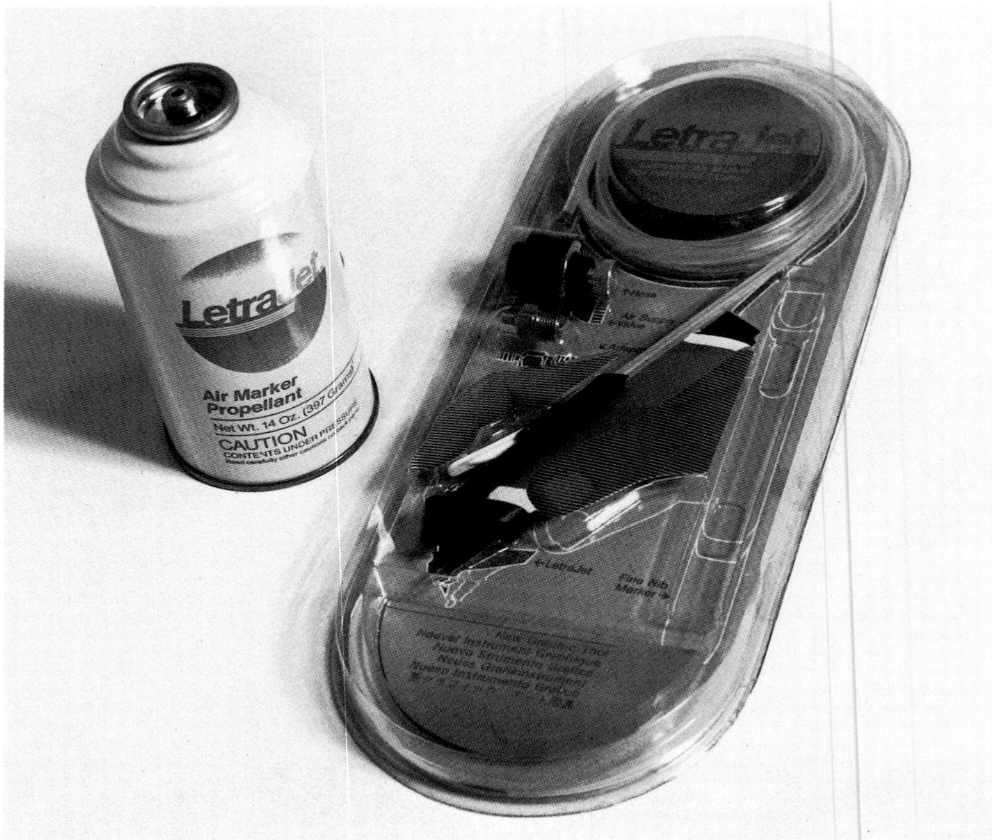

The LetraJet fits easily into your hand and requires little technique to master. First you should explore making consistent patterns with the tool and also become acquainted with its limitations. Its main drawback is its inability to create large areas of color evenly.

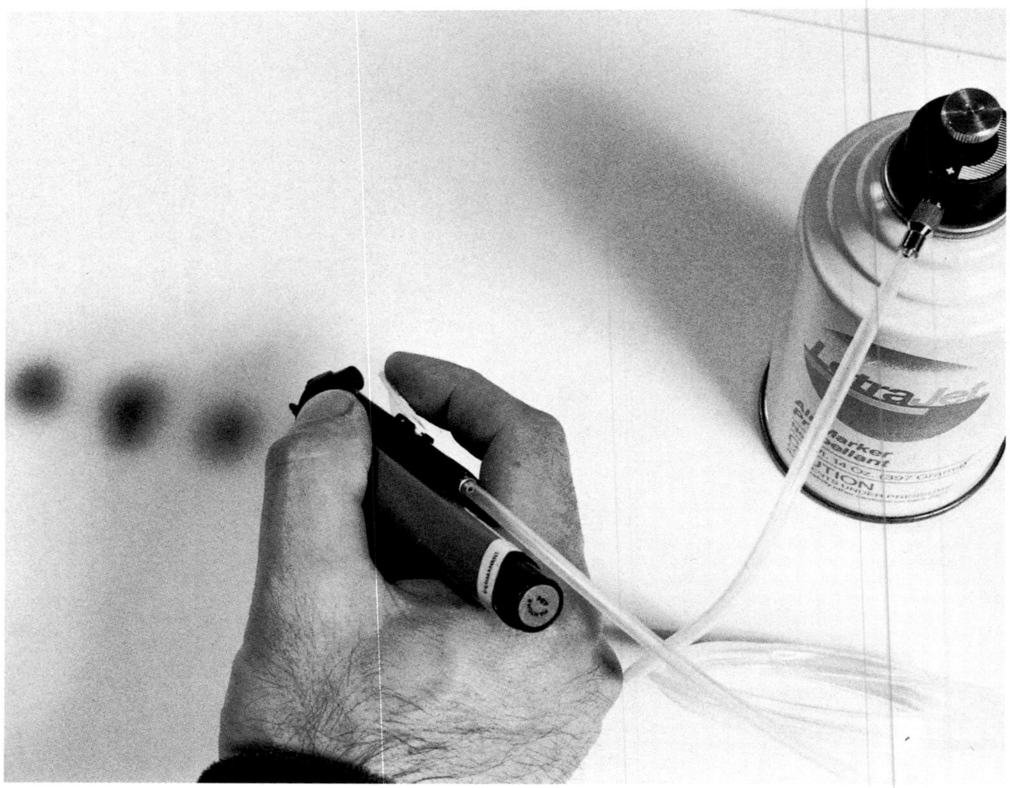

You will find that the LetraJet works best with sweeping motions and a sensitive finger on the control lever. A good learning technique is to make a series of stops and starts as a definite pattern and then try to duplicate it.

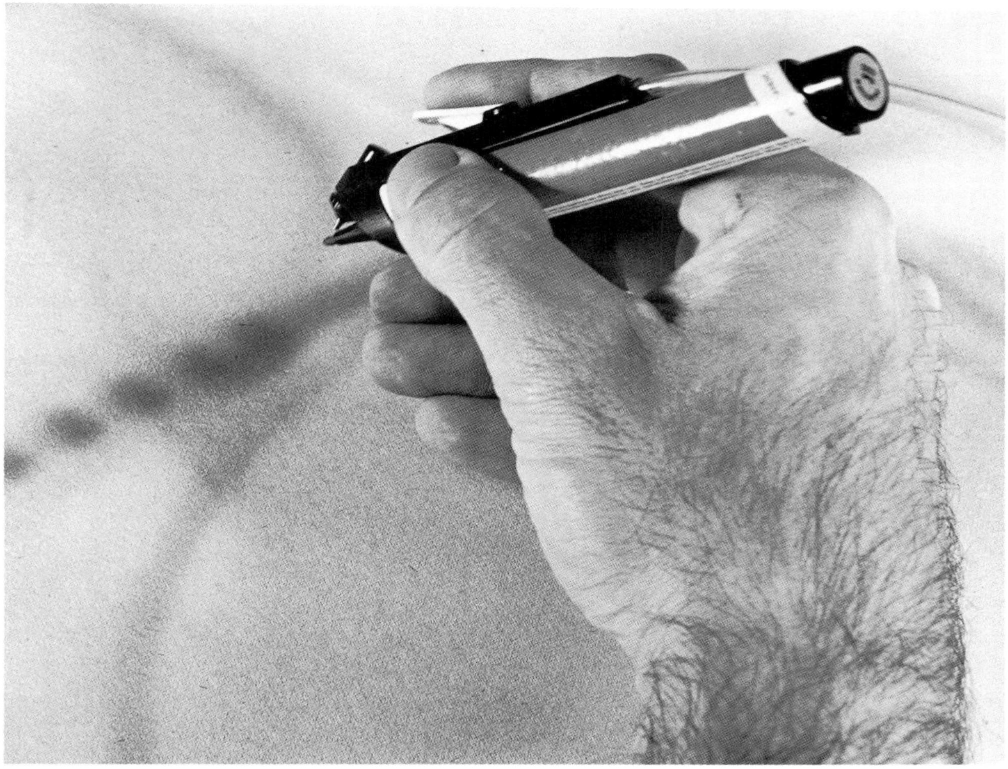

The LetraJet can create a sharp edge when masked with removable tape or simply the edge of a piece of paper.

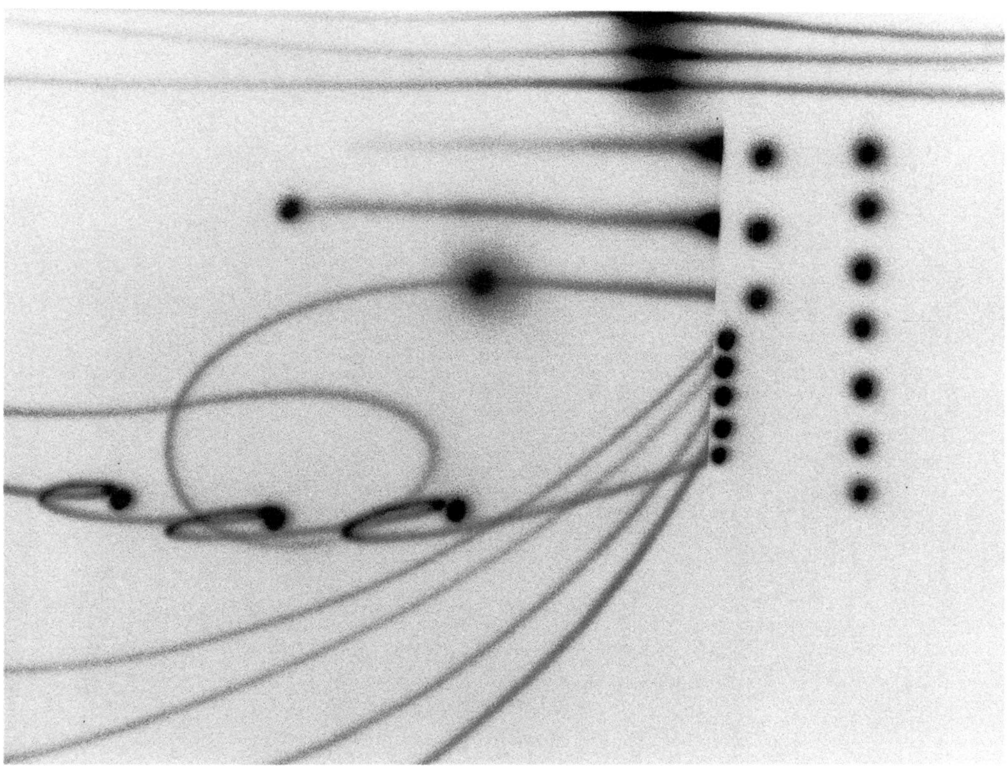

This glassware was quickly rendered on tan paper with a minimum of black lines to start. Then I added LetraJet spray into the areas that I would later highlight with white gouache. The tonal variations are controlled by the length of spraying time. (See color picture on page 106.)

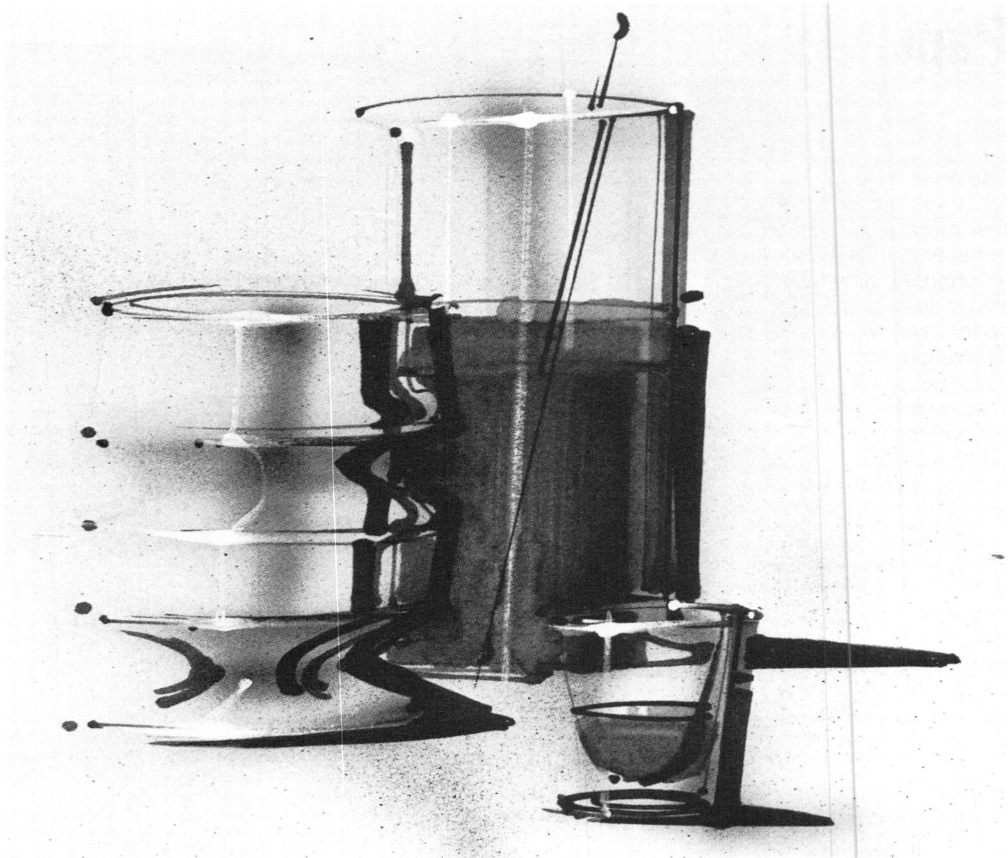

Here is a good example of the LetraJet being poorly used. Although the product itself may look fine, the blended background is too large an area for the technique. Pastel chalk would have served as a better medium for the vignette.

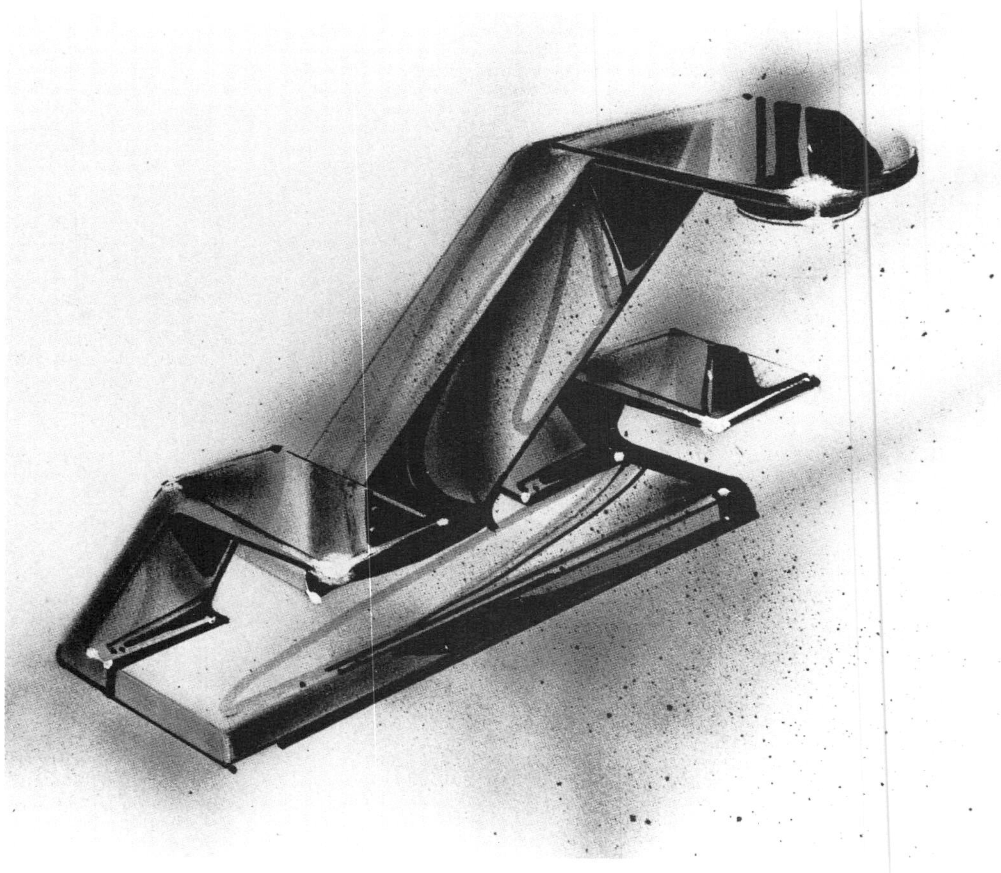

Paper and Pads

The paper manufacturers offer a vast array of products that interact well with pencils, pens, and chalks. In addition to ordinary drawing papers and pads, there are more specialized products such as illustration boards, tracing vellums, marker pads, charcoal and pastel papers in various colors, watercolor papers, and photo reproduction papers. All of these products will accept dry markers and pastel chalks with various levels of success. You need to gain experience applying mixed mediums to the different surfaces so that you can judge the effects and choose those most appropriate for your presentation.

Recently there has been an influx of products that promise specialized results, like the marker pads that do not "bleed through" to the back side or onto the next sheet in the pad. I tend to use these pads, although I have had great success on inexpensive papers such as newsprint. (If you use newsprint, be sure to use an impervious back-up sheet of vellum, such as Clearprint 1000HP–10 or an equivalent. The bleed-through will be stopped before it affects the next sheet in the pad.)

I find a good all-around pad is the Ogilvie Press V-120 engineering sketch pad. This is a smooth, semi-transparent vellum that can be worked on both sides with pencil, pen, or dry marker. Another choice, which is also excellent, is the Letraset A2 marker pad. This is a fine-quality smooth stock that is brilliant white and accepts dry markers extremely well, particularly intense black tones. Its only drawbacks are that it can only be worked on the top side and that it is rather opaque. A third choice would be Beinfang marker pads. They accept pens and markers well, and are also quite favorable toward the blending of pastel chalks, producing smooth, streakless areas of color if desired.

The vellum and the marker pads mentioned are excellent for all forms of concept renderings, from quick sketches to formalized presentations to management. Colored papers may also be used in preliminary renderings, although concept drawings on these papers tend to have a more formal look. This is especially true of the dark shades, such as black or blue. I prefer Mi Tientes pastel paper by Canson. Again the varieties of products in this market require you to test to your own personal tastes. The smooth, high-quality grades are always recommended because of their ability to stand up under duress and because of their acceptance of different mediums, such as pastel chalks, dry markers, and gouache.

Both brownline and blueline reproduction papers can be used as effective backgrounds for renderings that rely on strong black lines and bright white highlights. Since these papers tend to absorb ink, they accept gray or light-toned markers only marginally.

Pantone offers a variety of colored paper that has a graduated tone. The intensity of color as well as the degree of tonal gradation can be selected from basic variations available. The papers also come in two surfaces: glossy (coated) and matte (uncoated). Both kinds can be used with dry markers or LetraJet spray. The glossy surface will accept pastels to some degree, but the matte surface will absorb the chalk.

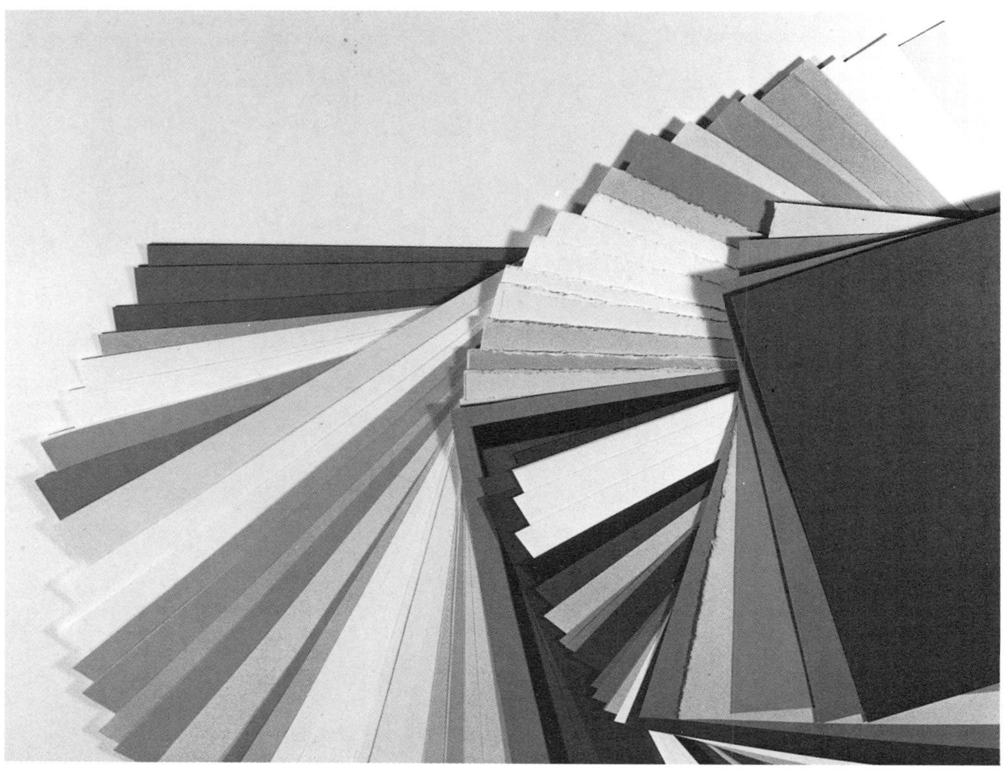

Colored papers can offer a dynamic background to a mixed-media rendering. The entire sheet becomes the middle tone and a fast concept can be created simply by adding the light and dark tones. You should definitely stay with heavy stock that has a light tooth to the surface. An excellent choice is Mi Tientes pastel paper by Canson.

Dark values and highlights were all that I added to the middle-tone value of this rendering on colored paper. You will find this technique easy, since many of the lines are created by merely dragging a sharp Pink Pearl eraser through the pastel chalk areas. (See color picture on page 102.)

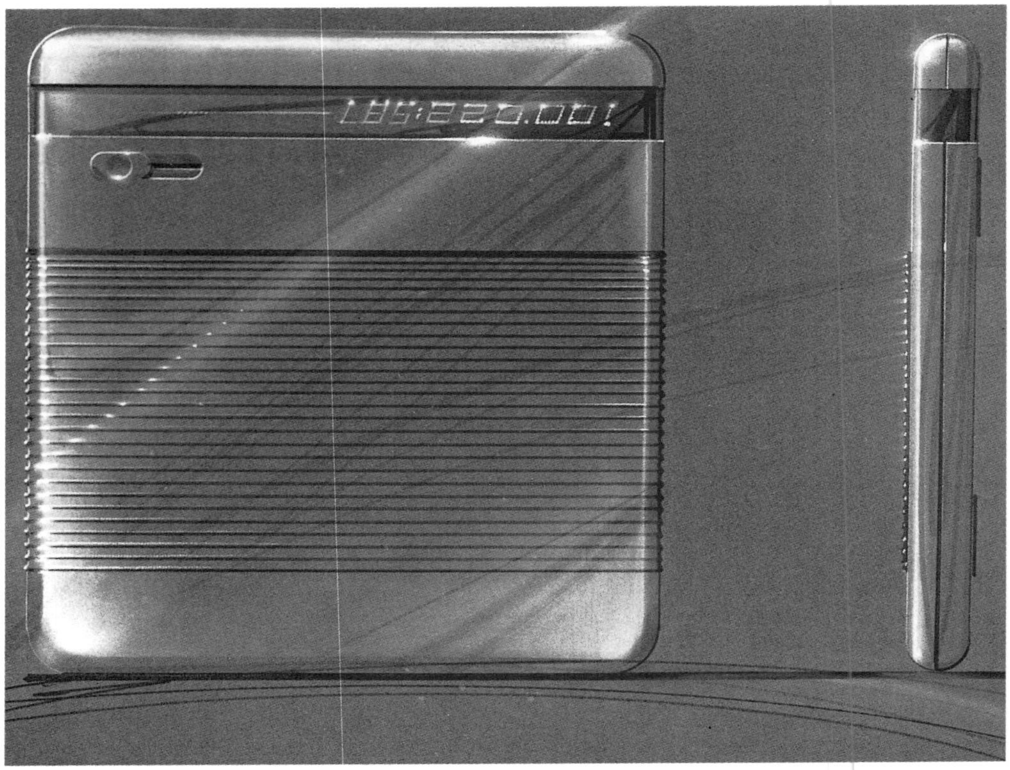

Pantone graduated color papers by Letraset can save time with certain kinds of renderings. The paper has color blended on either side in various proportions to produce a ready-made air-brush effect. In this rendering of a paper copier, I used the effect to focus attention on the display area of the product.

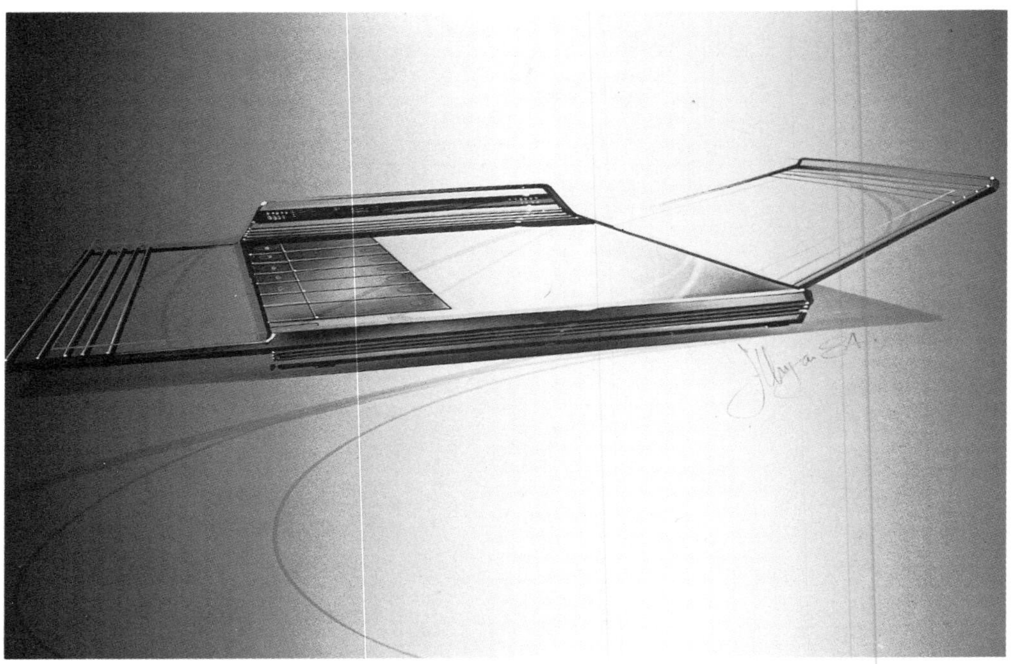

Evaluation of Paper

It is necessary to keep abreast of new products as they appear in the marketplace. You should evaluate new papers by asking the following questions and then testing a sample pad:

1. Does the paper accept ink or dry markers without bleeding to the back?
2. Is there excessive bleeding along inked lines, or do the edges stay crisp and sharp?
3. How well does the paper blend both light-tone and black dry markers?
4. Is the paper translucent enough to see layouts placed beneath it?
5. Is the paper smooth enough to blend rubbed-on pastel chalks into streakless gradations from light to dark?
6. Is the paper stock thick enough to allow its usage when not attached to the pad? Many papers are too thin and will often require a back-up sheet or two of white paper for presentations. Thin papers are simply too flimsy to withstand handling by several people, which is commonplace in the design office.

The marketplace has included a wide variety of paper pads suited to your special needs as a designer. You will want to experiment with new products as they come out. I try to evaluate each product in relation to the various media I will be using with it.

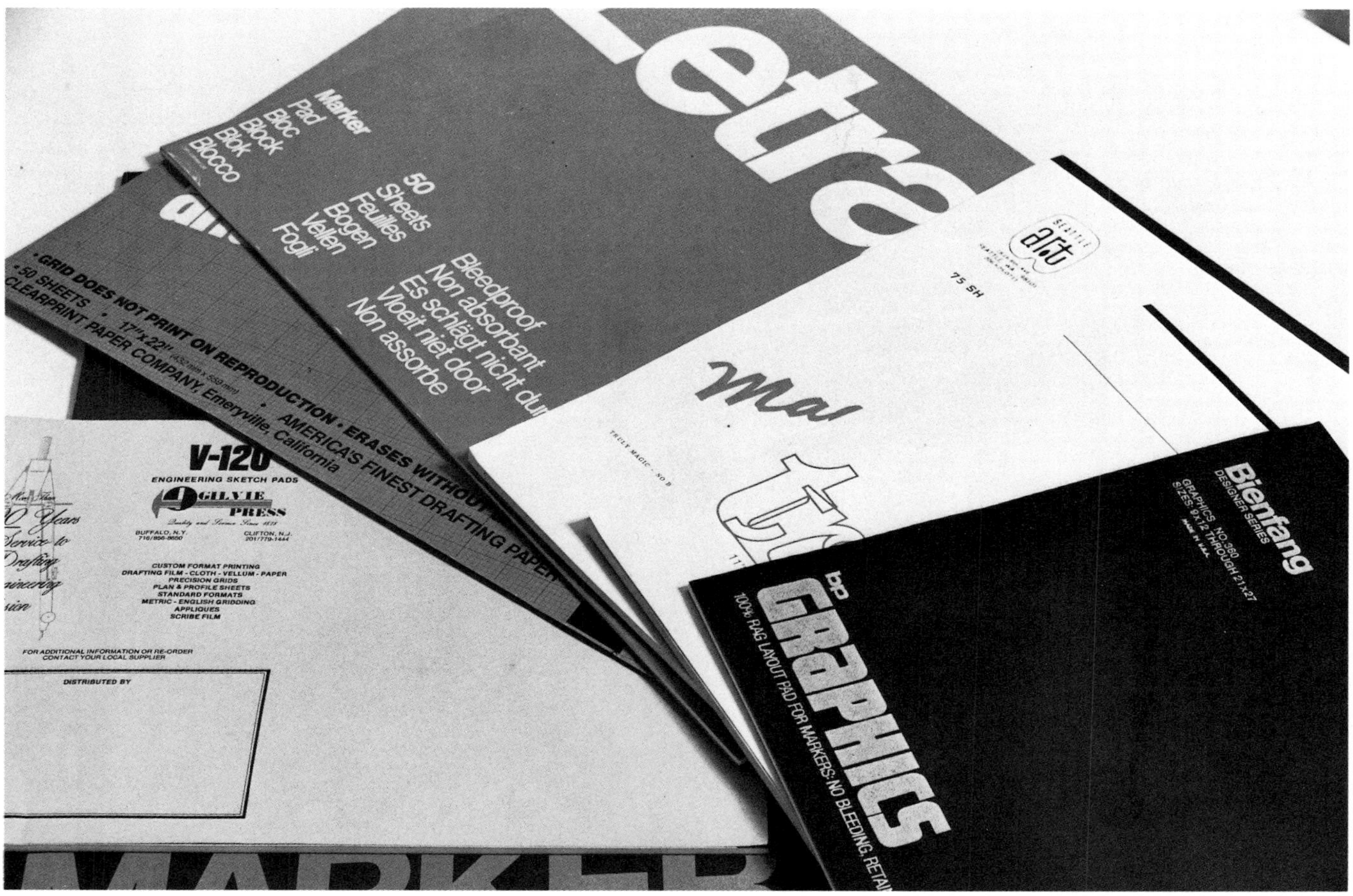

Masking and Drawing Tapes

The general use of masking or drafting tapes to secure a drawing while working on it can be extended to use as a frisket. I have successfully used drafting tapes as a device for blocking in backgrounds on marker pads. Drafting tapes, however, cannot be used for masking areas on reproduction paper (such as brownline) because that paper tends to tear as you pull the tape up.

Technology strikes again with the recent introduction of Scotch-brand removable tape #281. This is a good masking frisket for dry mediums and for certain multi-media such as lighter-fluid/pastel-chalk combinations on vellum. This tape will pull up from almost all papers, including repro, without tearing the sheet. Unfortunately, it does not have the sealing strength for masking such mediums as FloMaster inks and cleaners. (For that purpose, I use Scotch Magic Mending tape, suitable for use on vellums only.) The Scotch #281 tape comes in a variety of roll widths up to 6 inches. I recommend that you get several 1-inch width rolls and at least one 6-inch roll.

An interesting technique for developing lines that can be changed later is to use black photographic tape (3M #235). This is a flexible crepe tape that comes in 1/4-inch, 1/2-inch, and 1-inch width rolls. Chartpak also makes flexible colored tapes in various widths from 1/4-inch down to 1/32-inch wide. These tapes are relatively sticky and allow you to create curved or straight lines. They are great for making fast large-format line drawings, such as full-size automobile profiles, computer work-station analyses, human-factor studies, and so on. They do tend to tear papers when lifted, so they work best when applied to vellum.

There are also rigid tapes in a variety of colors. These can be used in renderings of orthographic views, if you are limited to straight lines only.

Masking tapes have evolved considerably in the last decade, and the recent introduction of removable transparent tape by 3M has made many new mixed-media techniques possible. Experiment on small pieces of your paper with a chosen tape before you use it, or you may ruin an entire rendering because the tape will not come up later. Armak or 3M black photographic tape is essential for masking large areas of vellum, especially when using wet-medium techniques (See Chapter 6).

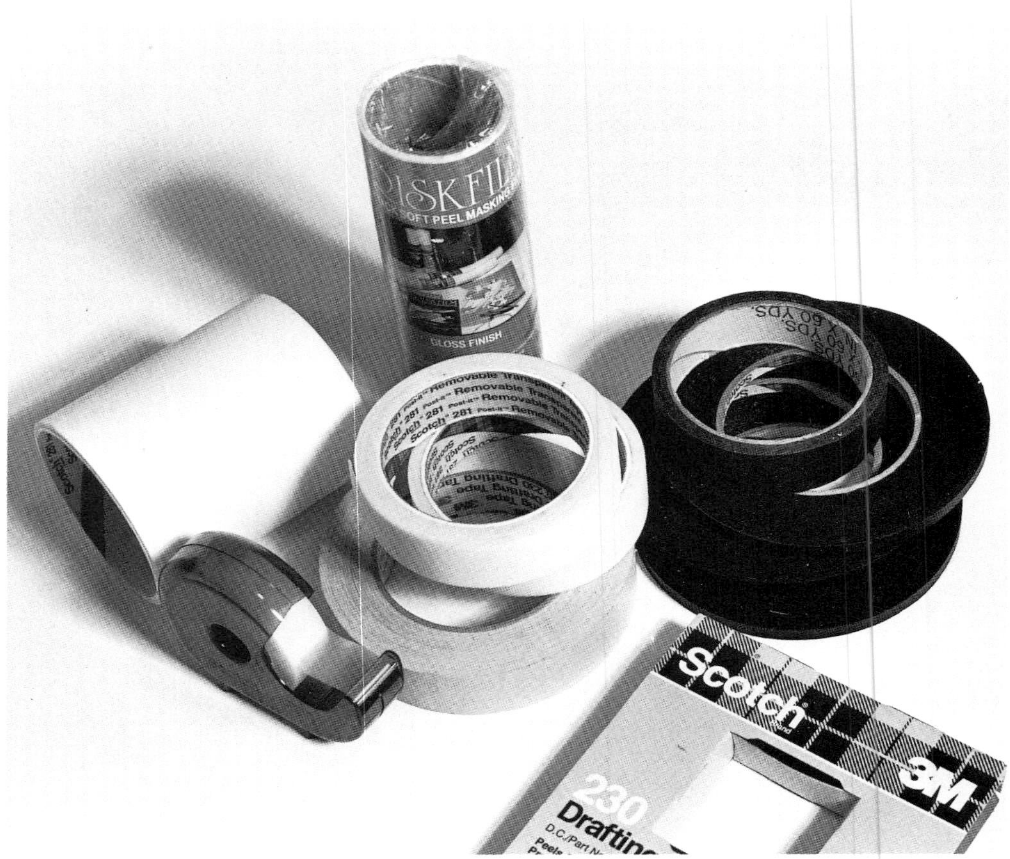

Masking the surrounding areas with tape before applying dry marker will create clean edges. This blended vignette was created by swabbing ink solvent onto the paper after the dry-marker ink was laid down.

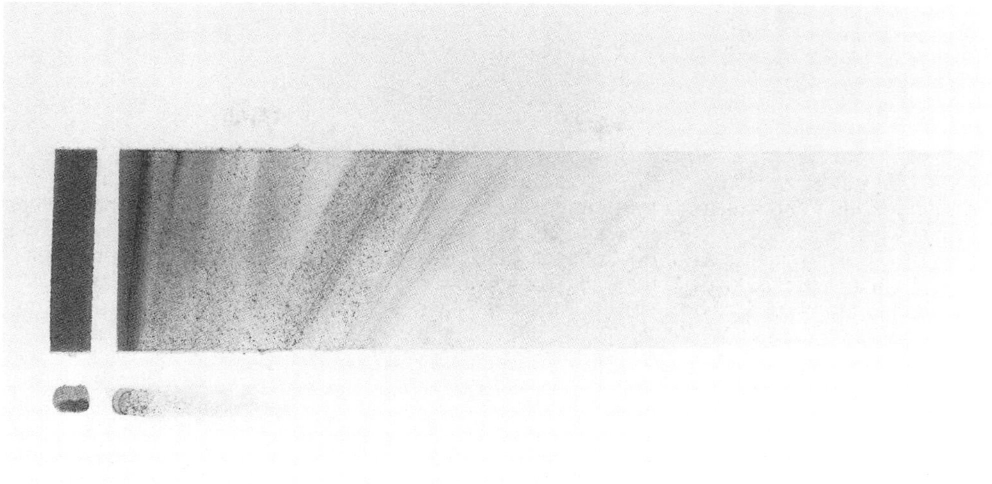

Removable tape allows the masking to be done on marker-pad paper, which would otherwise tear as the tape is removed. Here, darker shades of dry marker were blended over lighter shades.

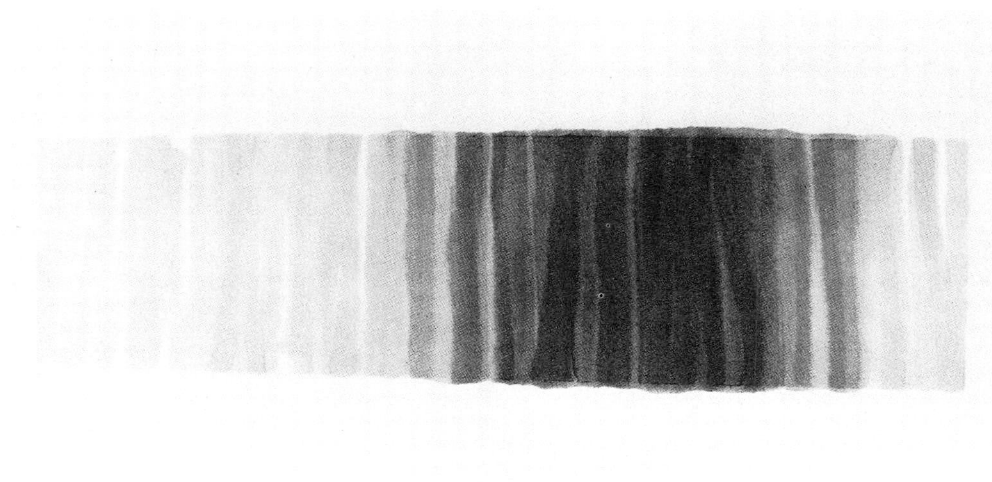

Simply spraying over rub-down letters such as Letraset and then removing the letters with masking tape can create nice blended graphics. This technique can be used in order to create title blocks on finished renderings.

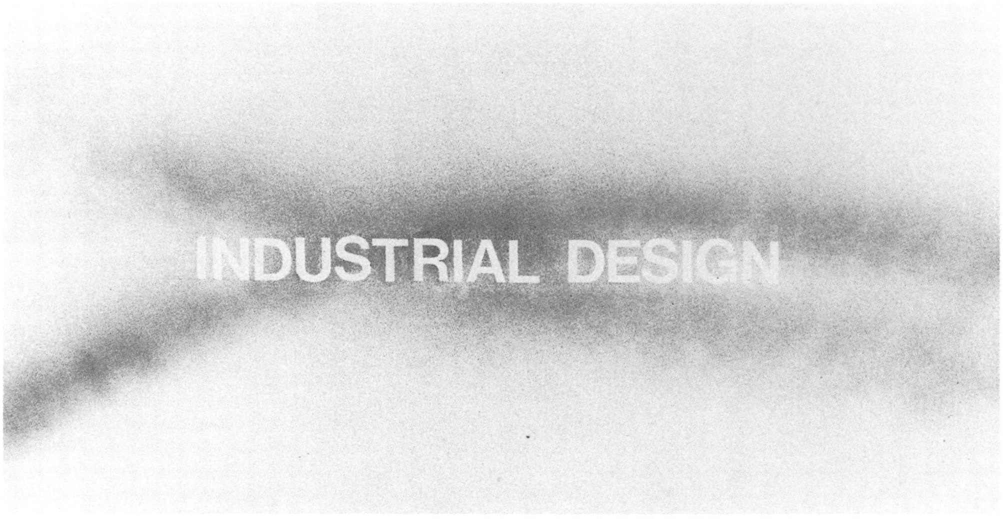

This rendering of a medical cart was created on vellum. The background was done with dry markers over an area masked by simple drafting tape. After the illustration was done, the tape was lifted off, creating a dynamic background.

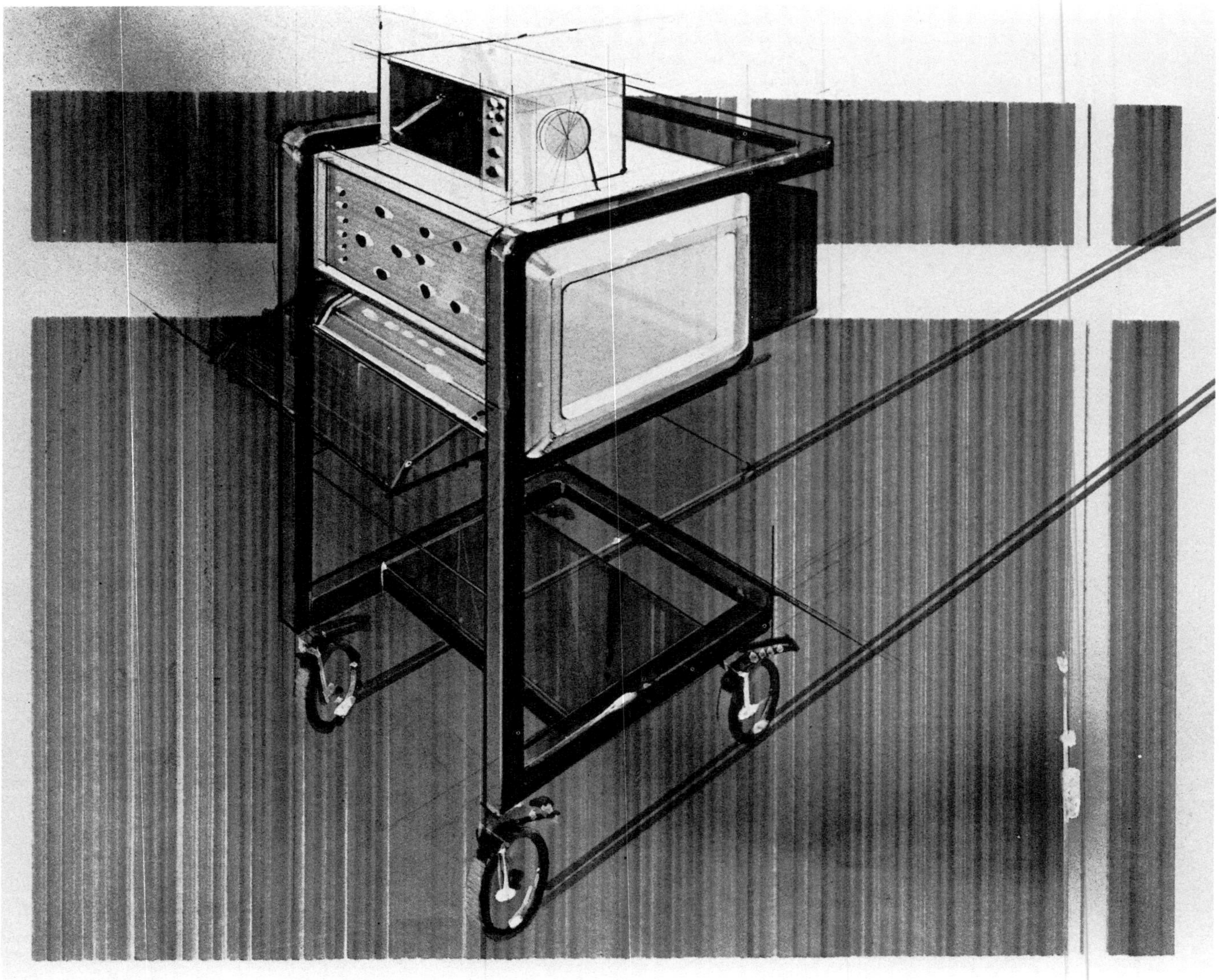

Black photographic (crepe) tape can literally be drawn with. The various widths range from very thin lines to lines 1-inch wide. Experiment with them as a drawing medium as well as a masking medium.

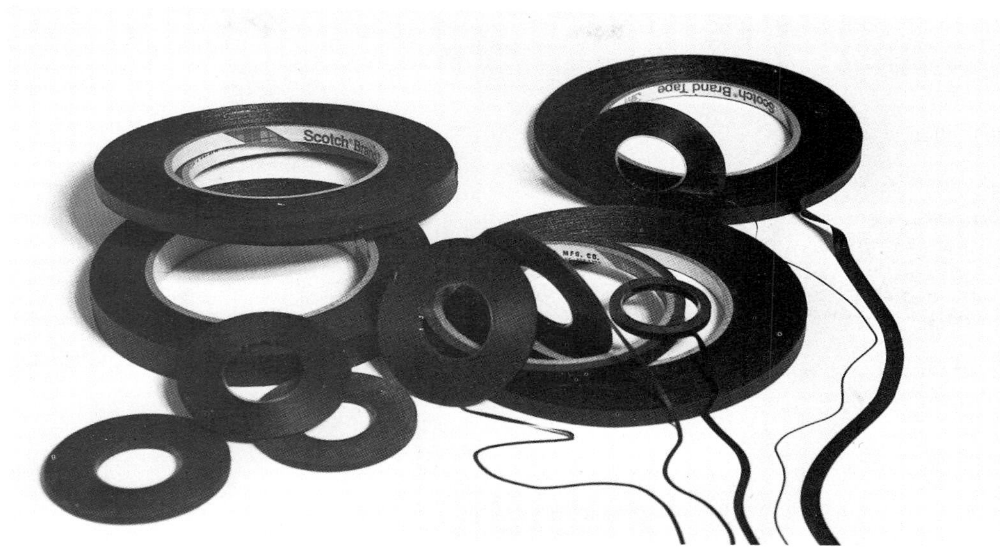

This early concept of a supermarket check-out station was drawn entirely with 3M photographic crepe tape. It is obviously limited in tonal value but has strong graphic interest.

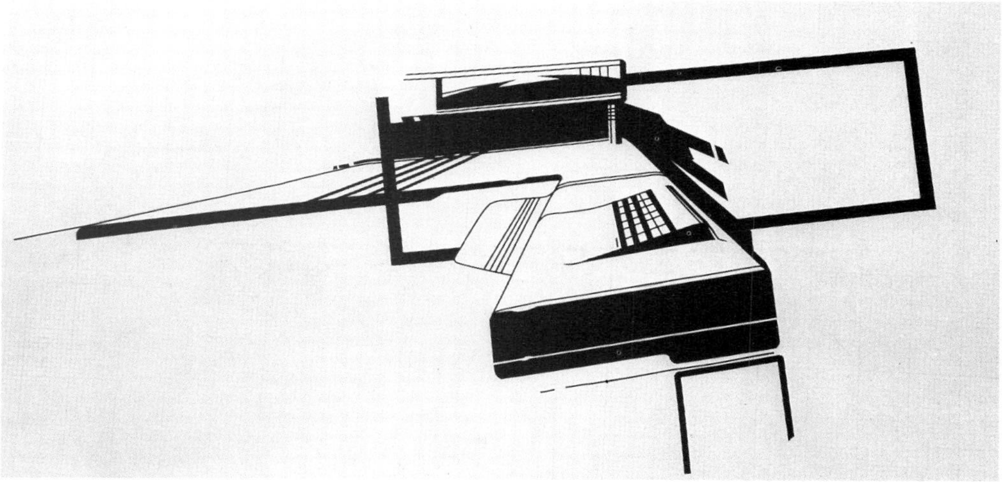

This ergonomic (human-factor) study for a computer work station was drawn entirely with photographic crepe tape. Curvilinear forms lend themselves to this technique. Adjustments and changes can be made easily if the drawing is on vellum. Simply lift the tape lines up and place them down until the design is right.

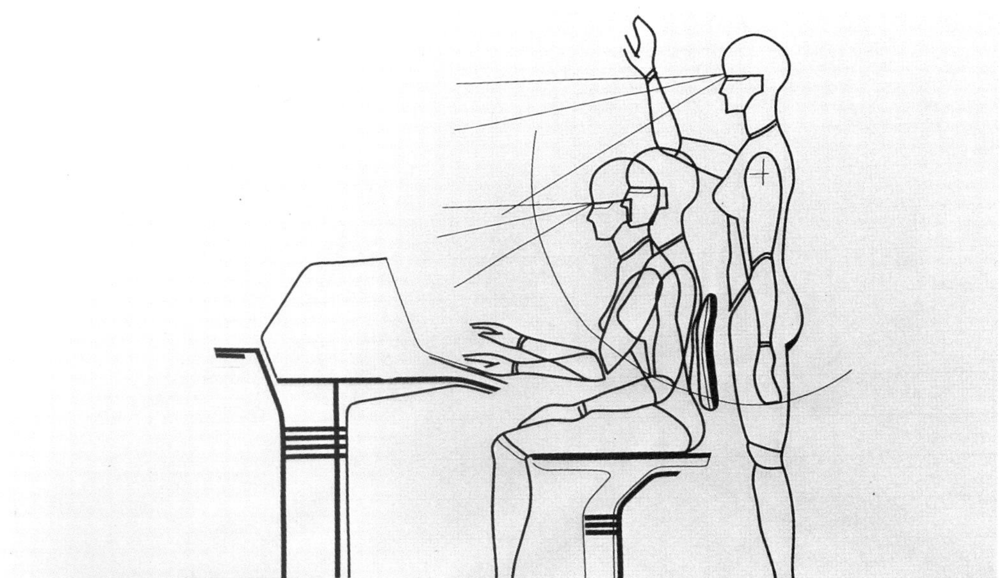

Films

Sheets of films for blocking in large areas of even tone can be found in almost any art-supply store. Letraset has what it calls the Pantone Matching System (PMS), which is probably the industry standard in terms of both tonal consistency and color options. The Pantone system offers dry markers, films, and papers that match each other based on a numerical rating system. If you buy a Pantone 548 blue marker, for instance, the PMS 548 paper and film match. You can also buy films in percentages of tints. These tonal options can be quite effective for shading or blocking in large areas of color.

Both flexible and rigid tapes will adhere well to the slick surfaces. However, special inks and drawing pens are required for working on glossy film surfaces, and such work requires extra time. For fast sketch work, I generally use films as blocks of color without additional ink work.

Drawing tapes and films can be used together to create many effects. The Pantone Matching System (PMS) by Letraset correlates films, papers, and markers to an overall color-matched scheme. The films can be selected as percentages of the parent color, as can the dry markers and papers. Since the films do not take dry markers, I use them as backgrounds or fill-ins where solid tones are needed. Application is simple because the films are adhesive-backed.

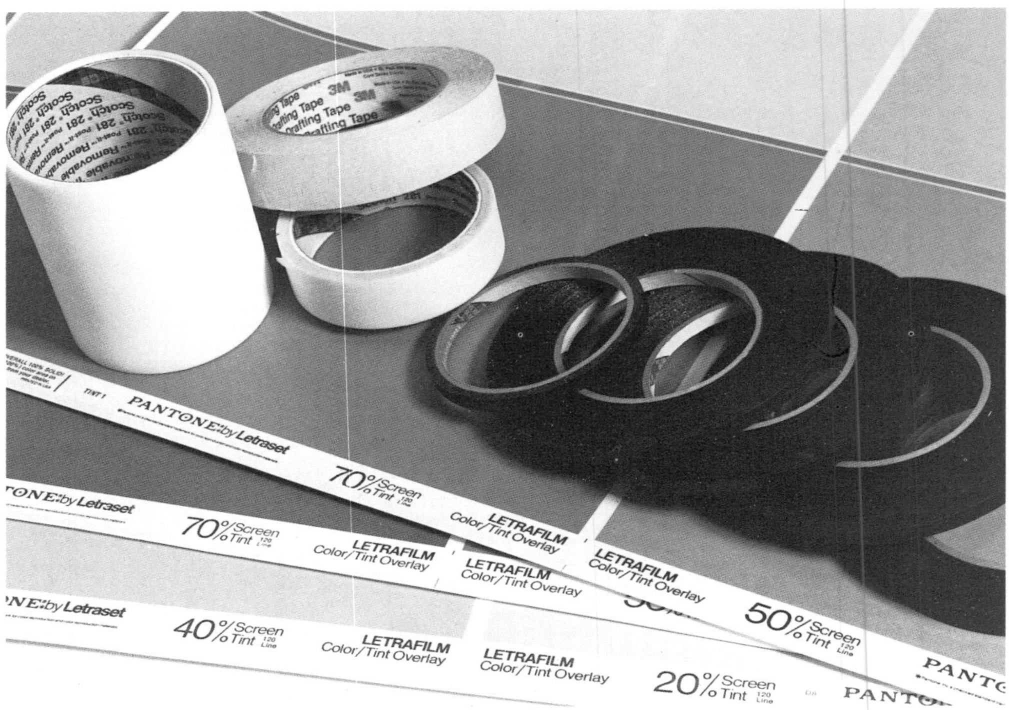

These cigarette lighters were illustrated first with dry marker and pastel; then Pantone film was placed over the rendering and selectively cut out, resulting in an evenly colored background area.

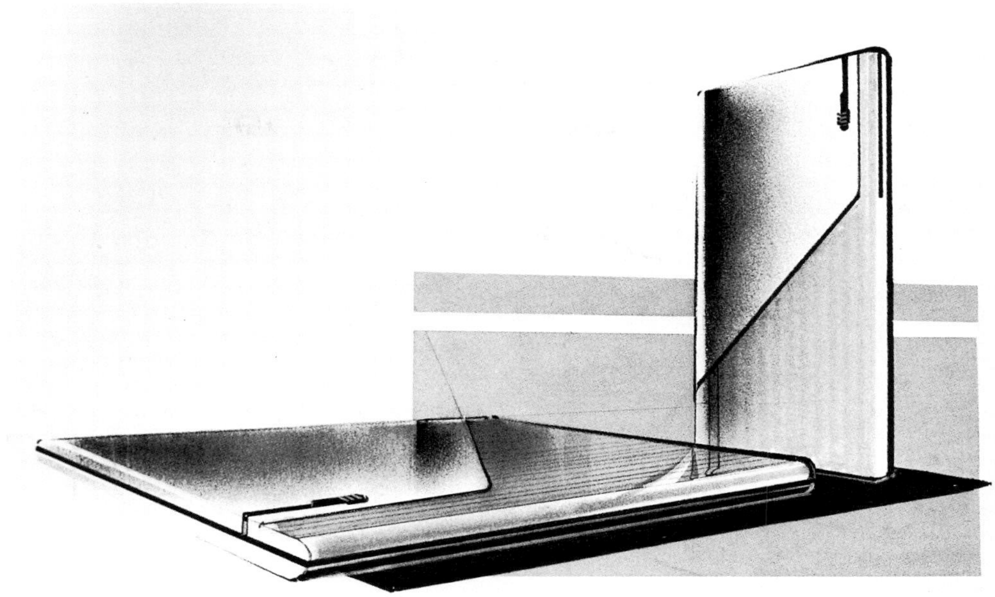

Colored film here serves as a dynamic movement across the background, adding visual interest to the rendering of the lectern.

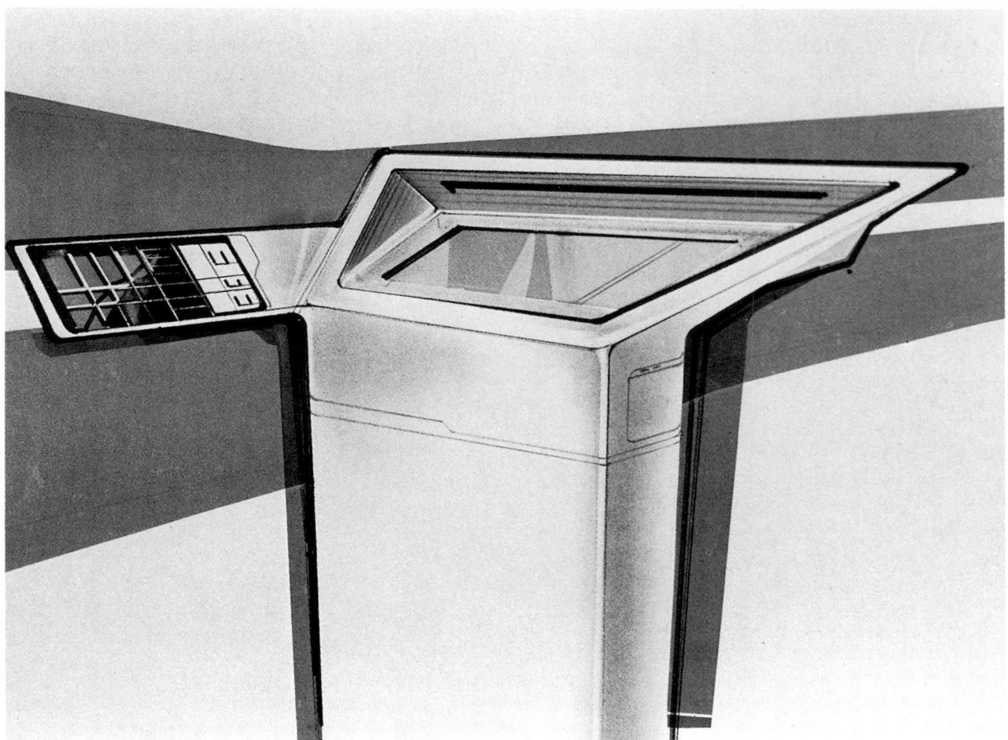

Wet Media

Perhaps some of the most dramatic results in product rendering can be achieved with the application of wet-media techniques. The visual impact can be both powerful and intriguing. In terms of design time, the incorporation of wet-media techniques can tend to burden a schedule, since they require some amount of preparation and clean-up. Once you are comfortable with the process, however, you will find that the results cannot be matched with any of the faster rendering approaches and your efforts are more than compensated for.

The wet mediums involve both water-based and petroleum-based products, and each group can be used with or without their accompanying masking techniques.

There are many products within each of these groups, but my experience has shown a few specific brands to work exceedingly well for design presentations. Within the water-based group, I use Luma Brilliant Concentrated or Dr. Ph. Martin's Synchromatic Transparent watercolors (which are both dye concentrates), Winsor & Newton designers gouache, and Liquitex fluorescent poster colors. I use the gouache primarily for opaque, white highlights; the fluorescent colors for bright, electronic effects; and the dye concentrates for large, translucent background areas.

The water-soluble dye concentrates can be airbrushed onto vellum or applied with watercolor brushes or with special pens. Because vellum will wrinkle if too much water is used, direct application with brushes or pens limits the effects to simple strokes and lines. The use of watercolor techniques on watercolor paper, however, allows the creation of various tones and wash effects.

The intense chroma value of the dye concentrates can provide an almost luminous quality to a rendering. To apply watercolor techniques, choose a paper that is receptive to wetness, such as D'Arches hot-press watercolor paper. Single sheets of paper must be stretched before use, but the stretching technique is easy. Simply wet the paper and smooth it over a sturdy, flat board, like Masonite. Then use gum-backed postal tape to secure it to the board. When the paper is dry, you can wet it again and apply the concentrated watercolors such as Luma or Dr. Martin's. (See pages 113 to 115.)

Experiment by applying the concentrates to the wet watercolor paper in various ways, using both an eyedropper and a sable brush. If undiluted color is dropped directly on the paper, the effects that are produced at the contact point may or may not be desirable. Results can vary, so continue to experiment.

The petroleum-based media include FloMaster or Marsh T-Grade marking-pen inks and Krylon or other lacquer paints. Petroleum-based solvents—such as FloMaster or Marsh ink cleaner, Bestine rubber-cement thinner, and Zippo or Ronson lighter fluid—are also useful. (It should be noted that all of the petroleum-based products require *good ventilation*! Use them for as little time as possible within the rendering process; proper preparation will make this easier. Also take note of other warning labels on these products—they are extremely flammable and must be kept away from heat and flames.)

Intense coloration can be created on vellums by the application of FloMaster or Marsh inks onto a background surface that has been dampened with the ink solvent. The inks can be used on some marker papers also, particularly papers with limited bleed-through. Coloration on more absorbent papers is less intense.

Apply the inks with eyedroppers, brushes, or Webril pads. The pads will give a smooth wash-effect such as seen in watercolor work. When using the pads, however, make sure your skin does not come in contact with the ink. (See pages 119 to 121 for illustrations of the technique and the vivid coloration that can be achieved.)

One of the most interesting techniques is to scrape pastel chalk sticks into a powdered form and then use a solvent, such as lighter fluid, to mobilize the pigment into a fast-drying medium. Webril Handi-Pads by Kendall can then be used to transport the pigment as wash onto vellum or marker-pad paper. (See pages 116 to 117.)

Aerosol cans of lacquer or other paint can be used as a background effect or as a means to render a large color area. These sprays can be used freehand or with masking friskets. Different effects can be found by experimenting with various types of pressurized paint sprays. One method for attaining the exact "corporate" color is to have a quantity of paint custom-mixed and then use it in a jar equipped with an aerosol power unit. Products like this, such as the Preval Sprayer, can be found at art-supply and auto-paint stores.

Finally, experimenting with non-compatible media—such as lacquer paint applied to water-soaked paper, or FloMaster ink combined with Bestine solvent—can add interesting options to your techniques for developing dynamic backgrounds. If overdone, these startling effects can overpower the focus of attention, which should be on the subject of the rendering. Here again, experience will guide you. (See pages 122 to 124.)

Wet media are those that are worked before they dry on the illustration surface. It is from this group that the most exciting mixed-media techniques are derived. The interaction of wet mediums with each other and with dry media provides a visual element that is only partially predictable; hence, you will have a lot of fun experimenting with them.

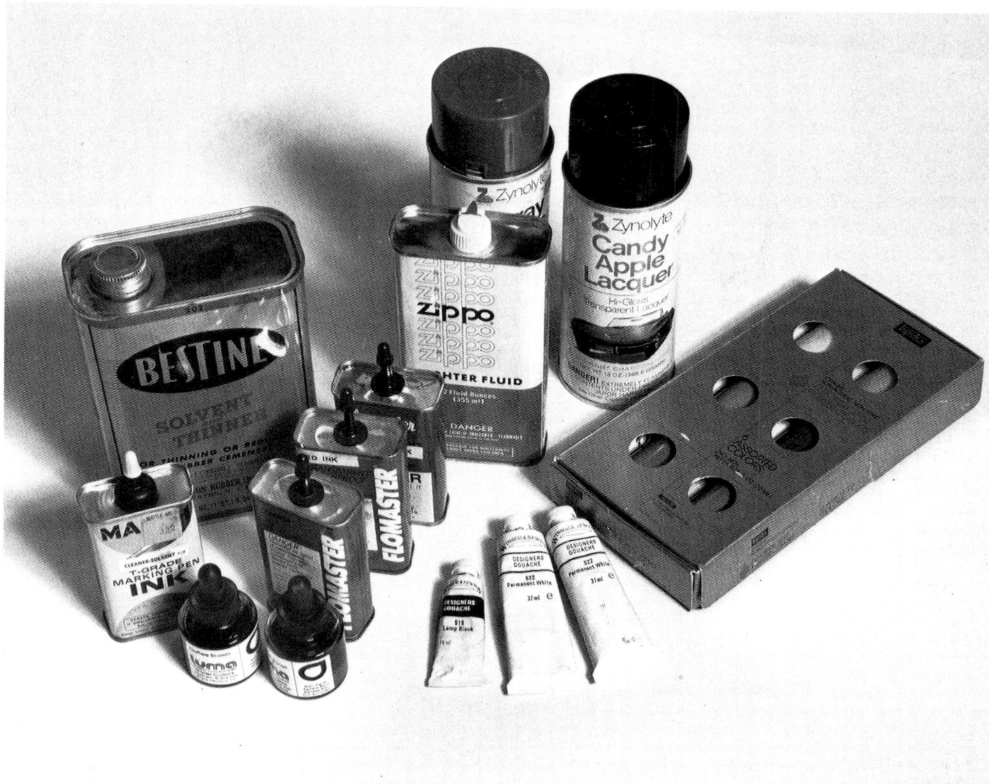

Aerosol lacquer or enamel sprays come in a variety of colors. Your client's corporate color can be matched and custom-mixed at an auto-paint store and then applied to renderings with a reusable spray gun, such as the Preval Sprayer shown. Lacquer sprays often require longer drying times than others and must be used with adequate ventilation.

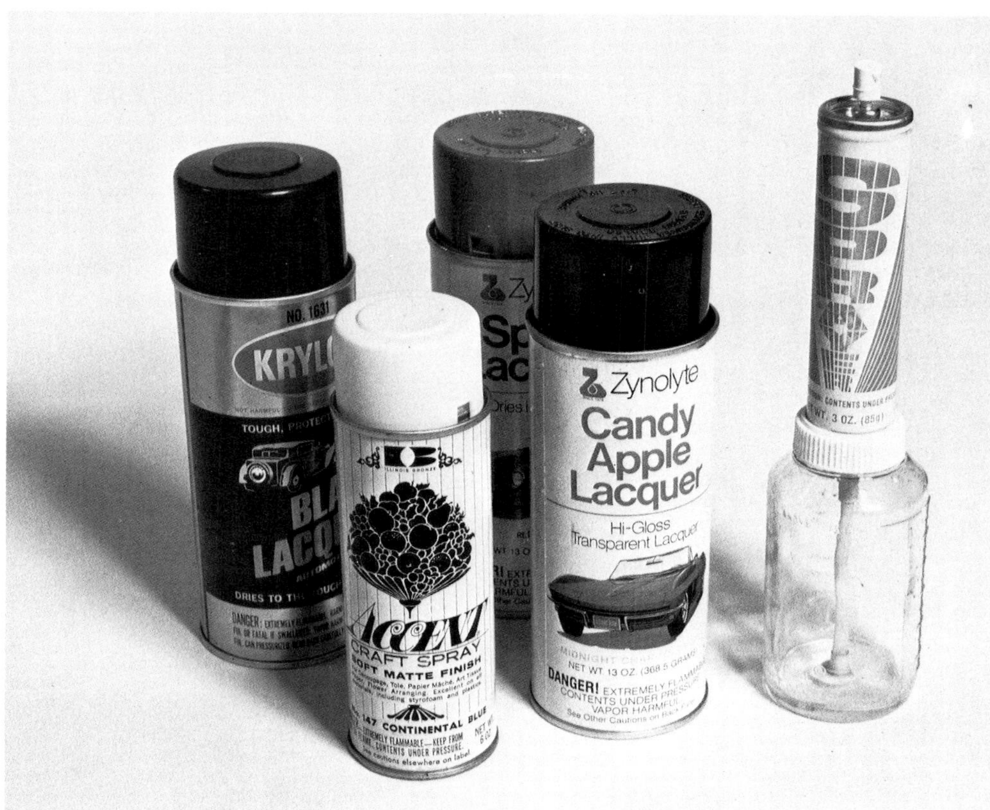

Concentrated watercolor interacting with a water-soaked #200 hot-press illustration board provides a soft, flowing effect that becomes a counterpoint to the crisp, linear lines of the product, a wall-hung computer. The product was laid out separately, then transferred to the dried board as line work, and finally rendered in place with dry marker and pastel chalk.

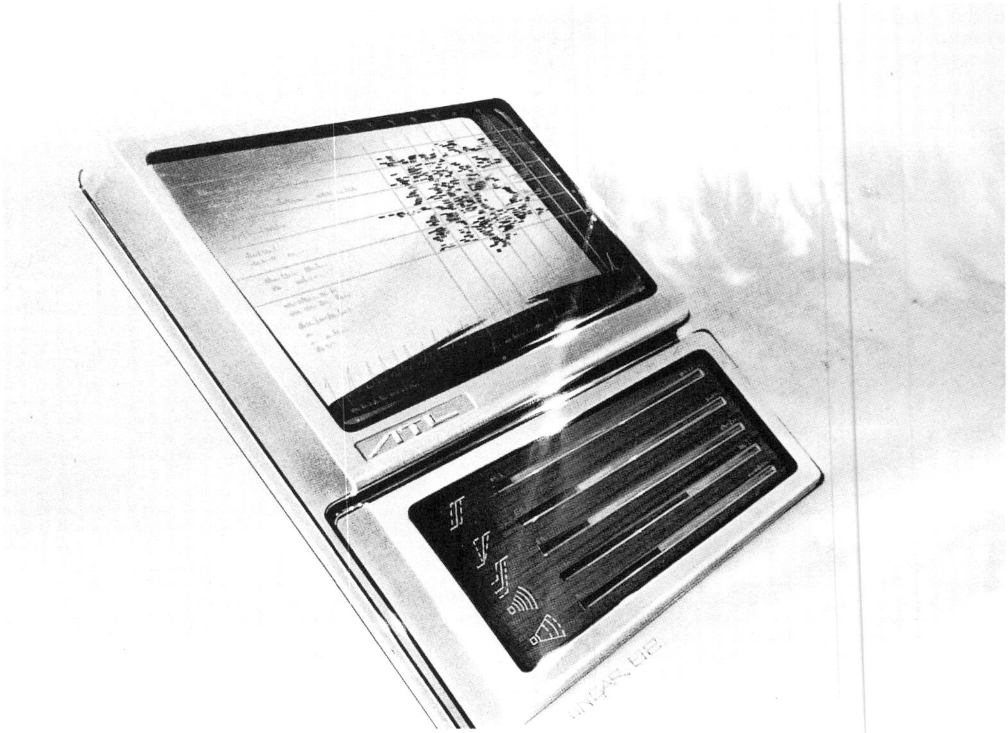

This background was developed using Luma concentrated watercolors on hot-press watercolor paper. The product was then rendered directly onto the background by using dry markers, pastel chalks, and white gouache. (See color picture on page 132.)

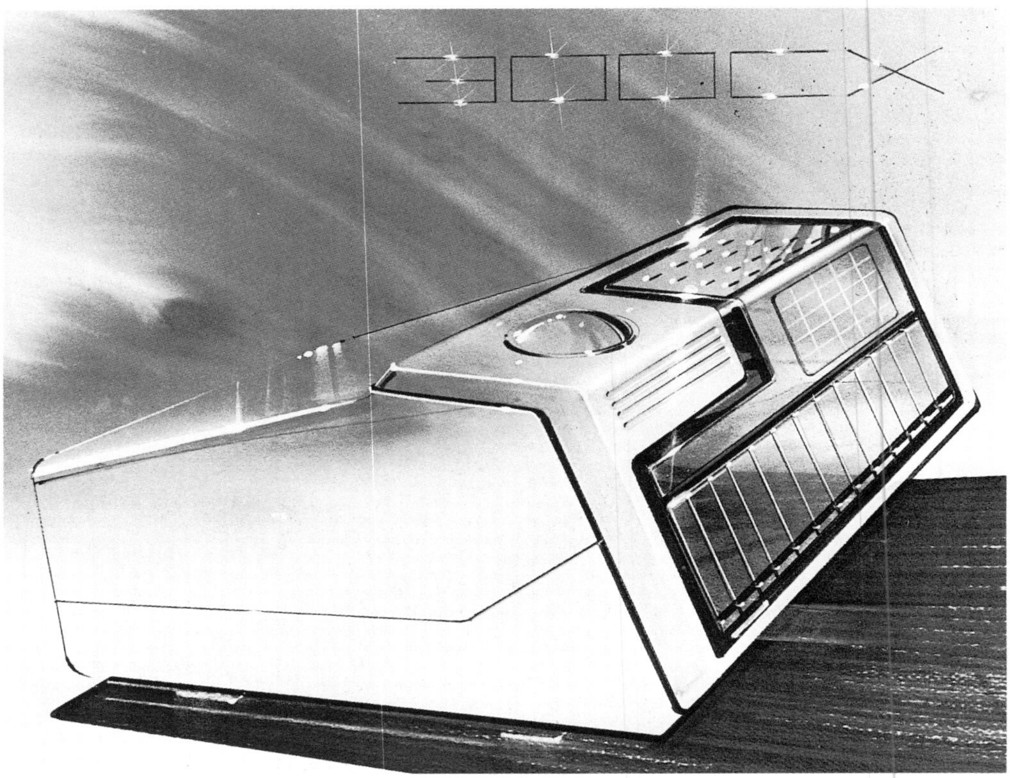

In this case, a general wash of FloMaster marking ink was blended over hot-press illustration board that had first been dampened with FloMaster cleaner. The medical cart was then rendered directly onto the dried background.

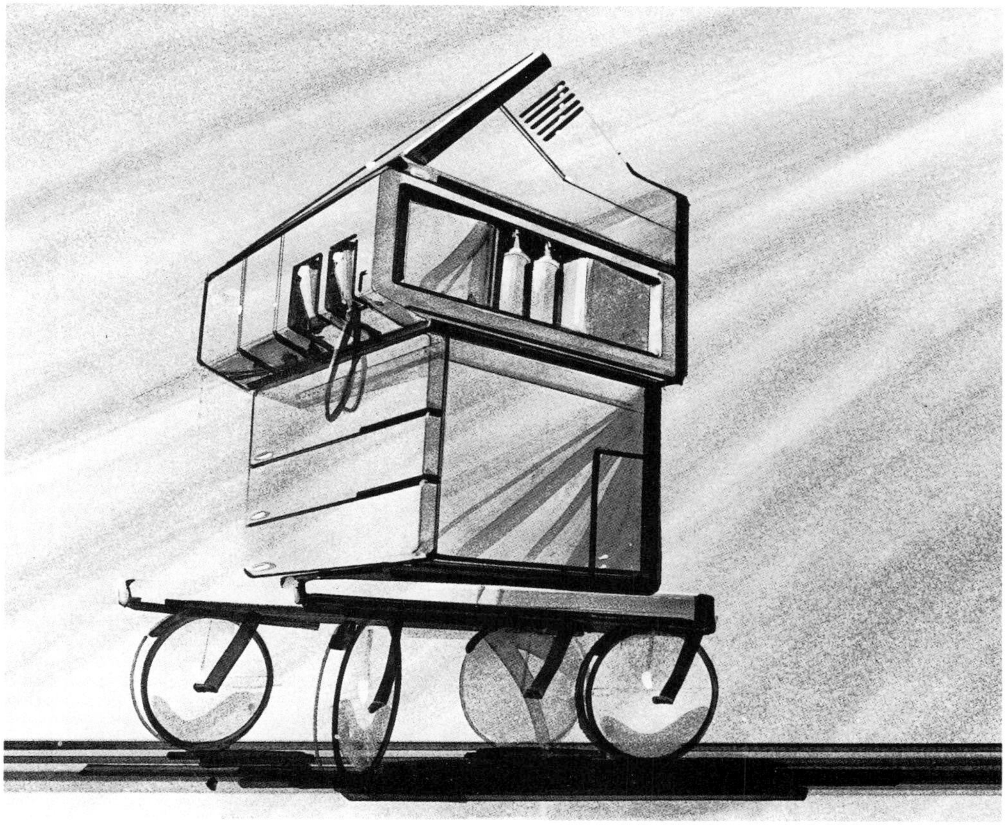

This mobile computer is based on a plot generated from Jim Hennessey's Industrial Design Drawing Programs software. The selected plot was reproduced onto vellum and then lighter fluid and pastel chalk were blended over the plot. This allowed the final rendering to stand out from other similar, uncolored plots.

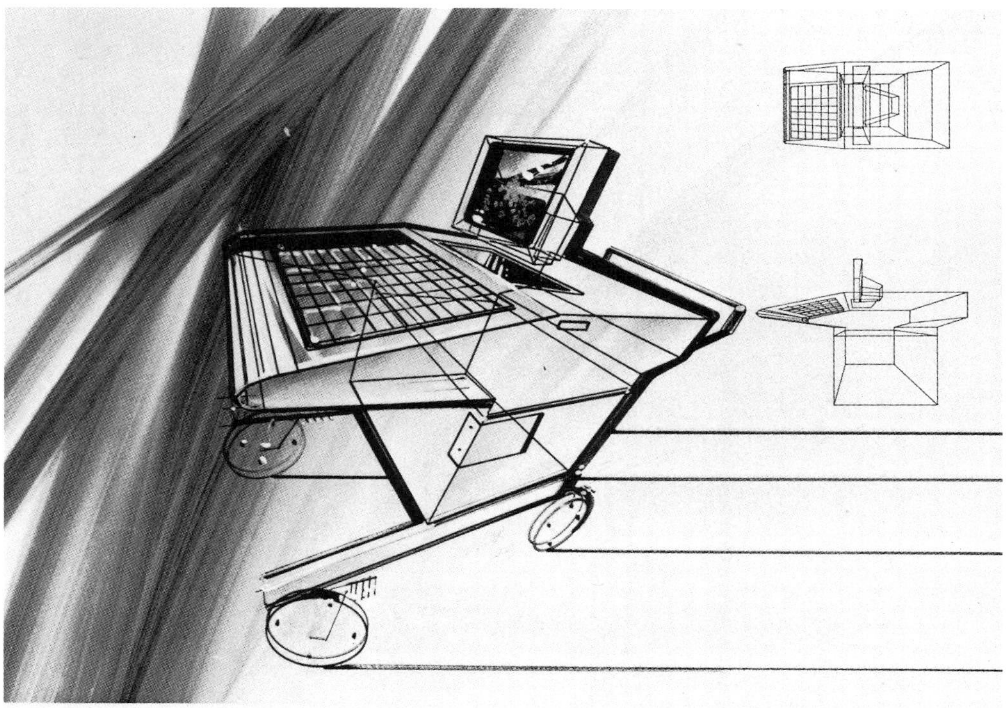

The Complete Studio

The mistake designers most often make in product rendering is two-fold: First, I believe they use incorrect materials, or correct materials on weak or incompatible surfaces; and second, I find that many designers are intimidated by materials and will not experiment with techniques they have not previously used.

You should find the following media-interaction matrix very helpful for remembering what media are compatible and work well together. All of the materials you will be working with in the ensuing chapters are readily available in larger art-supply stores, but just in case, there is a source guide in the Appendix for the harder-to-find products.

Mixed-media matrix
Use this chart as a handy guide to see at a glance which media effectively interact with various kinds of papers. Throughout this book, you will be using all of these combinations as a means to create fast, clean concepts. You should definitely explore all of these possibilities and experiment with new interactions as new products become available.

	Graphite	Pastel chalk	Lighter fluid/pastel	Colored art pencils	Dry markers	Liquid marker inks	Rubber-cement thinner/marker ink	Dye concentrates	Gouache	Fluorescent poster paint	Photo tape
Dry-marker pad		●		●	●	●	●		●	●	●
Vellum	●	●	●	●	●	●	●	●	●	●	●
Newsprint paper	●	●	●	●	●				●	●	●
Copy-machine paper (white bond)	●	●	●	●	●				●	●	●
Brownline repro paper		●		●	●				●	●	●
Blueline repro paper		●		●	●				●	●	●
Colored paper for pastels		●		●	●	●	●		●	●	●
Watercolor paper		●		●	●	●	●	●	●	●	●
Pantone graduated color paper				●	●				●	●	●

2 DRAWING THE LINE

The simple analysis of how the human eye perceives a two-dimensional image serves as a good starting point for learning how to effectively produce fast, exciting, and highly representational concepts. Communicating within the framework of lines and tonal gradations can appear to be extremely complex and simply unobtainable to the uninitiated. Good artwork is commonly attributed to a mysterious quality called "talent."

I contend that anyone can draw to excellent levels if he or she can see sensitively and hold a pencil at the same time. Like anything else, it is simply a matter of breaking things down to their common denominators and then building them up again. This chapter will show how you can create the illusion of depth and dimension with a simple line drawing. These techniques will be invaluable later, when you will combine dynamic line work with pastel chalks and exciting backgrounds.

Simple line work on this sofa rendering implies a softness that is set off by the solid shadow and the sharply contrasting marker background. Blended vertical streaking of dry markers can create a dramatic backdrop to such freehand sketches.

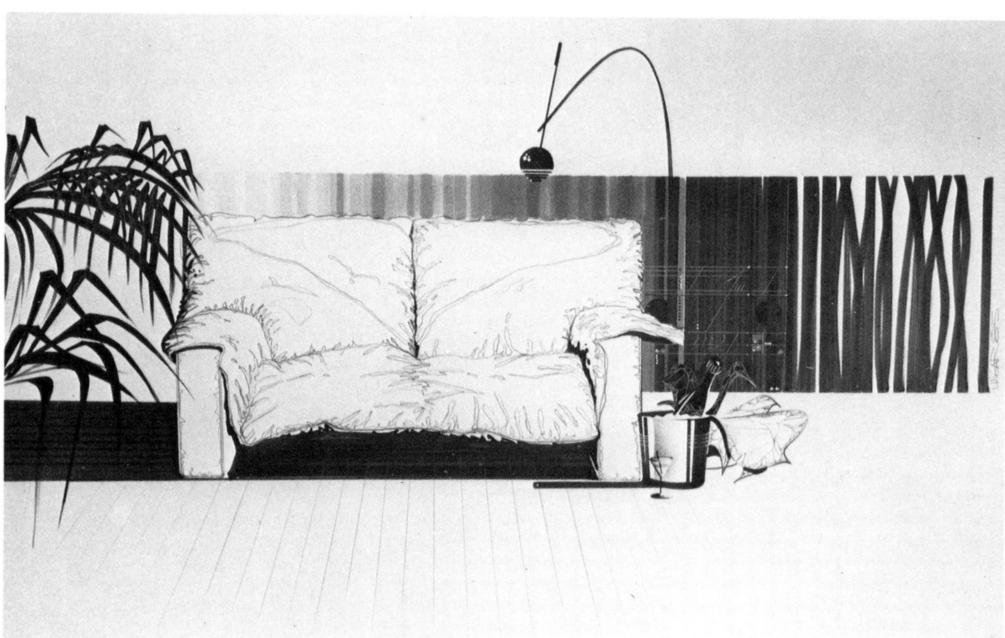

The Viewer's Role

The human mind will first process an observed image as a single entity; an accumulation of points, lines, and shapes merge into one cohesive image. You can think of this as a very "subjective" data base. At the moment of observation (which may take less than a second for a simple drawing), the concept drawing either works or it does not. The image at hand is either recognized as a very impressive concept of, say, a hair dryer, or it is not. It is only moments later that isolated parts of the drawing may be appreciated for their own merit. These parts will be seen as either individually successful design elements or well-illustrated components of the complete drawing. If the concept as a whole lacks impact, however, the excellence of the details will not matter. The overall concept of the product must be visually strong. It simply must have graphic muscles.

The Designer's Role

Effective product design strives for functional solutions that meet both project constraints and contemporary aesthetics. Is there any reason to have the presentation of one's ideas fall short of this? A fundamental problem with many designers, no matter what the discipline, is a failure to recognize the following: From initial, preliminary concepts to final presentation work, the renderings are a means to obtain the final design solution. They should have the same strength of professionalism as the finished hardware. Graphic excellence should be mandatory from day one in the design process. Good ideas are often lost or overlooked because they have been presented and conveyed with an inherent lack of graphic confidence.

The first step toward achieving graphic strength is to recognize that the most successful renderings are often the simplest. Such renderings maintain an economy of line and of tonal values and strike a careful balance between the subject matter and the background. They contain just enough information—not too little and not too much. The total look is strong but does not overpower the subject matter, and it is tailored to the needs of the audience.

To be effective, then, a design concept should convey to the observer in the shortest time and cleanest manner the essence of your ideas. Therefore the conceptual designer's first axiom is this: The strength of a preliminary concept rendering lies within the designer's ability to leave out the obvious. Overattention to details will result in an overworked drawing and will weaken the overall impact.

In this drawing of a sci-fi highway, the car attracts all of the viewer's attention because it contains much more graphic emphasis than the rest of the concept. You could consider the car overworked or the surroundings underworked.

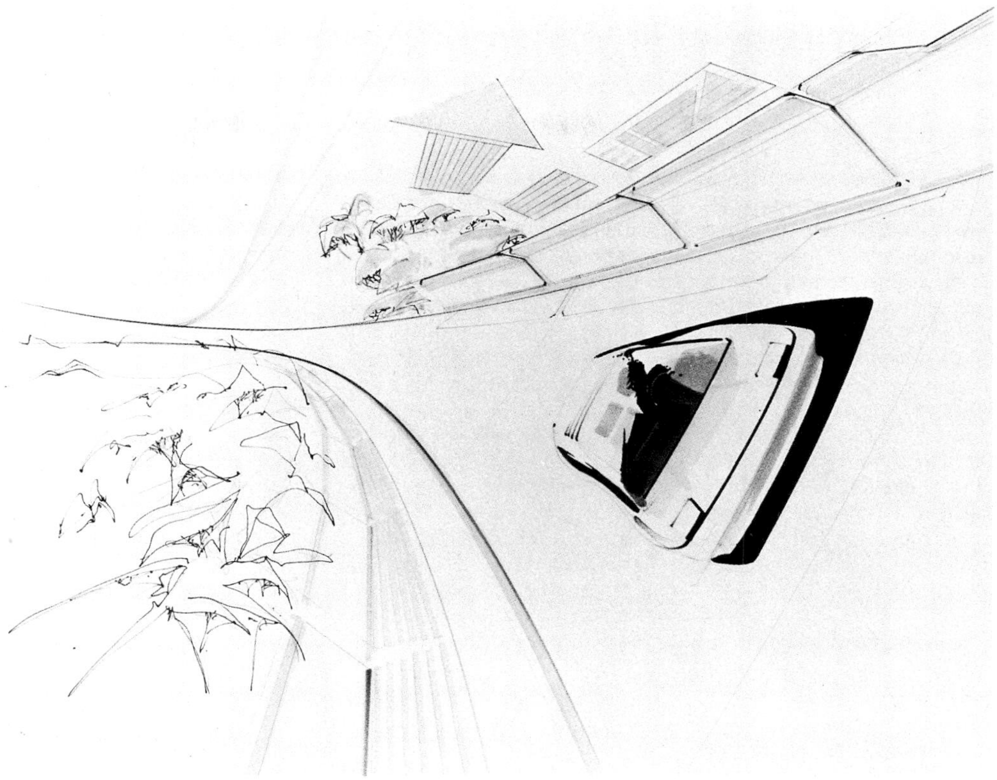

This drawing is more appropriate. There is a balance to the composition because no single detail is overemphasized. Do not be concerned if you consistently overwork drawings as you are learning the balancing process. The realization that a drawing is overworked is a healthy sign of your rendering sensitivity. And with practice and experience, you will know when to stop in future renderings.

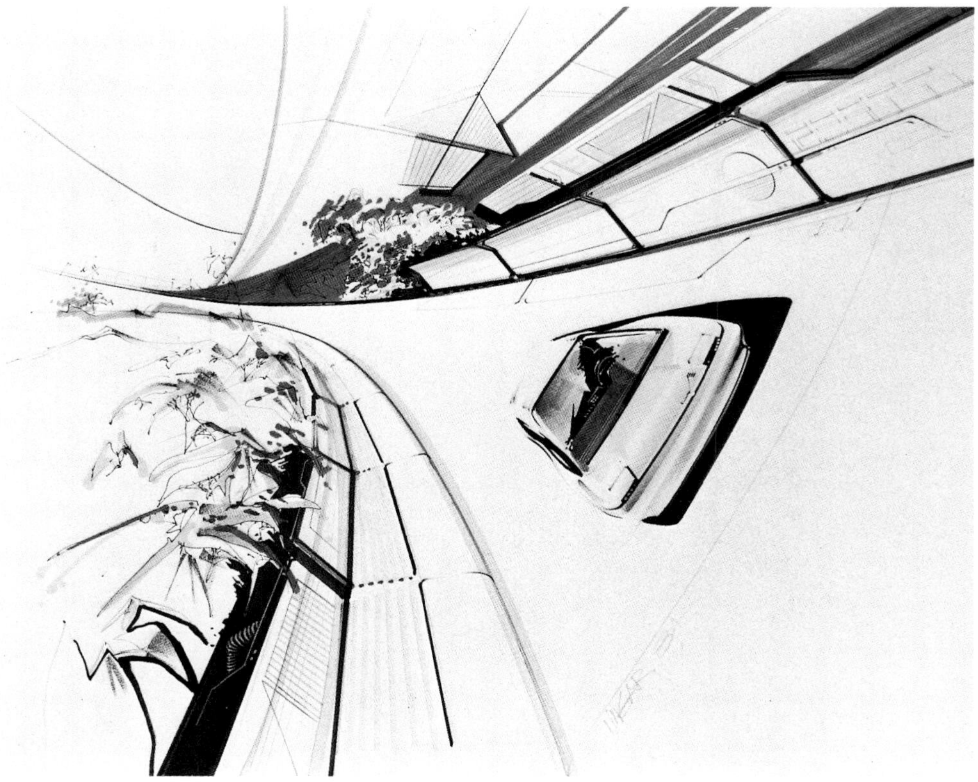

Objective: Do Not Draw the Obvious

Aside from the obvious aesthetic drawbacks, overworking a concept drawing can complete visual statements that are unnecessary and in fact limit the conceptual potential of the drawing. Judiciously selecting lines or shapes to "not complete" will allow the observer's image processing to complete them for you. This is very important. It allows a certain ambiguity to take place in the rendition of the concept—a kind of looseness to the illustrated thought-process.

The most important advantage in this ambiguity is the manner in which your audience will complete the lines and shapes for you. This usually takes the form of creative solutions and alternatives that your drawing has started to suggest to them. It is amazing how fast this interactive creative process can be dampened by the thorough construction of all the points, lines, and planes. Completing every facet of the concept will exclude these alternative possibilities!

In the preliminary stages of concept development, industrial designers have a distinct requirement to keep their initial design concepts as open-ended as possible. This allows other design team members the creative freedom to read other solutions into your illustrations. At the same time, paradoxically, the drawing of a design concept must be specific enough to graphically communicate your complete idea. Therein, again, lies the heart of the problem: The designer must know how to include enough information to make the concept effective and how to stop the visualization in time to prevent it from being overworked.

The industrial designer is, of course, not uniquely focused on this problem. It is common to all design disciplines, from product designers to architects, from interior designers to toy designers—wherever presentation drawings are used to communicate phases of design solutions to an audience, and in particular, to creative audiences with differences in their individual abilities to generate drawings themselves.

Initial design ideas should not be rendered in too much detail. This allows other team designers to extrapolate their own ideas from unfinished details of your renderings. Important new directions often come from this effective technique. Here, a limited amount of detail defines the shape and form of a home entertainment system.

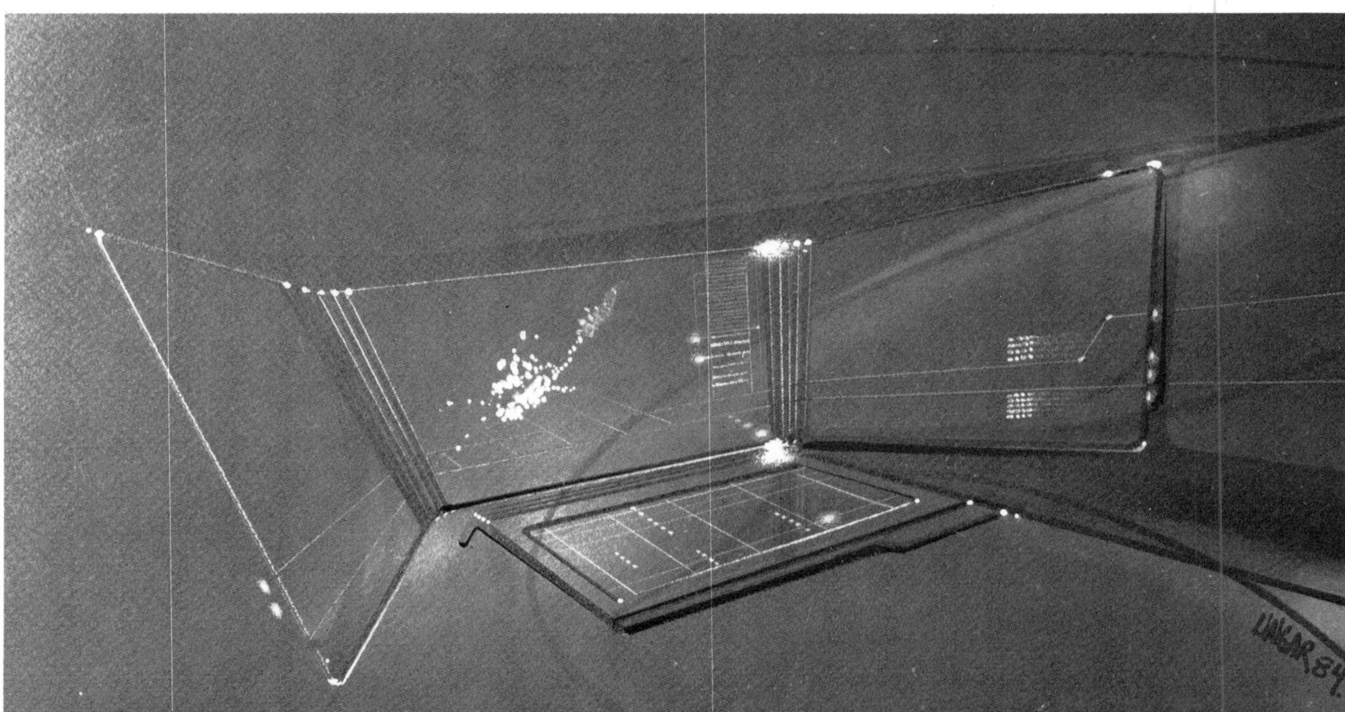

The Need for Rapid Visualization

Within the corporate design world, my experience has been that the management audience will not in the least be swayed by the artistic merits of a group of renderings. They effectively focus on: (1) the time it may have taken to generate the concepts (or the perceived time, since in the business world, time translates directly to money, or overhead on a project) and (2) the content of the drawings—what ideas do they portray or suggest; how much do they imply? It is only after these considerations that the impact of a "polished presentation" will have a positive effect. This principle is particularly important in the early phases of concept rendering. The reality is this: Contemporary illustration techniques are of value in the business marketplace only to the extent that they convey ideas rapidly and efficiently.

Drawing the Cube

Learning rapid and effective visualization techniques naturally should start with a discussion about fundamentals. The cube is as good a place as any to start. Think of the following examples as progressions in development. The illustrations will demonstrate several rapid-visualization techniques: appropriate viewpoint and estimated perspective; weighted lines (light, medium, dark); tapered lines (line-point extrapolation); and incorporation of bold, outlining shadows.

Try to copy each step in the demonstration. To start with, use a simple soft-lead graphite pencil or a black Prismacolor pencil on plain, white bond paper. First outline a solid cube in two-point perspective. Never mind about shading just yet. Each of the six drawings, through line weight and viewpoint, will unfold an increasingly interesting visual, starting with the most boring (and the most commonly found species) first and proceeding to a relatively successfully drawn cube.

A fast, simple drawing of a cube drawn in two-point perspective shows the essential form. This typical "eagle's-eye" view is a common one and probably the most boring. Also, there is a complete lack of visual interest to the illustration.

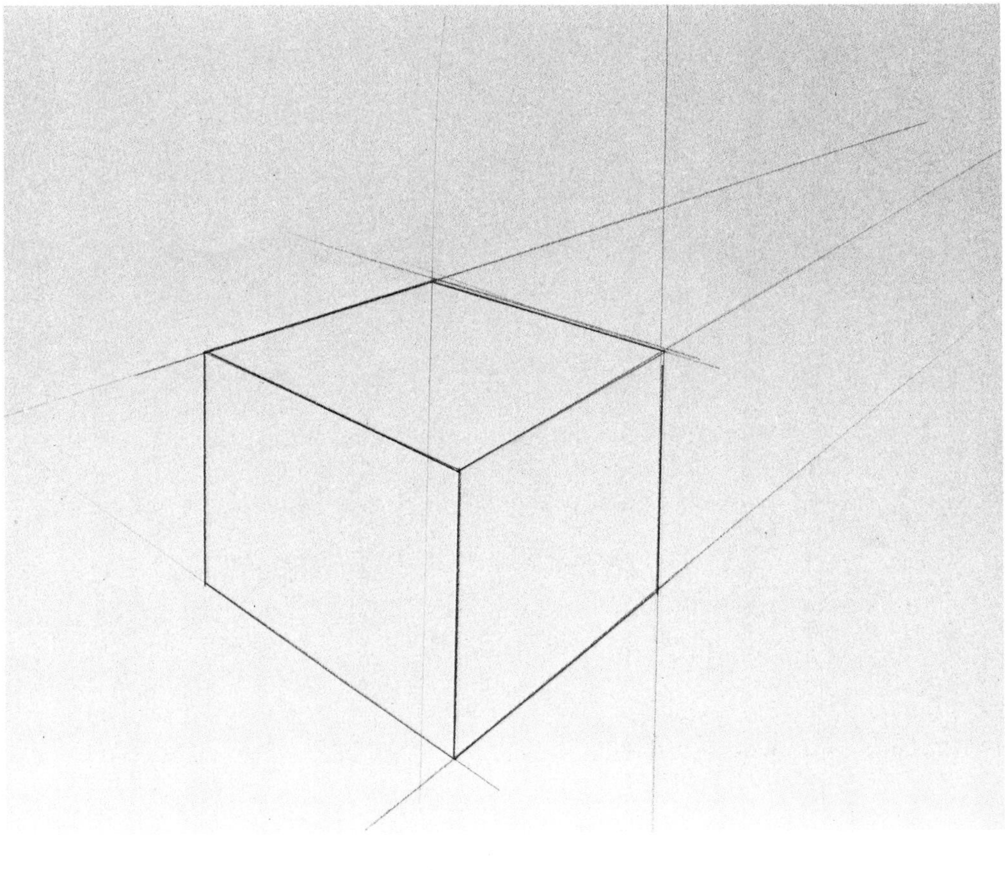

Drawing the Cube

In this layout, I have used a lower viewpoint but to the detriment of the product—in this case, the cube shape. You will want to develop a sense of knowing just how much to exaggerate a perspective without compromising important details of the concept.

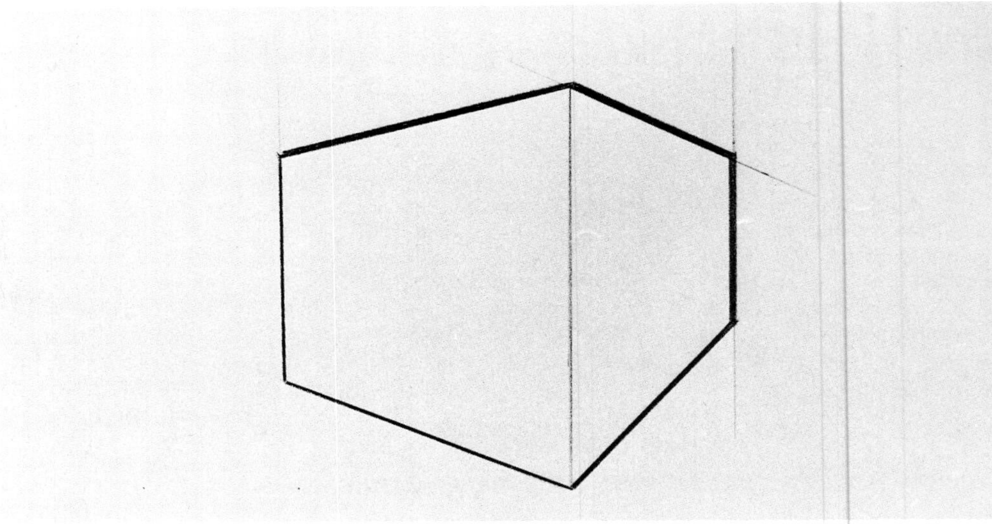

This is a better viewpoint for this shape, and also a variety of line weights are used. If you have at least three line weights (light, medium, and dark), you will effectively lead the viewer's eye around the product. The line work will "flow" as it moves from plane to plane.

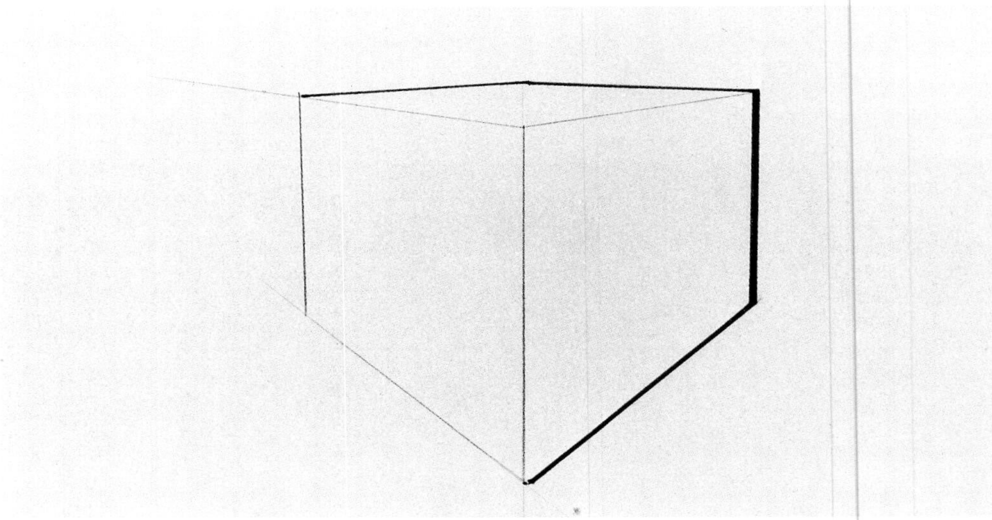

This quick sketch has the same information as the previous cube drawing but has a much lighter and faster-looking style. Your eye completes all of the visual statements where the lines taper to a point.

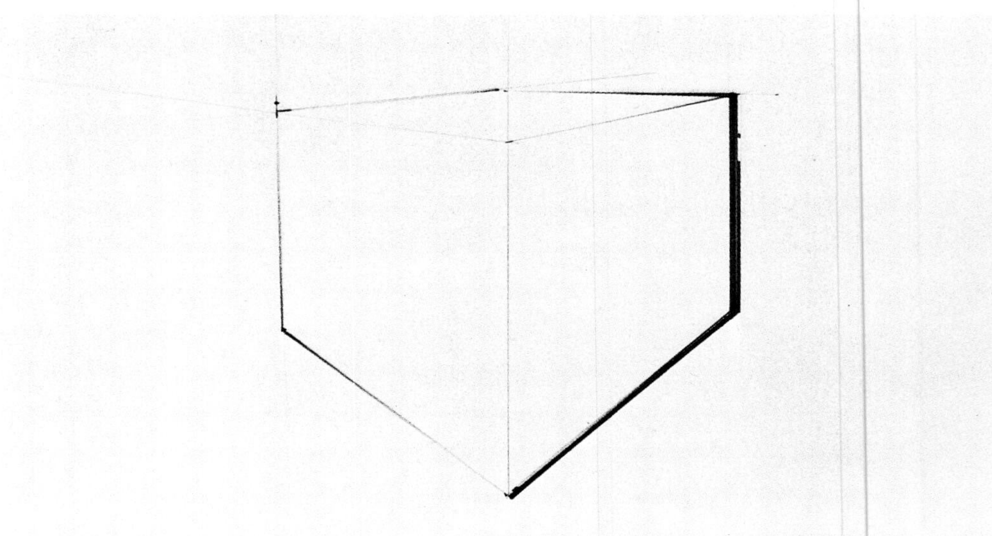

The addition of a shadow or outline visually sets the concept onto the drawing surface and gives the shape three-dimensional presence. The shadow detail is defining three sides of the cube, so lines may be omitted there to save time.

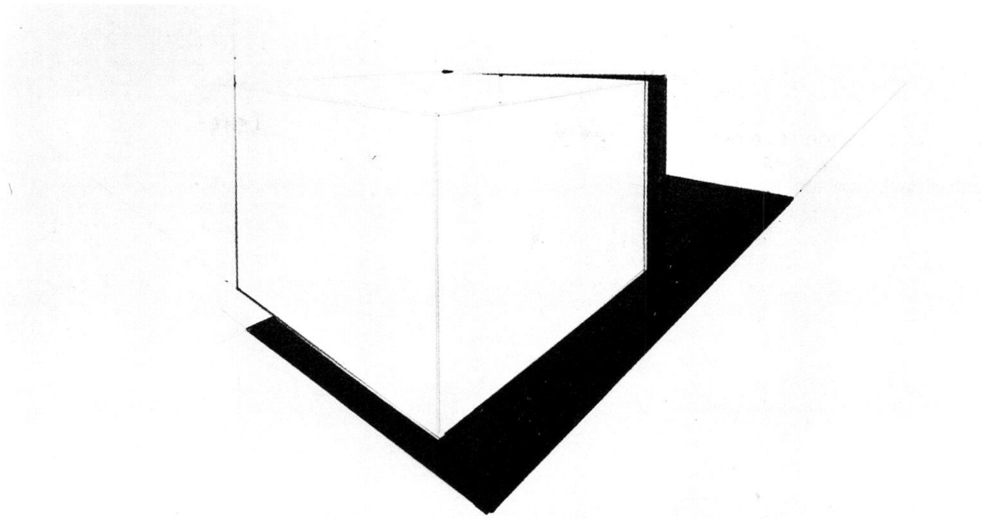

This group of cubes took only thirty seconds to draw. Each has a different viewpoint and three line weights. At this point, you should quickly draw twenty cube shapes, each with a different perspective. To get the feel of quick, estimated perspective, hold your straightedge loosely and draw all of your lines without plotting any vanishing points on the page.

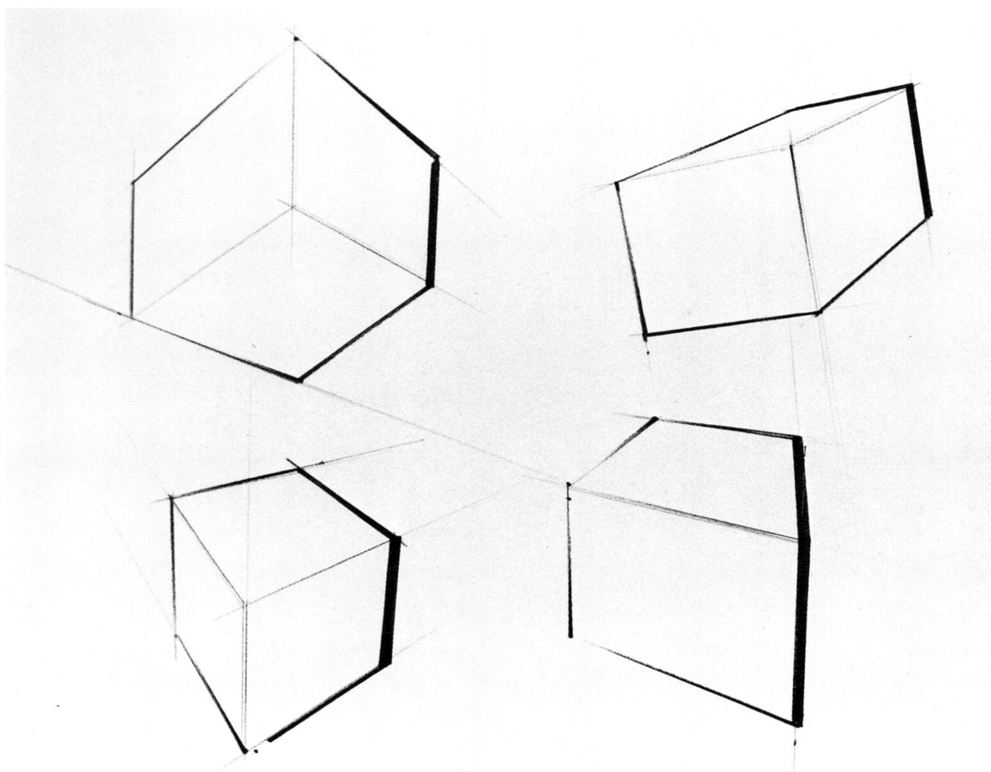

Weighted Line and Line-Point Extrapolation

Do you see the evolution from a simple, boring line drawing to a dynamic expression of line weights and form? The simple, expressionless single-weight line drawing of the cube shape takes just as long to draw, if not longer, but it holds our attention the least. The drawing with varying line weights is more forceful. The drawing with tapered lines, however, commands the most attention by allowing the mind to do a major amount of the work. The drawing succeeds because in processing visual information, the mind will connect a line section to a point and read it as a continuous line even though the line was never completed. This is especially true if the line weight broadens to a heavier weight as it moves away from the point. I call this effect "line-point extrapolation."

Line-point extrapolation is especially effective for the quick generation of several related concepts. The line-point technique allows the suggestion of planar development without shading, and illustrations show a certain "transparency" as the concepts develop.

Line-point extrapolation is a quick way to illustrate shape and form without rendering all of the complete lines. Your eye will move along a tapering line until the line disappears and is found again at a not-too-far termination point.

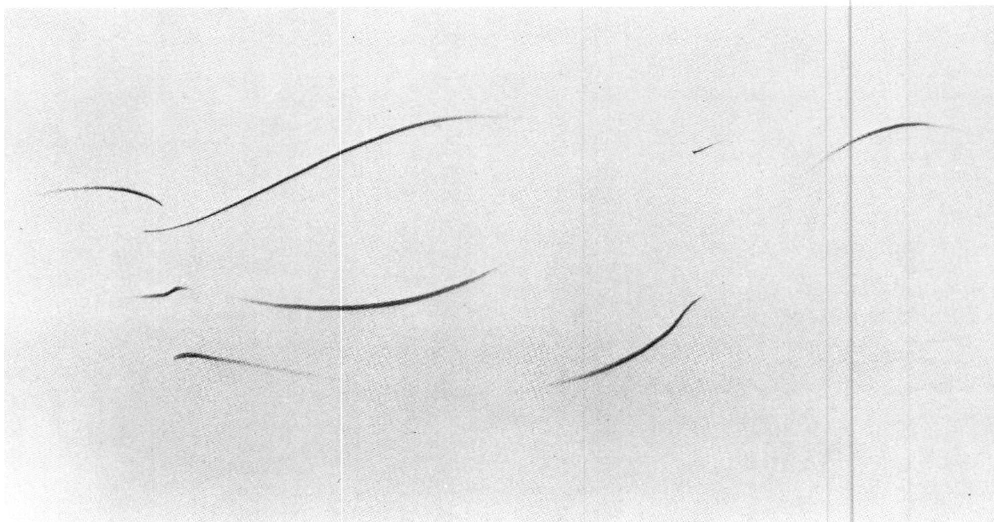

I quickly roughed in the curvilinear shape of this holography wristband by using line-point extrapolation technique. The exclusion of extraneous details allows the viewer's attention to be focused on the significant part of the wristband.

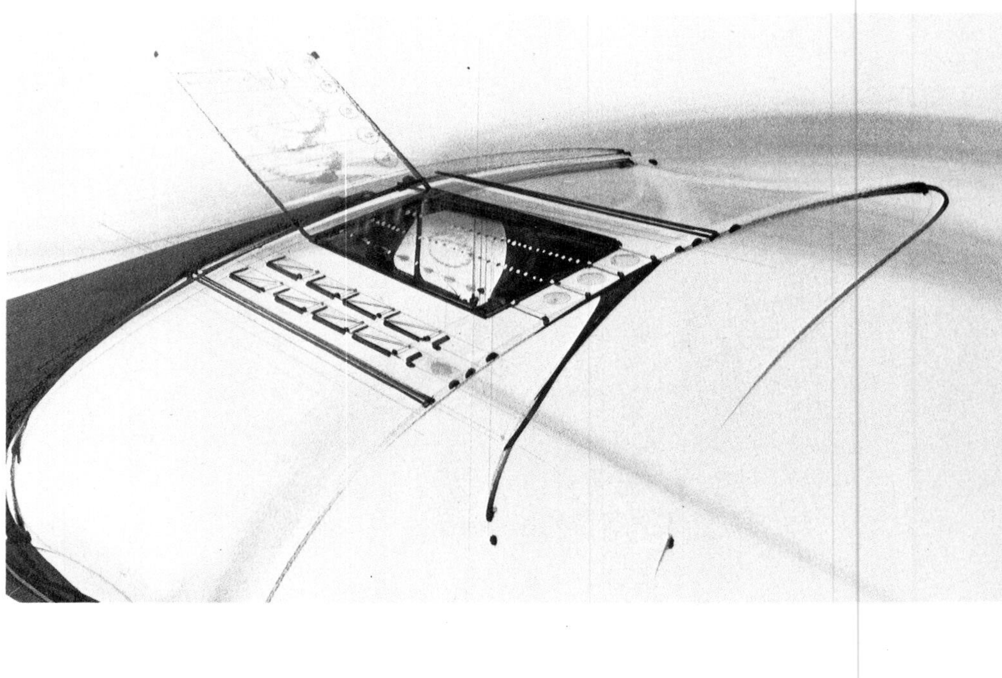

Line-point extrapolation works well with straight lines. The viewer unconsciously connects tapering lines to ending points even though the two may not be connected. Planes can be delineated rapidly using this technique.

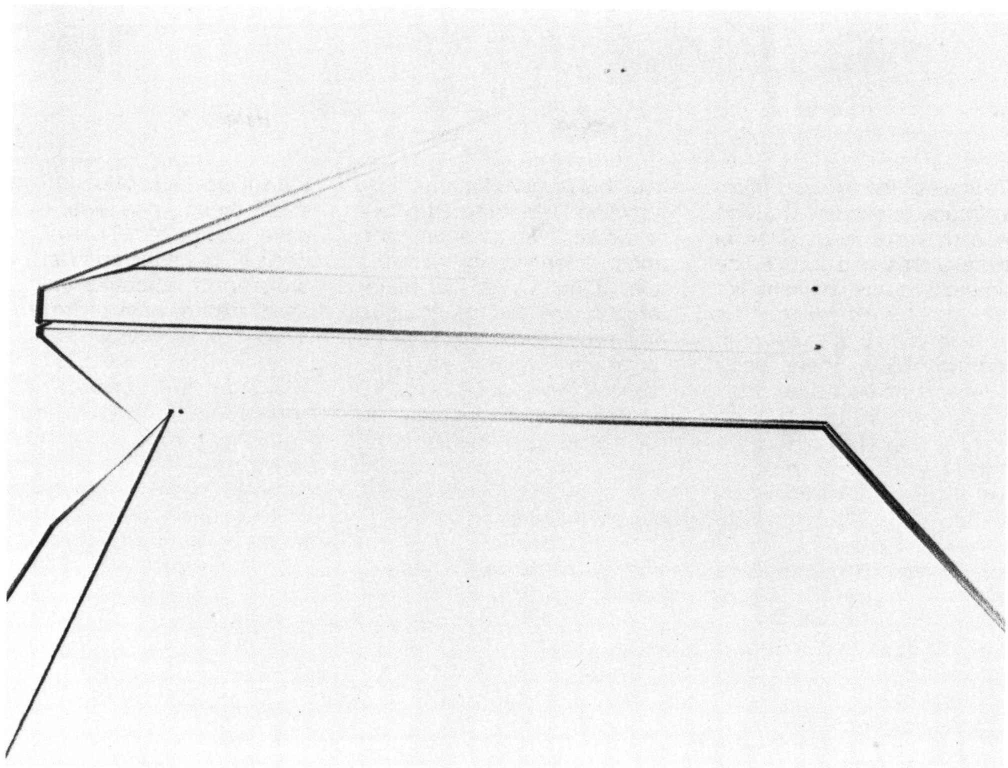

The female figure here was quickly created by using tapering lines that widen at the prominent parts of the body. Your eye will complete the rest, and the detailed product, the synthesizer, is thus emphasized.

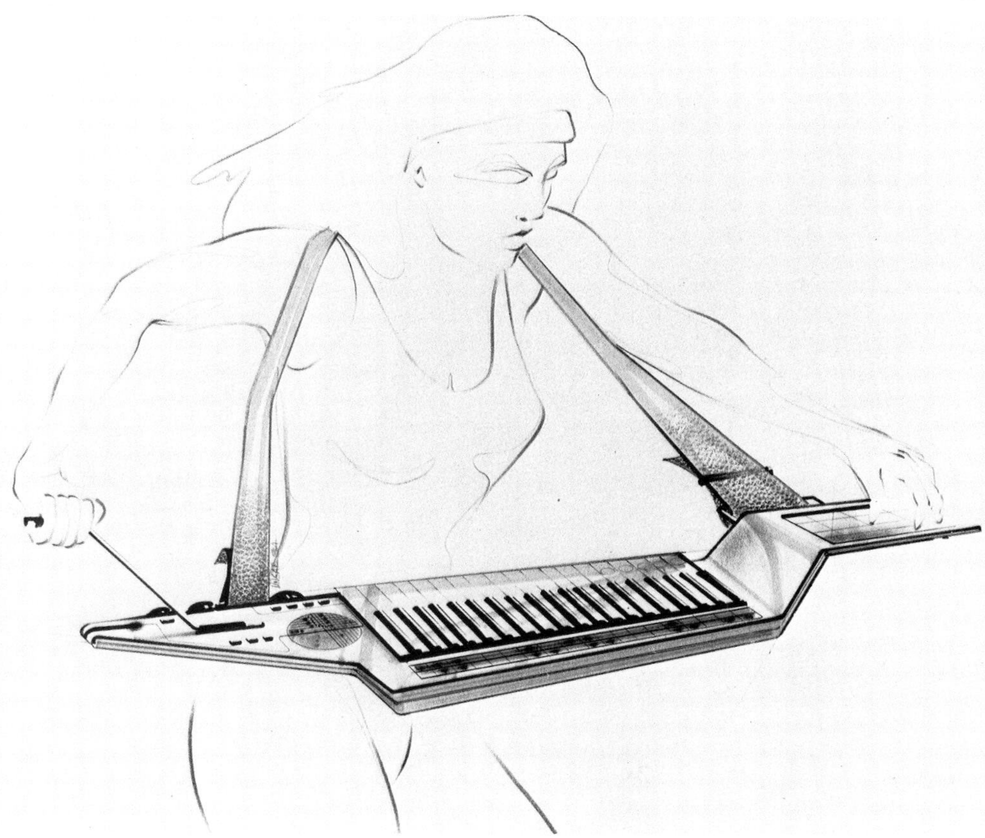

Estimated Perspective

The technique for estimated perspective is both fast and simple to do. First, you will want to tilt the drawing surface so that it is normal (90°) to your line of sight, or as close to that as your drawing desk will allow. Then, begin by estimating vanishing points toward the right and left of the leading edge of the object for two-point perspective; also add a vertical vanishing point if you are using three-point perspective. (Three-point perspective is useful for creating the illusion of tallness; the tapering of vertical lines to a common point slants the sides of vertical planes, such as those found in a skyscraper or the high walls of a room.)

For quick-sketch layouts, your vanishing points need to be only roughly accurate. If the resulting lines vary slightly, say plus or minus 5°, from those you would have obtained by using the real vanishing point, no one will notice, and the freehand style will increase your drawing speed.

It is important to keep the drawing surface normal to your line of sight to prevent the creation of a "perspective of your perspective." If the board is tipped away from you, there is a tendency to exaggerate your eyeball estimations, and the lines drawn near the top of your page may be inaccurate.

The reason for estimated perspective is simple: speed! I have seen designers evolve four or five quick concepts while a colleague is still setting up his vanishing points!

In the following examples, you will see the use of rapid-visualization techniques in the development of solutions to typical design problems. Each concept was first outlined lightly using a red or blue Verithin pencil and estimated-perspective technique. See if you can emulate the process.

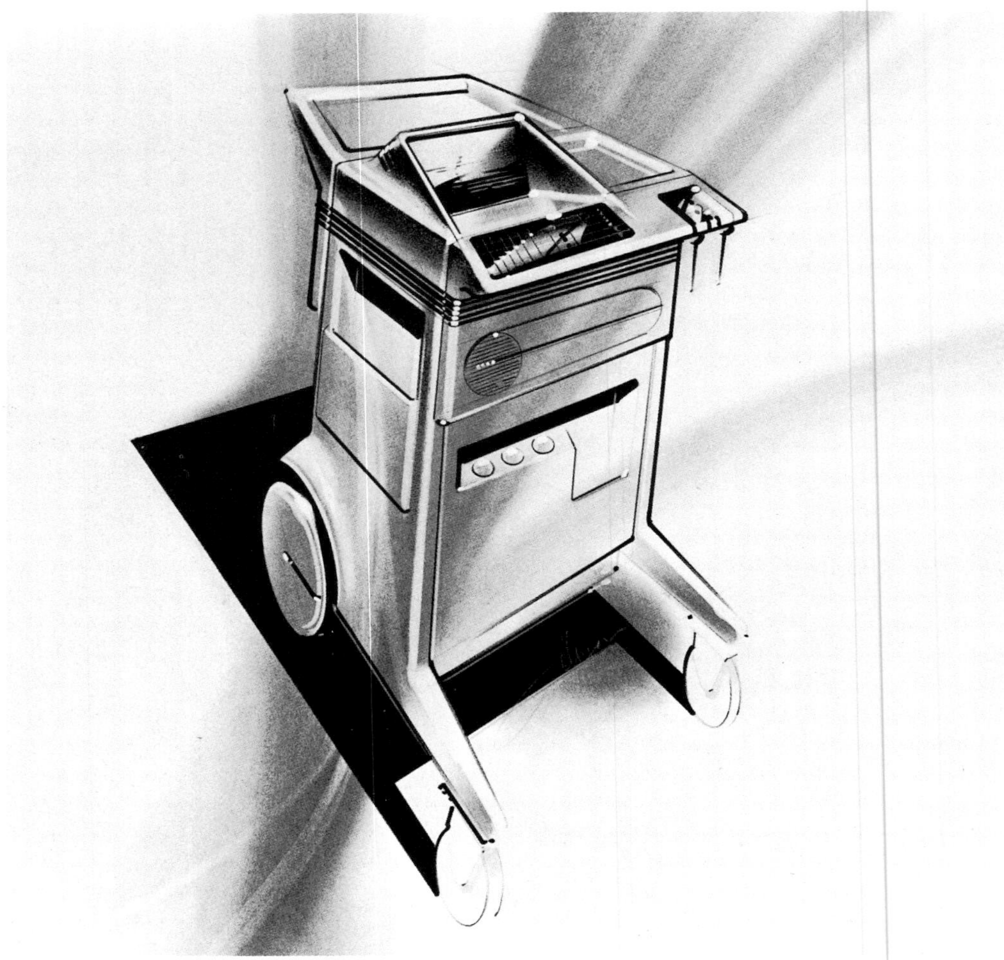

Although this medical ultrasound cart seems complex, it was rendered quickly by using estimated perspective and line-point extrapolation. To complete the drawing, I used a simple light, medium, and dark shading style (see page 63). Even the most complex objects can be analyzed and drawn effectively with this combination of techniques.

This series shows how a simple layout can evolve rapidly and cleanly with estimated perspective and line-point extrapolation. The layout for this communication device was first drawn lightly on the paper. The delineating shadow area was considered early on as an element of the whole composition. As the lines were finalized, heavy tapering was used to lead the viewer's eye around the edges of the product.

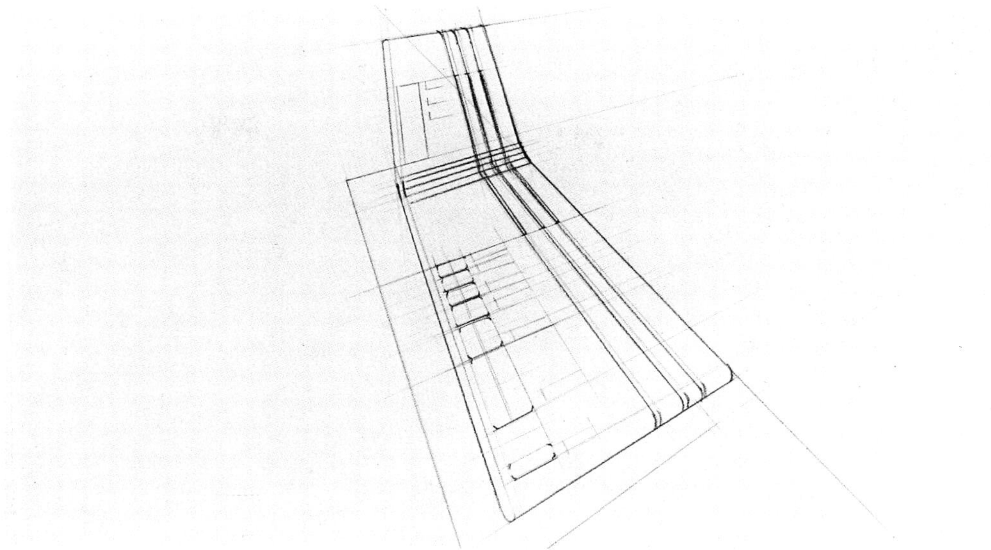

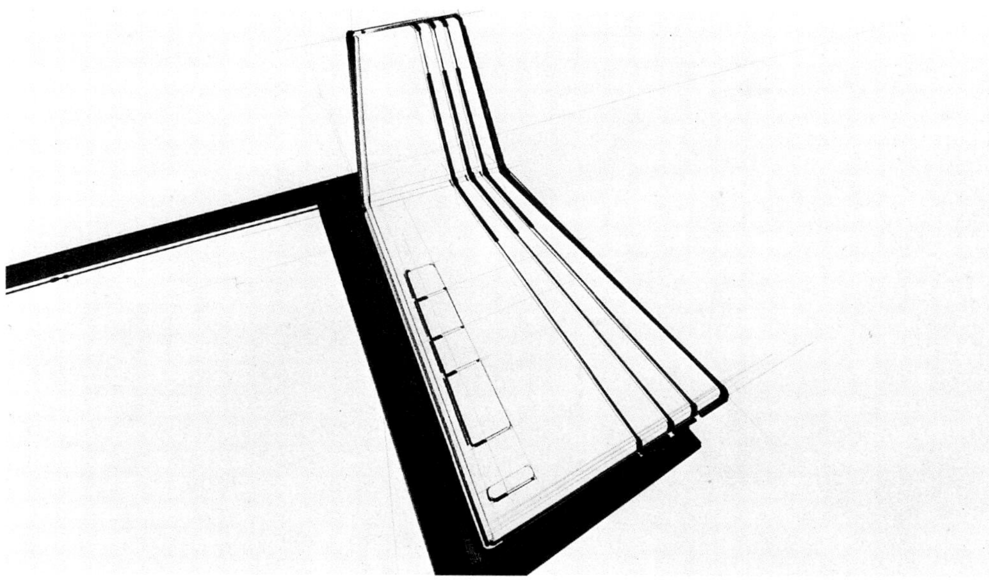

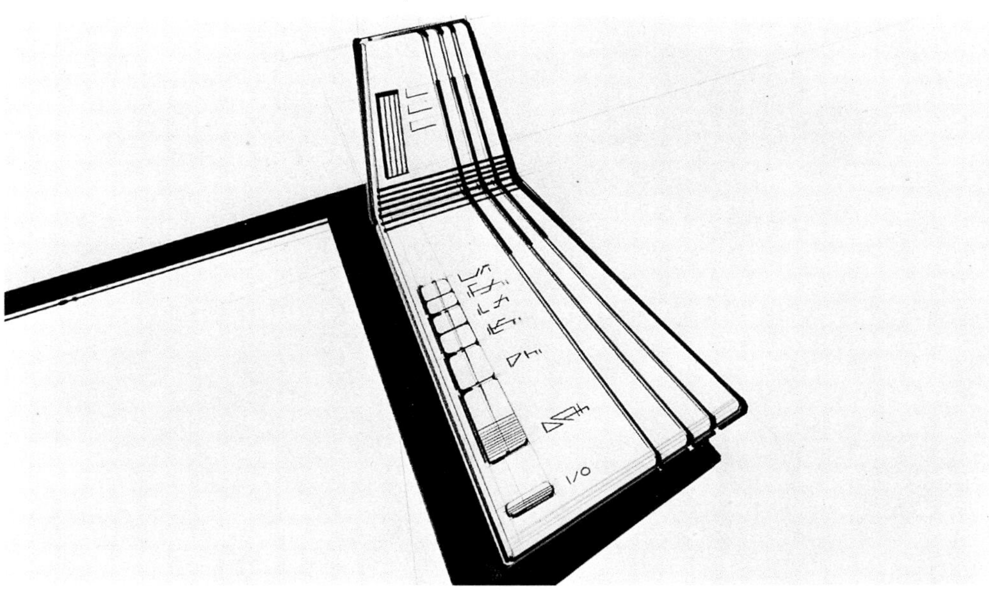

After this restaurant menu-display product was laid out on a marker pad with Verithin blue pencil, I emphasized the major lines and the areas closest to the focal point, which I wanted to be the display area itself.

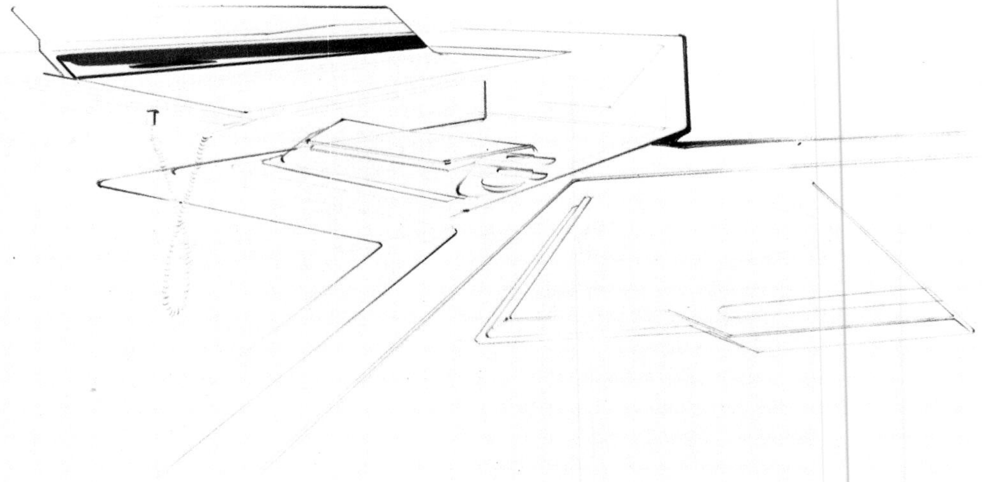

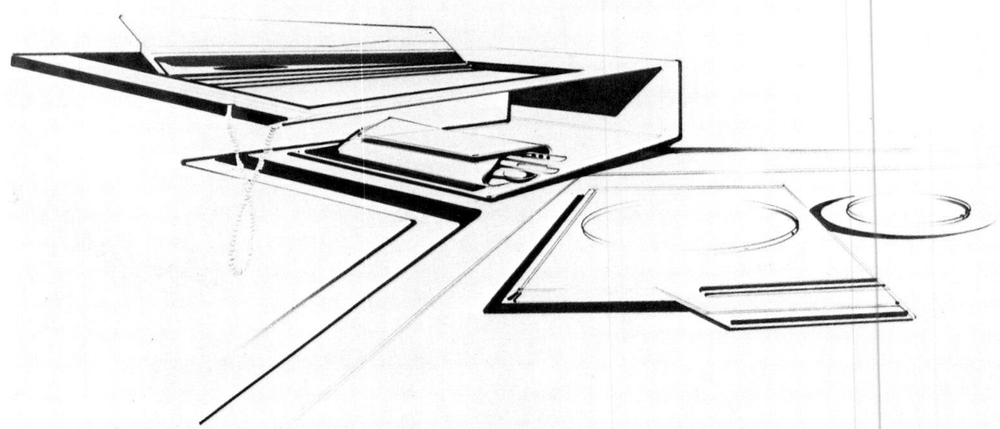

The final line drawing has a suggested level of detail that works thanks to the fine lines drawn in with Prismacolor silver pencil and black ink.

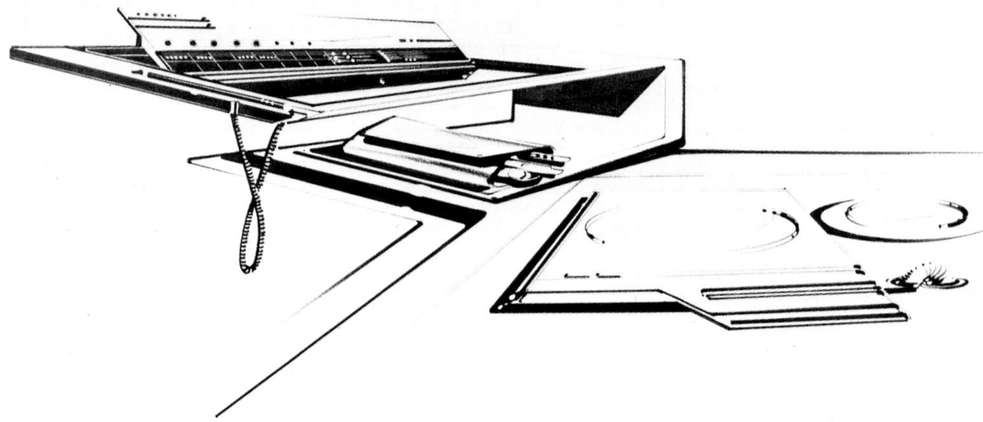

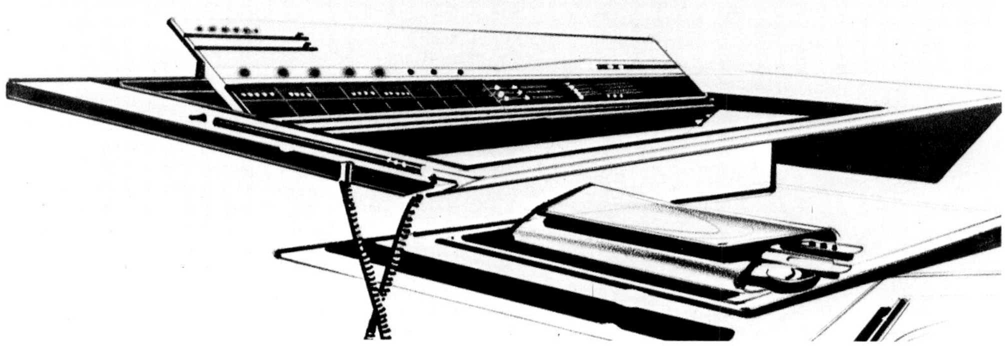

Estimated Perspective

This communication console was laid out quickly by using estimated-perspective technique. The major lines were then emphasized with black Prismacolor pencil.

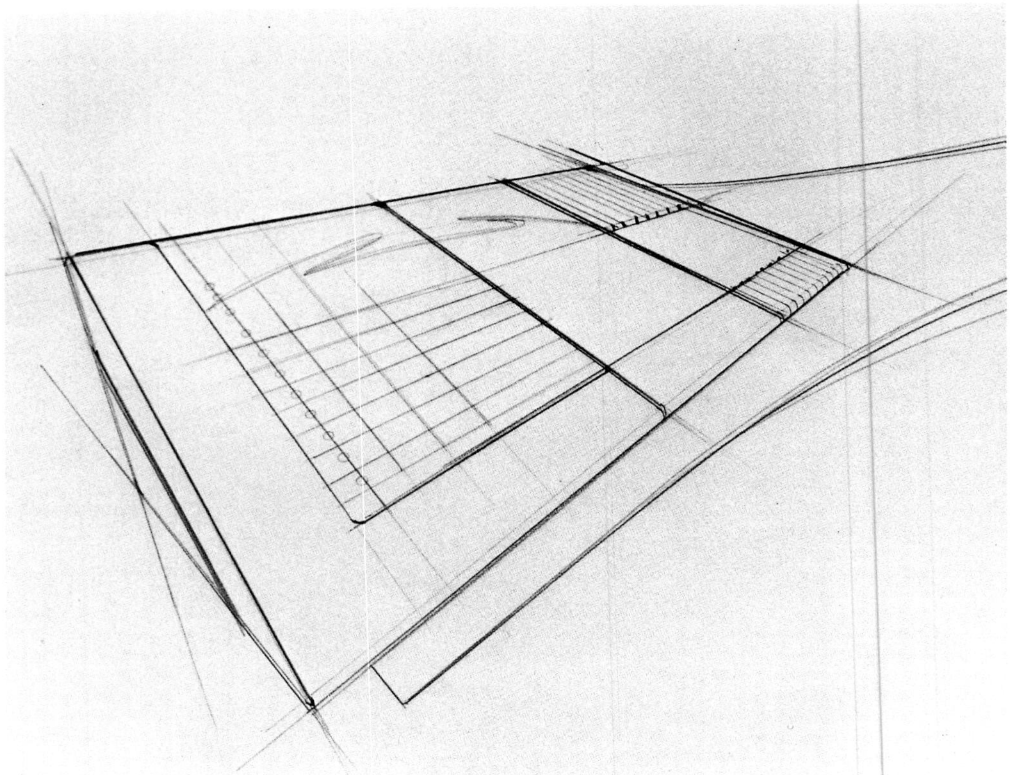

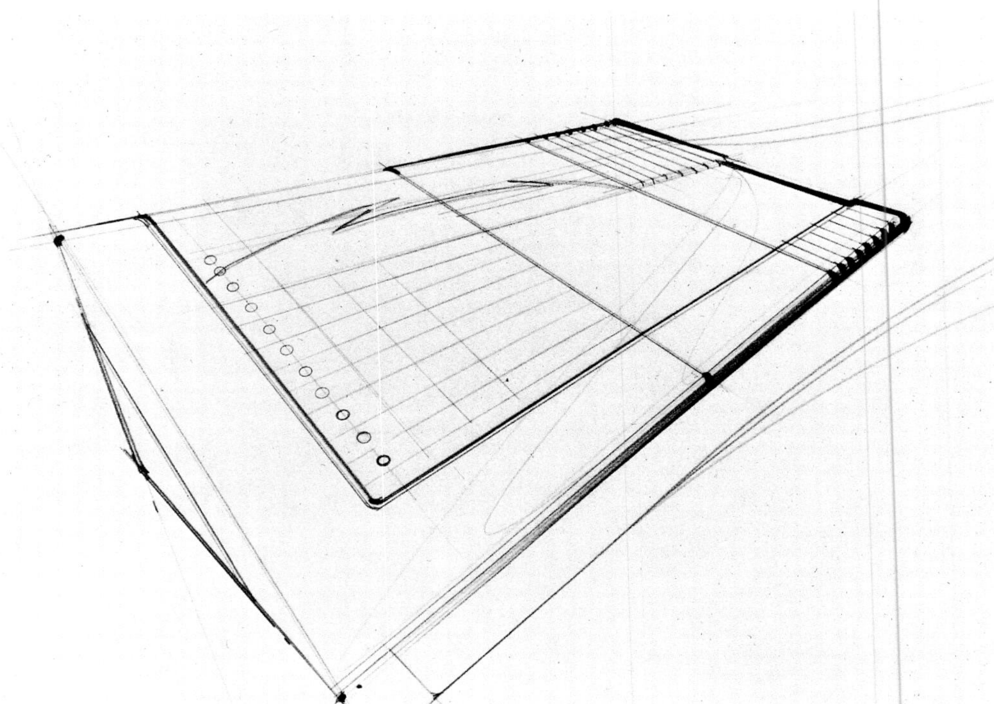

After the reflective areas were penciled in lightly, I filled in the solid areas, including the delineating shadow, with Pantone black marker and Sharpie black pen. The final concept is a strong line drawing that has a certain suggestion of detail. I like to take the shadow area to the edge of the paper on line drawings so that the concept is not "floating" on the page.

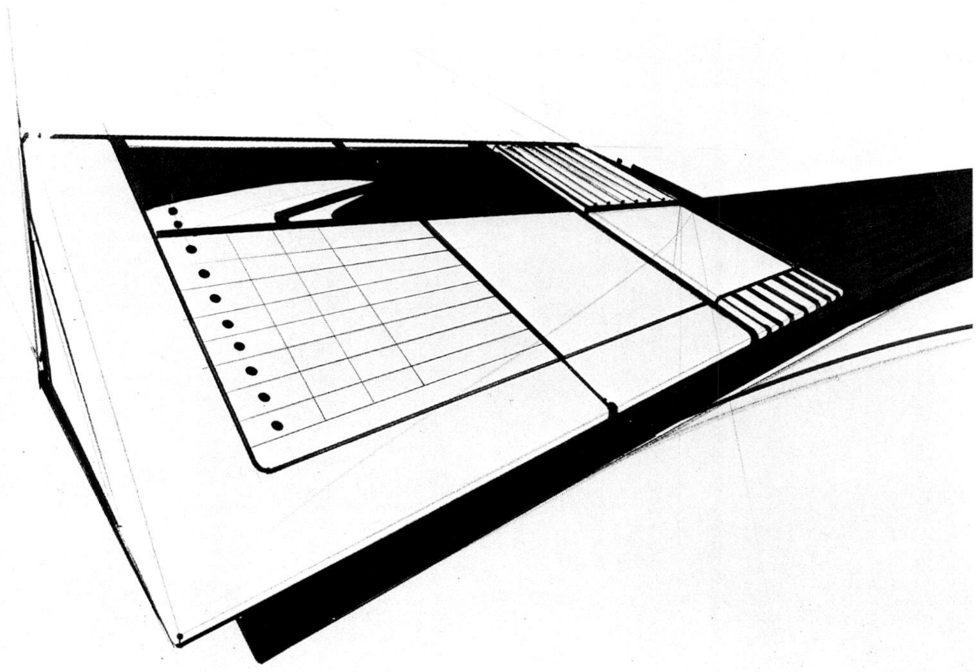

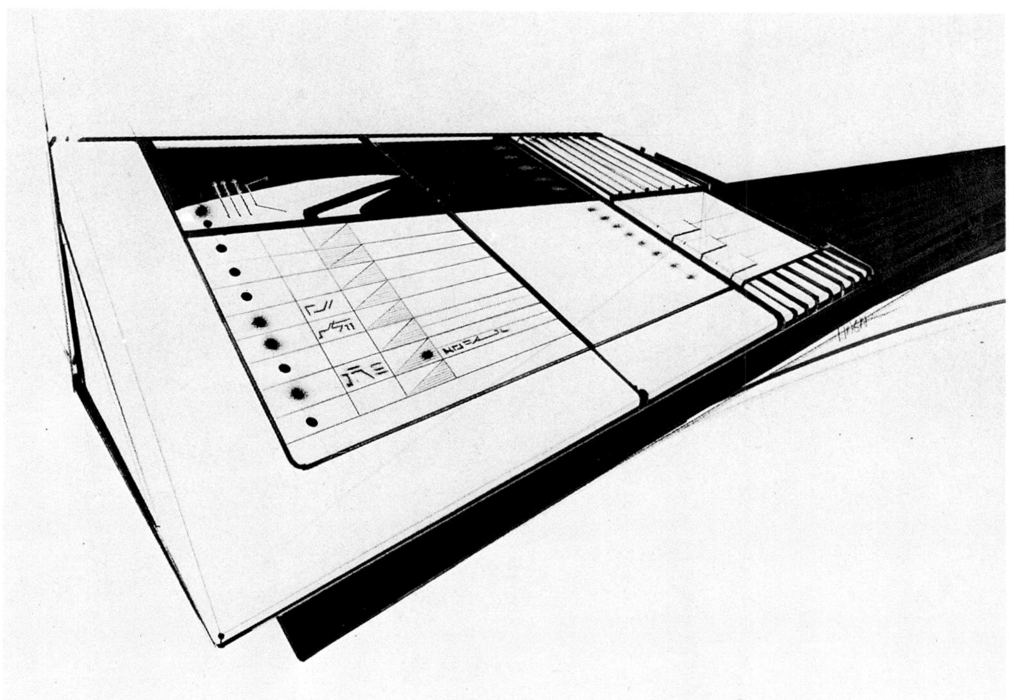

Estimated perspective and line-point technique allowed rapid visualization of this digitizer pad. The delineating shadow is curvilinear to offset the rigid lines of the product. Again, the tapered lines allow detail to be read into the rendering.

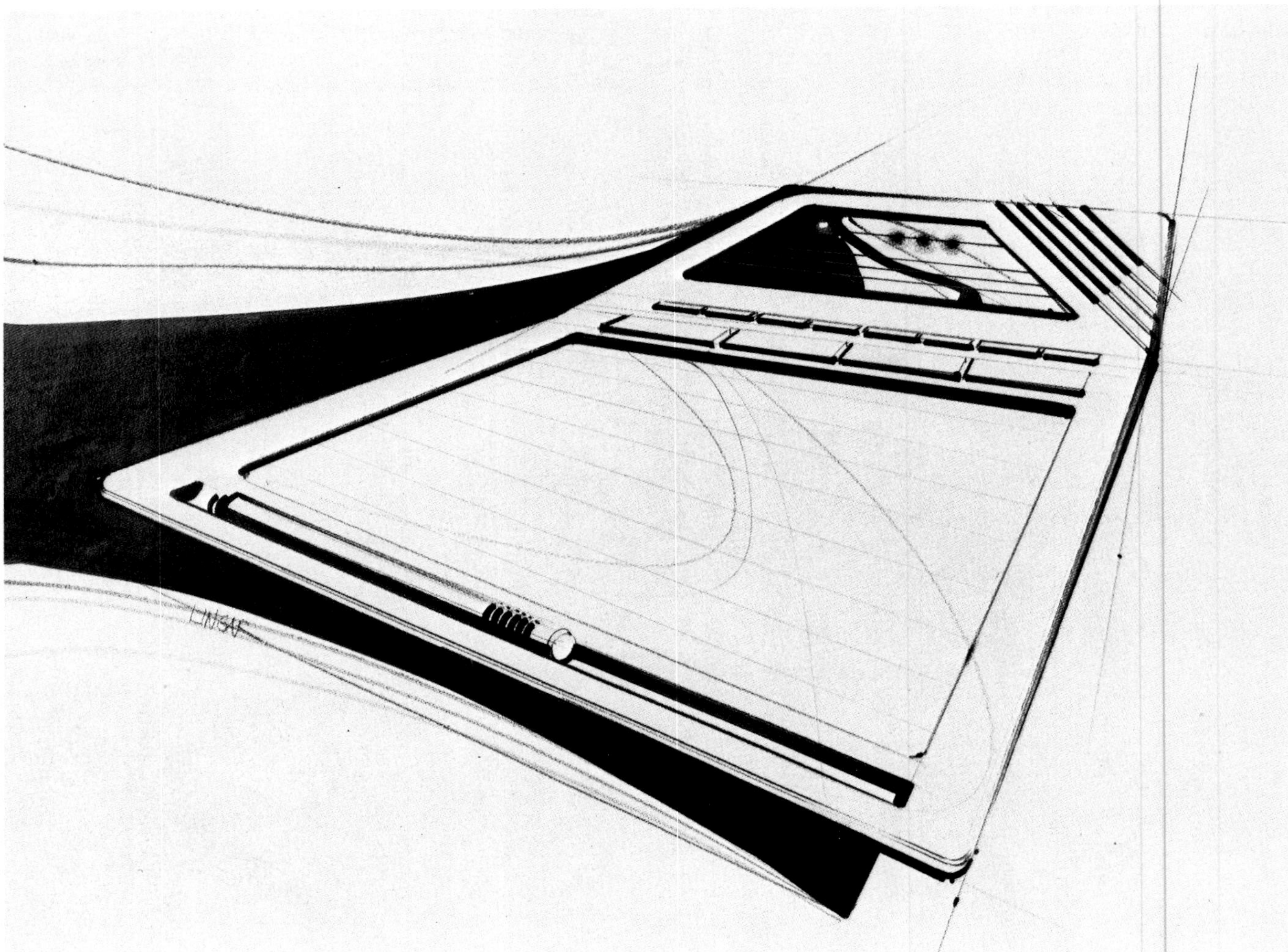

Exploded-View Drawings

Weighted-line technique is also very helpful in the spatial delineation of exploded-view drawings. Estimated perspective will work particularly well here, since the multitude of lines in an exploded view makes these drawings very time-consuming. This is especially true if they are plotted out by hand rather than by a computer plotter. Please avoid simple isometric projections because they do not exist in our perception of the real world!

A nice exploded view rendered in two-point perspective is usually easier for the mind to process and accept, since there is an illusion of reality to the drawing. Weighted-line technique is effective for all types of exploded-view projections. Heavy lines on the outer edges of each part will emphasize the uniqueness of each piece of the exploded-view illustration.

Exploded-view drawings help engineers understand the assembly and structure of a product. This drawing of the digitizer pad fails in that sense, because the viewpoint chosen blocks important details. Be sure to watch for this early in the layout stage, before you invest too much time in the illustration.

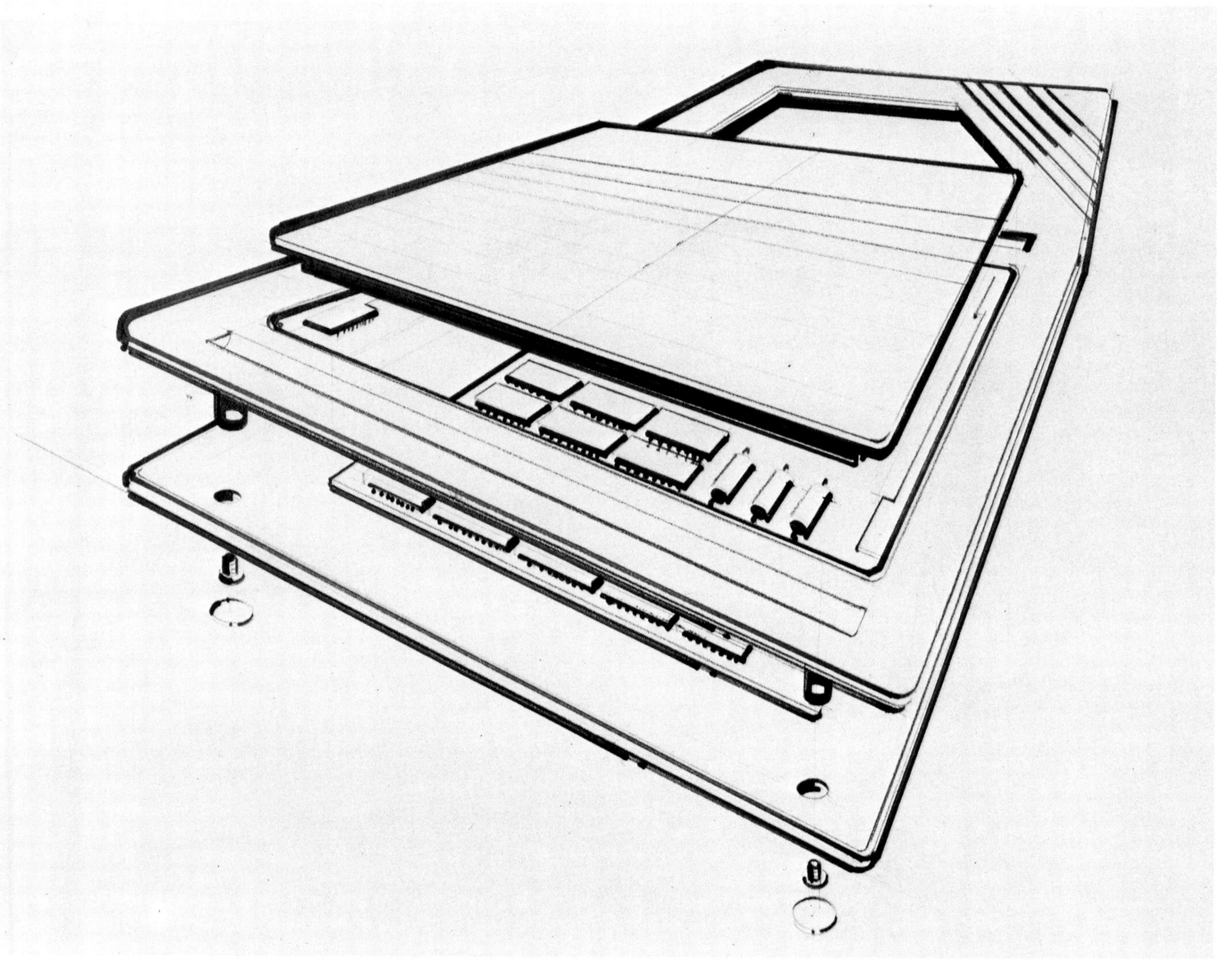

The first of these exploded-view drawings received criticism because overlapping areas were hard to understand. To avoid confusion, I reworked the edges of all the parts, outlining them in a heavier black to contrast with the lighter lines. The weighted-line effect individualizes each part better, yet the exploded view still works as a whole.

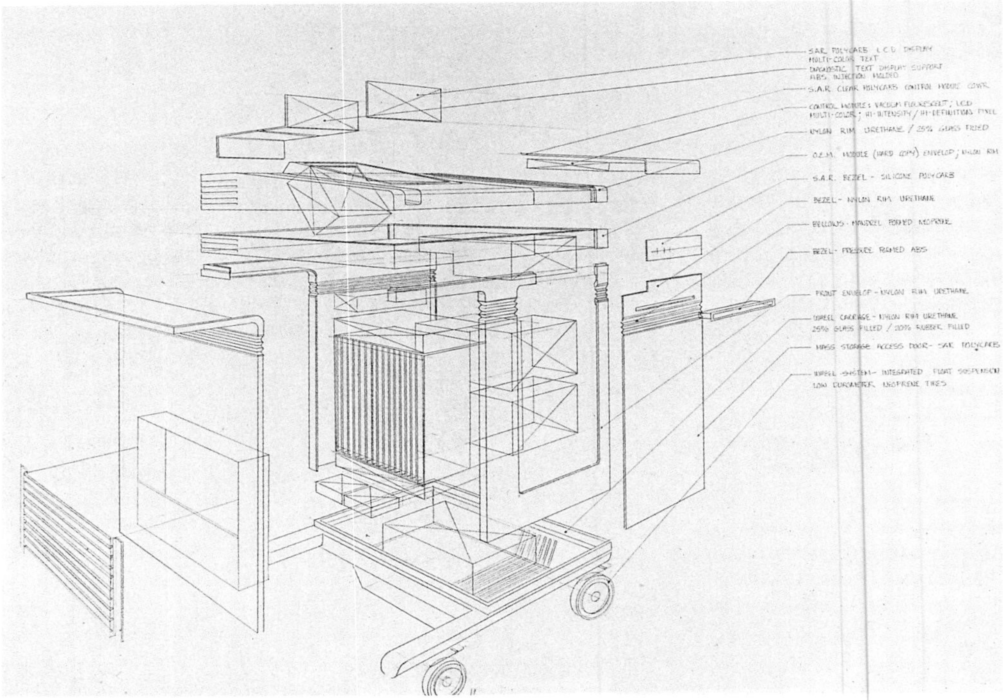

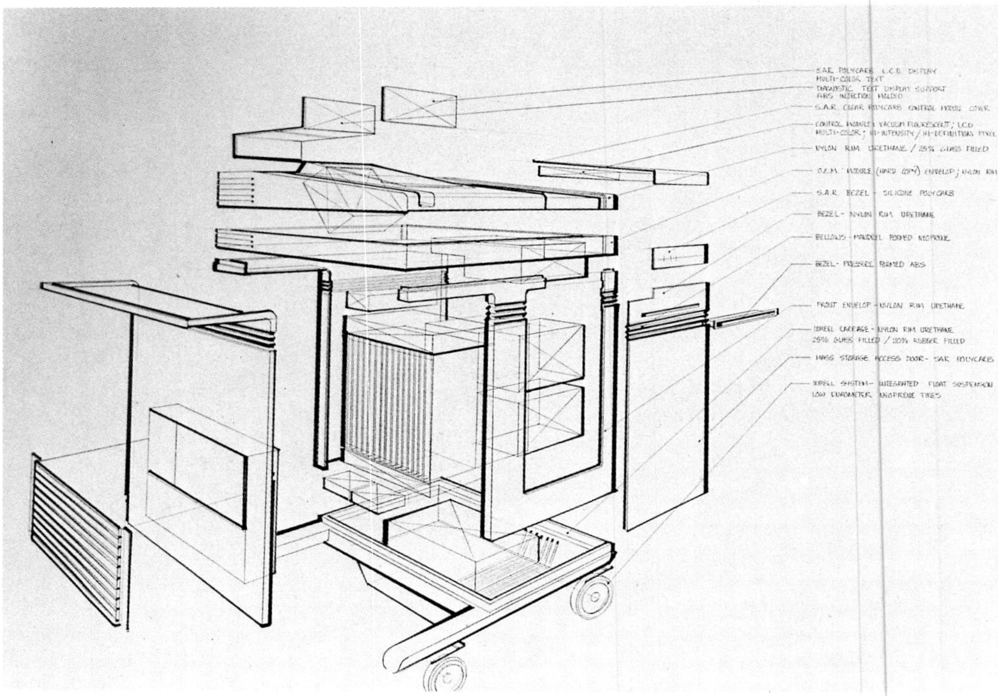

Quick Sketch

Expressing ideas on a page is most quickly accomplished by abbreviating lines and simplifying details, so that the drawing process is fast. You should try to have the background help define the form and the content of your concept. A composition of several ideas can be effective if you use a quick-sketch approach. One approach you may take is to place several concepts on one page in sketch form and then shade only one in detail. This will highlight a single concept, yet show other options at the same time.

When laying out a quick composition that shows several products, you should try to see the entire drawing surface as a whole. The composition should be visually balanced, with the focus of attention on the products. Here the various desktop clocks were all basically drawn with a Sharpie black pen and a black Prismacolor pencil. The black shadows help define the forms. A small amount of pastel chalk was blended in to provide a unifying backdrop and to make the reflections look more real.

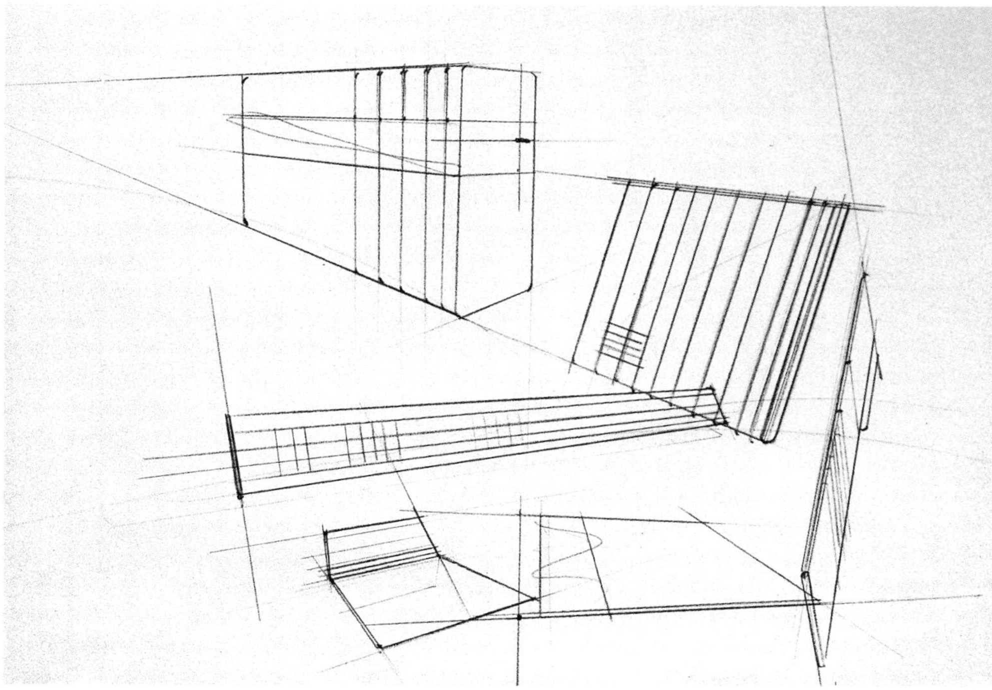

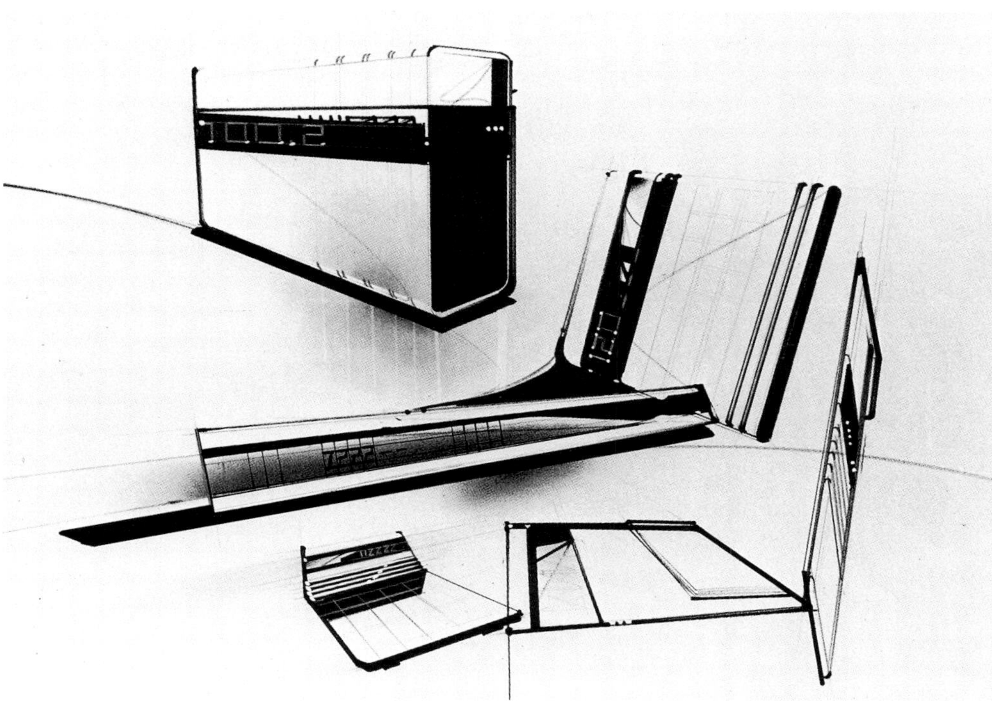

Even unlikely media can be used for fast renderings. These autos were drawn on paper napkins while I was waiting in an airport restaurant. With simple basic tools, such as a fine-tipped pen and a Pantone #2 gray marker, you can create nice renderings.

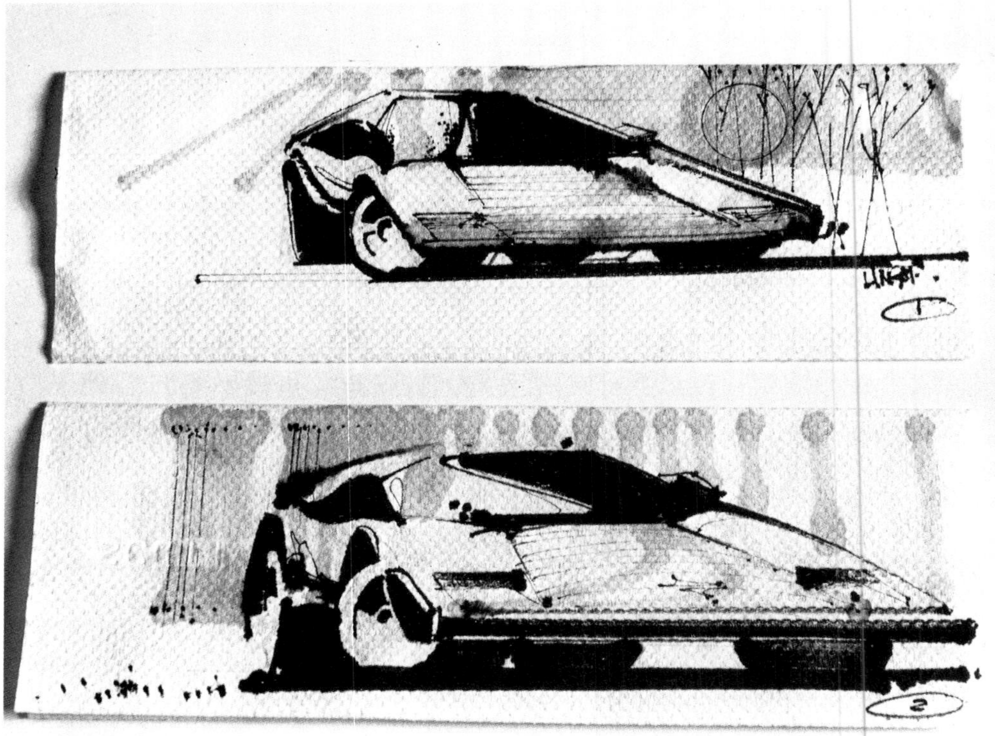

Using only a Pantone black marker and #2 and #4 gray markers, I created a future disco. The illusion of detail and the exaggerated perspective allow the observer to move into and out of the rendering smoothly.

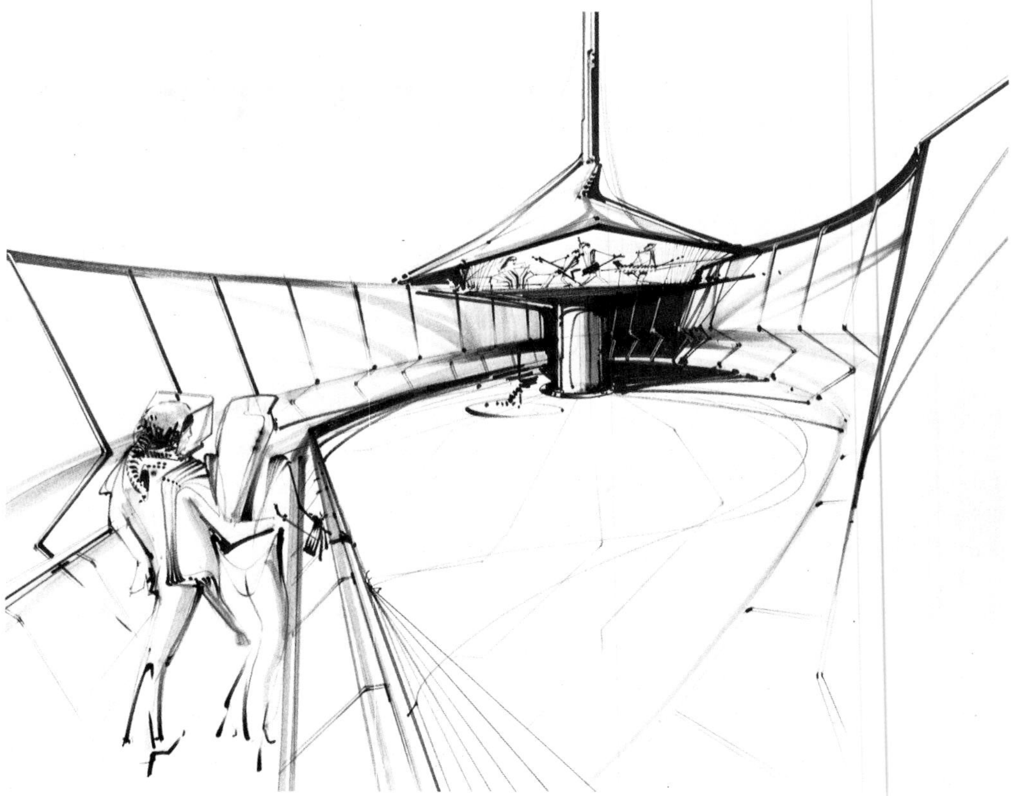

People

Figures can be effectively delineated using line-point extrapolation (the tapering of a line to a point). It is usually desirable to give secondary emphasis to renditions of people so that the primary focus or attention is on the product. By the same token, you do not want to underemphasize the human form, or it can take on an animated, cartoonlike feeling. Tapered, curved lines, with end-point nuances, can give you an effective presentation, suggesting human likeness and form.

Easily obtainable copy-machine paper is a good medium for quick sketches. Here, I used a light-gray dry marker, a fine-tipped ball-point pen, and a Sharpie black pen to visualize a radiology reading room. The human figure was lightly drawn in with marker and then emphasized with a heavy line on the outside contour. This keeps the viewer's focus on the detailed hologram image in the foreground, which was done with gouache.

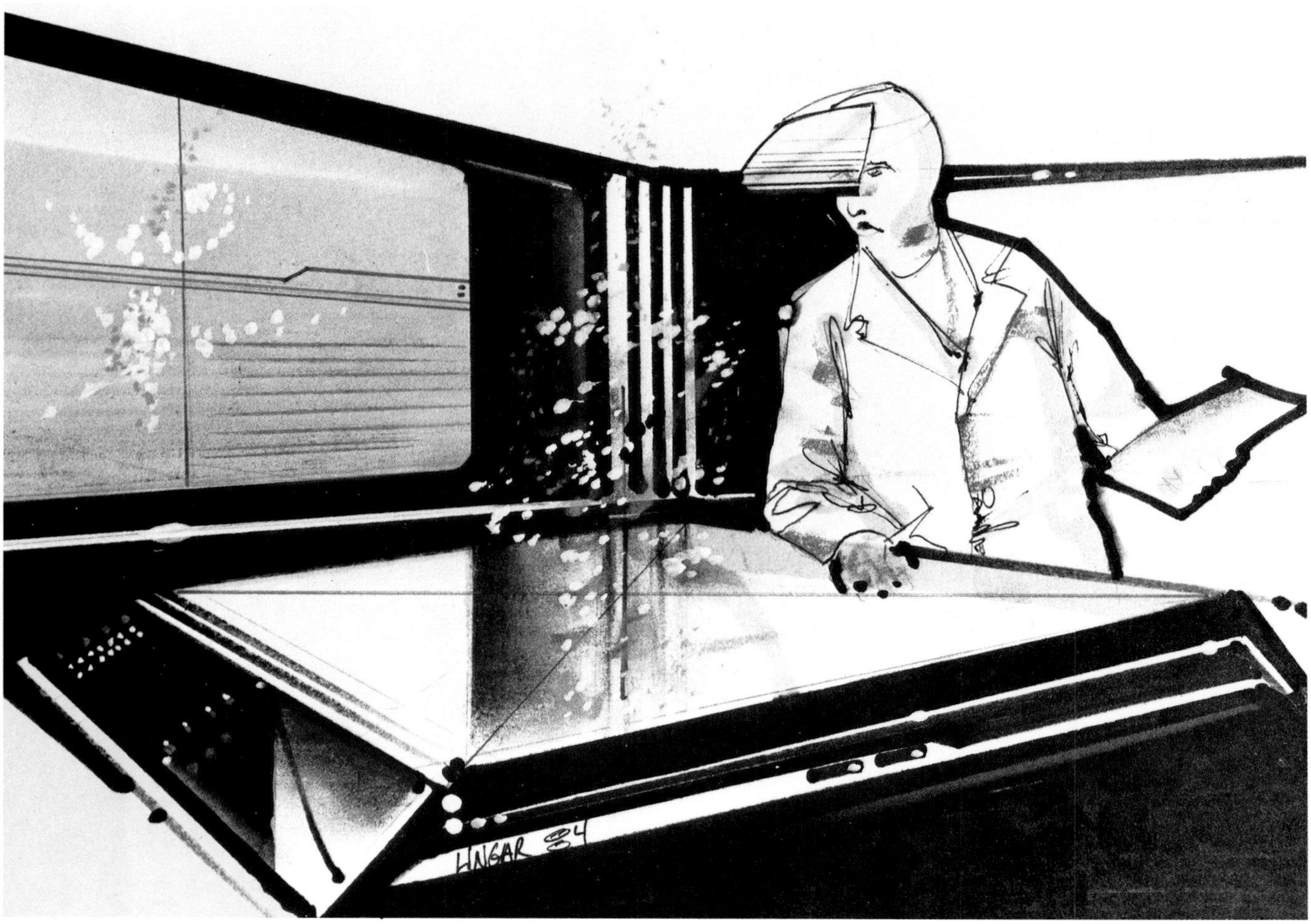

To emphasize the tennis racquet, I encouraged selective focusing by using light-gray dry markers on the figures and harsh, fine lines on the product. The people are there, but they are appropriately understated.

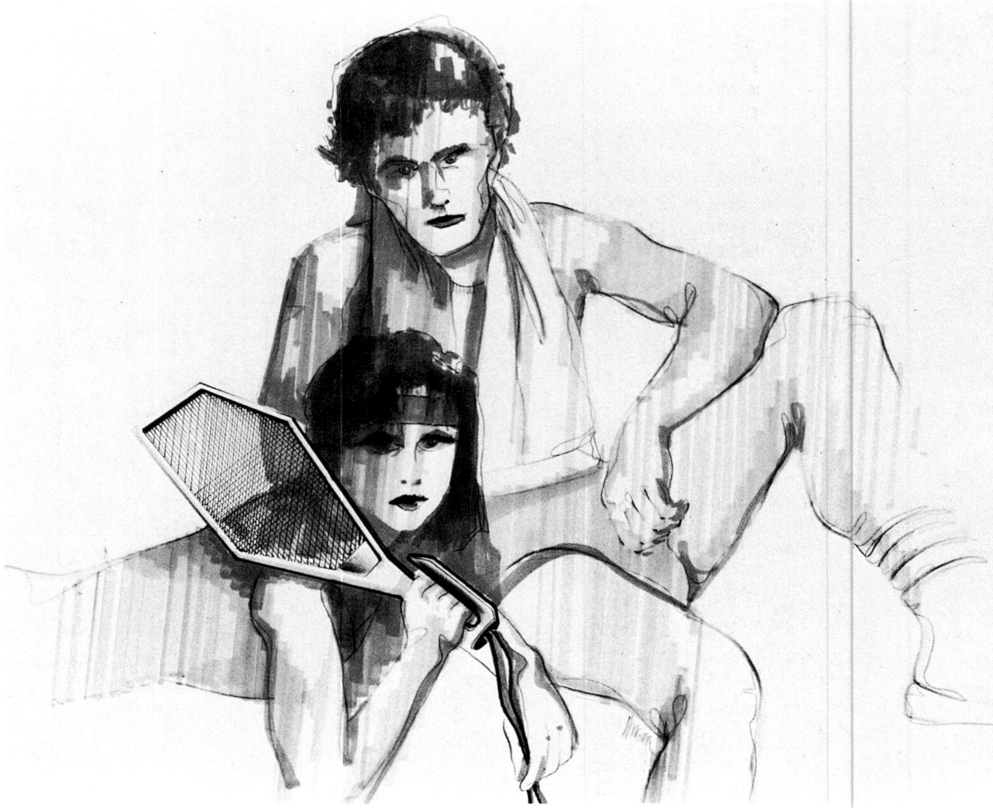

Here, the children were lightly sketched in over a layout of the product. Adjustments were made until the perspective was correct. Then the wagon was rendered in using black lines and blended chalk, and the children were understated with light-gray dry markers.

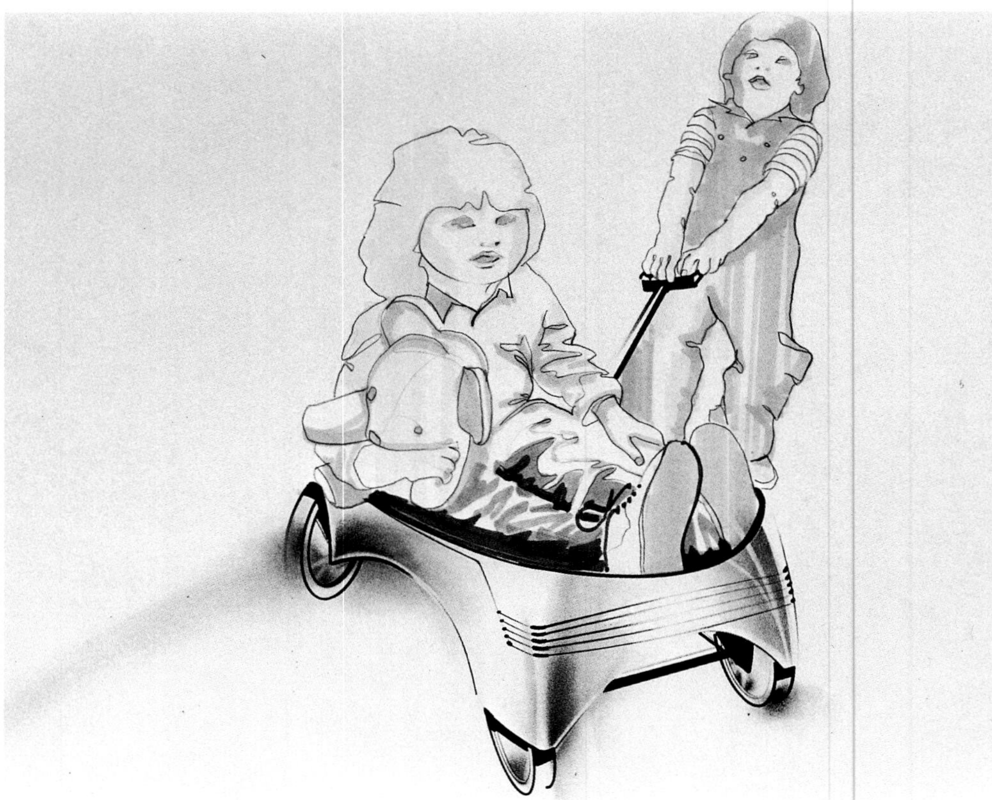

A communication device marketed as a jewelry item required that the illustration include a woman's neck. After the layout was created, I darkened the essential lines with Prismacolor black pencil. Fine details were achieved with gouache and a Winsor & Newton #00 watercolor brush. The heavy shadow lines accentuated the product against the human form, which remained as simple tapering lines.

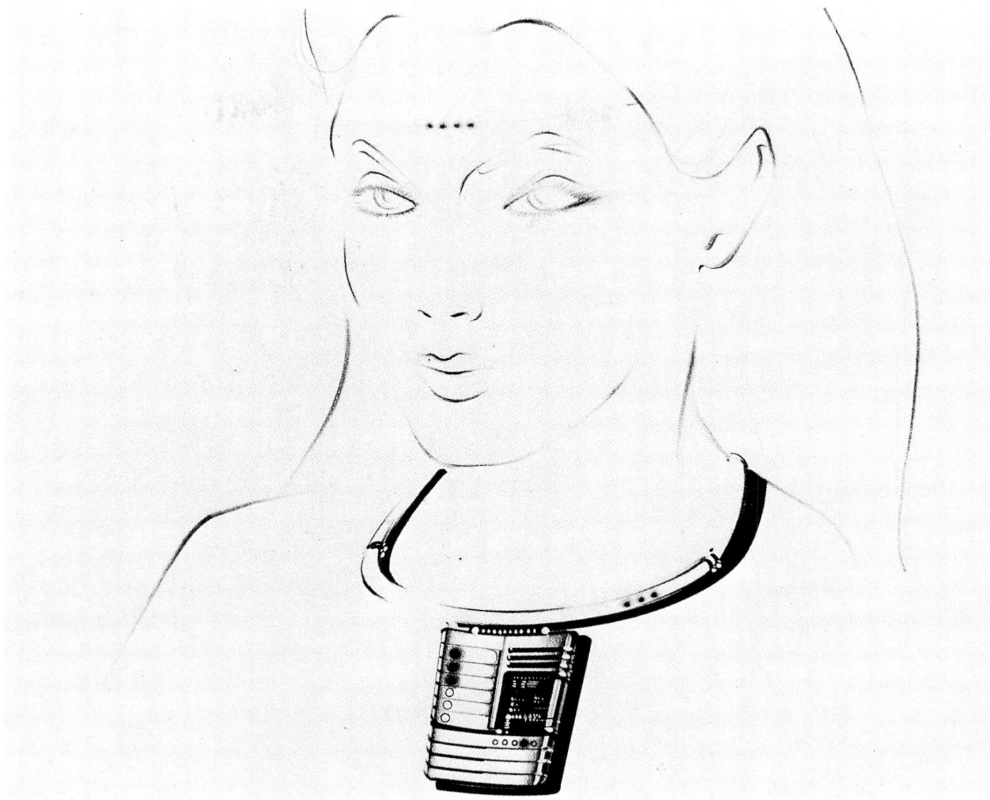

In this human-factors drawing, I used tapering curvilinear lines to make the figures effectively transparent. A multiple-exposure effect can be developed to show overlapping figures seated and standing without obscuring important information from the drawing.

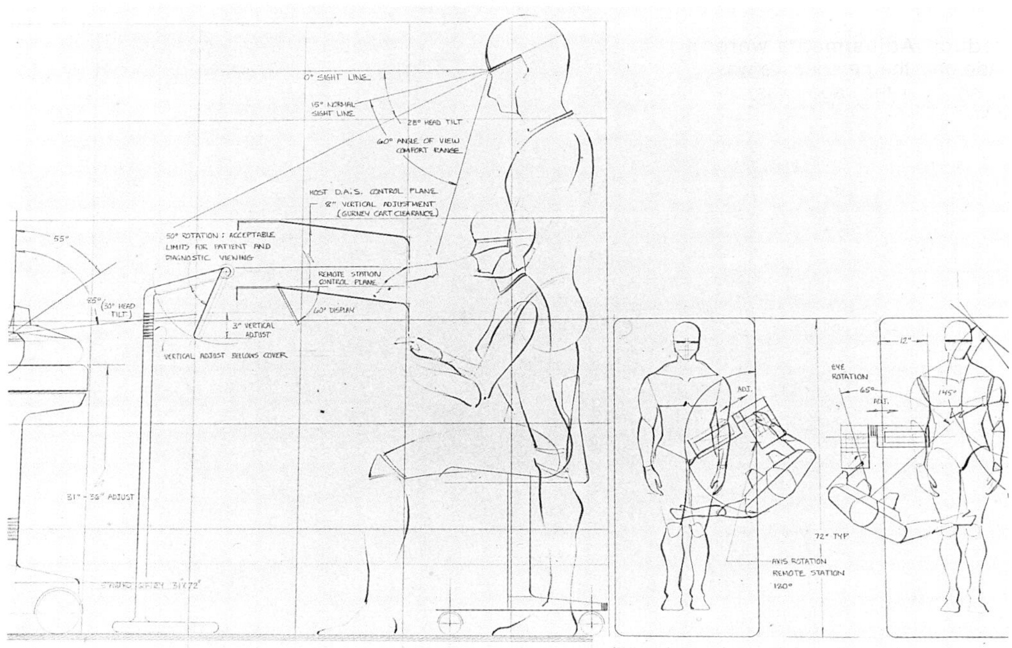

3 SHADING

By now you should be showing off. No? Well, keep moving that pencil across the page. It is true that illustration techniques can be explained, discussed, and shown, but nothing can substitute for the hours spent with the proverbial pen to paper. That so-called talent your mother talks about is or will be nothing less than miles of ink and lead applied to paper. Mastery will require literally hundreds of hours of drawing.

Lines are lines are lines. The excitement starts when a twist of illusion is thrown in: shading.

Nothing renders the illusion of form as shading does. Shading conveys a certainty of form and shape, and when properly done, it imparts a kind of life force and strength to the rendering. This applies to everything from the smallest product concept to the most complex architectural drawing. The rules never change. This chapter will explore what these rules are and how, as a designer, you can use artistic license to make shading a powerful visual tool.

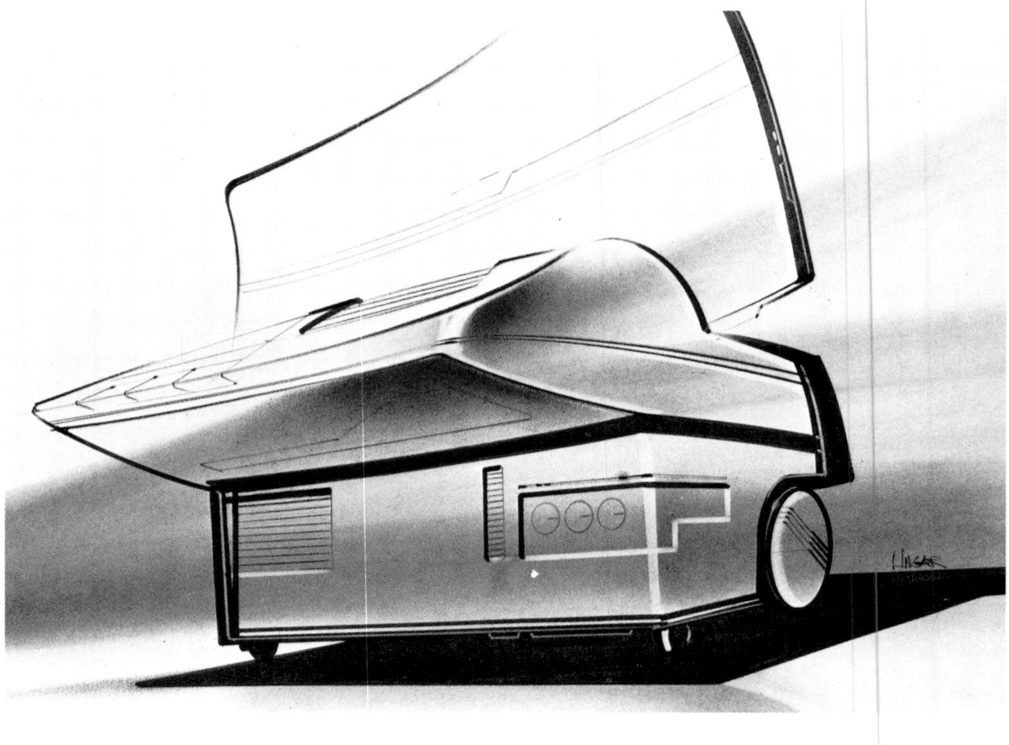

A large mobile TV display was rendered with black lines and pastel chalk only. Some chalk was removed with erasers to create areas of high contrast where I wanted the viewer's attention. Note the angle of view, which imparts a dominating feeling to the product.

Shades of Refinement

You should note that as light falls on a subject—the solid cube, for example—there is an obvious falling-away of illumination on the surfaces furthest from the light source. Every drawing book in the world explains in great detail the scientific principles of light, medium, and dark shading of a cube. This concept cannot be overemphasized. Areas that receive the most amount of light are rendered in light values; areas that receive little or no light are rendered in dark values; and areas that receive partial light are rendered in medium values. The darkest values are reserved for the shadows cast by an object, and the lightest values are reserved for highlights on reflective surfaces.

Shading can be analyzed as a complexity of interactions the results of which are as dependent on the light source as they are on the surface composition of the object. Diffused reflection occurs on matte surfaces, while "spectral," or concentrated, reflection occurs on hard, glossy surfaces. In each case, the values are worked and blended to bring out the three-dimensional form, only the values differ in intensity.

Diagrammatically, the value changes blend from light to dark across each surface, as shown here, with the most contrast being the focal point of the drawing. Note, too, that the light, medium, and dark trick works just as well with cones, spheres, and other curved surfaces. The most intense light will reflect from a curved surface at the point closest to the source of light. In the case of a cylinder, linear reflections of light travel the entire length of the object and then blend to medium and dark values as the surface curves away on each side.

The most complex of subjects can be reduced to basic geometric shapes. Appropriate use of the principles of shading causes the eye to see a two-dimensional drawing as a three-dimensional expression of lights, mediums, and darks. With experience, you will instinctively be able to both understate and exaggerate shading to achieve dramatic results.

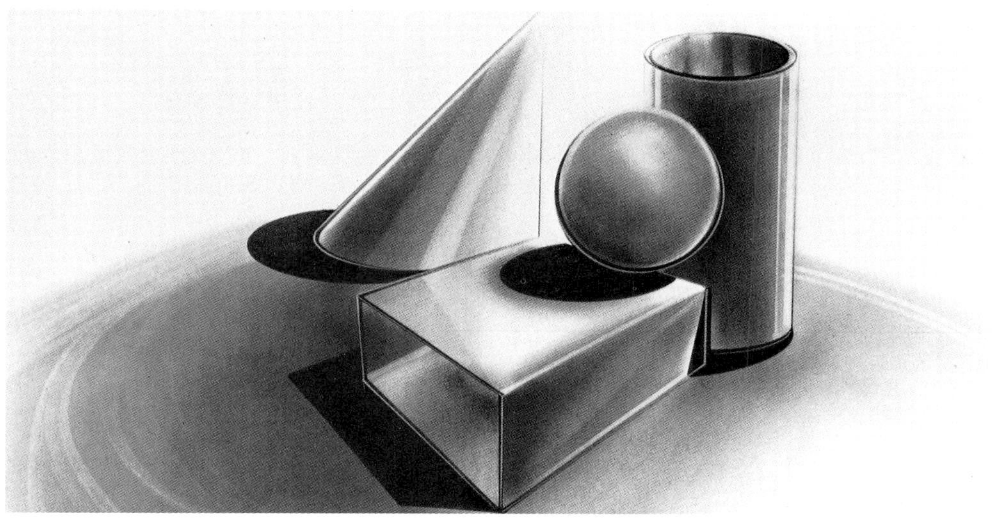

This simple analysis helps break down the shaded geometric figures into their elemental tonal values. If in doubt, you should do a simple analytical overlay such as this before you start on a complex drawing.

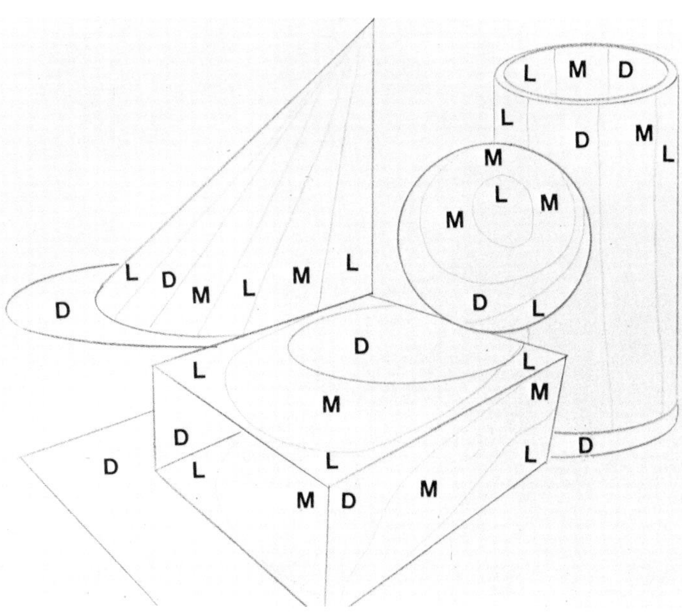

Shading the Cube

To create a smooth gray-to-black transitional blending, compressed pastel chalk can be used on paper, or graphite powder can be used on vellum or other nontextured papers. Webril Handi-Pads provide an excellent blender for the pastel chalks. Do not attempt to blend with cotton balls or tissue paper. Both are too absorbent, and they will not carry the pigment to the paper well.

The simplest method is to rub the chalk onto a separate piece of paper so that you can use the Webril pad to pick up the powdered pigment and apply it to the rendering. (You can also use a razor blade or an X-Acto knife to scrape the chalk into a powder.) Once you have swept the chalk over the line drawing, you can remove selected areas with an eraser, to show highlights or to emphasize leading edges. You can spray a fixative on the completed drawing if you wish, but I find this is usually not necessary.

Demonstration: Shading
This layout of a simple cube is first drawn with black Prismacolor pencil. Then a Webril pad is used to transfer chalk to the page. The straight lines of the cube enabled me to use a piece of paper to mask areas where I wanted extreme definition. (I used the same sheet of paper for the powdered chalk and for masking.)

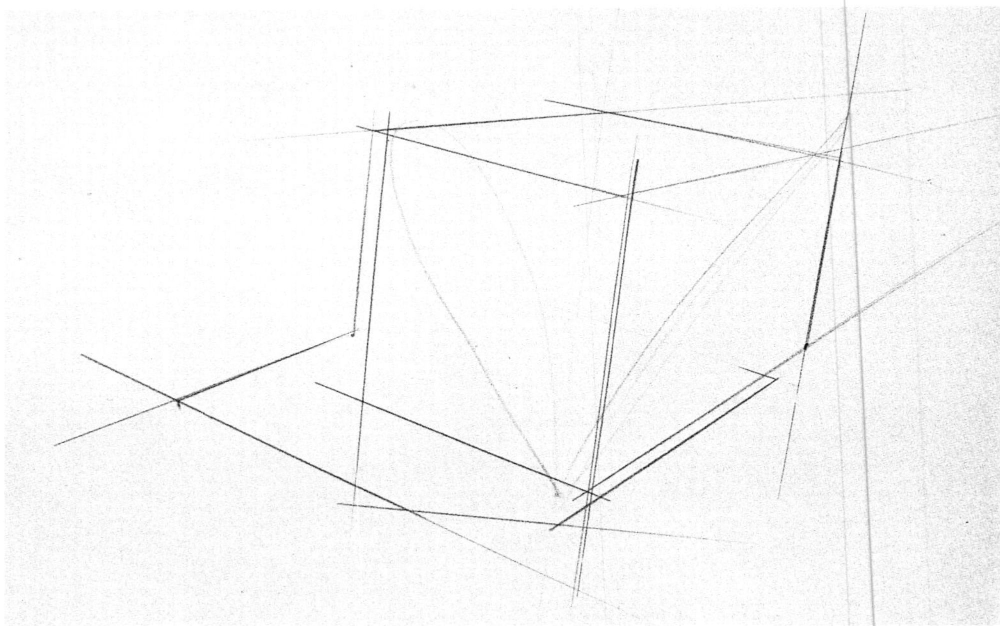

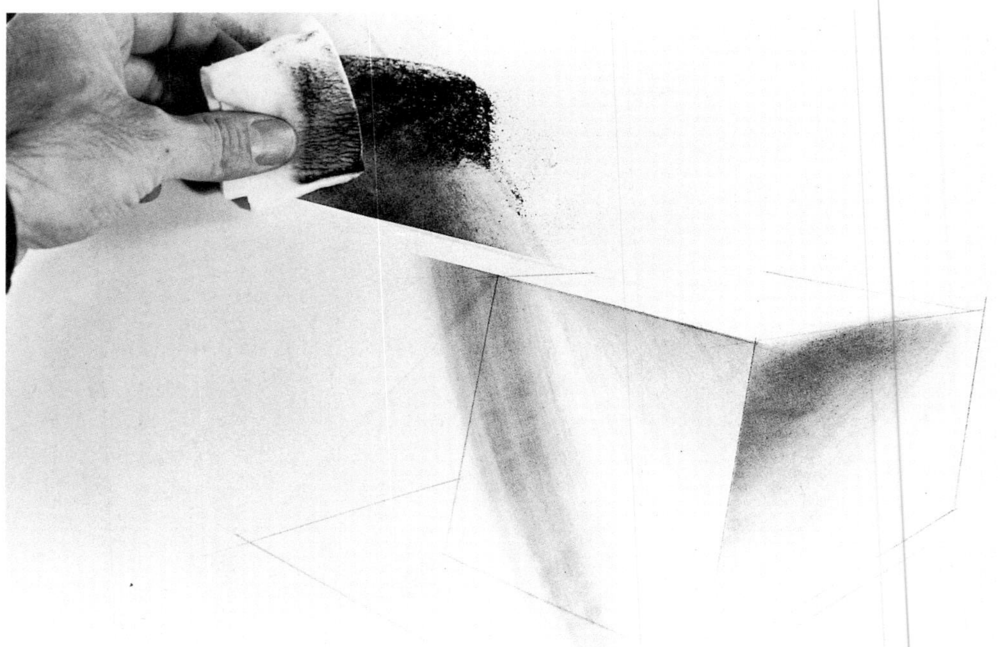

A background of gray chalk was swept over the cube, and a dark shadow and outlines were added with marker to create a compositional balance. Finally, leading edges were emphasized by removing chalk with an eraser.

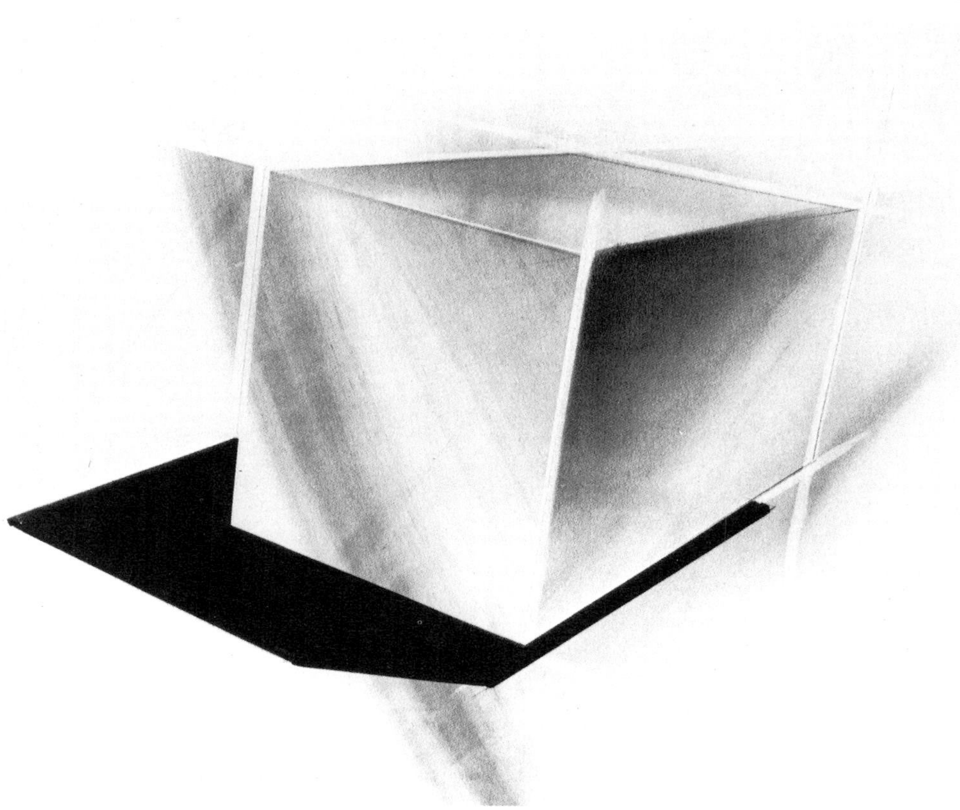

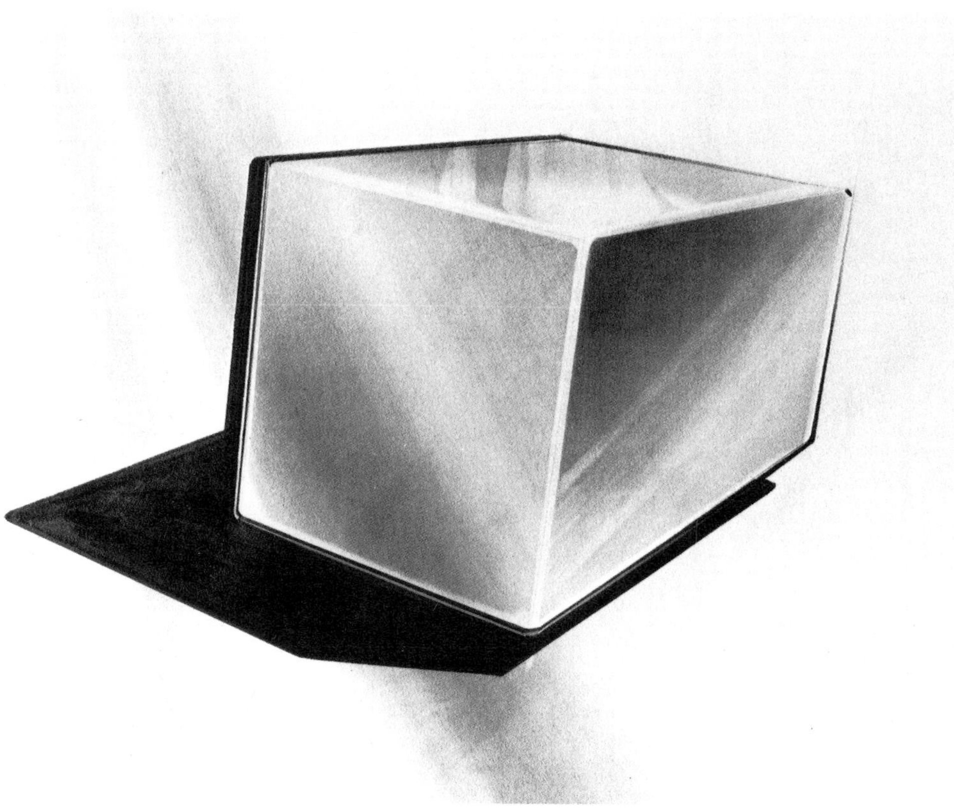

Shading the Cube

A group of cubes can now be shaded in mere minutes! Do not labor with this technique. You should master it so that it is quick and easy, and the results will be clean and crisp.

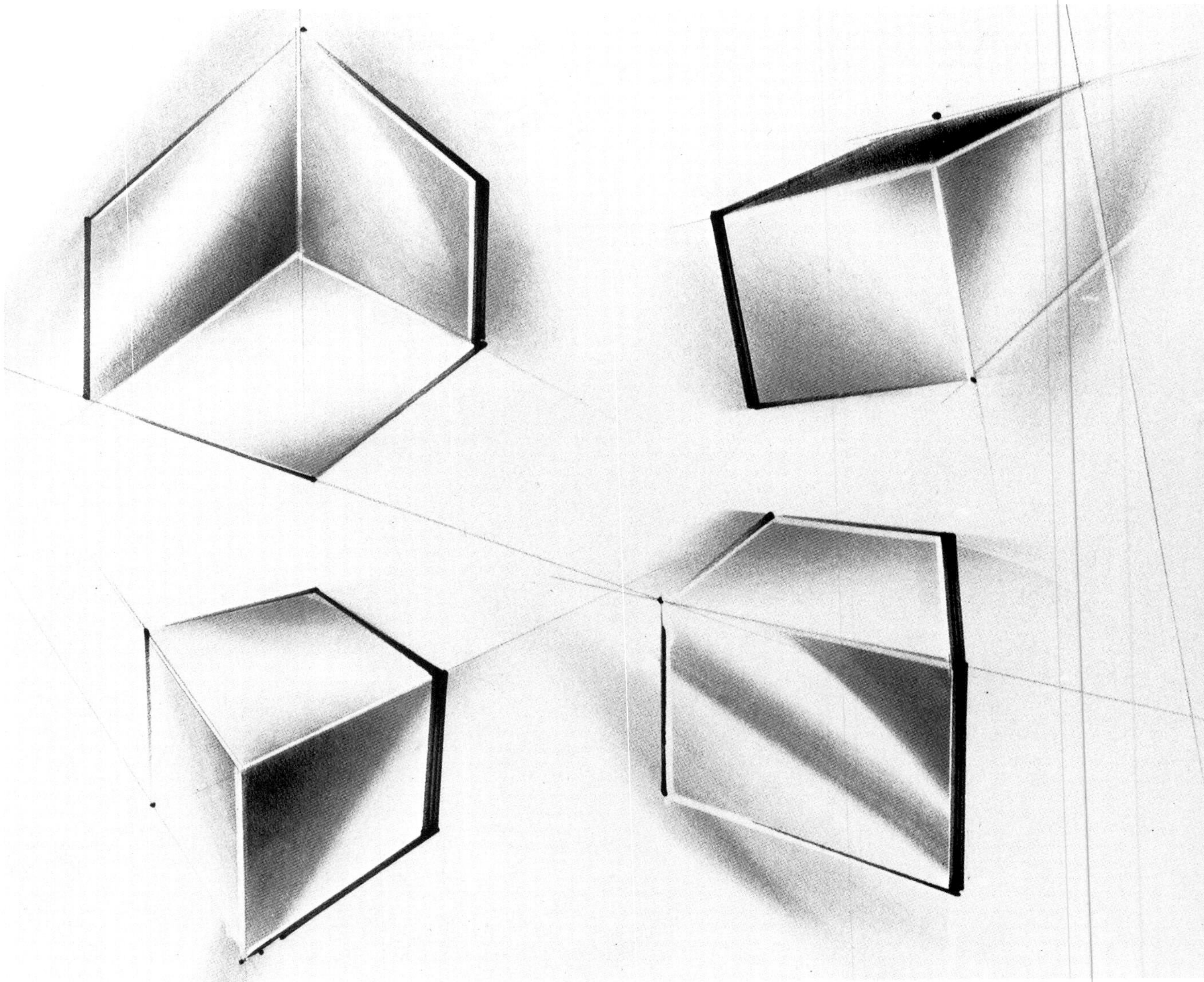

The manipulation of light, medium, and dark values is clearly shown in these views of a diagnostic ultrasound cart. Chalk was blended over the center of the page so that, by removing chalk where there were leading edges, a focus of attention could be created. Erasers cut at an angle work well for removing narrow areas of chalk.

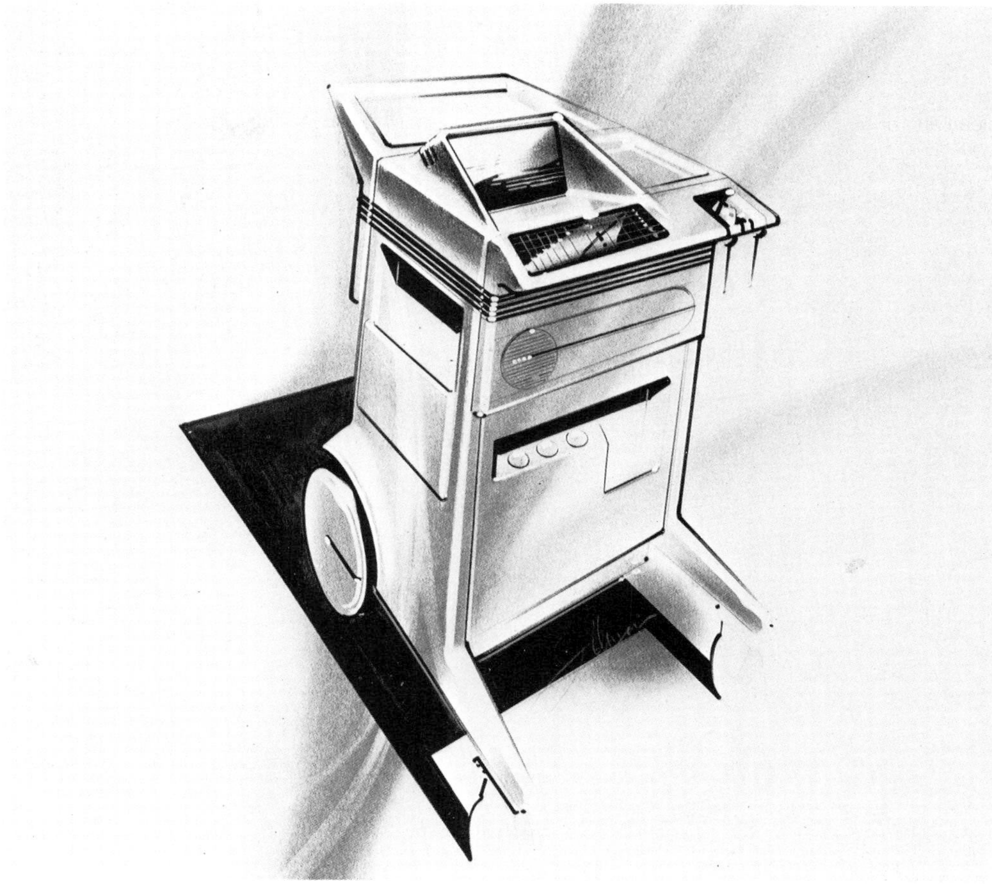

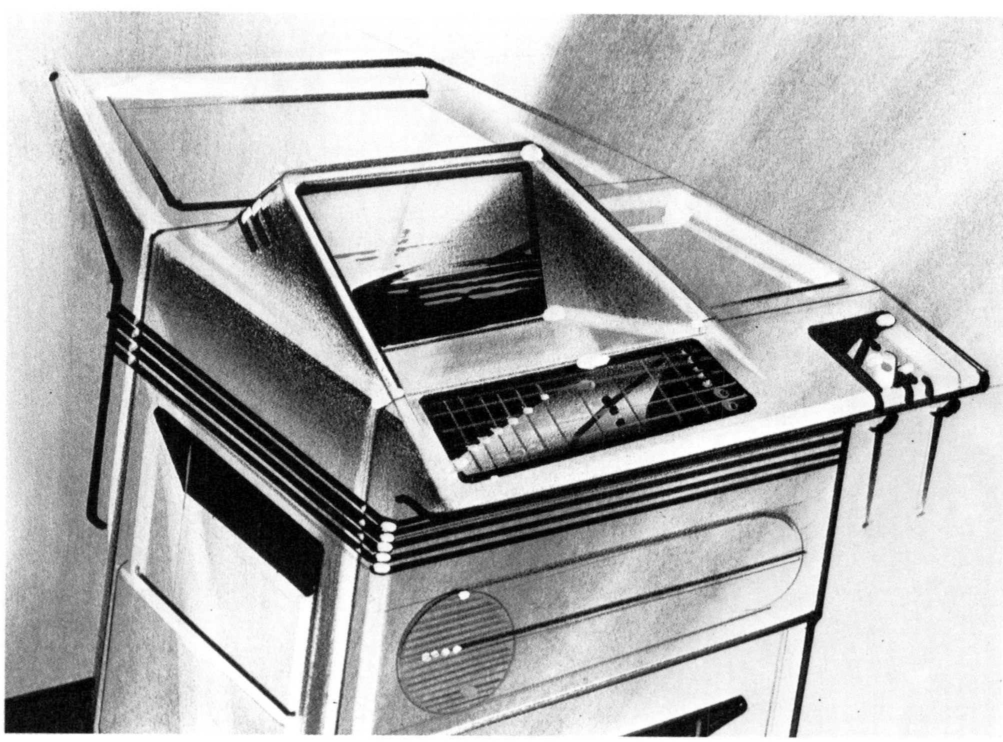

Exaggerating Tone

For quick-sketch techniques, you must think almost like an animator, exaggerating tonal values for effect and playing down or deleting line details that serve no visual purpose.

At the edges of extremely reflective objects, such as those made of glass or chrome, there is a double line which helps delineate the object from the background. I generally take some artistic license with this fact, however, and express this condition in almost all surfaces that are blocked in by a heavy outline or shadow. This not only adds interest to the rendering, but also helps relate the product to the background.

Reflections should try to follow the laws of physics as much as possible, although these rules can be stretched a little to exaggerate the three-dimensional aspect of the form. Many objects have no perceptible reflections at all, yet they may be drawn with just enough reflective areas to persuade the brain's image-processing department to recognize the surface changes.

Demonstration: Using tone to define geometric shapes

You should try to emulate the techniques used in each of these next five product concepts by rendering the products as shown in the examples. Note the use of tonal variations and the liveliness of the highlights. The first example is a clock based on the cube. The layout was done with a Verithin blue pencil just dark enough so that essential details could still be seen after chalk was blended over it with Webril pads. Chalk was then removed over leading-edge areas.

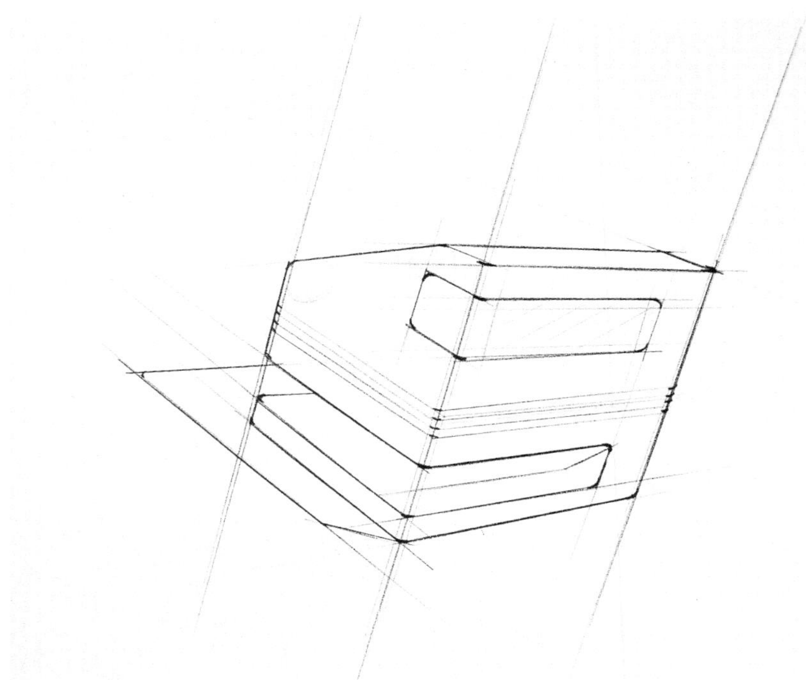

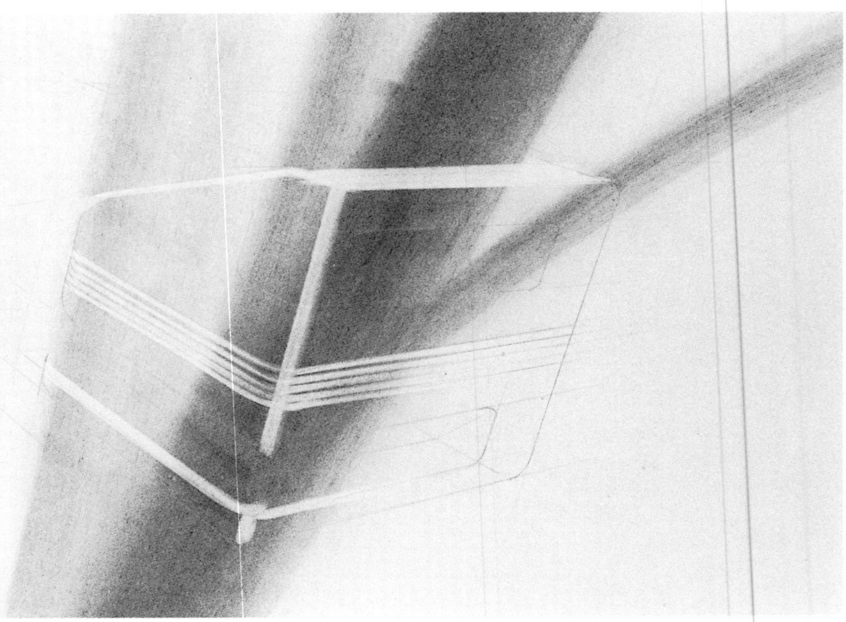

Areas that were to be black were outlined with a Sharpie black pen and were then filled in with a black Pantone dry marker. The concept was finalized by strengthening value changes at the leading edges and thus creating a strong focus of viewer attention.

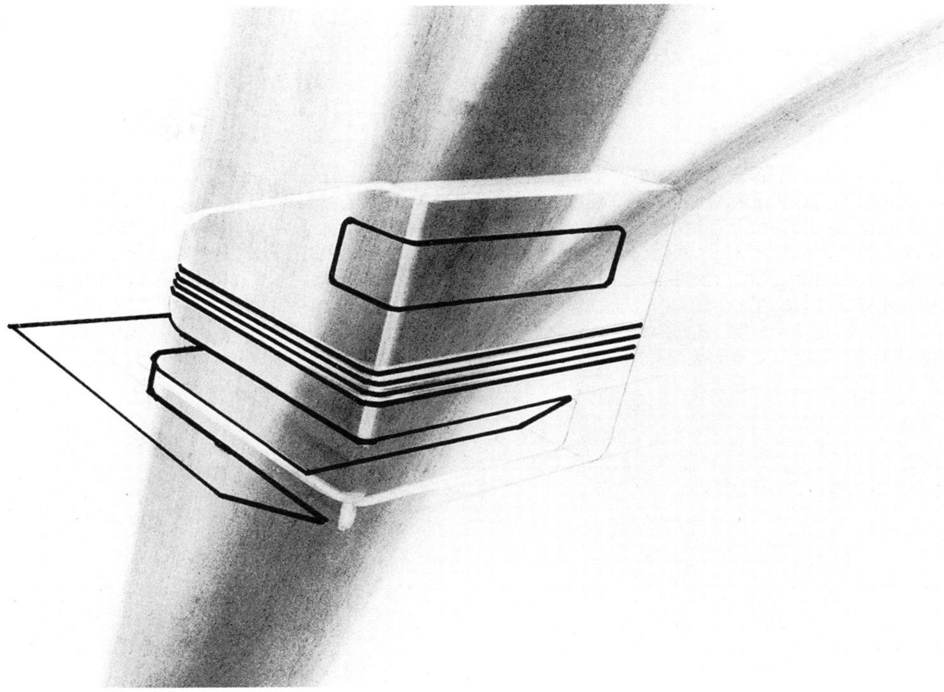

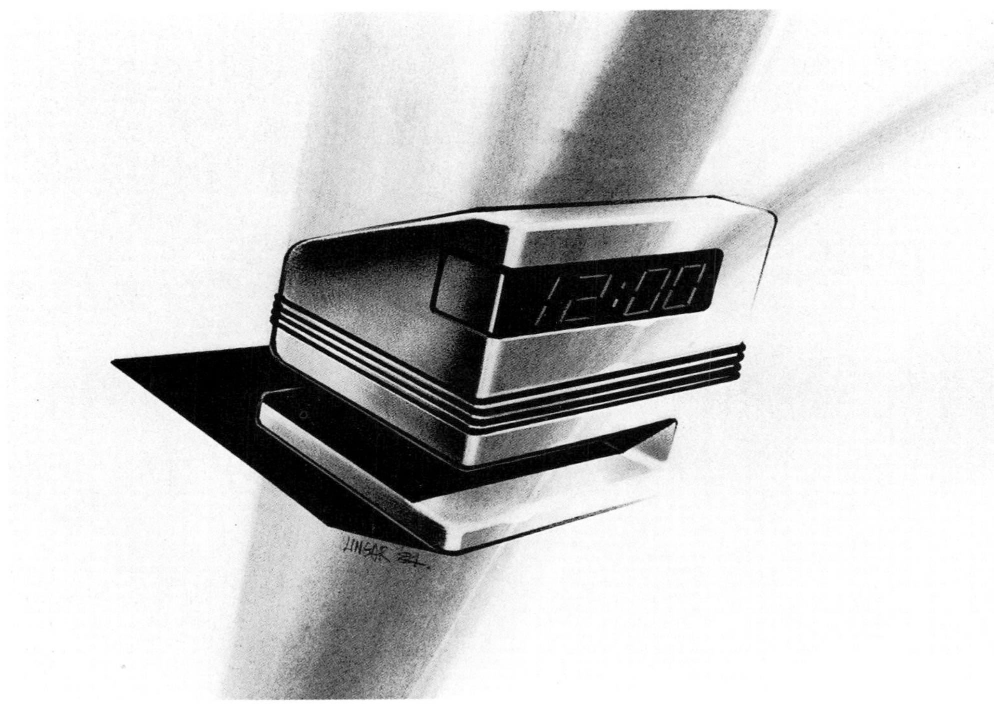

Exaggerating Tone

For this rectangular camera flash unit, parts of the layout were outlined in black; then gray pastel was blended across the drawing area. Medium tones and black shadows were then filled in, and leading edges were erased. I extended the blending all the way to the edges of the page so that the entire paper was involved in the composition. You should try to use the entire page whenever possible. With the addition of reflective nuances, the final concept achieves graphic strength without dwelling on unnecessary details.

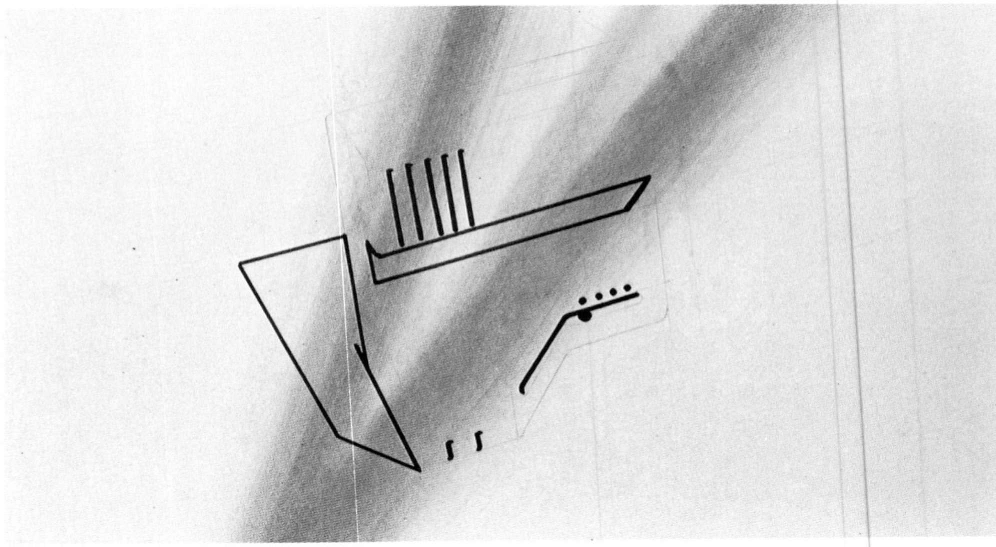

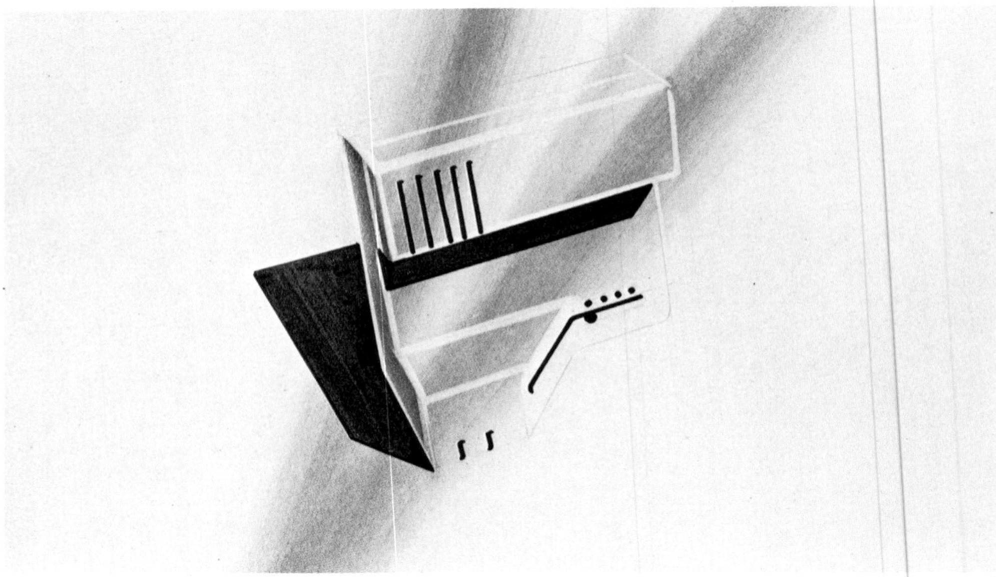

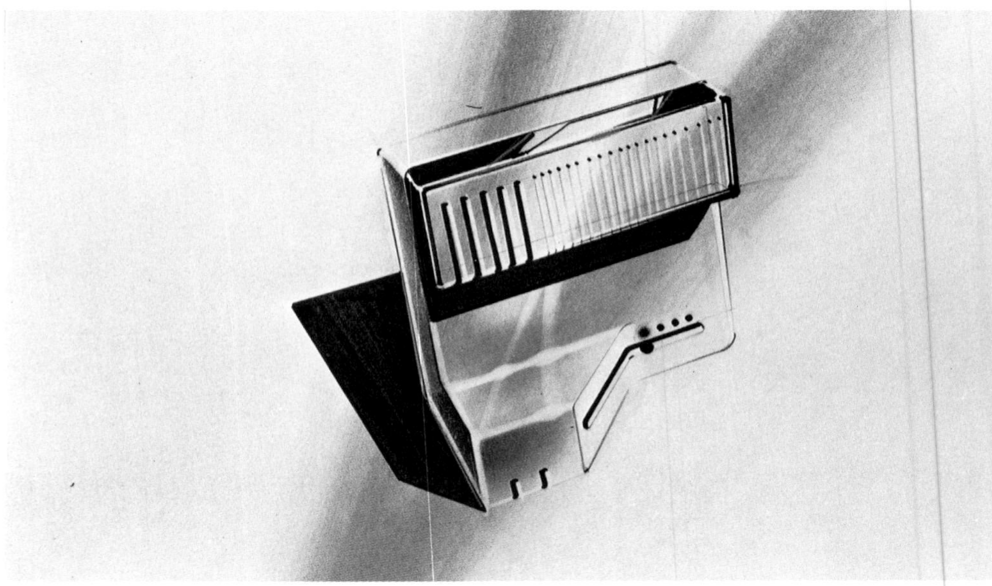

This handheld TV is also based on a rectangular shape. It achieves a certain realism because it uses a collage technique. A photo was cut out and pasted onto the rendering to act as a display. This can work for you if done with restraint.

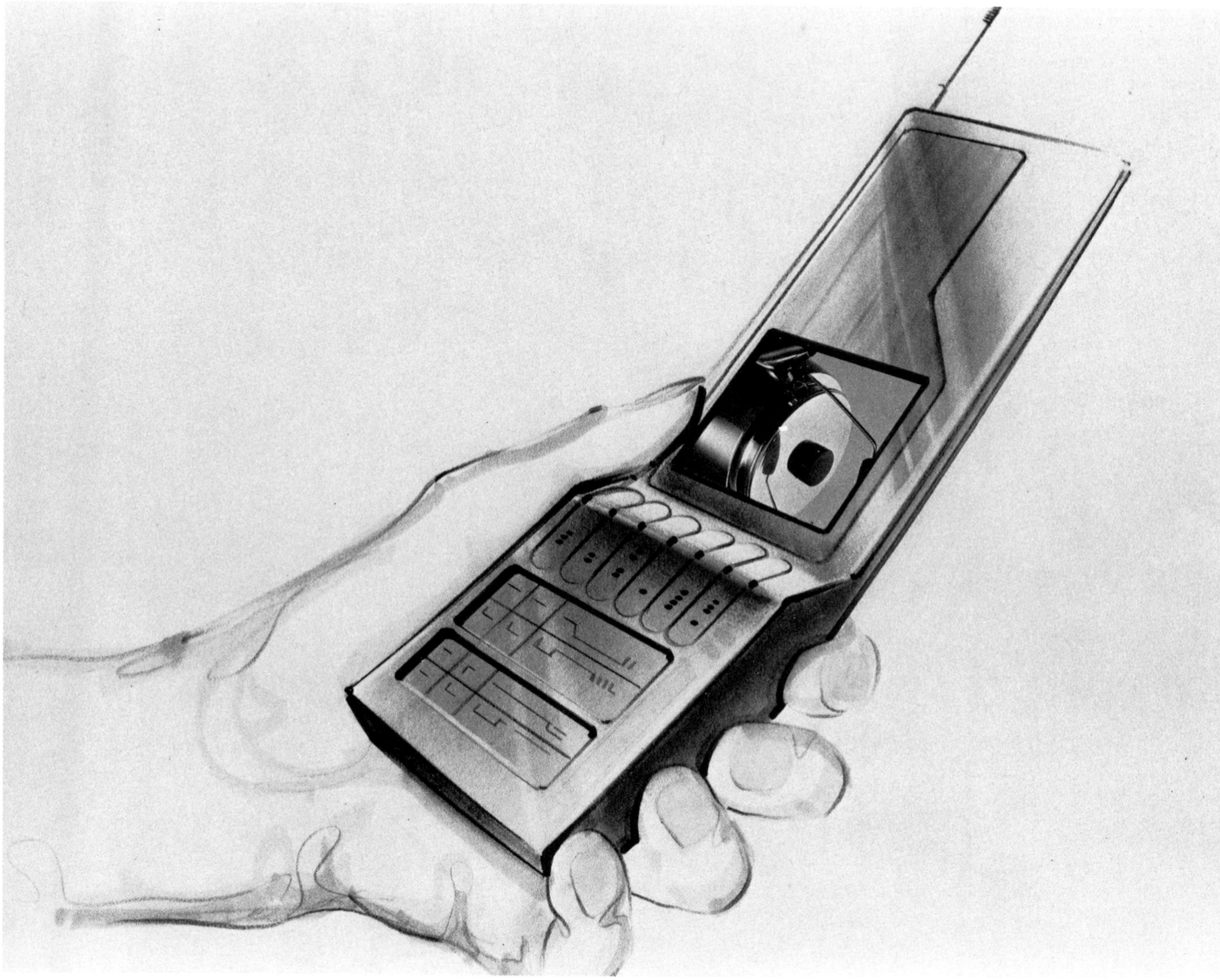

Like rectangular shapes, cylindrical shapes are usually easy to render; because they are based essentially on straight lines, masking is relatively easy. For this minicomputer, dark outlines were added to the initial layout, and chalk was swept through the shape with a Webril pad. The chalk creates a visual base upon which the product rests.

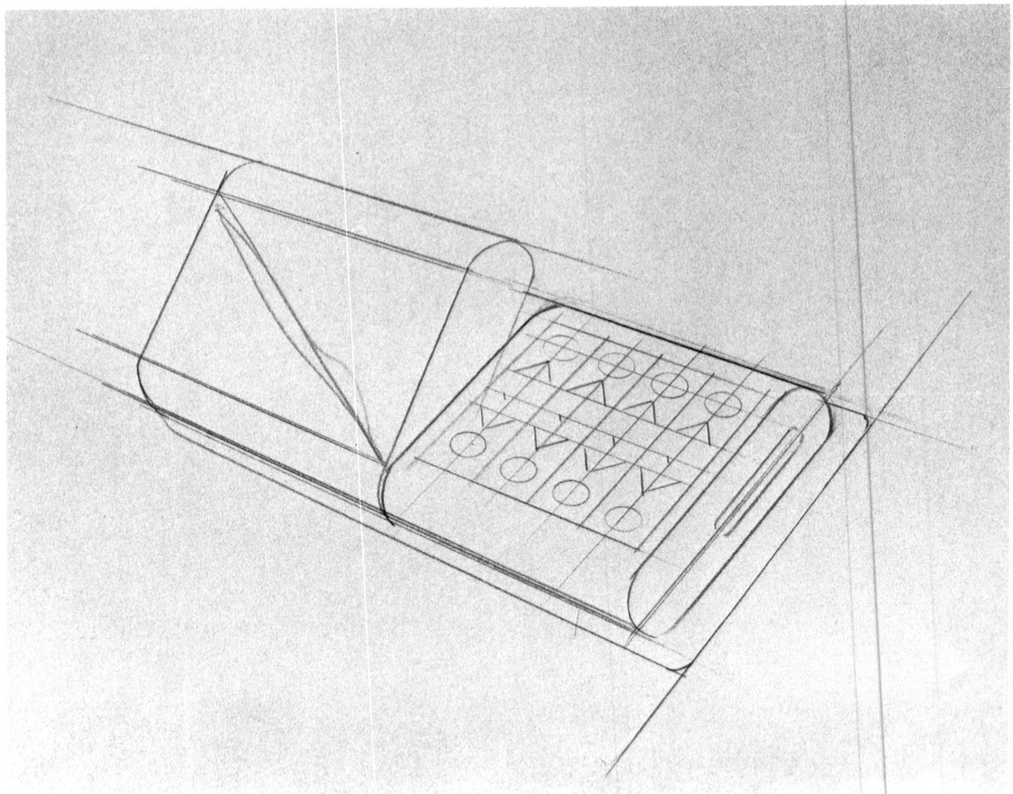

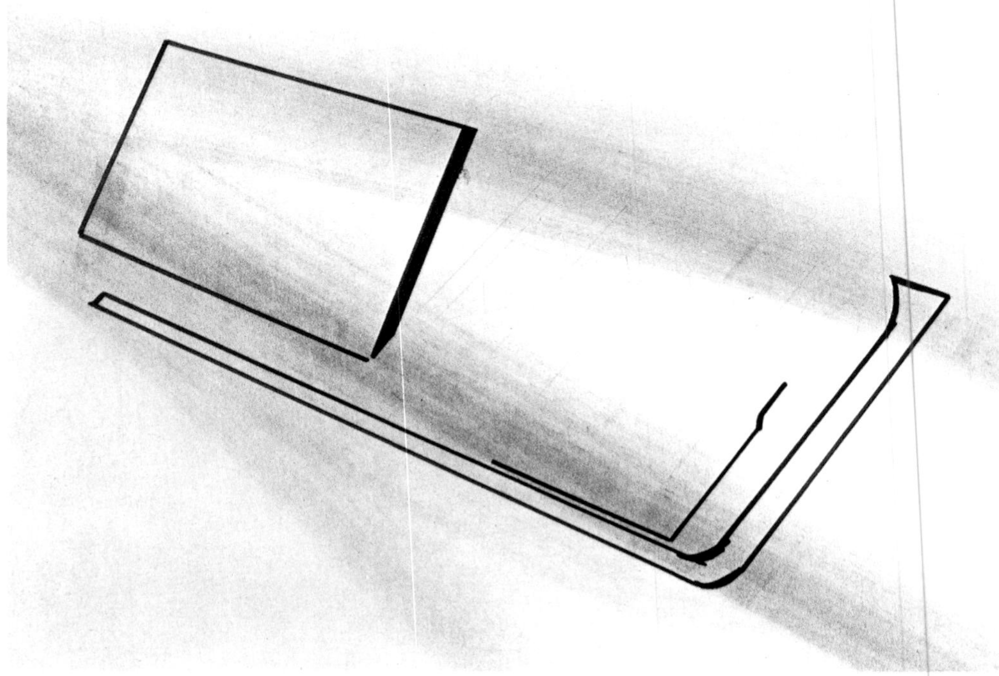

Medium and dark tones were added, highlight areas were emphasized by removing chalk, and appropriate details were added to complete the drawing.

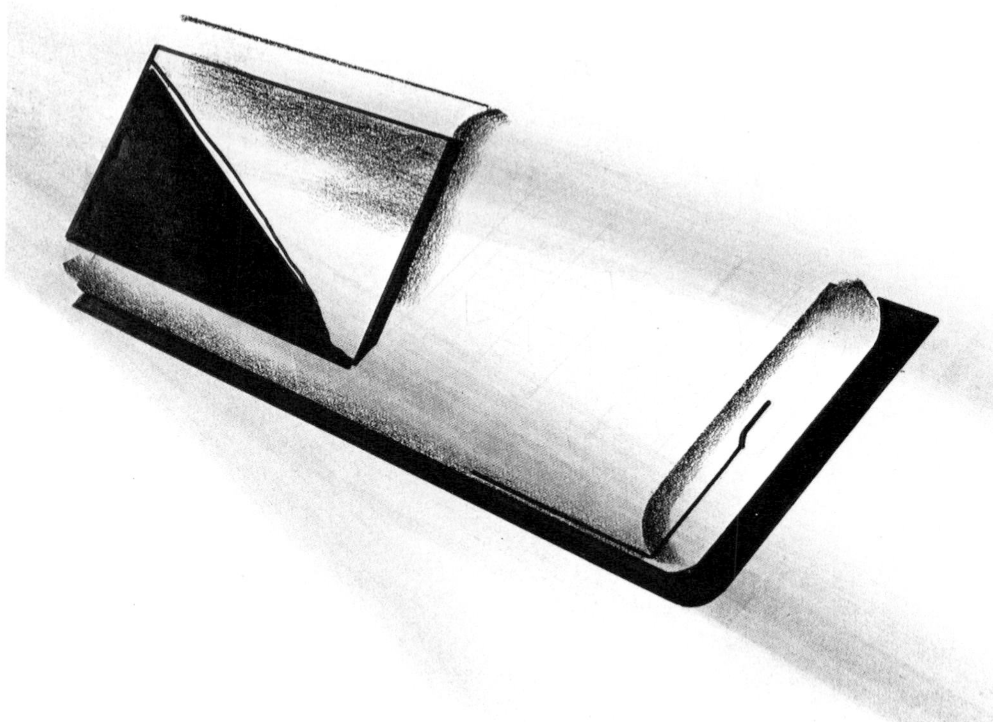

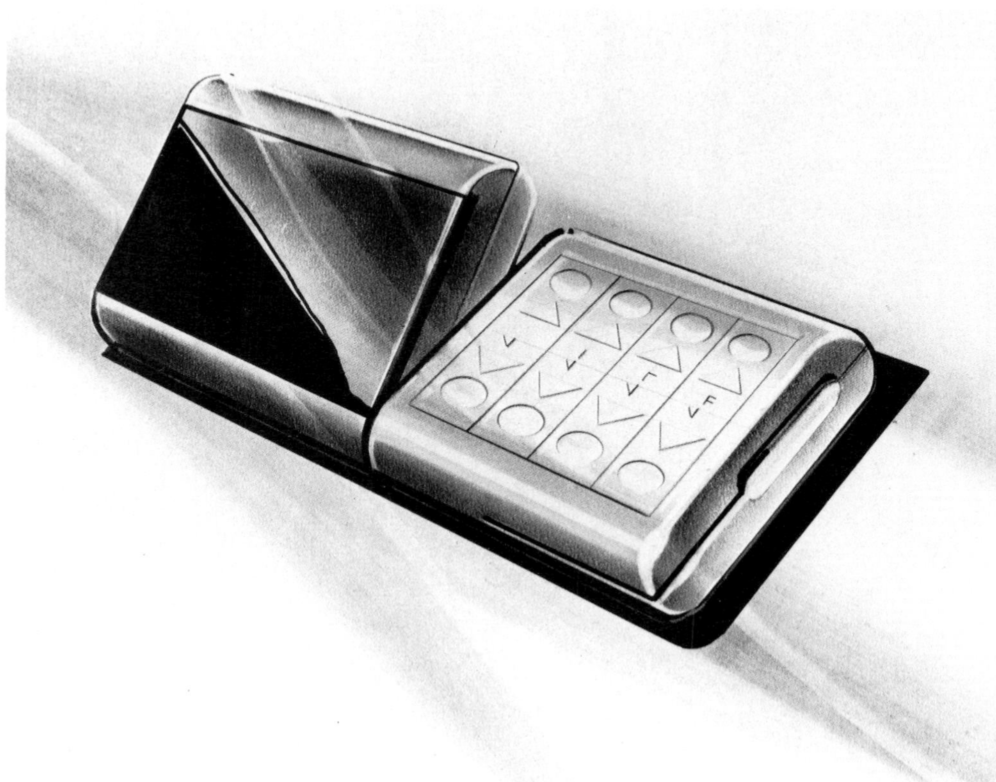

This football helmet with radio receiver is based on a spherical shape. First, the contours were rendered lightly with pencil; then, chalk was swept on, and major lines were darkened with black pen.

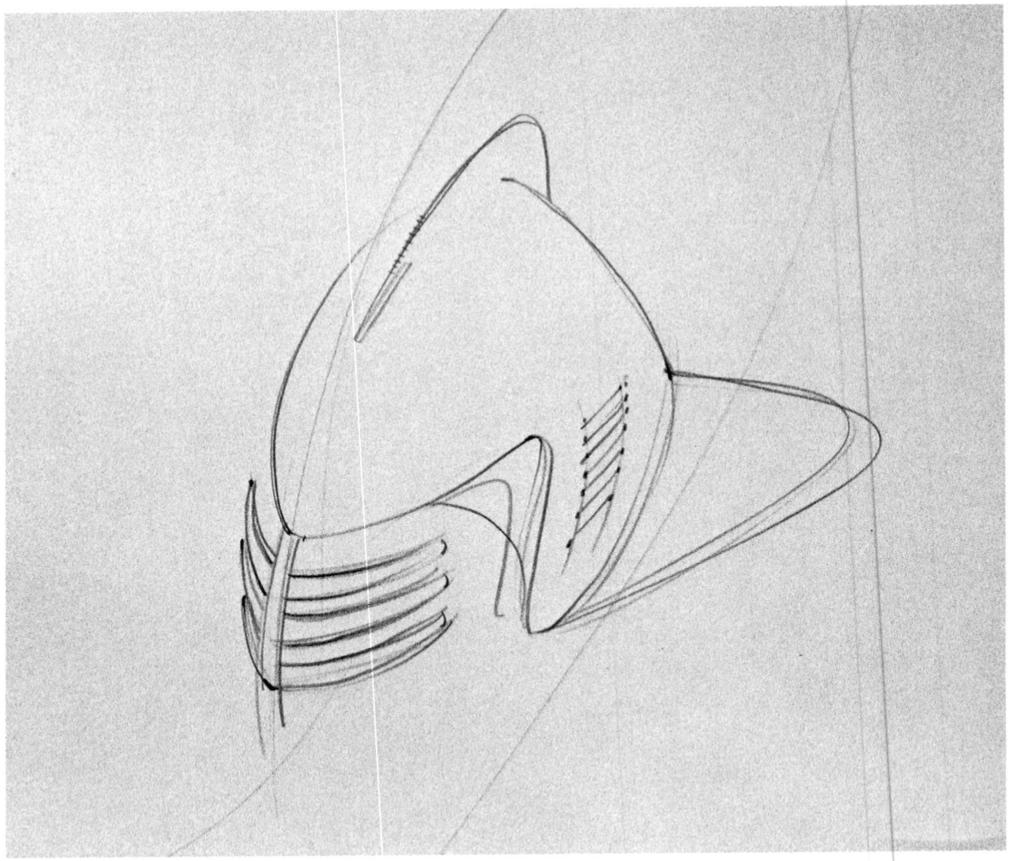

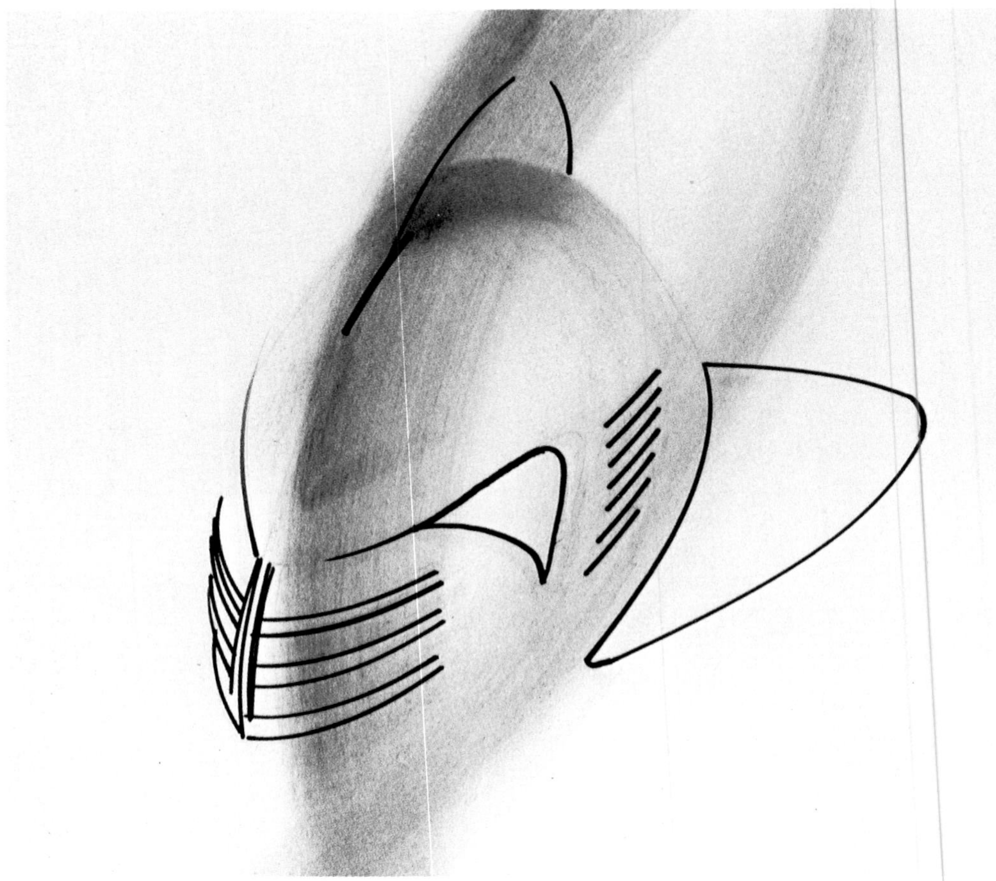

As the final shape was rendered, dark areas were blocked in. I ultimately used the background sweep of chalk to give the feeling of a spherical shape. Removing chalk with an eraser is helpful in a situation such as this, even though the reflective lines may not actually be there on the real product. This is "artistic license," exaggerating value changes to better communicate an idea.

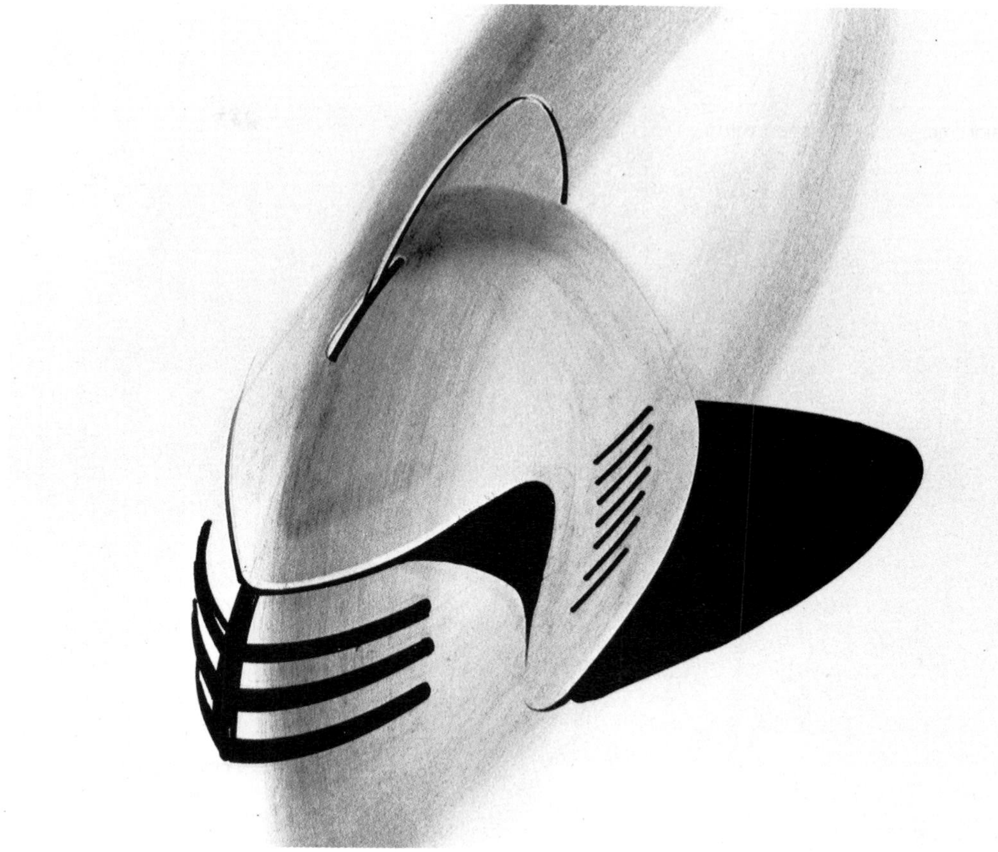

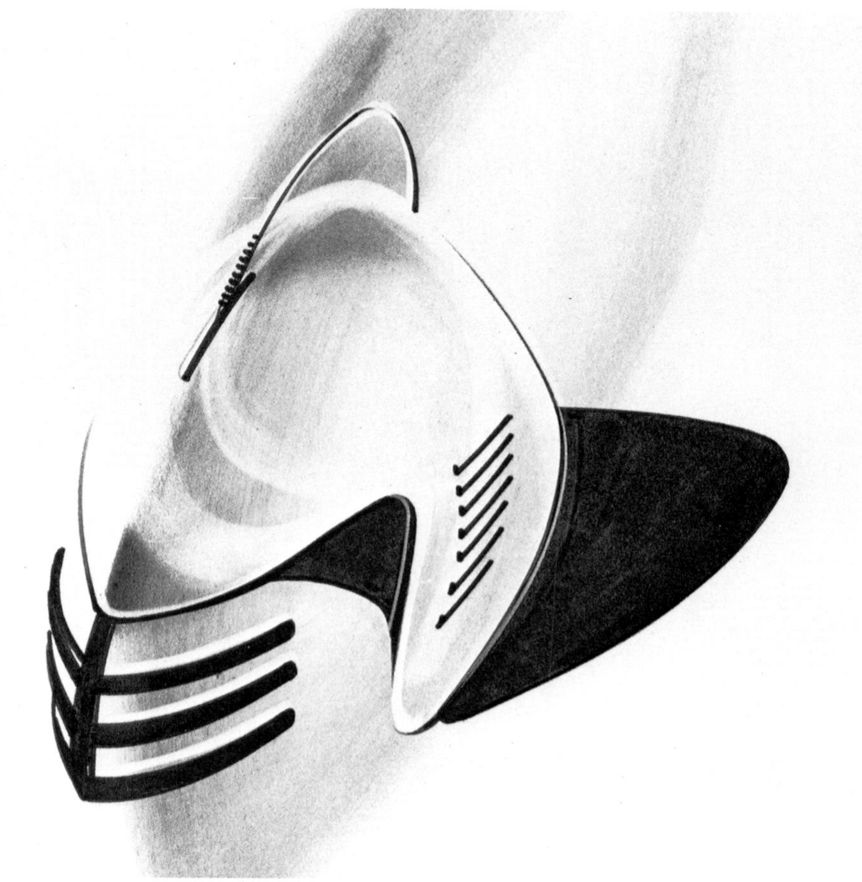

4 DRY-MEDIA TECHNIQUES

Mixed-media techniques produce perhaps the most exciting visuals. They are fast and adapt well to almost any two-dimensional paper surface. We have already been using mixed media in the previous illustrations by combining black marker and pencil with a gray chalk. Traditionally, designers often did not mix media, retaining the "intregrity of the medium" by using only dry markers, chalk, or gouache as the sole medium throughout the drawing.

I find that a designer's quickness in setting an idea to a page is more important to the business of design than his or her ability to accurately render an idea in a singular medium for the sake of historical purity.

The combination of dry markers and chalk can add another level of interest to a rendering and also shorten the time necessary to show reflections and nuances in general.

In rendering this living room, I used various dry media and a variety of line weights to add visual interest. The background consists of streaked dry marker; the carpeting effect was achieved by using a texture plate under the paper and then rubbing Prismacolor pencil over the paper (see Chapter 8). By choosing an eye level close to what a viewer's would be, you can make interior renderings seem more lifelike, as if the observer is "in" the depicted scene.

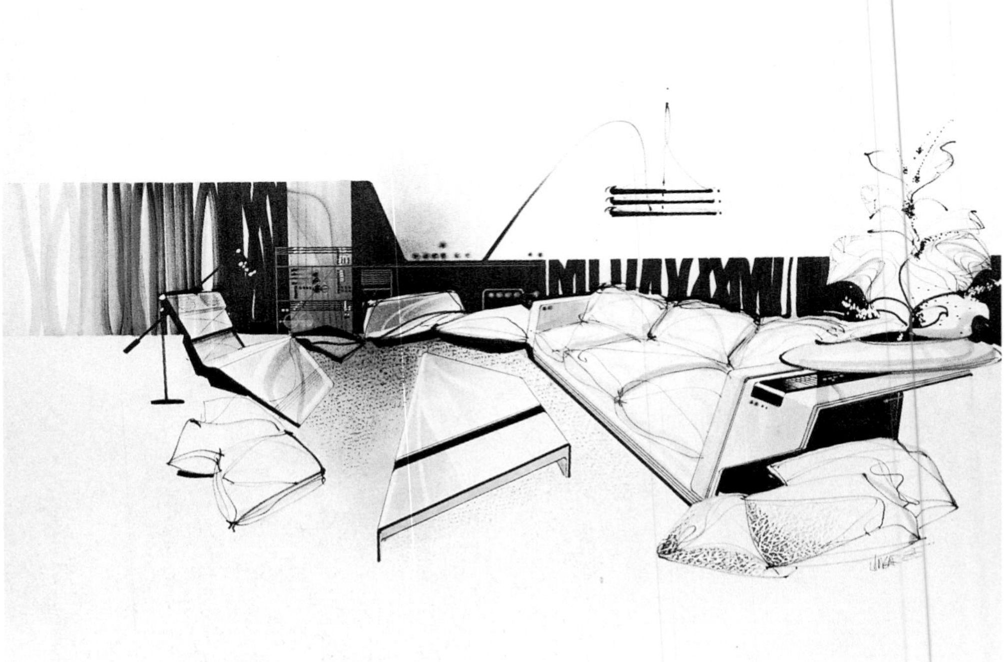

The effective use of dry markers can add vitality and realism to your renderings. This is especially true when markers are used in combination with pastel chalk and colored pencil. The flat, thin display and keyboard areas of this computer were rendered with these media.

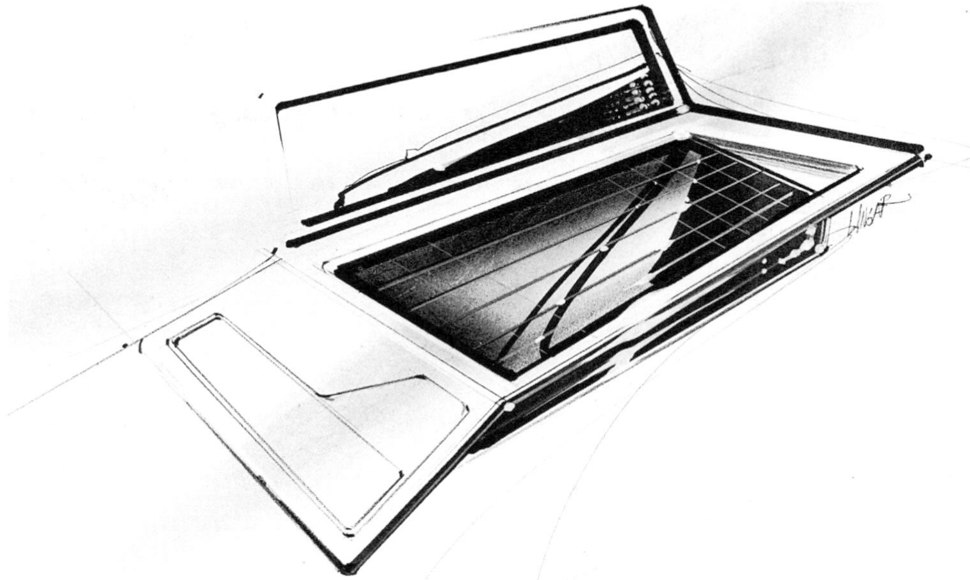

Dry marker and graphite were combined to soften the effect of the molded plastic in this bass fishing chair.

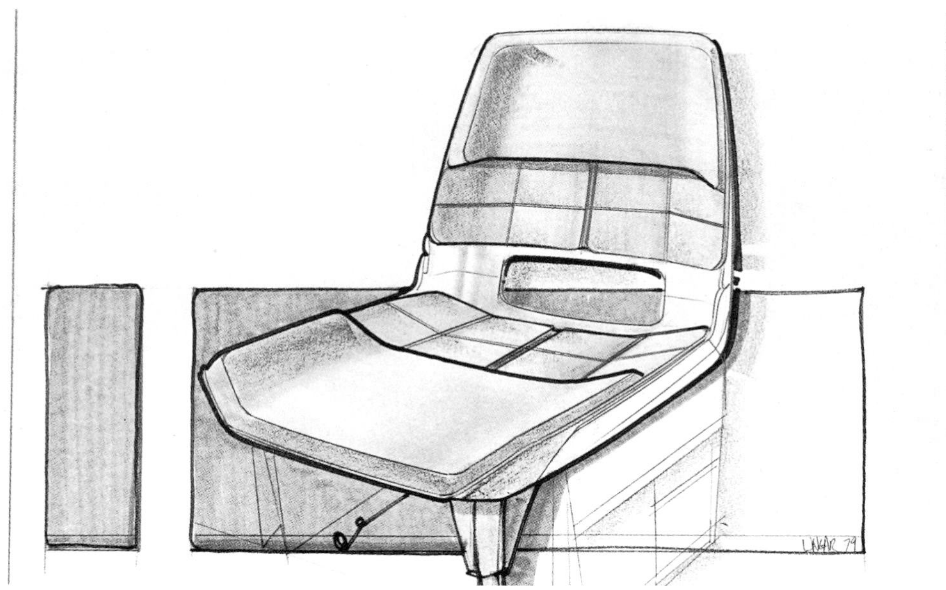

To develop this automobile, I used black Prismacolor, Sharpie black pen, and dark-gray pastel chalk, with black dry marker for the background and white gouache for highlights.

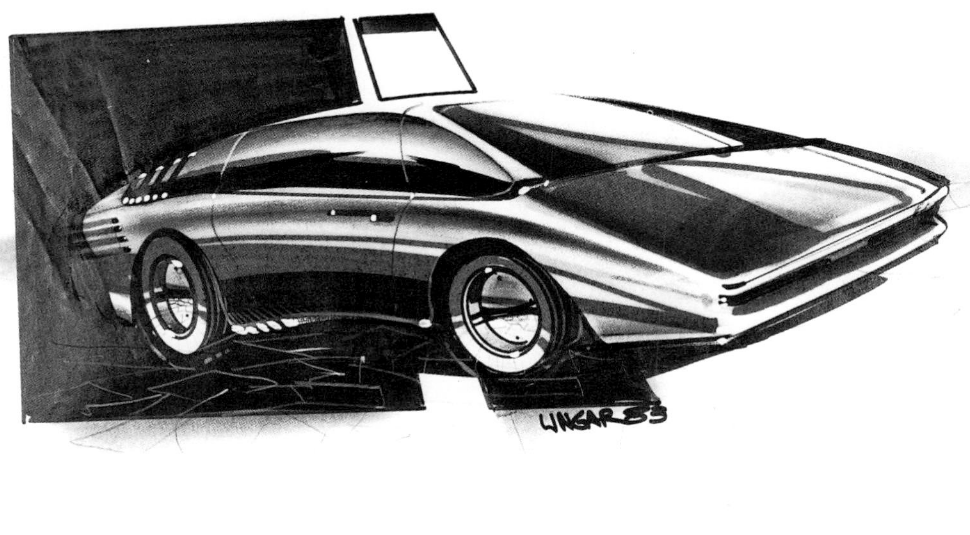

Marker and Chalk

There are several brands of dry markers, including AD marker by Chartpak and Design Art by Eberhard Faber. I usually use a set of warm-gray Pantone broad-nib markers, #1 to #10.

Because colored markers do not come in the same variety of shades as do the grays, they are more difficult to use for delineating fine tonal gradations. Hence, for color work, I usually create a drawing with gray markers and black pen and then blend colored chalk over the rendering.

Ogilvie Press vellum allows you to use the reverse side of the paper, as well as the front, for dry markers. Either gray or colored markers yield good results; a marker applied to the back of the paper will be seen as a lighter tone on the front.

Demonstration: Combining marker and chalk
This hand tool was started with a light Verithin blue layout drawn on Ogilvie Press vellum. This paper allows you to use dry marker on both sides. Next I turned the paper over to the reverse side and began developing the shaded areas with dry markers.

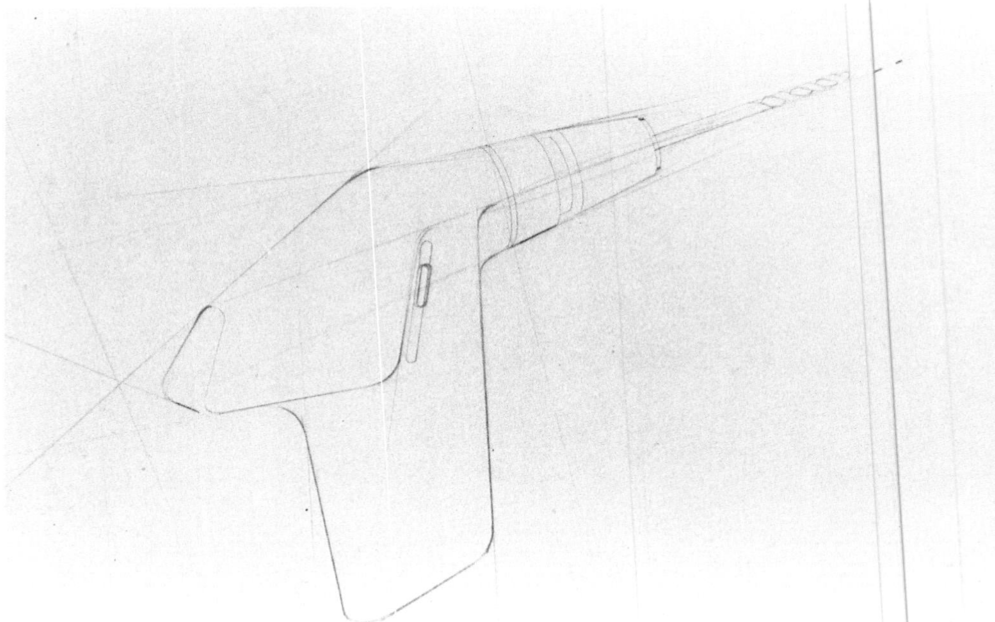

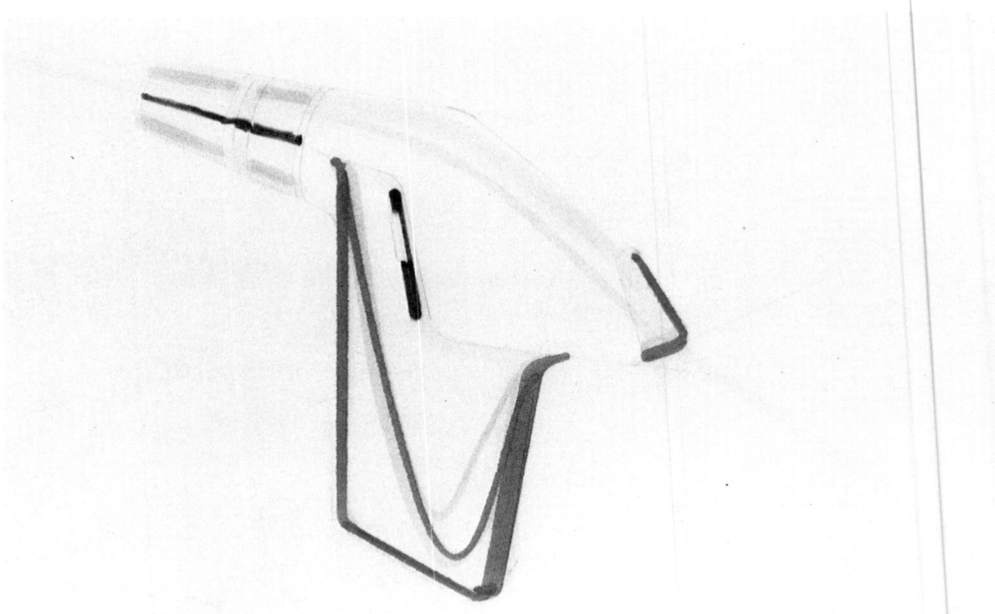

I turned the drawing over to the front side and darkened some of the major lines. I also lightly traced in the beginnings of a shadow background under the product, for placement study.

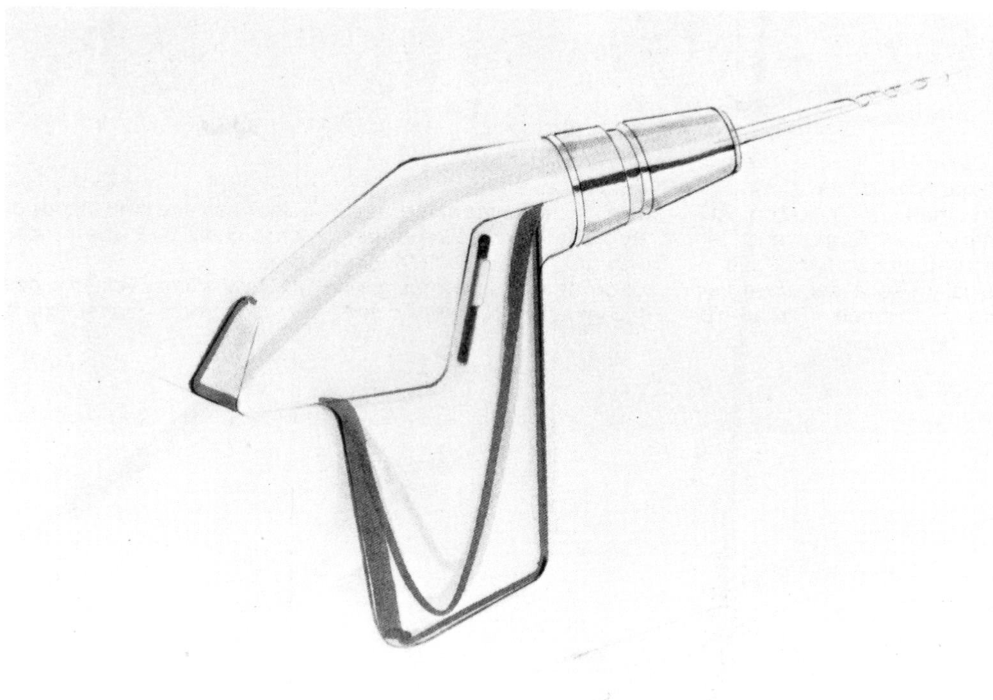

For the final rendering, I used gray chalk and added fine lines with black pencil and pen. I used black dry marker and white gouache highlights along the drill chuck's centerline to give the chrome a polished effect. The light in the handle area is a red dot fuzzed over with LetraJet red spray so that it appears illuminated.

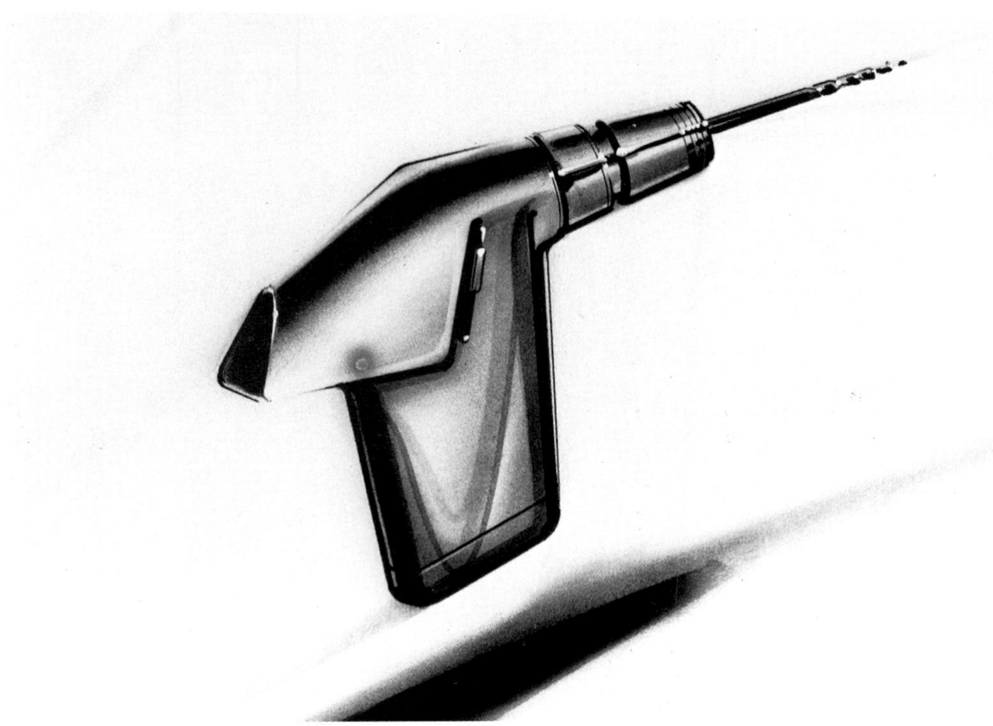

The chalk-removal technique helps define the horizontal surfaces of this sewing machine and the areas where the bend lines of the product are. Dry marker is used only as a subdued reflection across the front of the product.

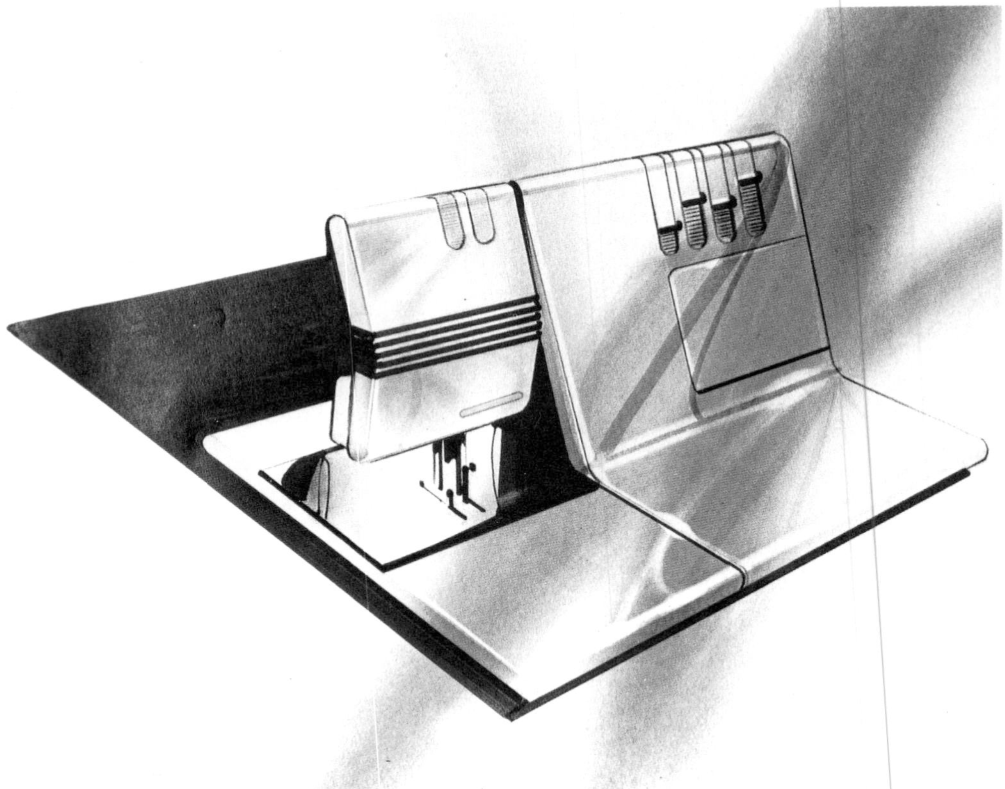

In drawing this medical device for measuring cardiac output, I used a dried-out black dry marker to create an interesting face to the product, with many tonal gradations. Over that, I then worked with a black Sharpie pen and pastel chalk to create reflections and detail. White gouache was added for highlights.

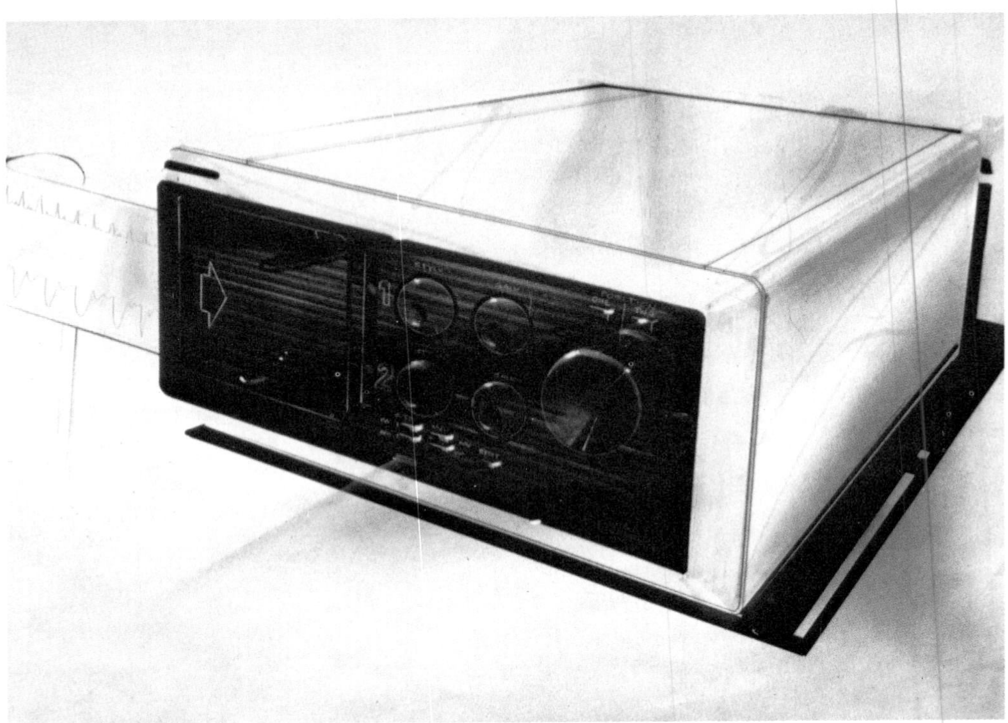

Highlights

The judicious application of white gouache to form highlights can have an amazing effect on a rendering. Highlights can take a relatively dry, lackluster drawing and transform it into a charged, expressive presentation. Anything good can be abused, however, and you should be aware that highlights are no exception.

Highlights are used to create the illusion of reality, not fantasy. Highlights should fall upon a scene or product drawing in a logical manner, based on the physics of light. I use artistic license with highlights only to further focus a viewer's attention on a particular feature, such as a leading edge or a series of edges facing the chosen light source.

Highlights can add a heightened level of realism to a rendering if they are not overdone. To create them, you should use a Winsor & Newton small sable brush such as a #0 or #1. White gouache, such as Winsor & Newton permanent or zinc white, is a good medium. For straight lines, use a straightedge, such as a ruler or plastic bridge created for this purpose, and guide the brush so that it makes a fine line. Apply more pressure to the brush wherever you want the highlight.

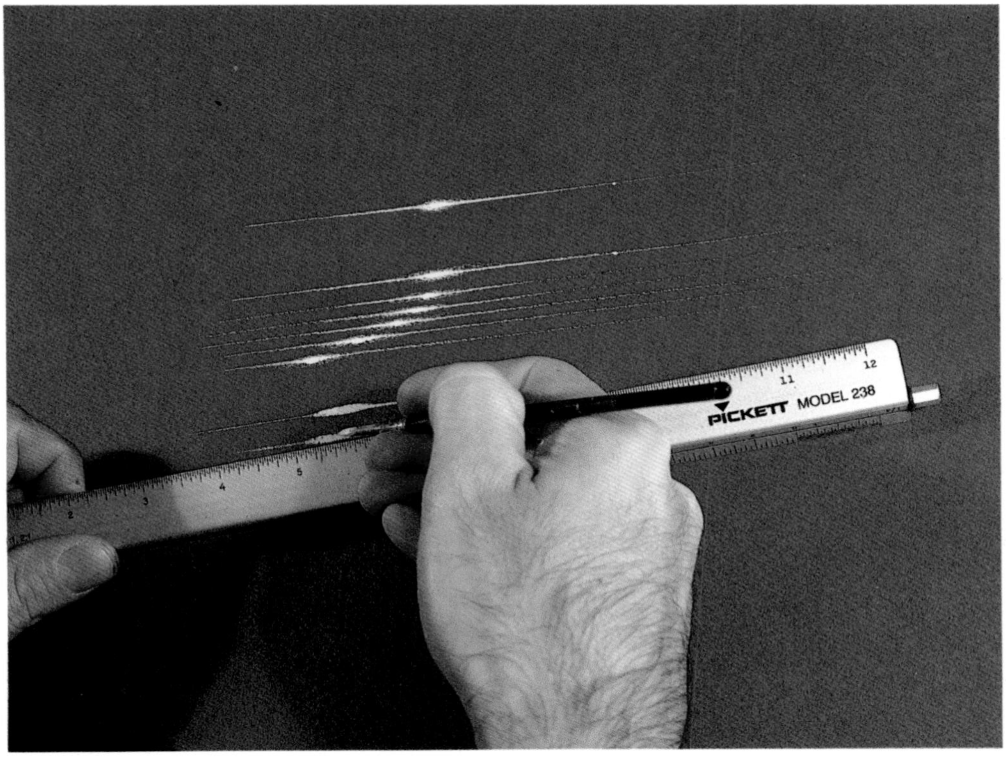

Note how the addition of highlights causes a drawing to "sparkle." To add gouache highlights to an area that already has chalk blended on it, you may have to mix your gouache with a little soap. Two products specifically designed for this purpose are Grumbacher's No-Crawl and Dr. Ph. Martin's Flex-Opaque. Here, gouache highlights were added to the brightly reflective earrings drawn in black and gray pastel chalks.

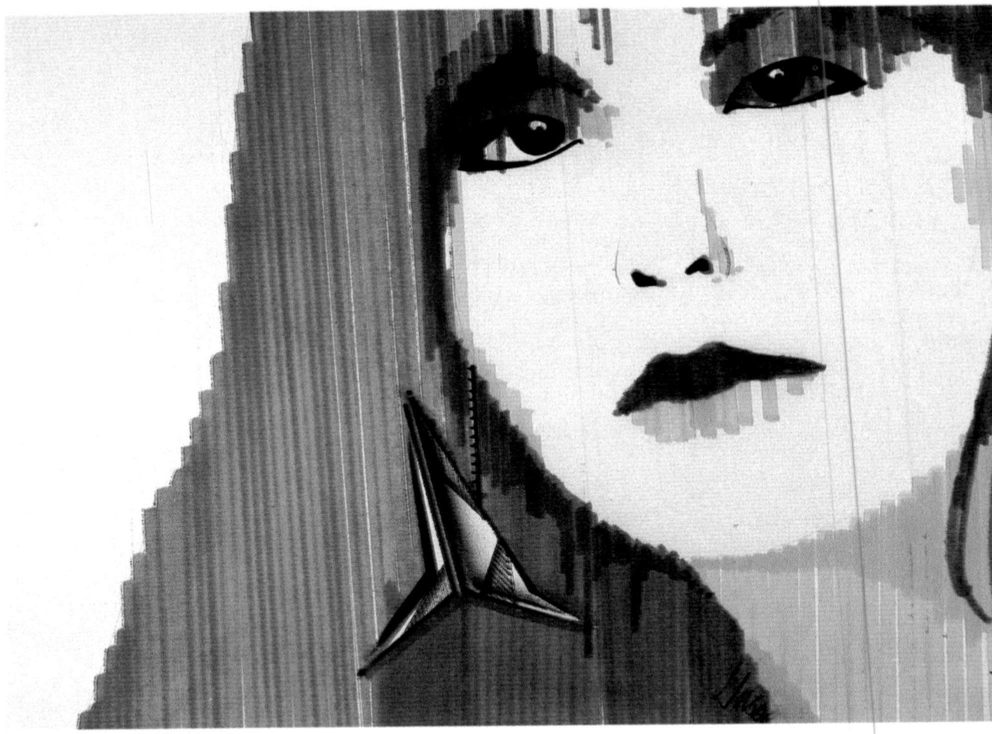

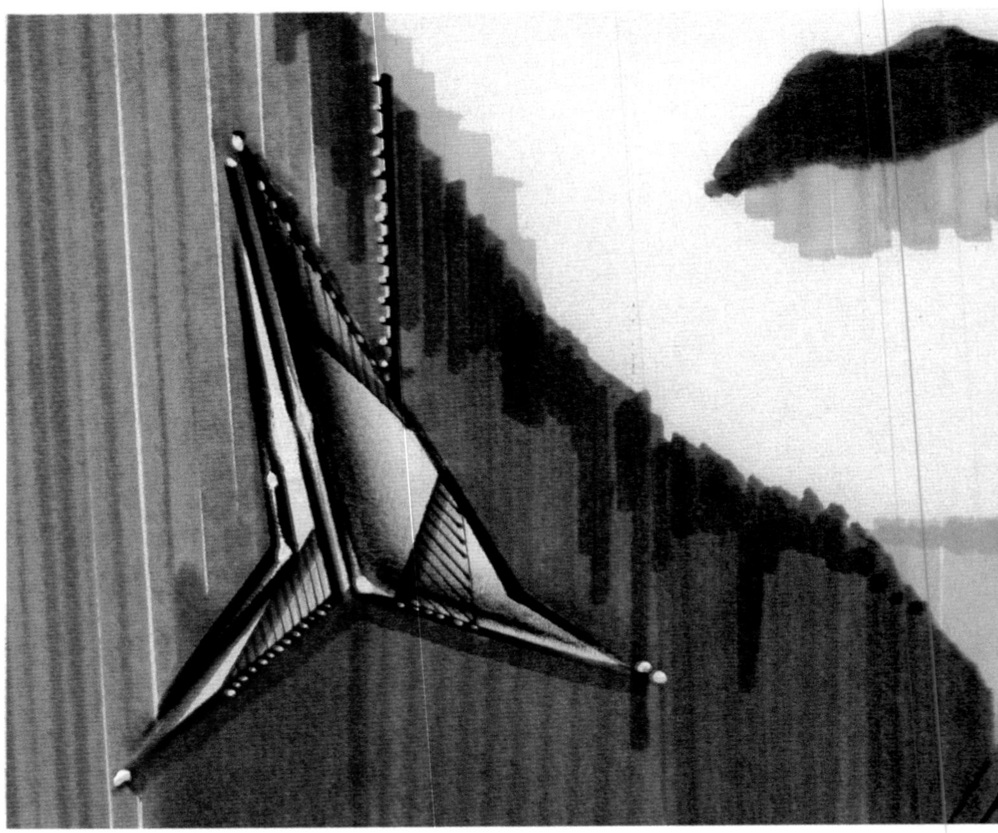

This hubcap is an example of the added realism attained by judicious application of highlights. The first example is before highlights were applied. In the second example, slightly more blue pastel chalk was added to achieve a higher contrast between the highlights and the product. Also note that all the highlights fall in a logical direction across the product.

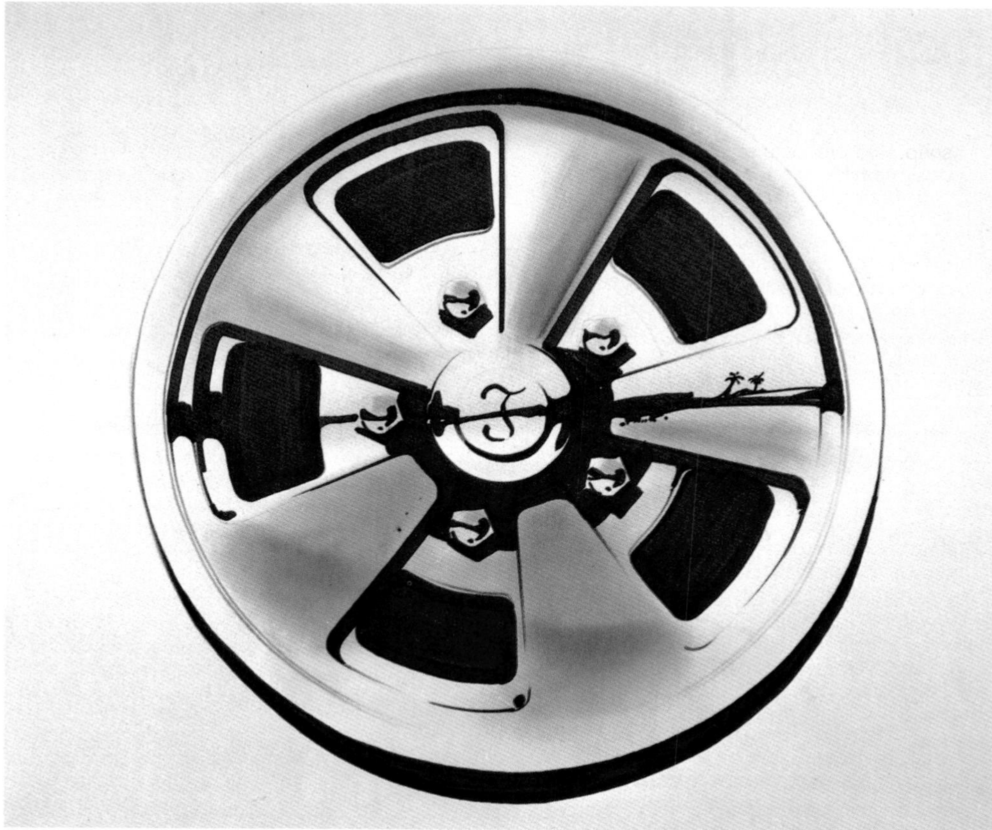

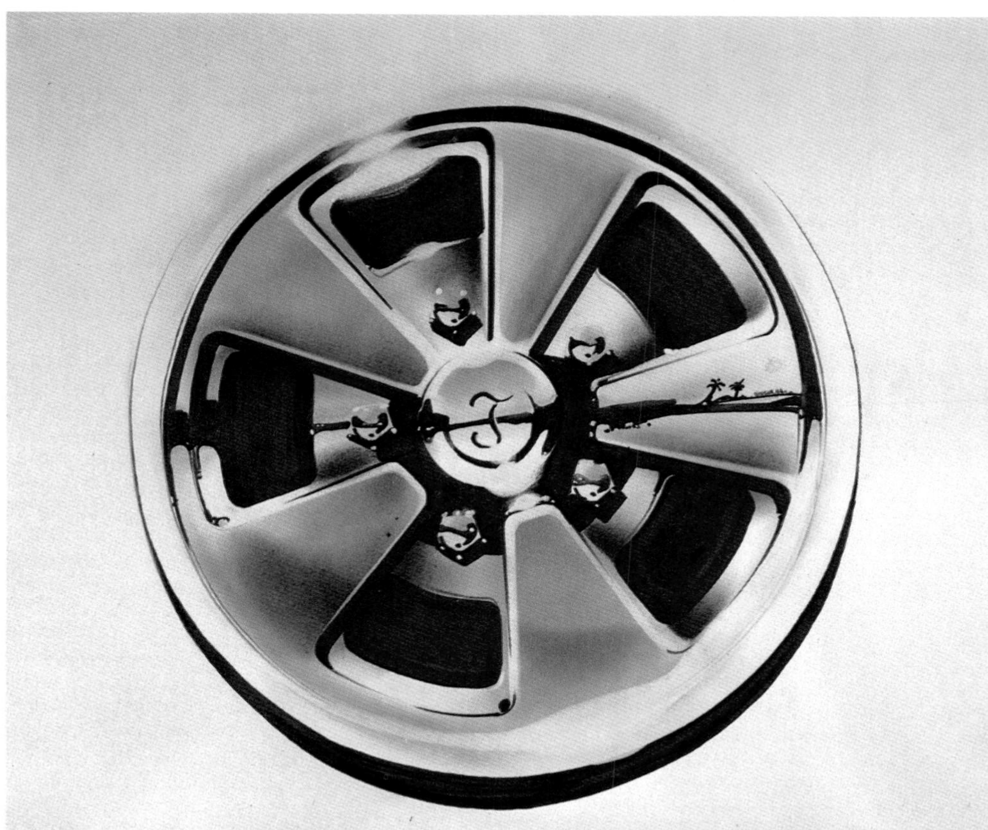

Marker Airbrush

You will find the LetraJet, a recent innovation, to be a handy tool. It provides a pressurized air supply that is good for about thirty minutes of continuous spraying. As a product-rendering tool, it is certainly limited, but it has a definite place, particularly for fast sketch work. I use it without masking for tonal effects on curvilinear or spherical shapes and to provide areas of color in black-and-white renderings.

LetraJet is designed for use with a Pantone fine-tip marker, but other fine-point markers will work if they are taped in place at the proper distance and angle to the airstream nozzle. I have produced interesting spatter effects by shooting the airstream close to chisel-point markers as well. Experiment! Markers used with LetraJet will tend to dry out faster than when in normal use, but a LetraJet should be kept on hand for special effects and fast sketching.

The use of colored marker sprays is rather limited, because they produce such a large, somewhat uncontrolled spray of color. However, for rendering a general background effect over a large area, spray cans are more effective than LetraJet. The small spray from the LetraJet nozzle is good for small bands or areas of color only.

Spray backgrounds achieve a blending effect that can enhance renderings of highly polished or reflective materials. The use of spray can quickly impart color to a simple back-and-white illustration.

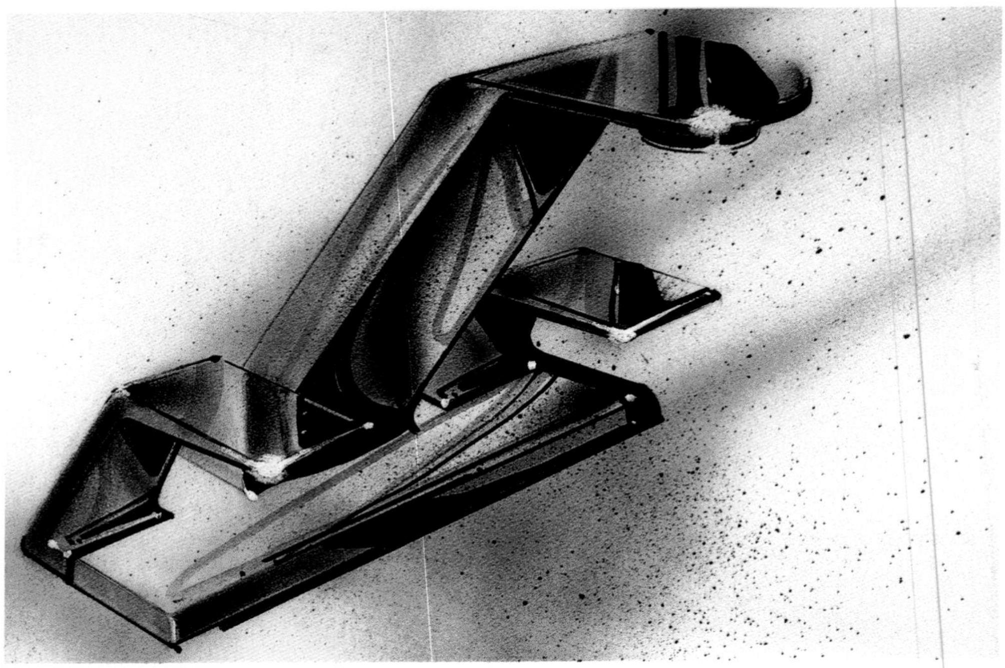

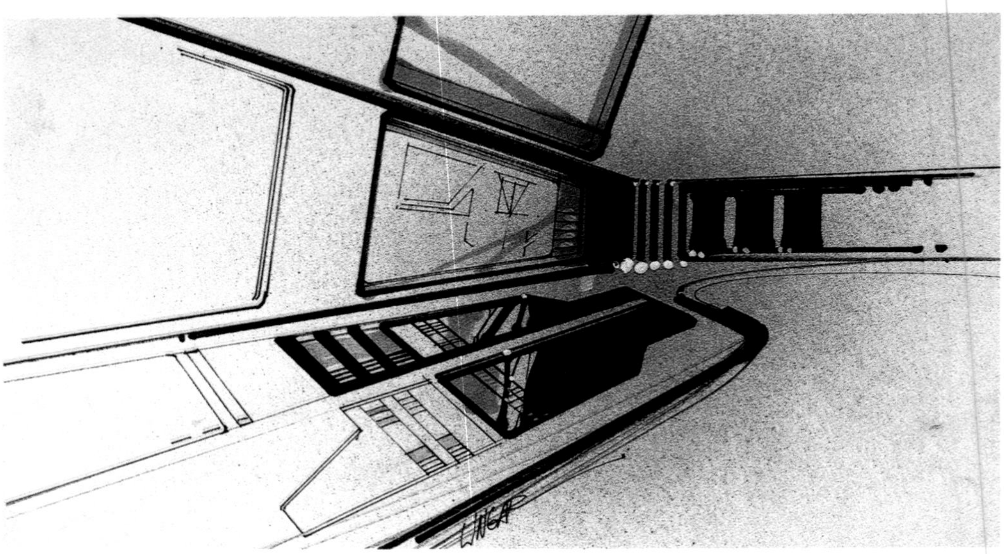

Color

Color, when used properly, can be a powerful visual stimulant that can liven up a rendering as nothing else can. It lends both interest and reality to a presentation, although if overused, color can become garish. It should be tastefully understated.

The richness of an innovative design concept must carry over into the presentation technique. If color is an important consideration, then it must be given tasteful attention in the preliminary, as well as in the final, renderings. Color can be incorporated into a drawing in several ways, such as through the introduction of chalk or of Letra-Jet.

One simple method is to use colored Pantone films over black-and-gray renderings. Another is to use a two-sided vellum. Apply your color to the reverse side for the middle tone and to the front side for the dark tone. By working back and forth, you can create two tonal values with only one colored marker or chalk stick. The lightest tone can then be added by blending a slight amount of colored chalk on the front side of the paper.

For a shade tone, use cool colors (blues and greens) as opposed to warm colors (yellows and reds). You can create interesting shade tones for an object having a warm color by first using a marker the color of the object and then blending blue pastel over the marker color. Shade tones for objects having a cool color can be obtained by adding gray to the original color. The use of cool shade tones also works well for illustrations developed in gray markers. Simply blend a cool blue pastel onto the shadow and shaded areas of the product.

The principle of using warm and cool colors in renderings is seen in this development of an orange cube. In this case the paper allowed the use of dry markers on both sides, so I first rendered the orange cube and the blue shadow on the reverse side.

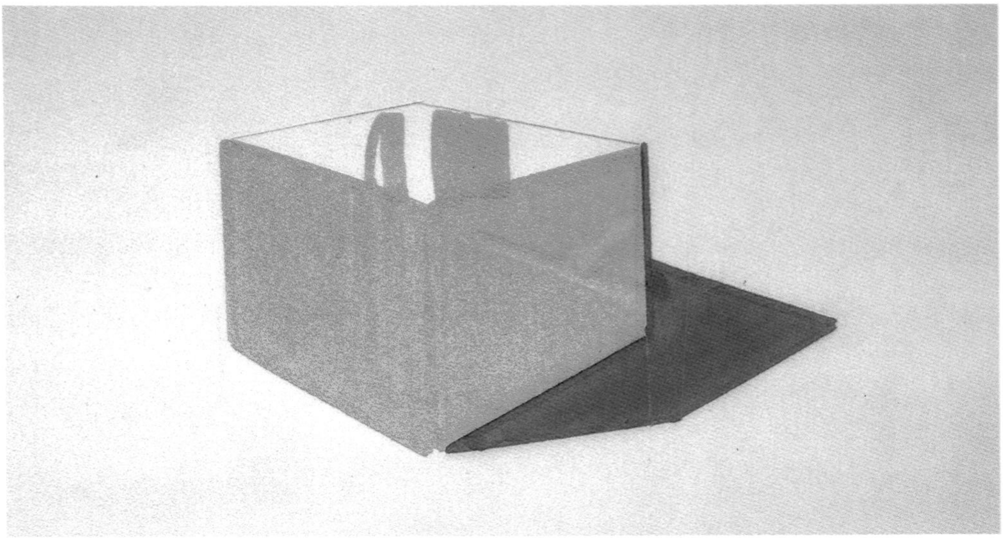

On the front side of the paper, the colors that had been drawn came through nicely muted. I strengthened the dark side of the cube by adding orange to it. Any additional light tones would be added with light orange or white chalk on the front of the paper.

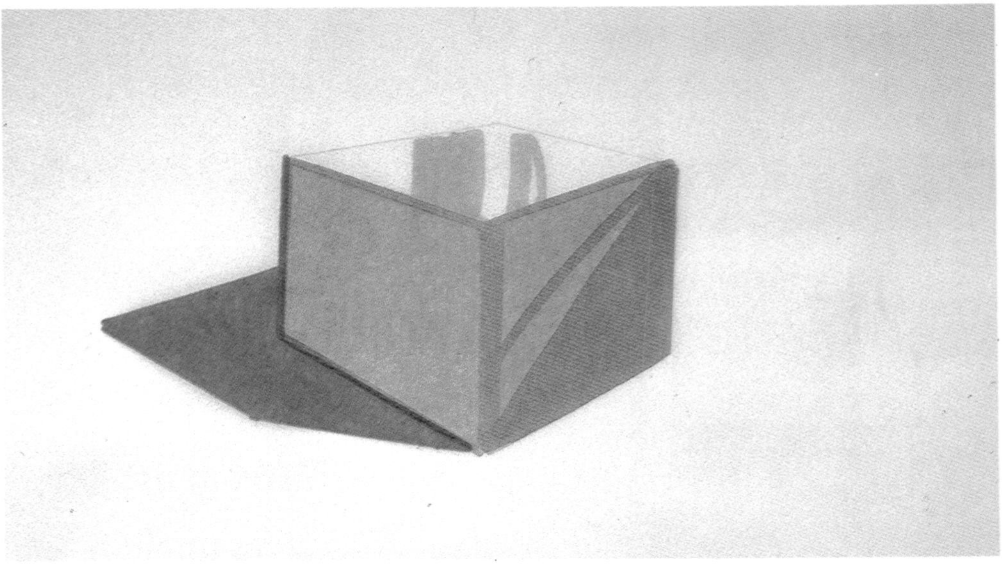

This architectural layout was done with graphite and black dry marker on vellum. The final rendering has pastel chalk added.

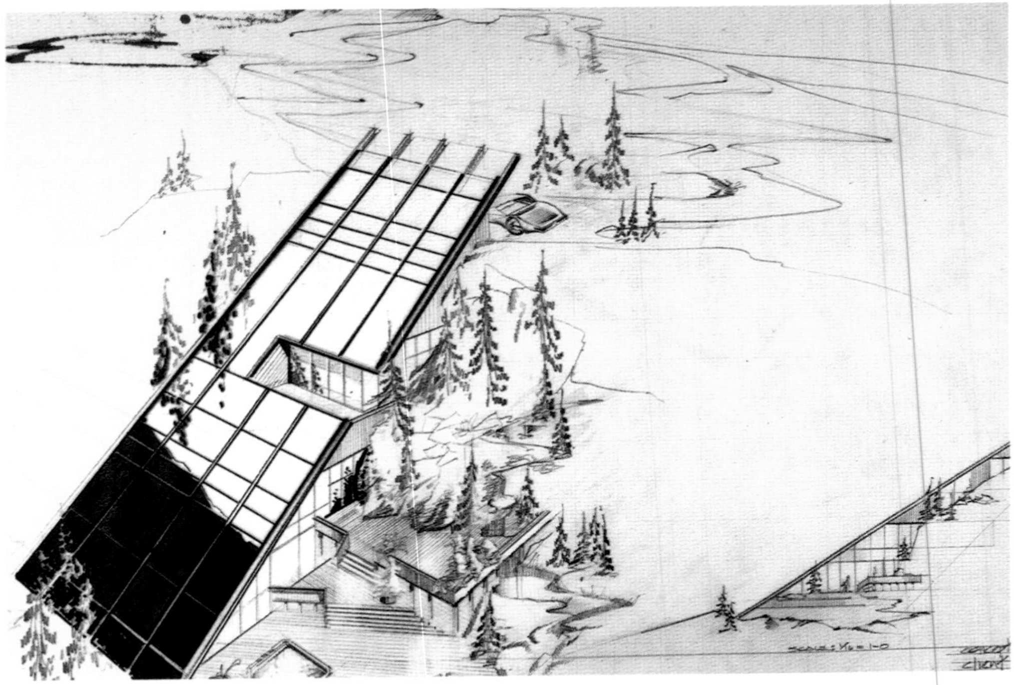

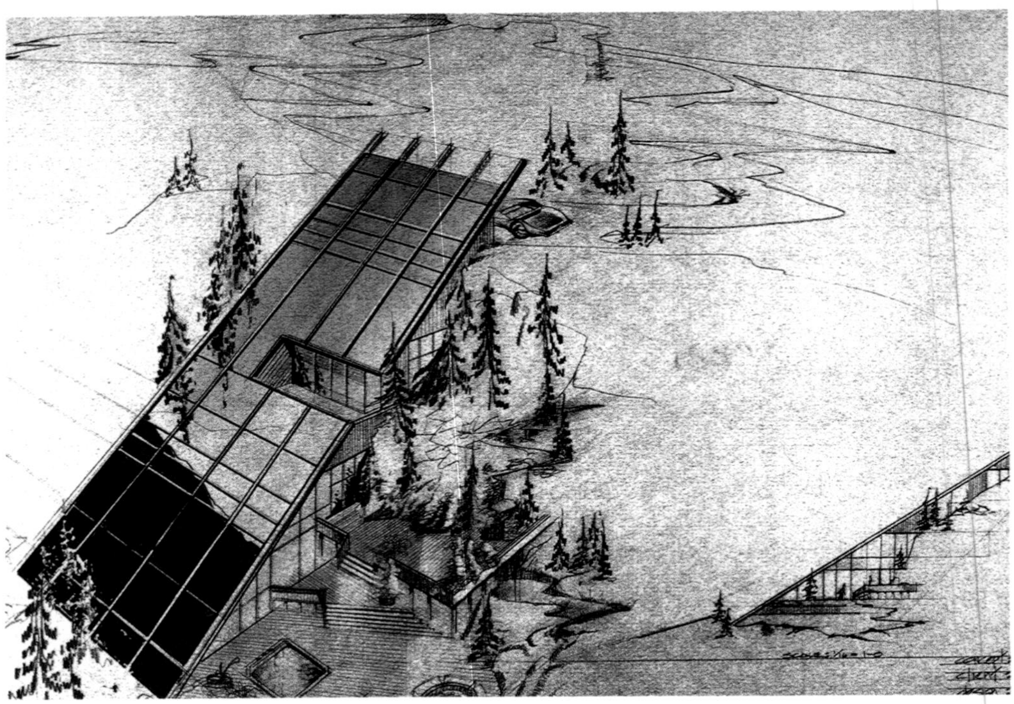

A complex illustration, such as this luxury bath environment, often has a variety of focal points within the drawing. If you keep the major portion of the illustration monochromatic, you can direct the viewer's eye with isolated areas of color. In this case, the blue water and blended blue background create a resting point for the eye. Black and cool-gray dry markers were used along with Prismacolor pencils for the electronic displays and fine details. The highlights on the water were applied with white opaquing fluid. The illustration was rendered on tan paper.

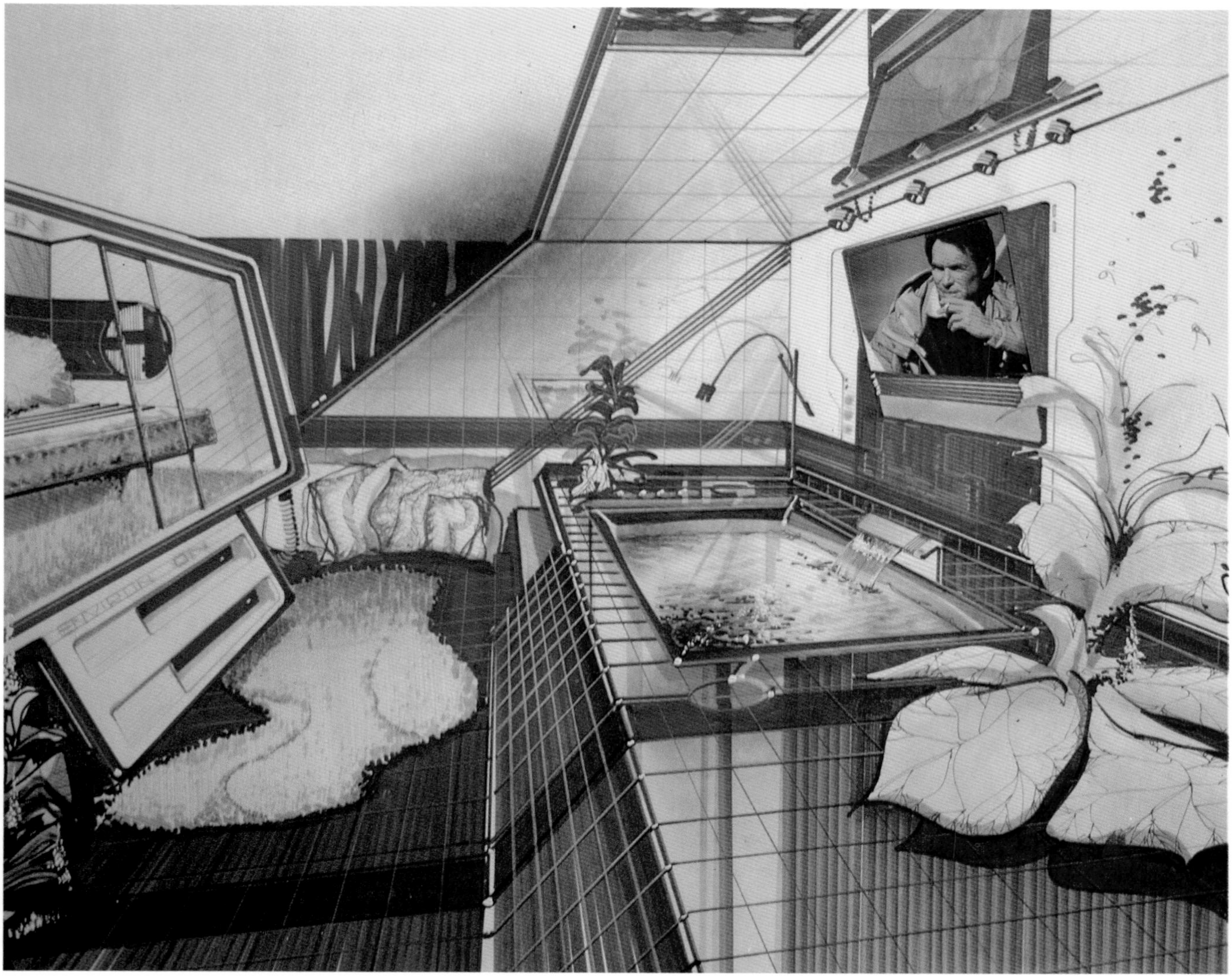

Quick Sketch and Color

The essence of a fast sketch is its economy of line and tone combined with a simple background development or shadow to help define the object. A medium-toned paper, such as inexpensive tan newsprint, works well for this. You simply have to add shade values and highlights, and you have a fast sketch.

For fast layouts, use a Verithin red pencil. Develop the product form quickly with gray dry markers. Next, add a blended area of colored chalk to create surface values or reflections. Weighted, dark line-work around the object will strengthen any undefined areas. Lastly, add cool-blue dry marker for shaded areas, and add white gouache highlights in logical spots, where light might fall across the object.

The color in a quick sketch can do two things. First, it can suggest the actual color of the object; and second, it can be used to link together several sketches presented in unison, so that they form a visual group when presented to a client.

Demonstration: Quick sketch with color

Follow this rendering of a miniature flashlight and emulate on a separate paper the progress from layout to final illustration. An analysis of the lights, mediums, and darks accompanies the layout.

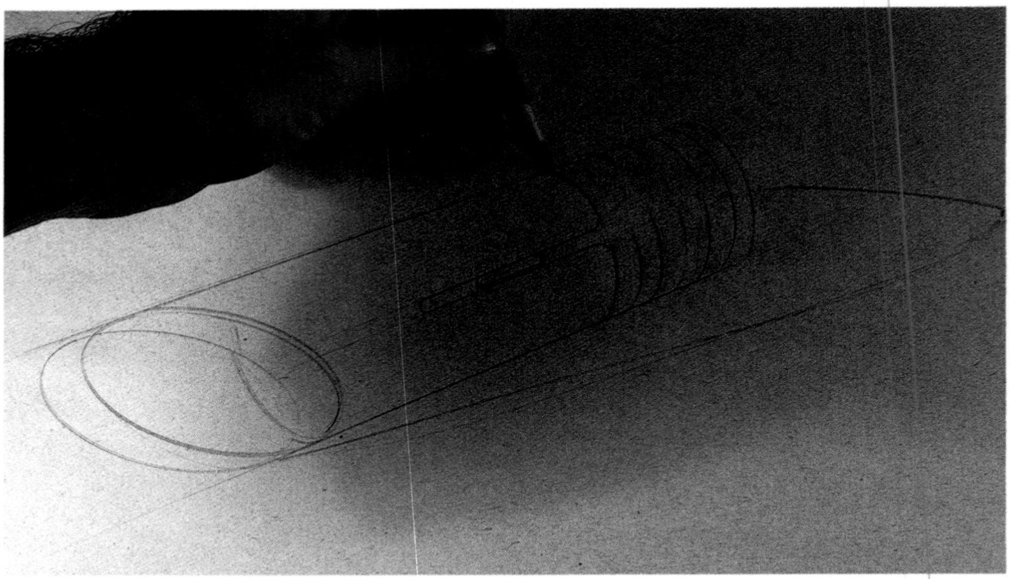

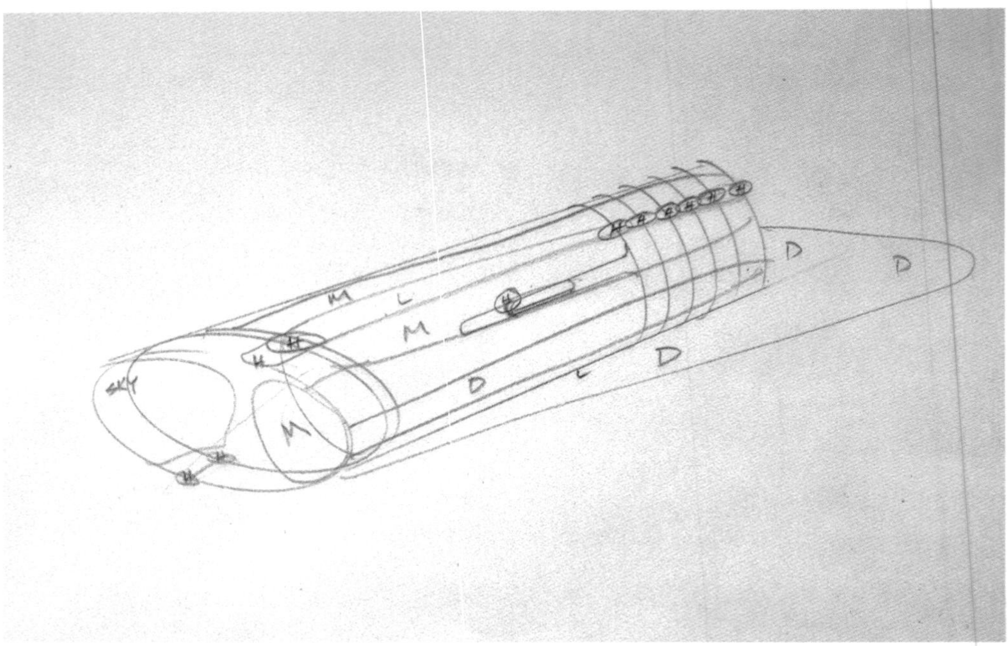

The form was quickly rendered with gray dry markers, and the shadow area was added with blue marker. In this case, a quick spray of orange was added with LetraJet for basic coloration. For the final rendering, tones of orange chalk were swept over the form; then penciled line-work and gouache highlights were added. (Always keep your paper on the pad while blending chalk, or the blending effect with Webril pads will be minimized.)

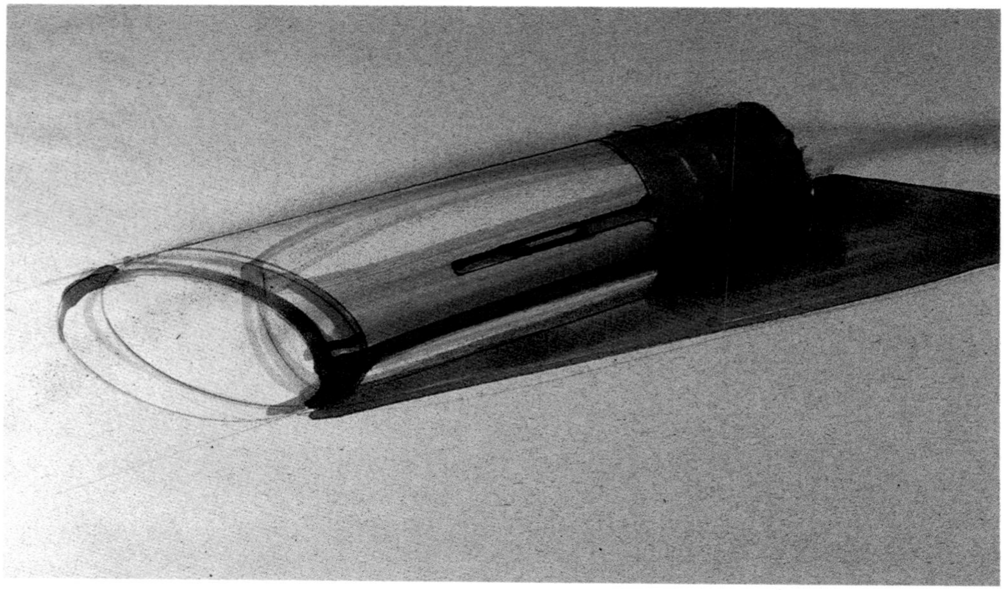

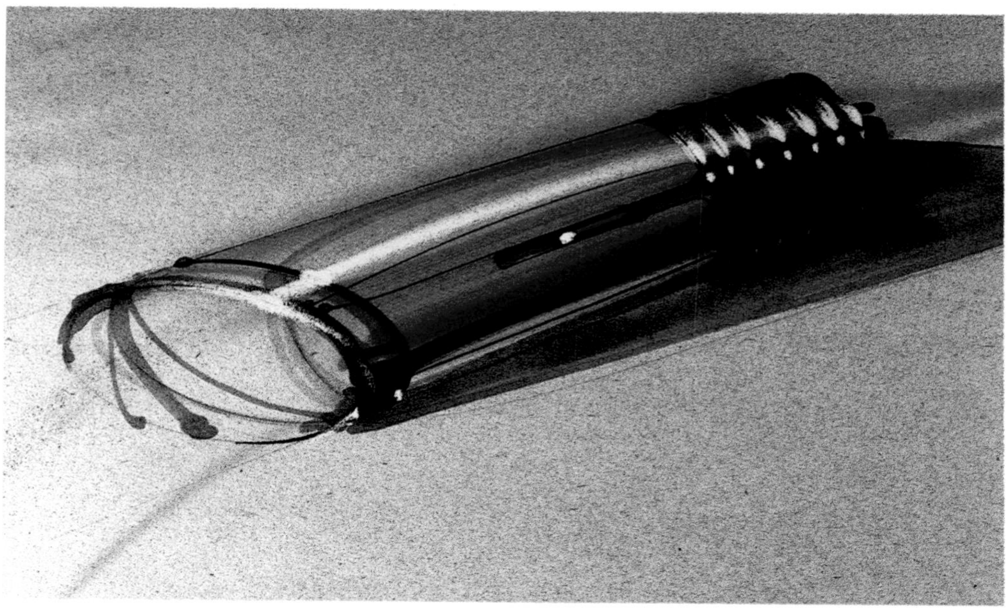

This value-analysis for an automobile design is a good preliminary start to a quick sketch of the concept. In this case, there are a lot of compound curves that can only be defined by the way reflections move around the surface.

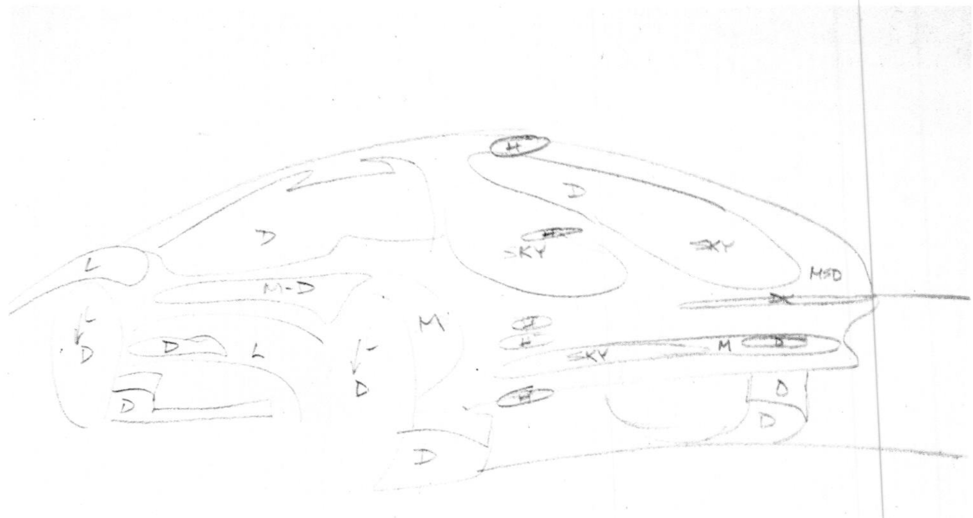

Reflections on the auto were done by applying warm-gray dry markers and blue pastel. A cool-blue dry marker was used for the shadow area, offsetting the warm coloration of the automobile (basically the color of the newsprint pad). You should observe nature and see how shiny objects reflect their environment; keep a log of these observations for later reference.

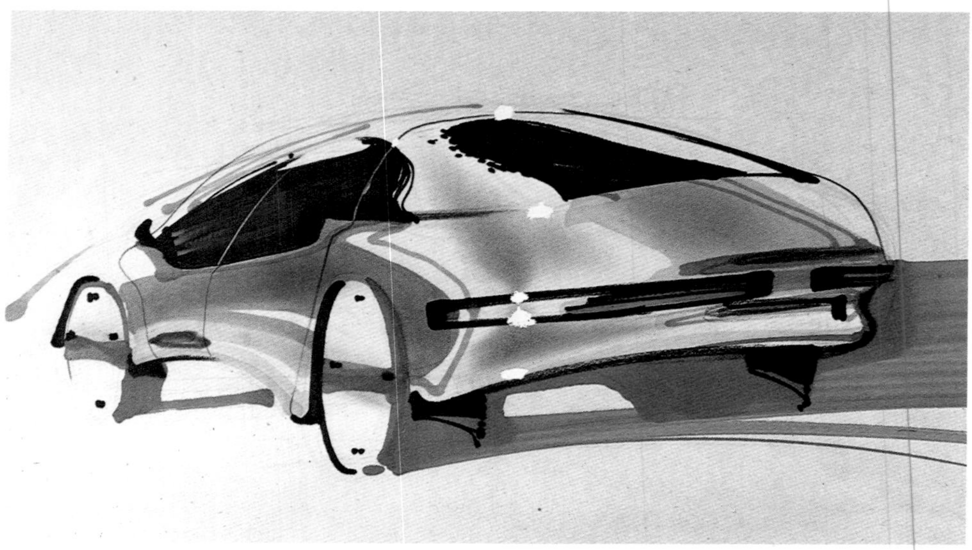

This is a similar quick sketch using the warm-gray and cool-blue dry markers. The darker reflections were created with a warm-gray pastel rubbed on with a Webril pad. Note that the dark reflections on the glass allow you to see into the automobile, whereas the light-toned reflective areas are opaque. This is a principle frequently used in automobile renderings.

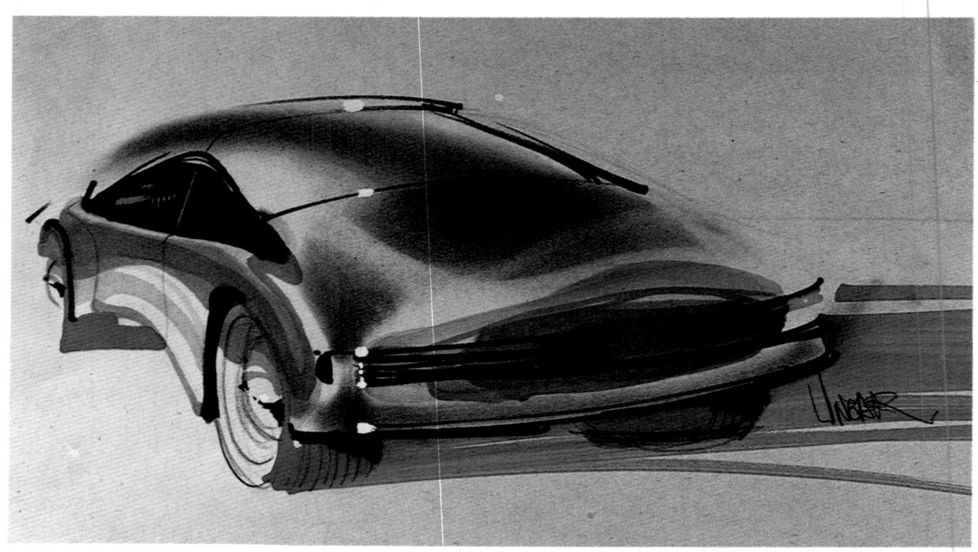

A quick sketch on simple copy-machine paper began with a fast layout in Verithin blue pencil and was developed with warm-gray and blue dry markers, black pen, and black Prismacolor pencil. A small amount of blue pastel was blended through the object and the background to tie the two together. The highlights were later added with white gouache and a fine brush.

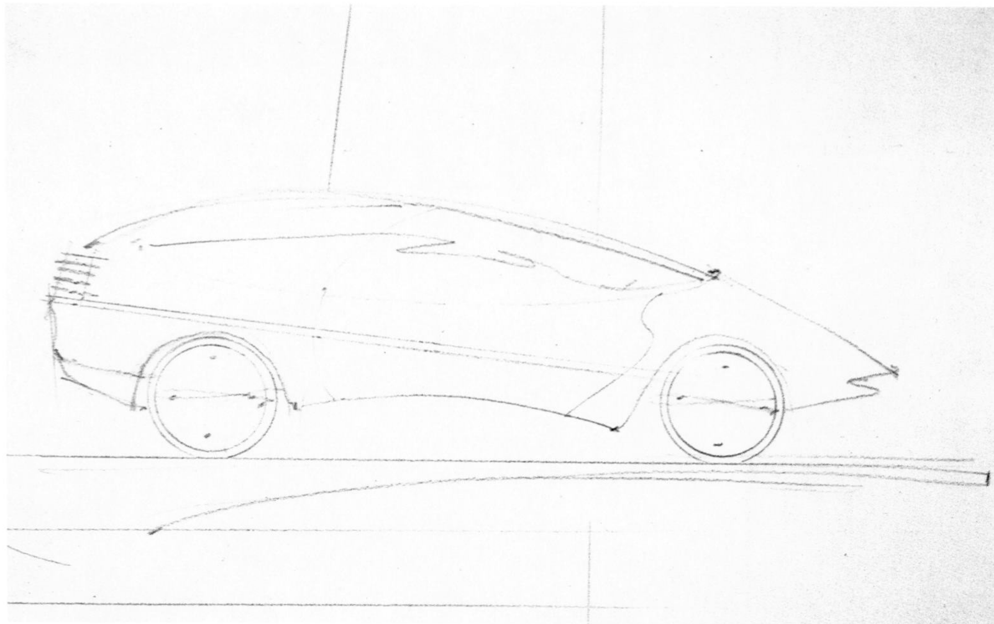

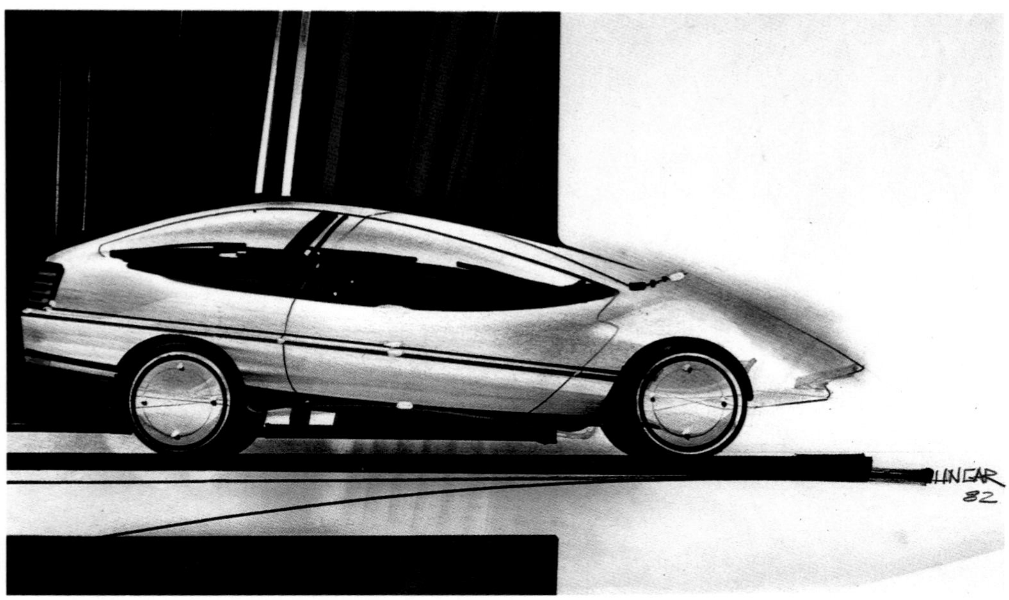

5 RENDERING BACKGROUNDS

Background development is a major compositional element in a multi-media rendering. It allows a focused subject to be "tied" to the drawing page, or integrated compositionally to the area around the subject. Backgrounds can also be informative and help define the product concept. Without background development, rendered subjects appear to float and remain somehow unattached to their surroundings.

Background Development

I usually design the background after I have rendered the product onto the page. This way I won't overemphasize the background by giving it an inappropriate amount of attention. With practice, you will be able to achieve a nice balance between the product and the background, as well as to maintain an interesting compositional structure.

Some backgrounds can serve to add meaning to the product—for example, a background setting of china and glassware can enhance the presentation of a flatware concept. For the sake of speed, however, most designers save background reference for the final illustrations only and let simplified, abstract areas of shadow or of color serve as backdrops for early sketches.

Although quick backgrounds can be created by adding blocks of colored papers or films, I think they tend to be flat and less interesting than backgrounds created with pastels, sprays, or dry markers. A background should be more than just a block of color. By having an interesting visual life of its own, a background can be a catalyst to focusing the viewer's attention on the subject of the drawing.

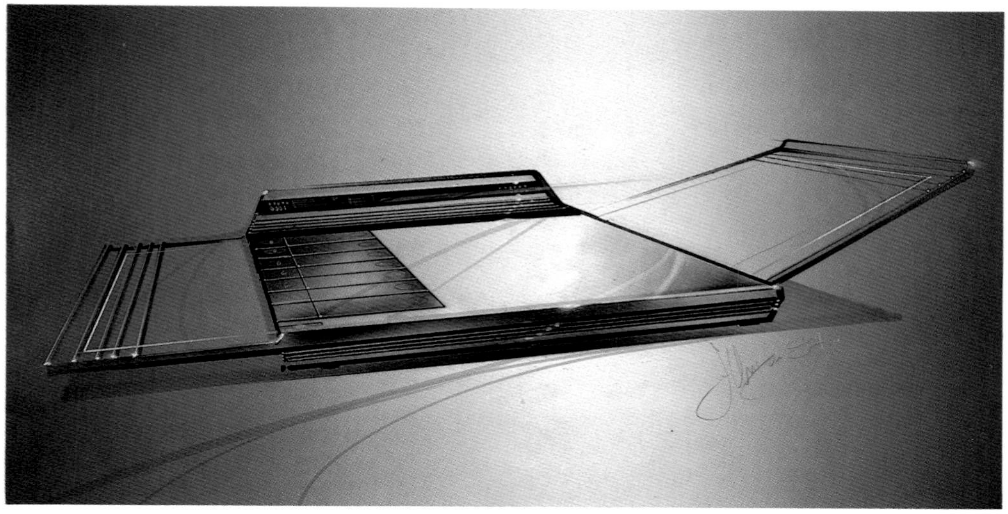

Backgrounds can be a powerful element in a rendering. They can work for or against a concept, and you must always be aware of the necessary balance that is required to have a strong focus to your illustration. For this desktop paper copier, I used a Pantone graduated color paper (process black, uncoated). This saved time because the background was essentially already developed. The product was drawn with light-gray and black markers, with highlights added later.

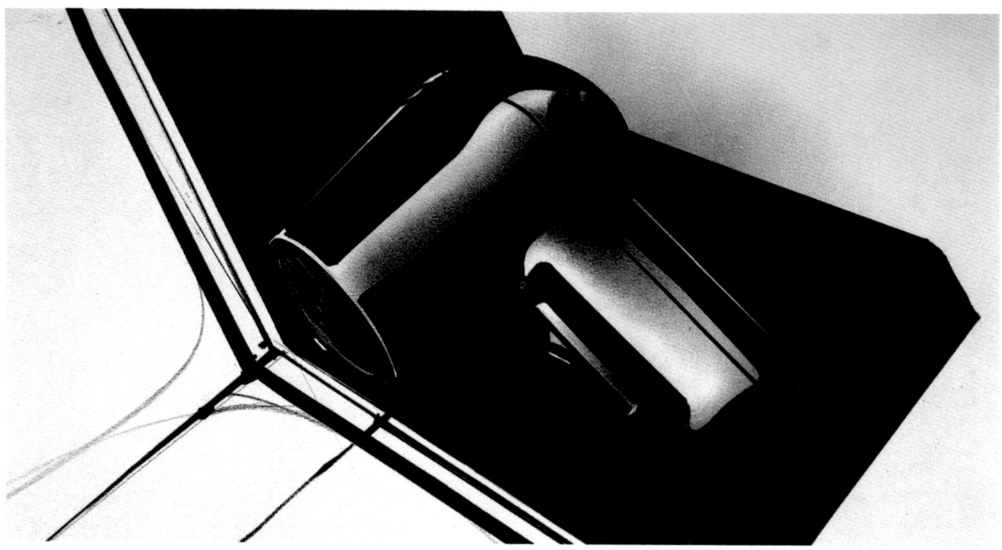

This hair dryer was created with a black dry marker and gray and blue pastel. The lines are black Prismacolor pencil. The dark blue chalk adds color to the product, and by mirroring the background color, it also helps to show the subject as highly reflective.

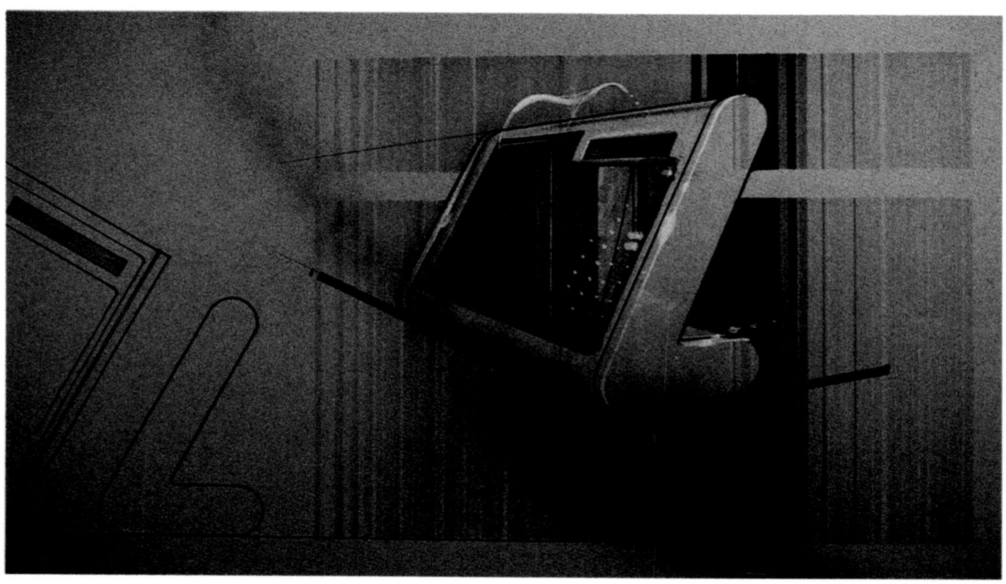

This desk calculator concept was rendered with dry marker on Canson colored paper. The background is dry marker masked with tape. The diagonal area of spray color is interesting but also somewhat distracting. It may have been better to omit the spray.

This wall-mounted, flat computer display was done with a black Prismacolor pencil, Pantone #2 and #3 warm-gray markers, and blended pastel chalk. The sweeping movements in the background balance the extreme perspective chosen for the illustration.

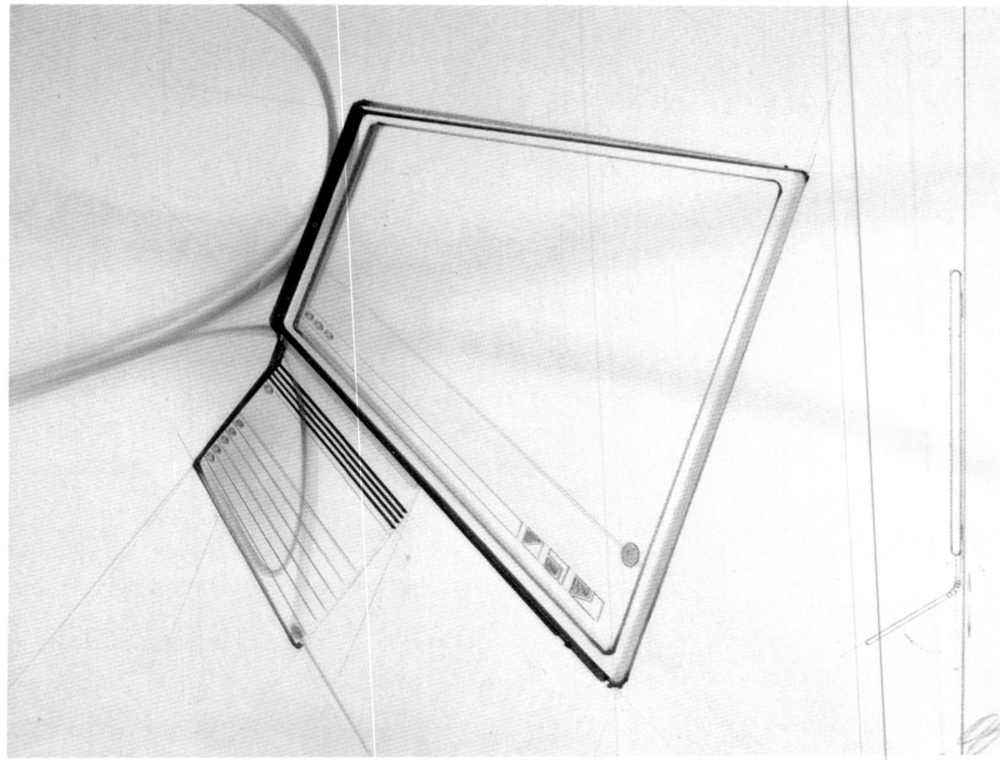

The sweeping blended-chalk background gives a casual, almost whimsical feeling to this rendering of a holographic wrist display.

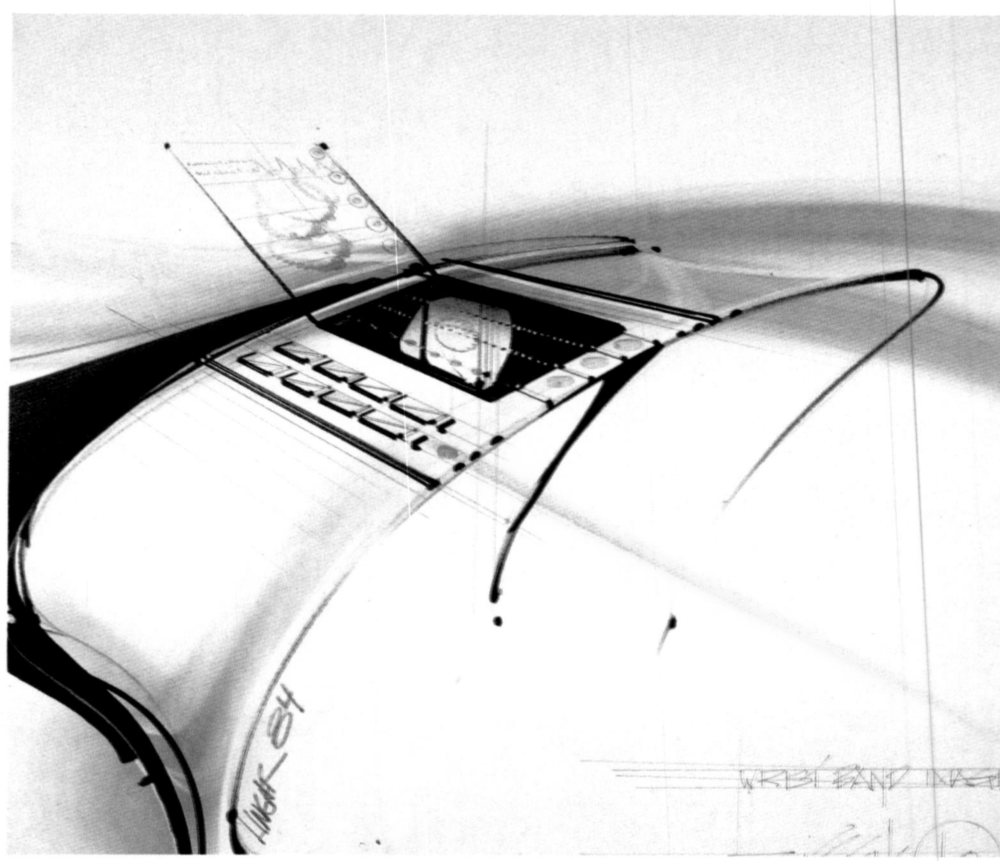

An almost-dry black marker gave the textural front to this illustration. The display information is done with a bright green Prismacolor pencil. Also note how the area of yellow color on the ground is picked up in the display as a reflected color. This is a good trick for you to tie the subject matter to the background.

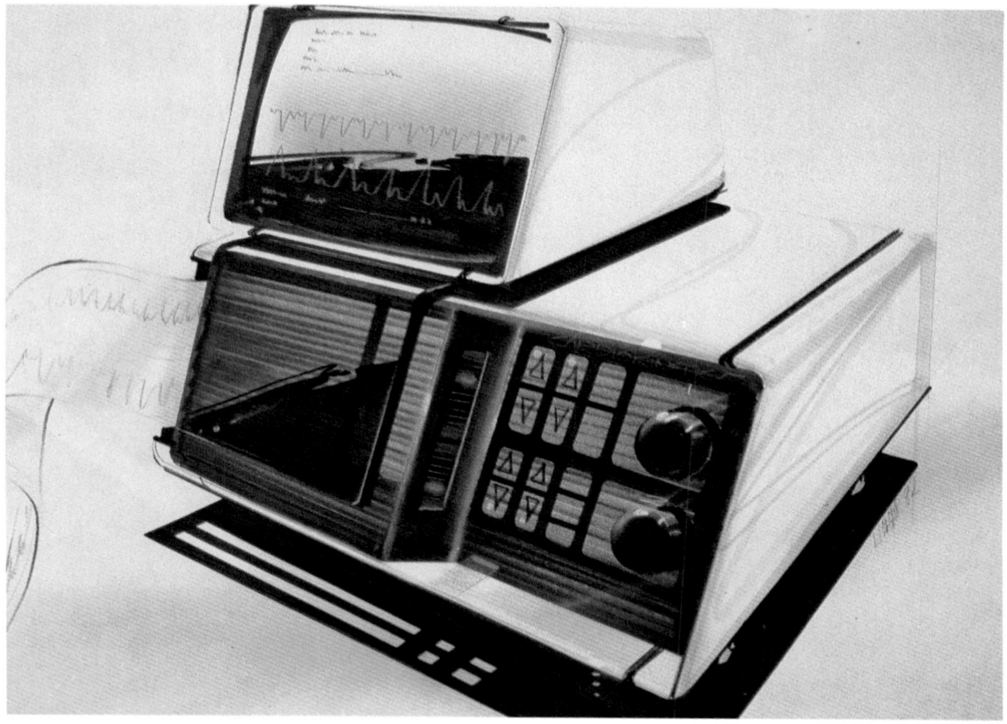

In this composition, several configurations of a portable computer are linked together by the shadow area, done in black dry marker. You can achieve interesting effects by linking several views of an object or scene in this manner.

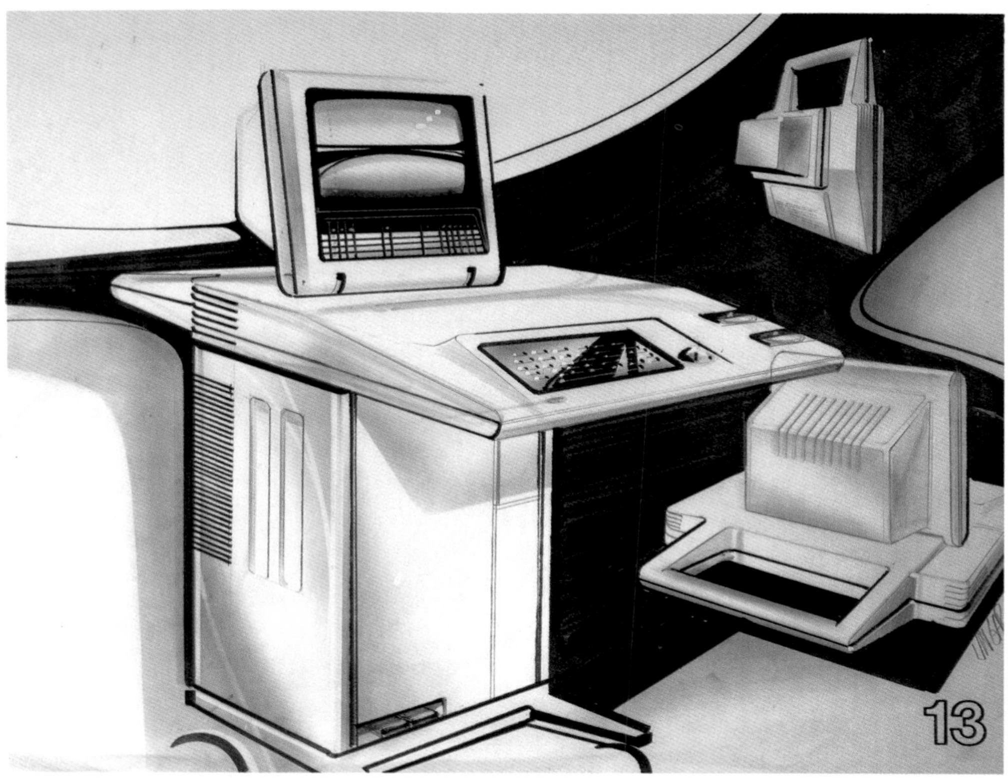

A sketch-pad drawing shows how a shared background area can link several ideas together. A simple sketch book can be less intimidating than large-scale rendering and can help you develop some of these techniques on a smaller scale first.

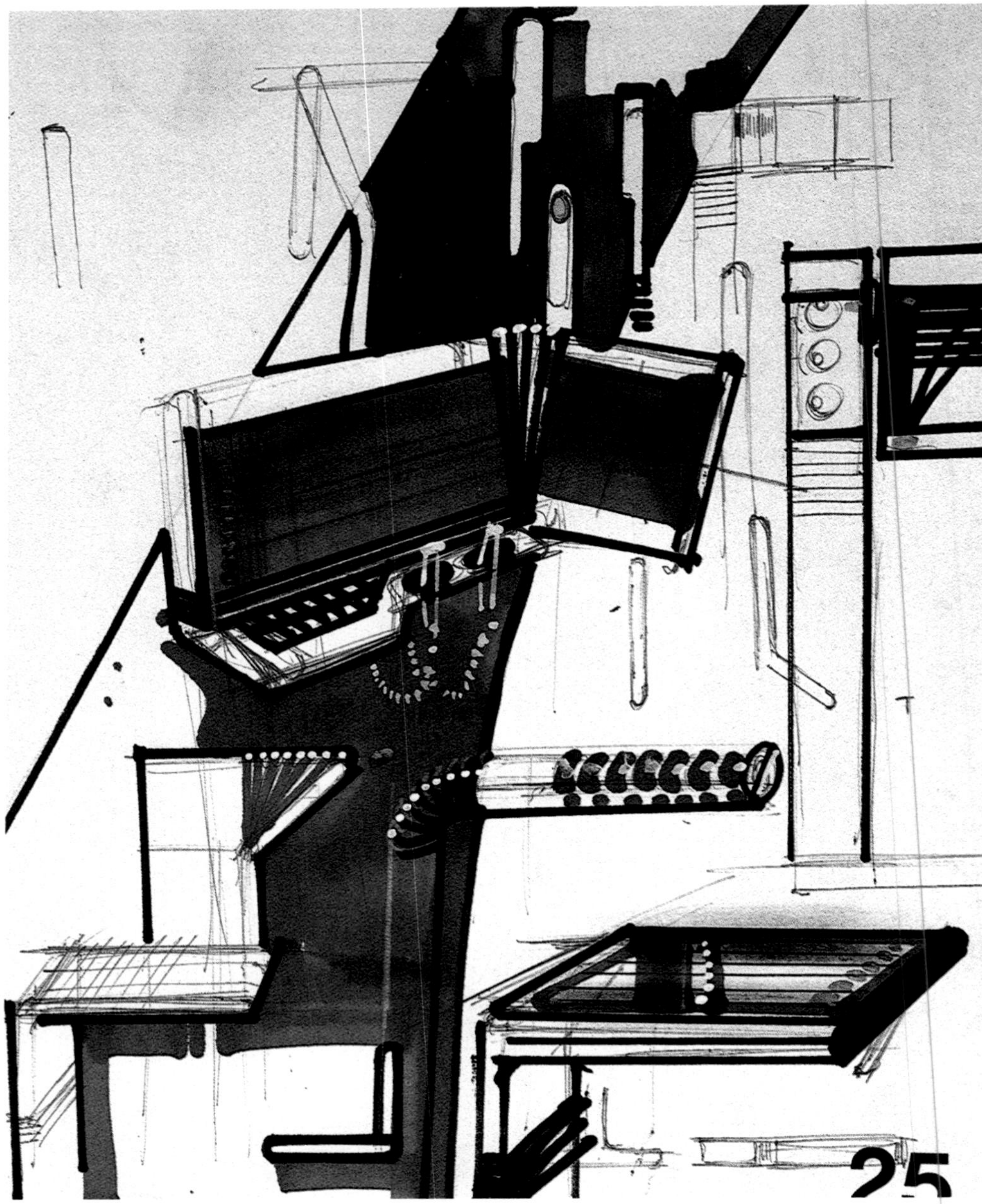

Colored Papers

One of the fastest ways of sketching and rendering is to use colored paper as both a medium and a background. Simple and quick expressions can be created by using the color of the paper as a middle tone and then adding dark tones, fall-away lines, background shadows, and gouache highlights. This technique can be used on a variety of paper mediums, from newsprint to reproduction papers.

The beauty of learning colored-paper illustration techniques is that you will be able to apply them to very inexpensive stock, such as newsprint, as well as to more expensive colored papers.

With light-toned papers, the addition of darks and highlights can give the illusion of realism to your rendering in a very short amount of time. The darker papers tend to offer a more formalized presentation. A high-quality dark paper, such as Mi Tientes paper, will accept blended pastel chalks with excellent results, and the luminous contrast of gouache highlights cannot be duplicated with other methods.

There are a vast number of colored papers to choose from in today's marketplace. Chalk blends well on papers that are of heavy stock and have little tooth to the surface. Canson's Mi Tientes paper is excellent for both pastel chalk and colored pencil.

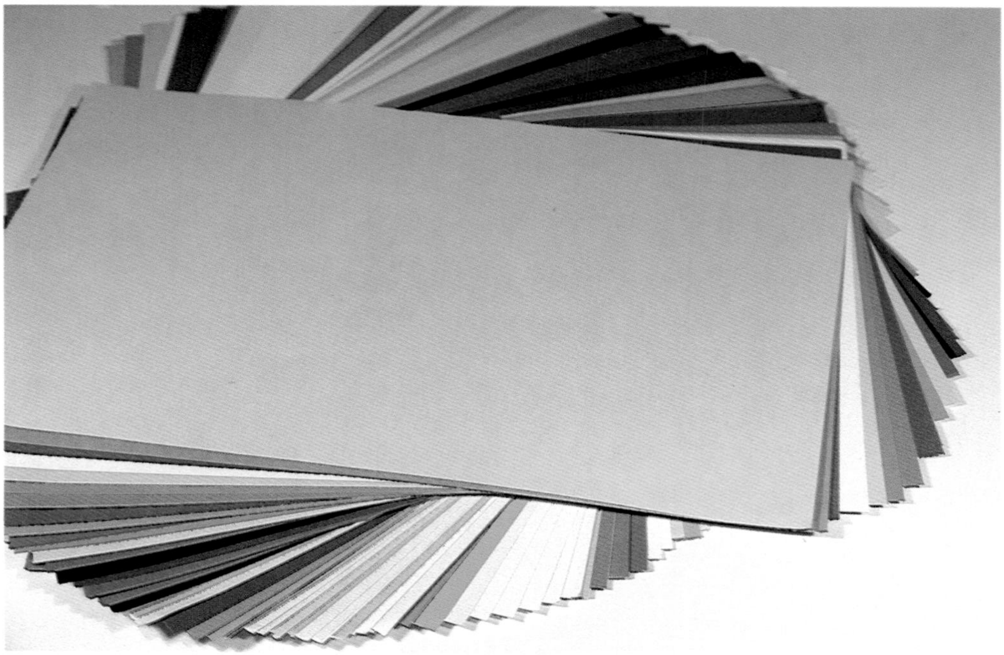

This basic exercise will acquaint you with the fundamentals of working with colored paper. By adding only highlights and shadow values to the paper, you can achieve the essential results that create a successful rendering. Try this with your own signature on colored paper.

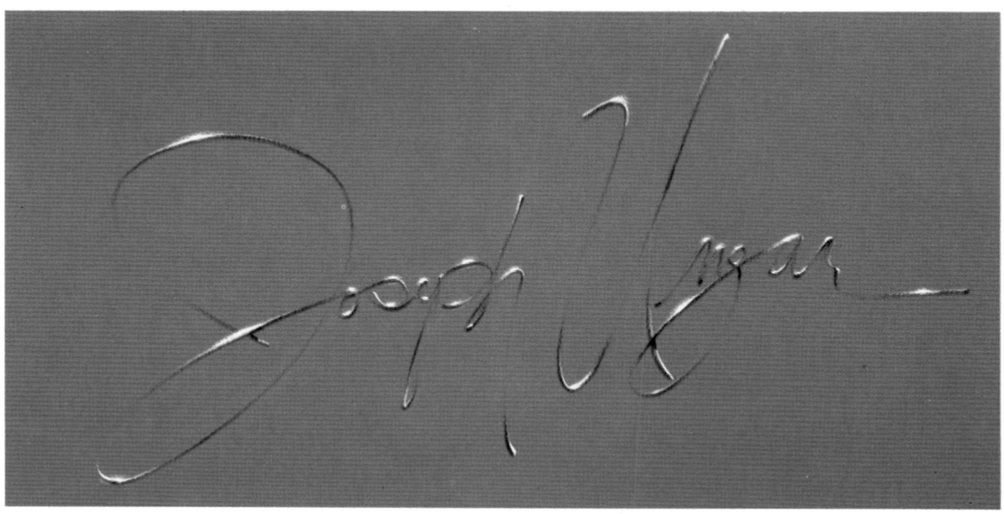

A quick sketch of a chair was done using the principle of adding only highlights and shadow values and letting the colored paper be the middle tone.

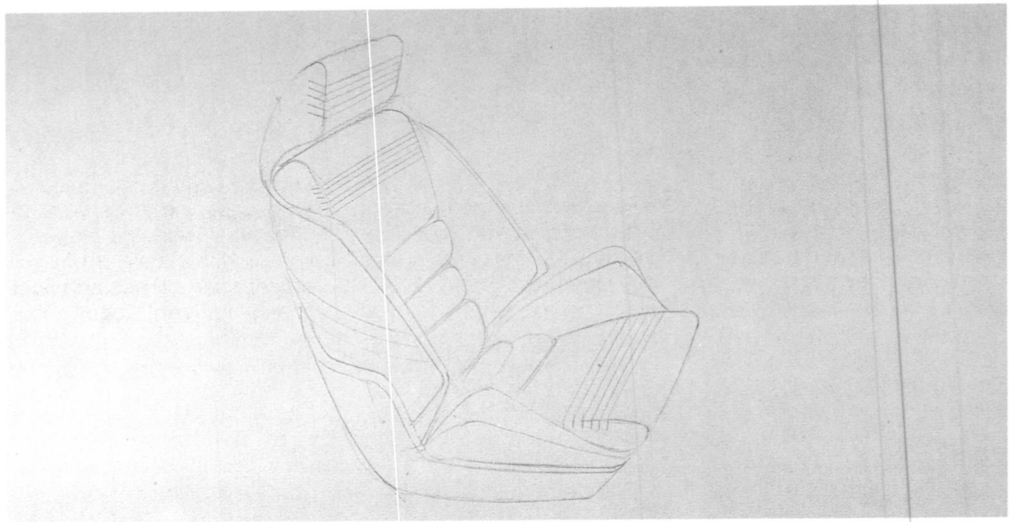

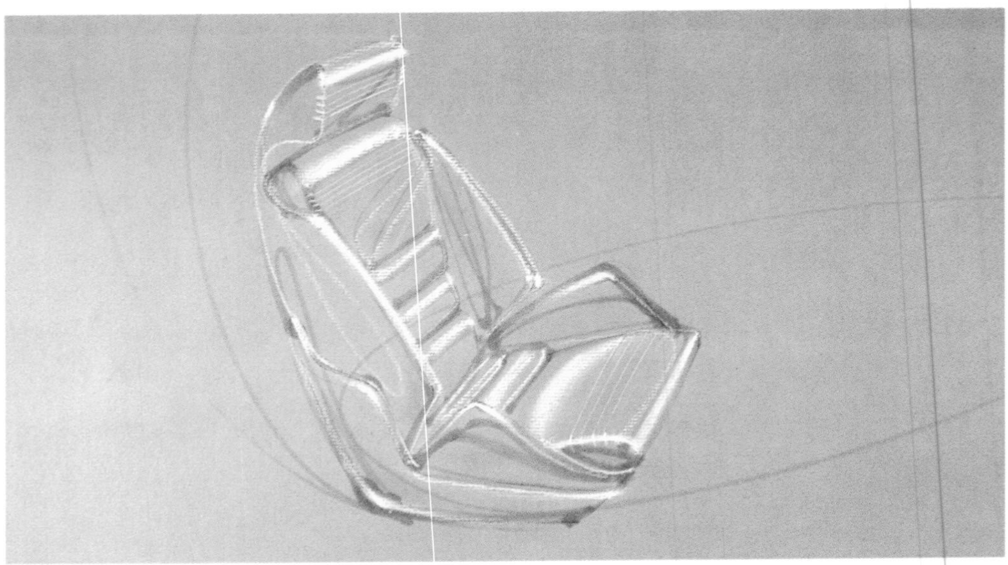

This computer controls concept was rendered with dry markers on gray Canson paper. Outlines for key areas were done using ocher and blue gouache in a ruling pen. A black marker-spray paint was sprayed across the entire field and then highlights were done by blending white chalk with the tip of my finger over white gouache spots.

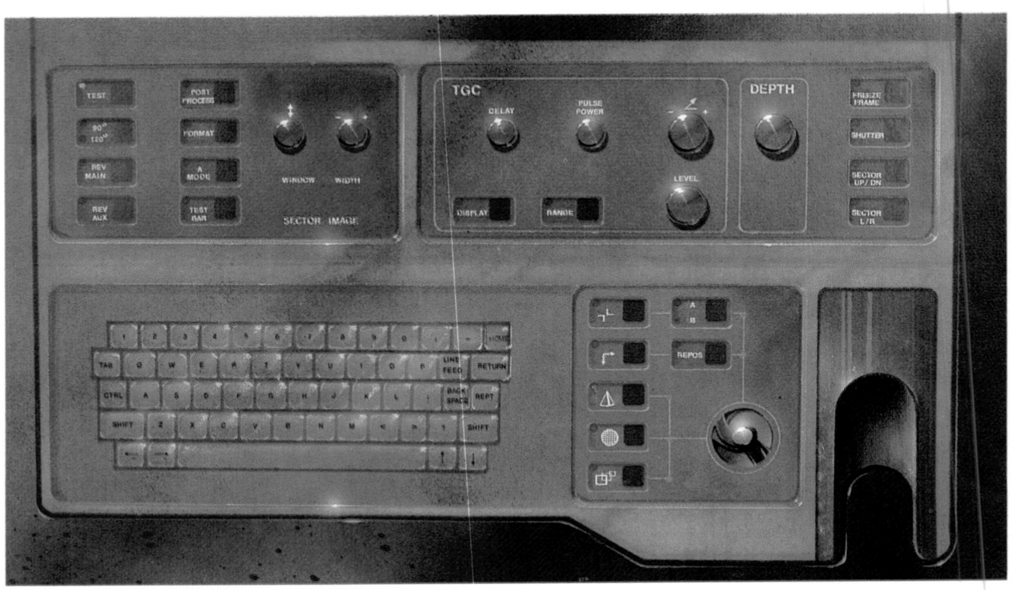

Rendering on Colored Paper

I find it easiest to develop a rendering directly on colored paper rather than doing a layout first and then transferring it over. However, if your concept is complex, it may warrant a preliminary layout done on a separate piece of vellum. The transfer process is easy. Simply use a pastel chalk that contrasts with the colored paper and rub the chalk on the back of a sheet of vellum. Then place the vellum chalk-side down on the colored paper, and place the layout on top of the vellum. With a third overlay of thin tracing paper, trace over the layout lines in a red Verithin pencil. The red color will show you what lines you have not traced yet. The resultant light lines of chalk that are transferred to the colored paper can be rendered over without smearing.

As in any quick sketch, the rendering of a concept on colored paper first starts by establishing the light and dark tones, followed by shadows and highlights. The middle-tone papers can be worked effectively with the application of warm-gray dry markers for shade tones and light chalks for light tones. The darker colored papers can dramatically show off the lighter shades of blended pastel.

You will find that even complex shapes rapidly take form on colored paper. Since the color of the paper serves as a general middle tone, you have only to render basically two of the three tonal values, and the net effect gives an otherwise complex drawing a rather clean, simple look.

You will also find that entire surface areas of a product can be emphasized by blending a background development into, or through, a subject area, with chalks, sprays, or dry markers. If you use chalk, you can then model the surface planes and create highlights simply by removing portions of the background.

Demonstration: How to transfer a layout to colored paper
This procedure allows you to transfer a layout to any kind of opaque paper. Simply rub chalk onto the back of a transfer sheet (bond paper or vellum) so that it can be used as a copying medium. Once this is done, you place the transfer sheet chalk-side down on the colored paper and place the layout on top of the transfer sheet. Then you cover the layout with thin paper and trace over all the lines with a red pencil, so you will know which lines you have already traced.

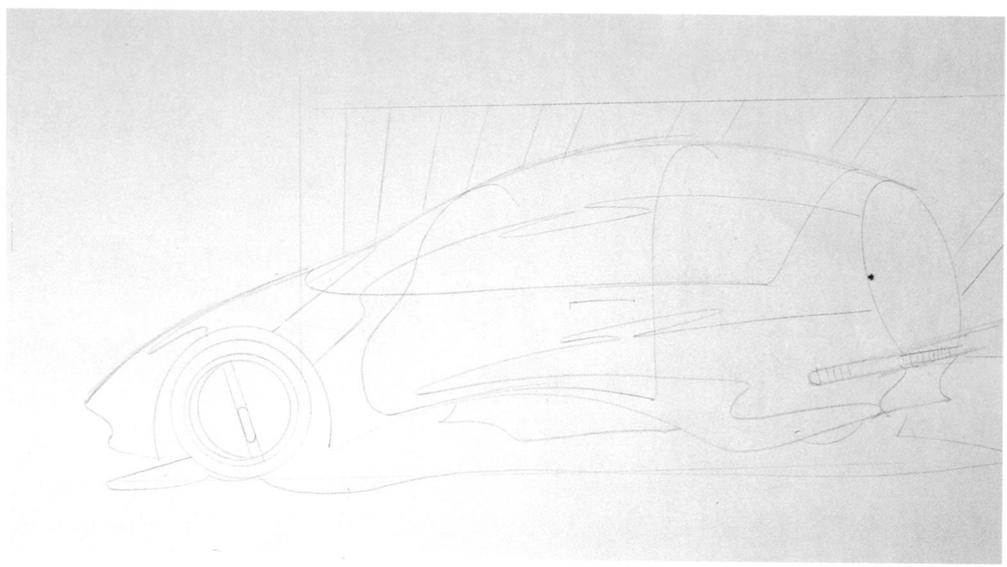

After the layout has been transferred to the colored paper, you can begin developing the surface values, as in this illustration.

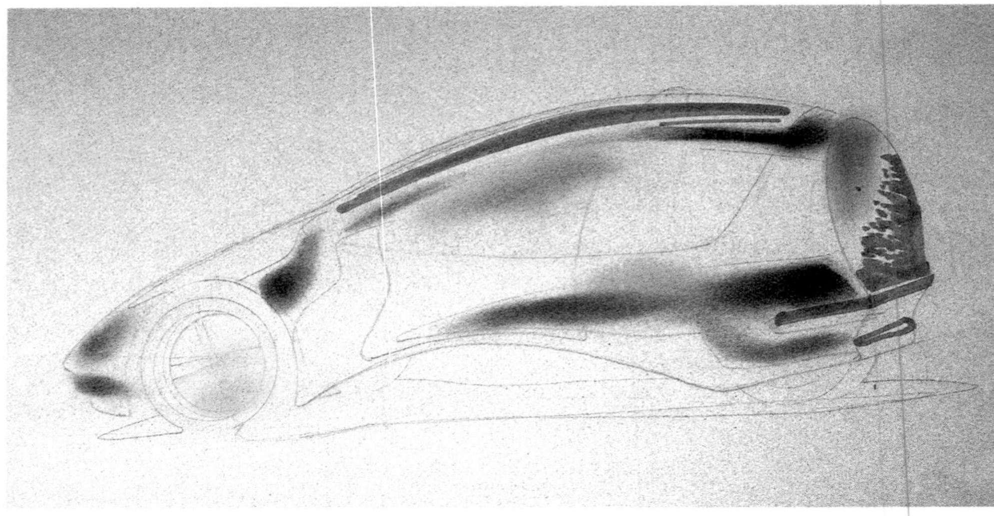

In this concept of a three-wheeled vehicle, I developed the reflective tones of blue, yellow, and gray first, with blended pastel chalk, and then outlined the black areas with a Sharpie black pen.

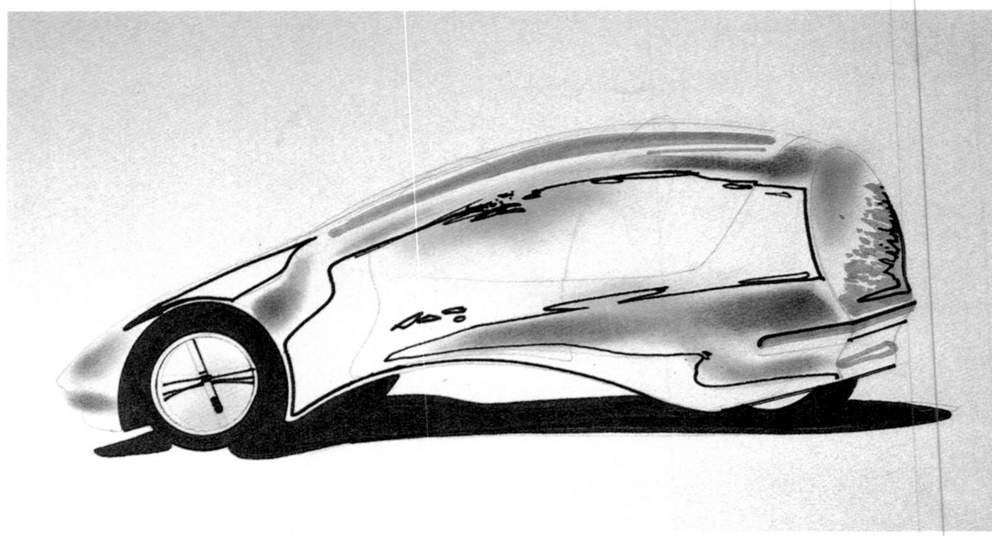

In the final stages, I filled in the black areas and added a background of gray dry markers to give the foreground more contrast. The reflections on the glass incorporate the orange of the setting sun.

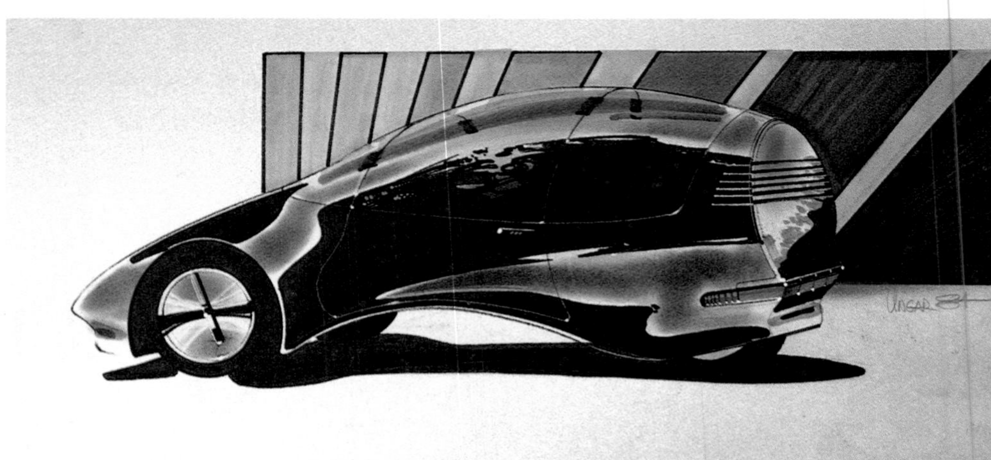

A mobile diagnostic cart was drawn with blended pastel chalk on Canson colored paper. Here light chalk was used as a spotlight effect on the floor. Some chalk was removed with an eraser, creating a shadow under the cart. Prismacolor pencil was used for fine lines, with fluorescent paint for control lights.

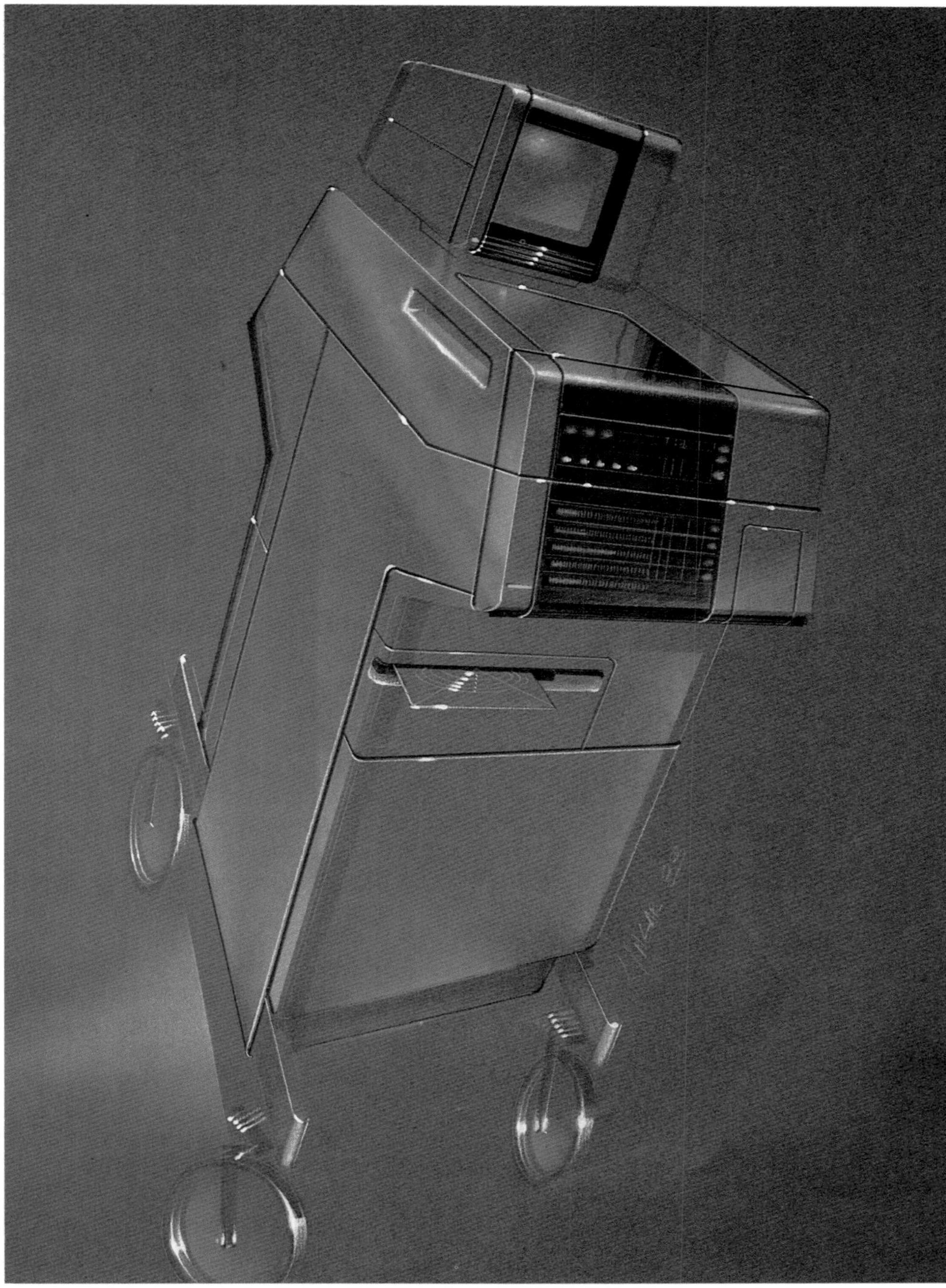

This phone set shows how blended white is used to indicate the light source of the highlights. Also, the pink color used in the background is reflected in the display, making the composition work as a whole.

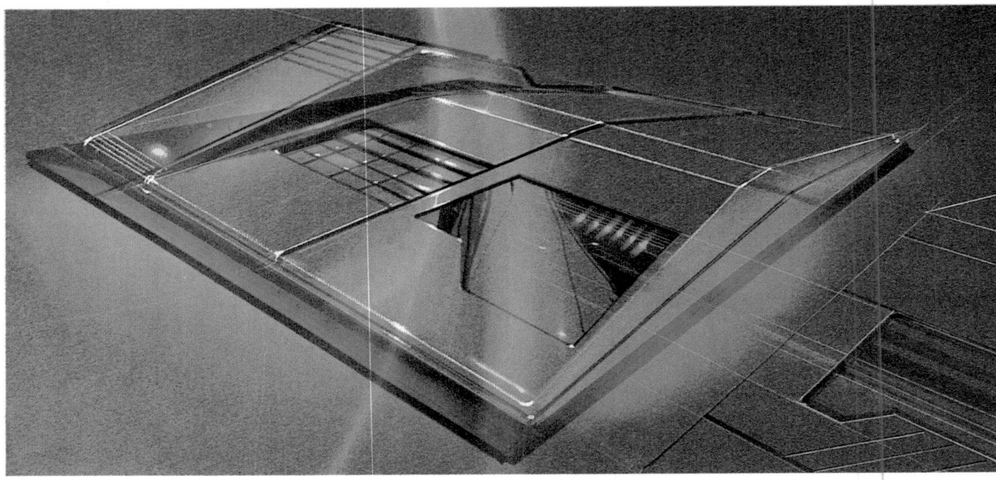

This bathroom scale, done with pastel and black and gray markers, uses the principle of highlights sweeping across a product. The display area was created with fluorescent gouache.

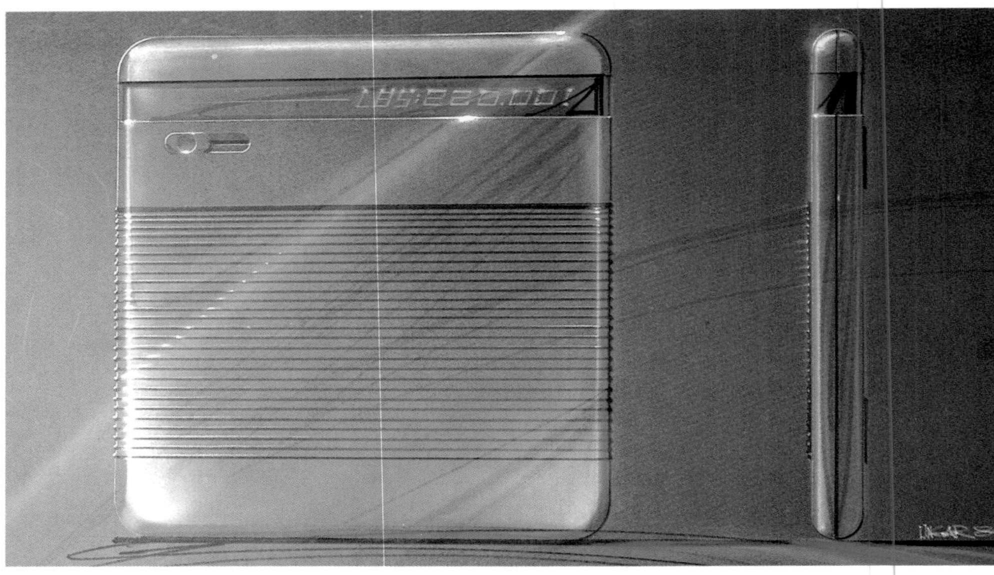

I rendered this television set by using pastel chalk, Pantone #2 gray marker, and black marker. The eye completes many details that are not drawn in great detail.

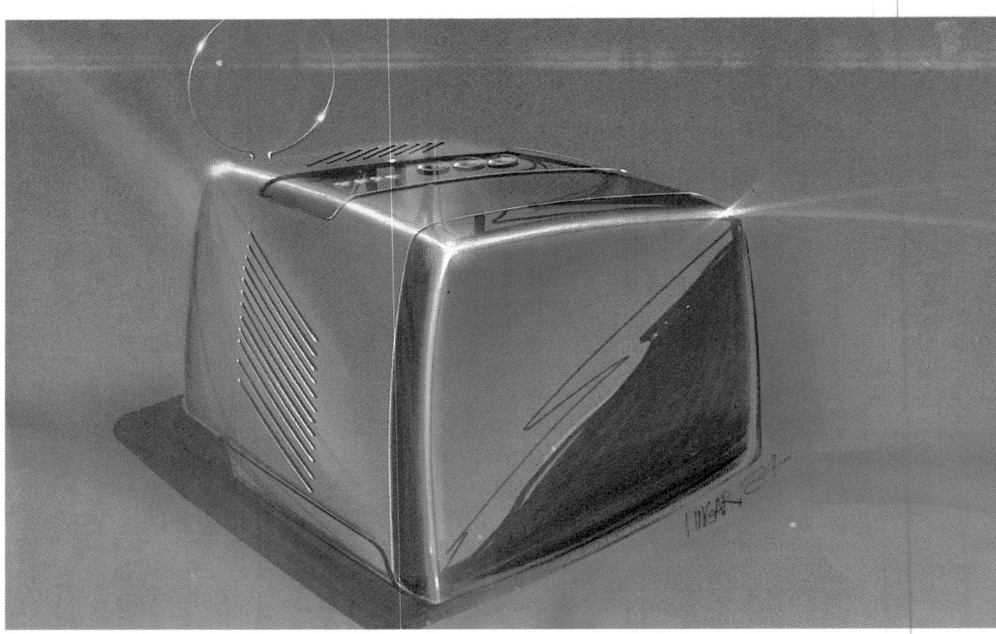

Reproduction Papers

Reproduction papers such as brownline, blueline, or blackline have a surface absorbent quality that causes some difficulty in using dry markers. I tend to use pastel chalk and black dry markers, with just a minimal use of the lighter gray markers. The paper tends to absorb inks rapidly, and dry markers will look dark on the paper until they dry to their normal color.

Reproduction paper starts out through its development process with an evenly toned, dark background. The development process removes background from the areas of the paper not occluded by your drawing on the vellum that is placed over the repro paper. The faster the paper moves through the processing machine, the less time there is for the background to be removed; the less development time there is, the darker the background of the final print will be.

If you use a normal speed of development, the black-marker drawing done on the vellum before running the print will show up as a rich, dark tone. This can be used as a nice outlining effect with the simple addition of highlights to the finished print.

If you use the darker shades of reproduction paper, obtained by running the paper through the developing cycle fast, be sure to rub your marker top on a clean sheet after each stroke. This will clean the marker, since it will pick up color from the reproduction paper.

For this exploded-view illustration, I used brownline reproduction paper as a middle tone and then added black dry marker for the outlines and the background shadows. White and blue pastel chalk helped bring out the leading edges of the objects in the rendering. Gray pastel helps define the surfaces.

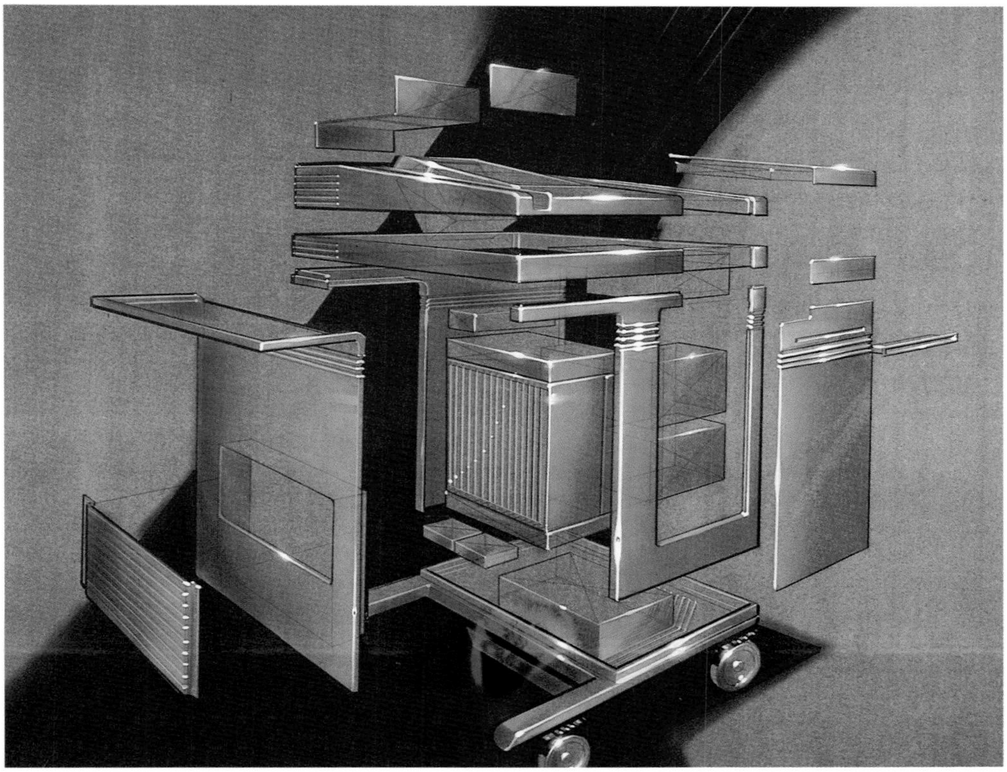

Demonstration: How to create an interesting multi-toned background with blueline or brownline reproduction paper
This stereo concept is started with a simple layout on vellum. A separate sheet of vellum is placed under the layout. This doubles the thickness of the layout vellum and will make the entire background twice as dark on the repro paper as using just the single original layout on vellum would make it. By taping more vellum (or bond paper or black tape) to the areas that you want to print darker still, and by cutting out vellum in the areas that you want to be lighter, you can alter the final tonal values at will. When you think the build-up of vellum and paper is correct on the underlay, place both the underlay and the original vellum layout on top of the repro paper, and send all three together into the diazo machine. Check the results and alter the vellum underlay to suit your purpose.

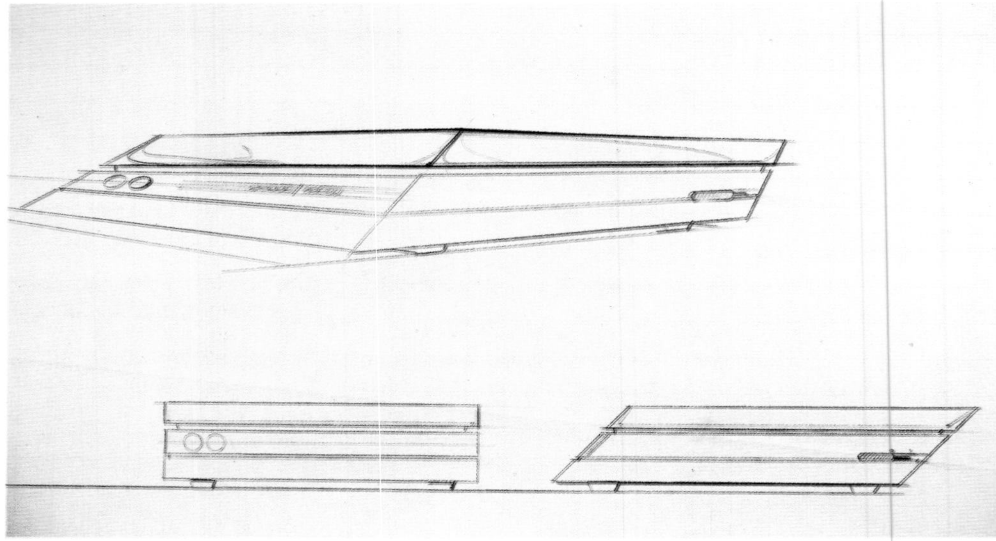

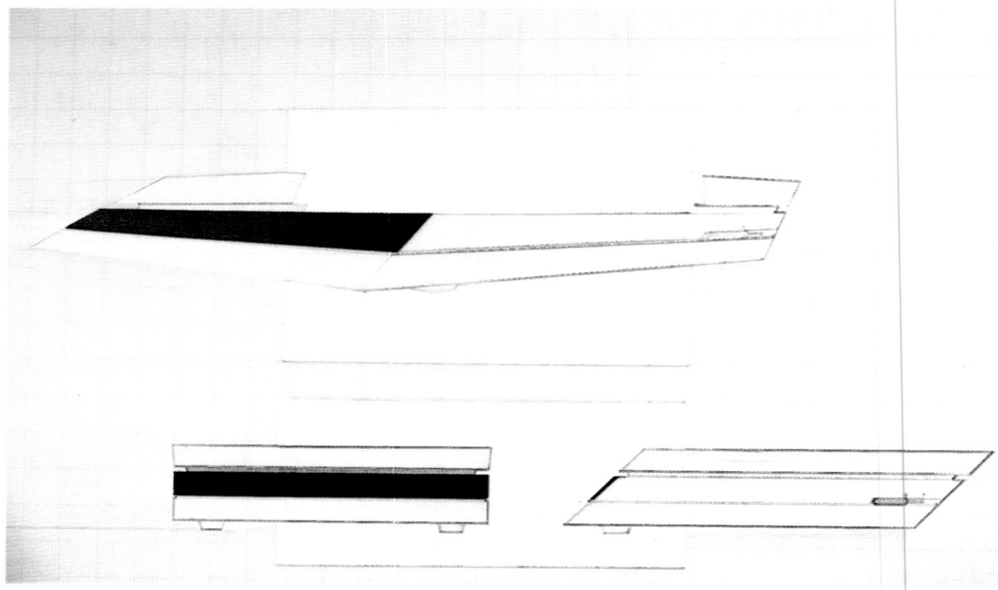

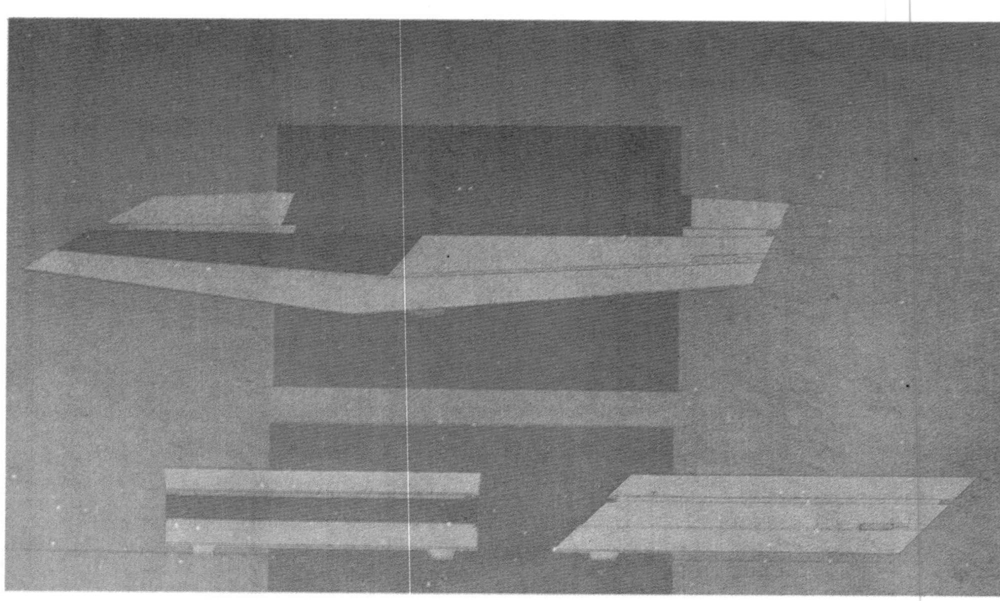

The final rendering was done by adding dry marker and gouache paint to the brownline reproduction paper.

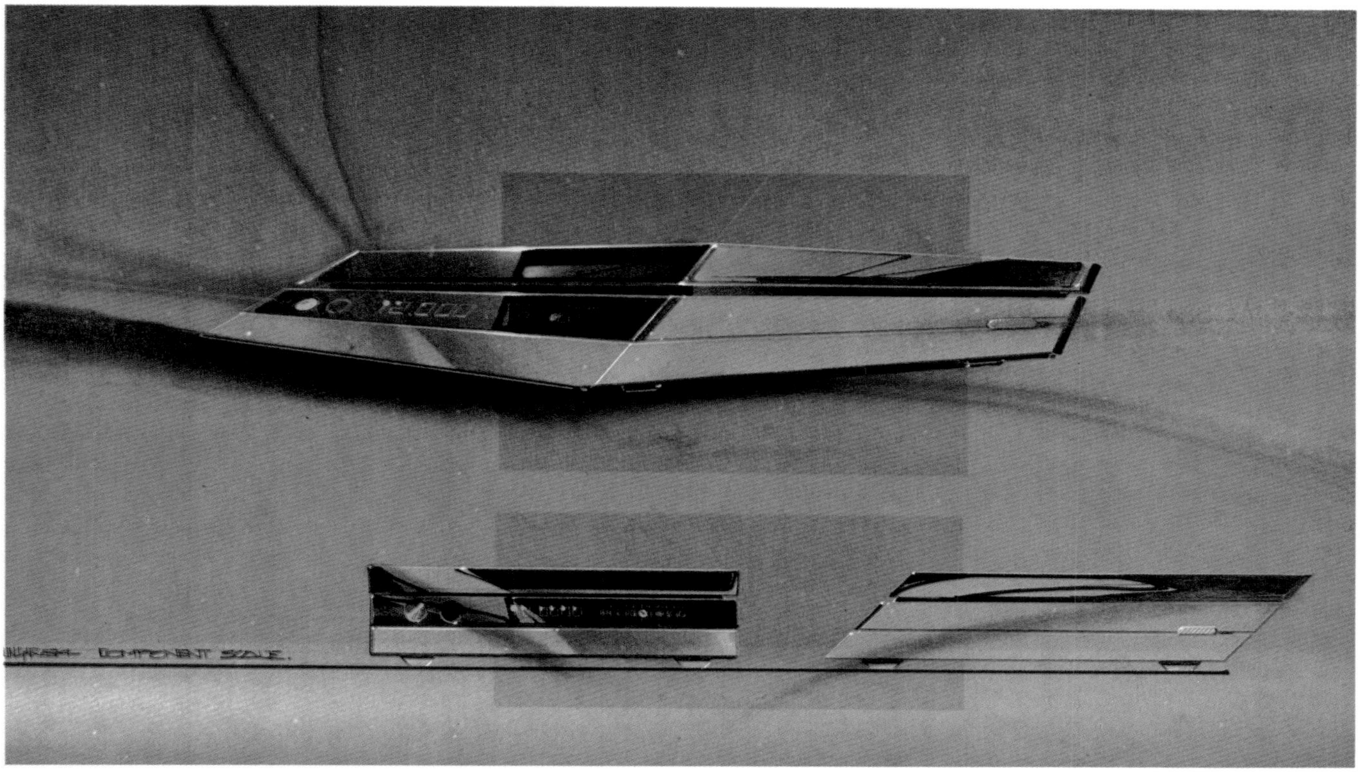

Marker Airbrush on Colored Paper

The LetraJet spray tool and spray-can marker colors in general work quite effectively on colored papers. With masking, a sprayed-on backdrop can "pop" out a subject from the page. LetraJet spray throughout a rendering can impart a suggestion of product coloration, with the neutral background of the paper color offering subtle contrast.

A rendering of an office-lighting product uses the LetraJet as a principal tool for modeling the shadow values on the cylindrical object. Overrunning the object with the spray ties the subject matter to the background and adds to the overall composition.

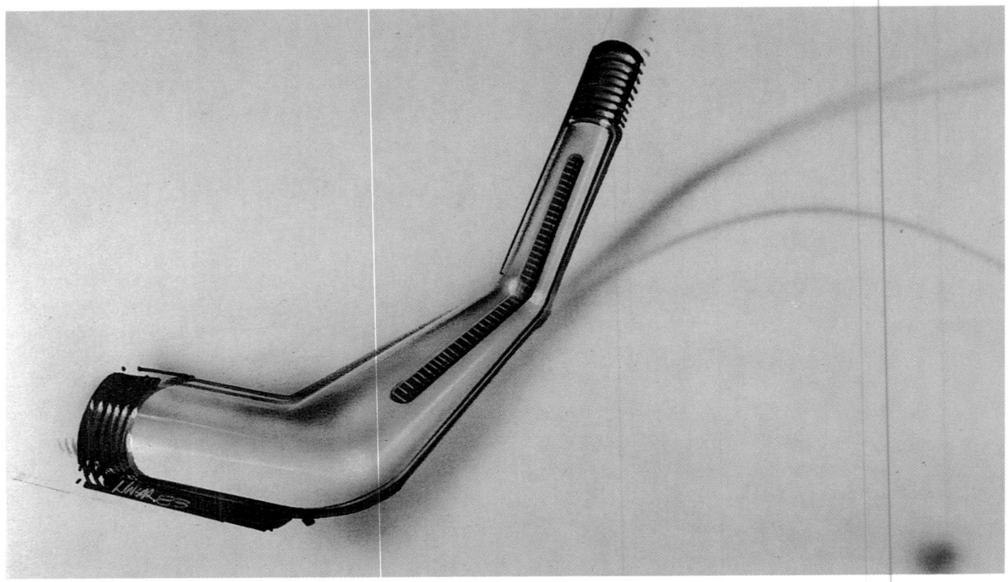

This glassware was quickly rendered while I was first testing the LetraJet's capabilities. You can save much time with this tool, although it can be easily overused in an illustration if you are not careful.

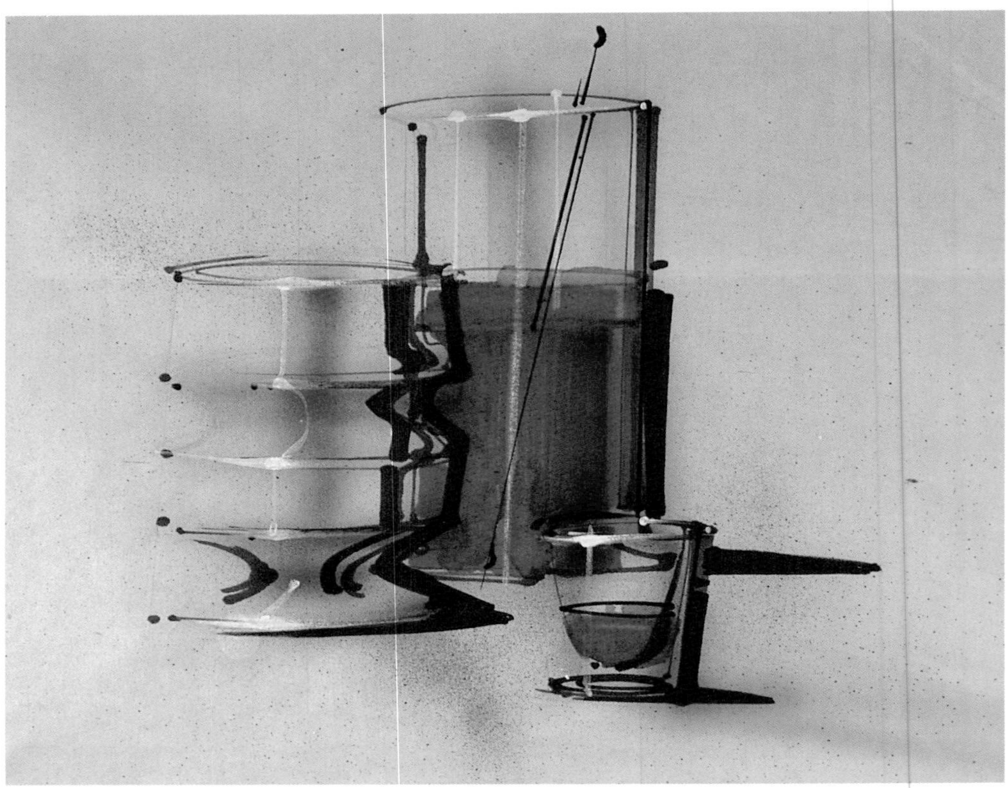

The initial rendering here was done strictly with dry marker and pastel chalk, with fluorescent gouache used for the display. However, because I felt that the contrast on the product where the horizontal surface meets the bend line was not great enough, I used the LetraJet to darken the area before I added highlights. The effect is subtle, but illustrates another use for the tool.

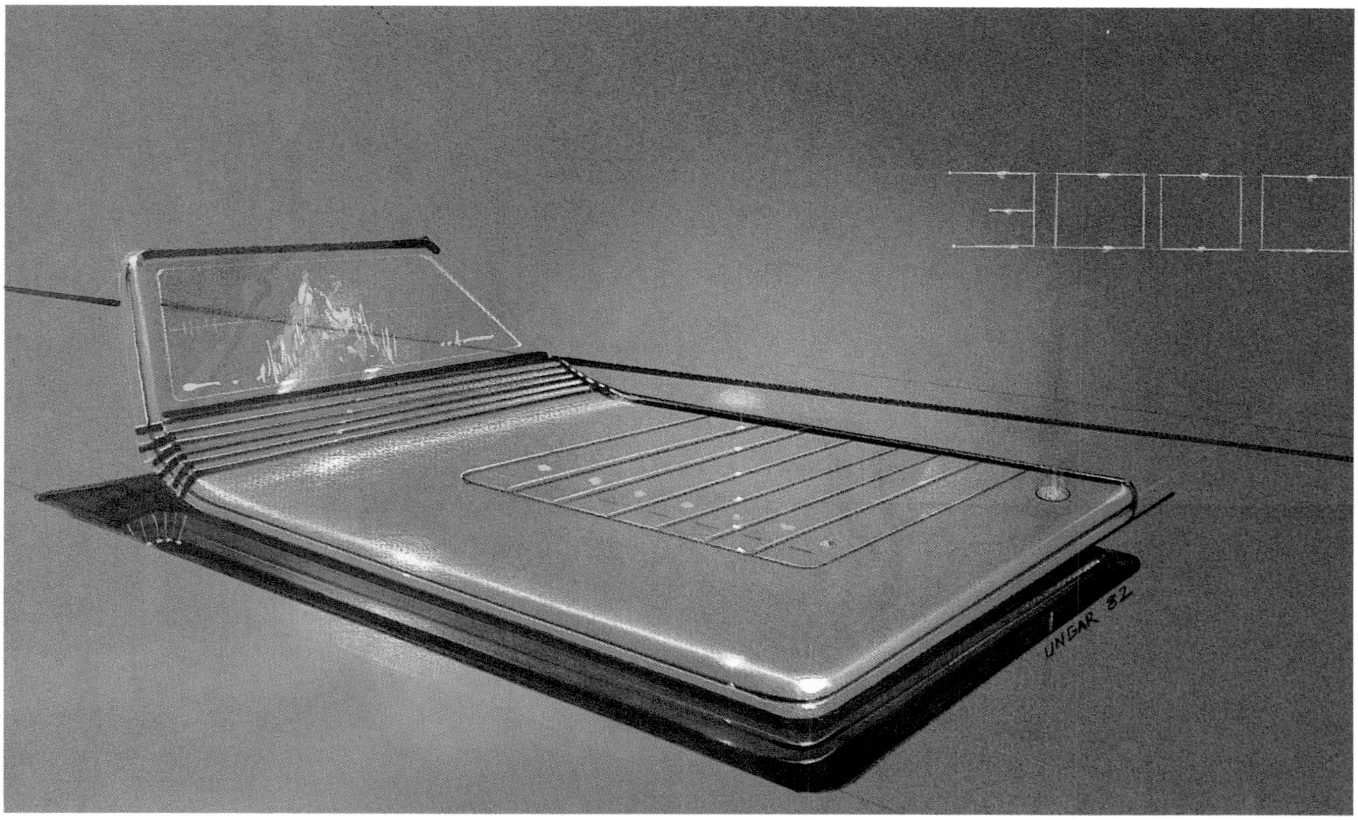

Black on Black

Black or very dark-blue paper provides dramatic backgrounds for renderings, especially for those that combine white chalk or Prismacolor pencil with gouache highlights.

The application of Winsor & Newton jet-black designers gouache to black pastel paper can give yet another level of shade tone to renderings on this medium. This is especially true if you are illustrating the effect of black reflections on a shiny black surface such as plastic or chrome. Lay out the areas that need the darker color, and render them in last with a small watercolor brush.

Fluorescent poster paint used for electronic lights on a product also shows up vividly on dark papers.

A rapidly drawn concept shows how black paper can be used as the dark tone by rubbing white pastel chalk over the subject matter and then selectively removing it with an eraser. Highlights are then brushed on with white gouache. This sketch took approximately three minutes.

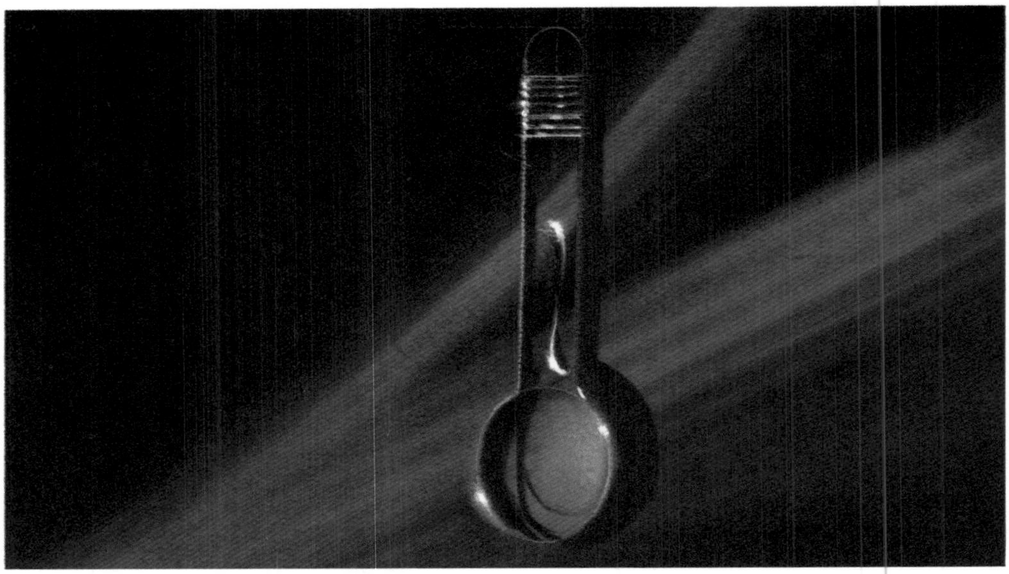

You will find that glassware rendered on black paper is fun to work with because the results are dramatic and immediate. Start with the layout either transferred or drawn directly onto the paper. Canson's Mi Tientes black paper is excellent for this technique. Render the highlight areas in first, then lightly blend in a reflective coloration with pastel chalk. The finishing touches are sparkling highlights brushed on carefully with white gouache. You should study the refraction and distortion patterns of real glassware before beginning.

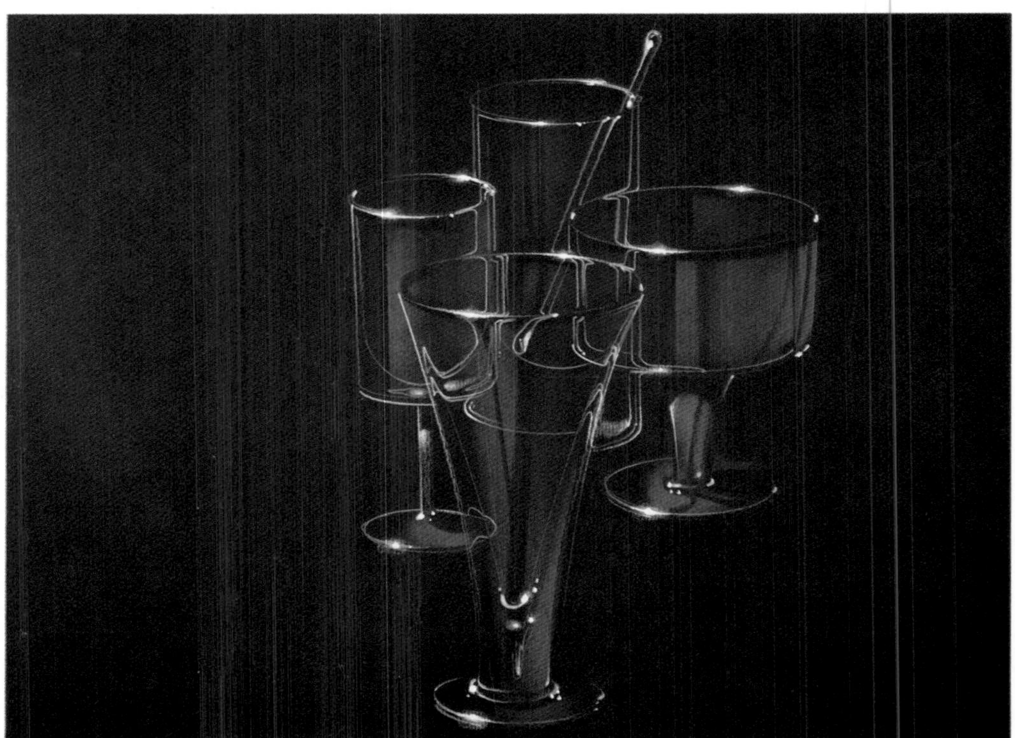

The black reflection areas of these cigarette cases and money clip were done by brushing in Winsor & Newton jet black. This is very effective, when working with black paper, to create darker values than the paper itself.

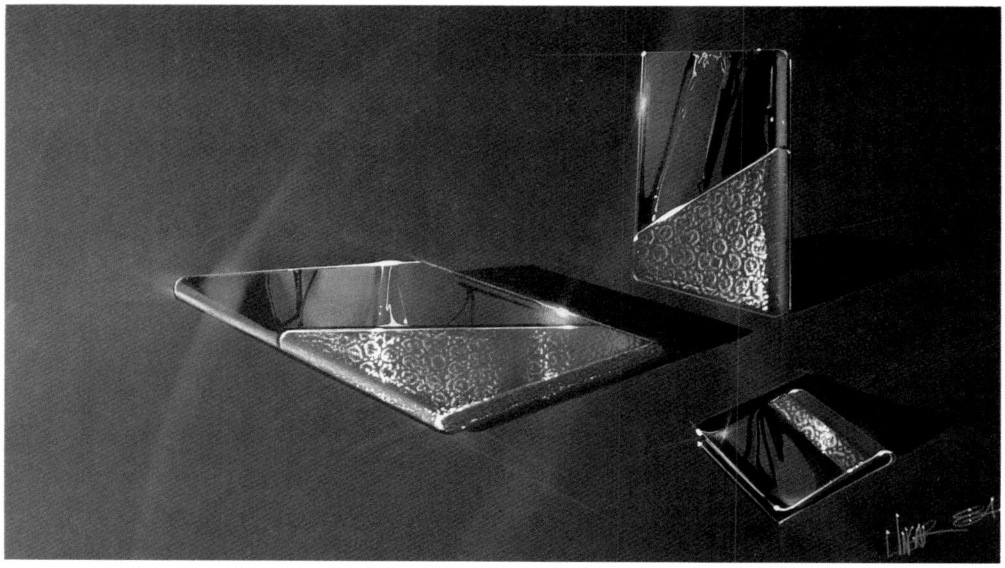

Winsor & Newton jet black was added to provide very realistic shadow detail to the knobs and buttons on the control surface of a computer. The drawing was pasted to a mock-up of the product.

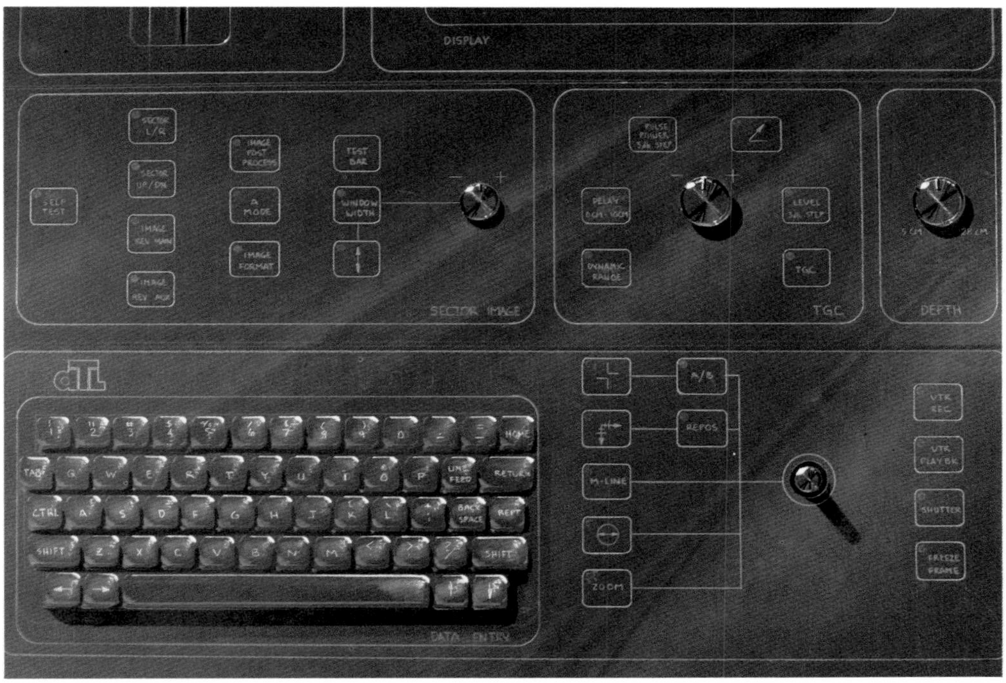

For this portable clock radio, I used white pastel and white gouache highlights, with some fluorescent poster color. The break lines in the product were created with jet black gouache.

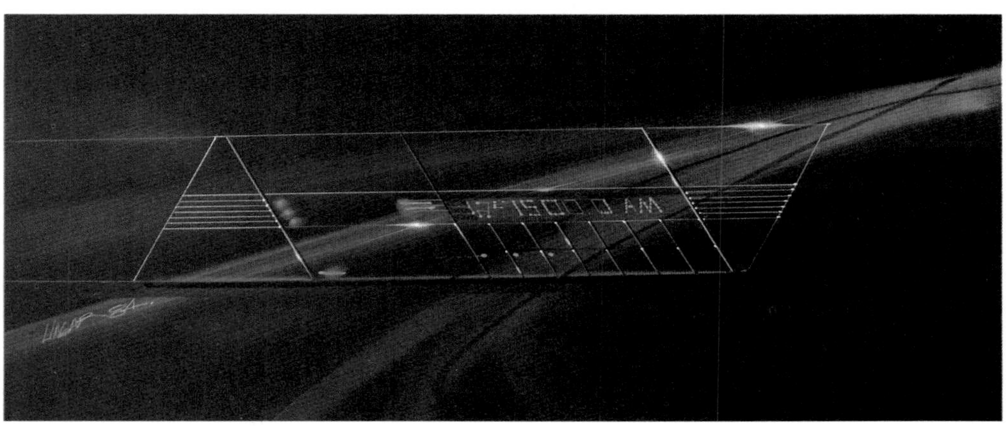

Using dark blue paper, this rendering of the control surface for a medical ultrasound cart focuses the viewer's attention on the highlighted areas—in particular, the display panel itself. Liquitex fluorescent poster color was used to create the electric effect on the display and the glowing light in the lower-right corner. Adding some of the fluorescent display color to the knobs reinforced the electronic effect.

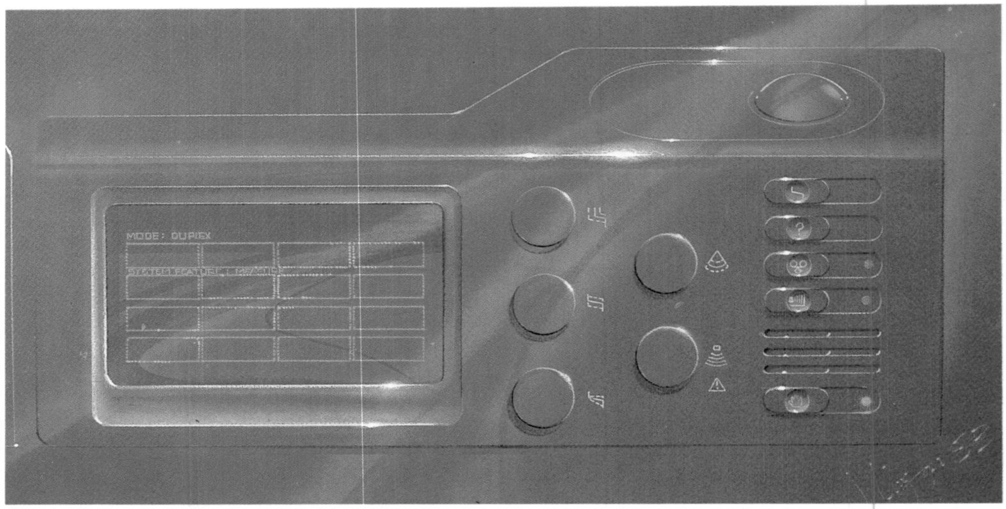

An automobile was quickly rendered on dark blue paper by using a Pantone #2 and a black dry marker with white Prismacolor and gouache highlights. The colored lights were added last with fluorescent poster color.

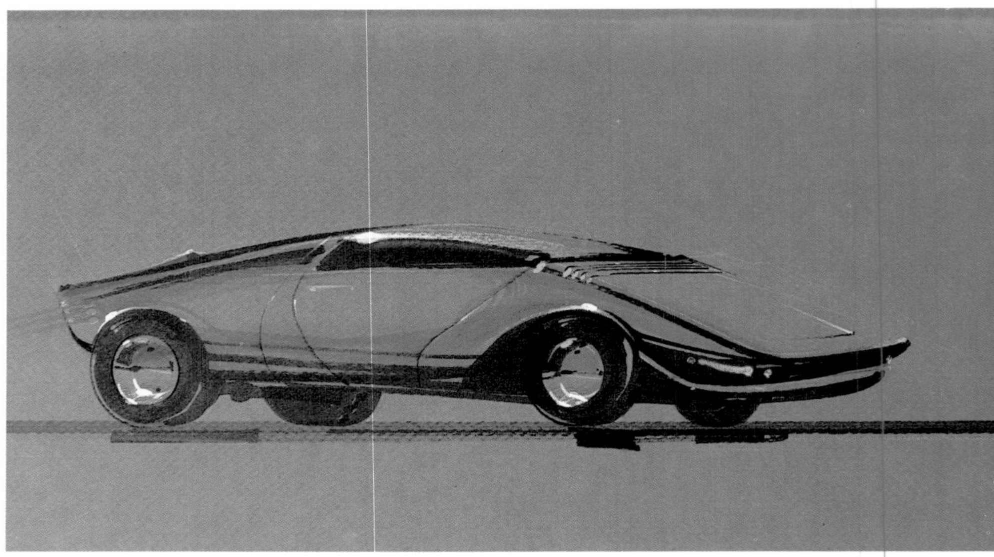

In rendering this home entertainment system, I used a limited amount of pastel chalk and gouache to achieve a dramatic effect. Notice how the perspective chosen uses the entire paper. You should always think of the whole paper as a composition and the product or scene as merely a part of it.

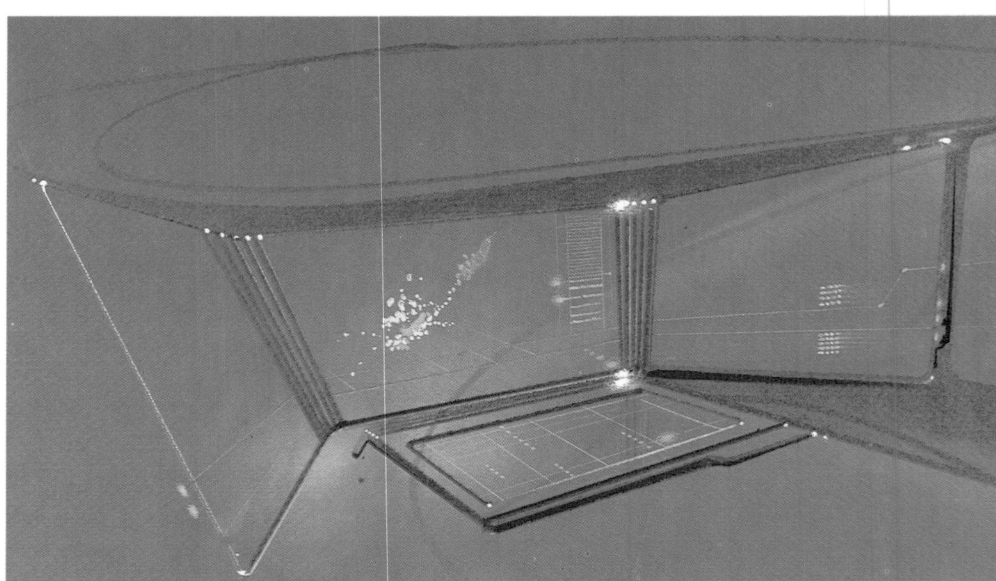

Although this background was created with Luma concentrated watercolors, the rendering of this miniature TV uses the same principles as working with colored paper. Use the background development as a middle tone and render the lights and darks over it.

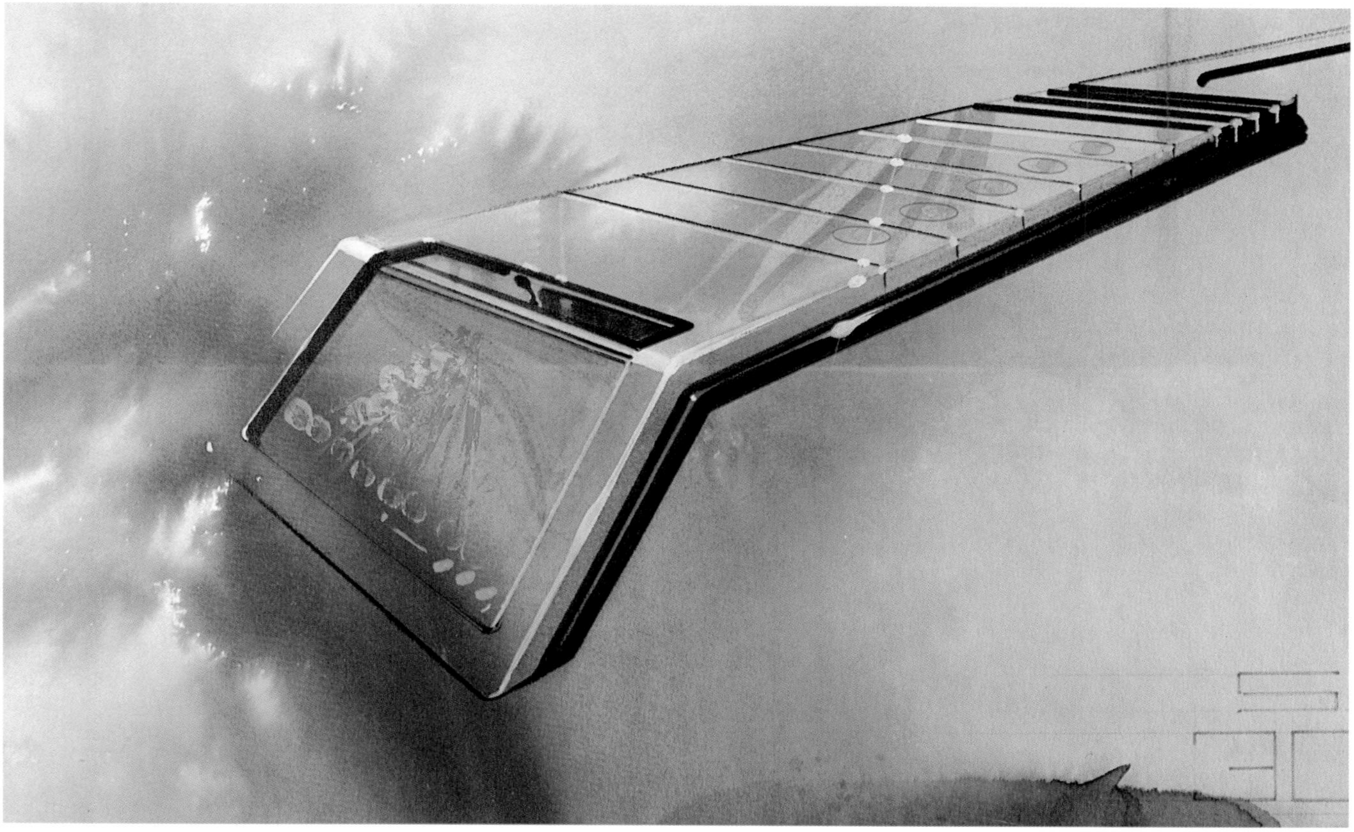

6 WET-MEDIA TECHNIQUES

Within the design process, there often comes a time when a final concept or a series of solutions needs to be expressed. These renderings should reflect a more finished format, as well as a quality of effort that comes across as both confident and dramatic.

Final concept renderings are reviewed by clients or top management with a great deal of scrutiny and, hence, should reflect your best effort. Fortunately, this does not mean that you need spend hours and hours on these pieces. This chapter will explain several wet-media techniques that can offer dramatic backdrops to your concept developments. The time invested in preparation and masking is minimal.

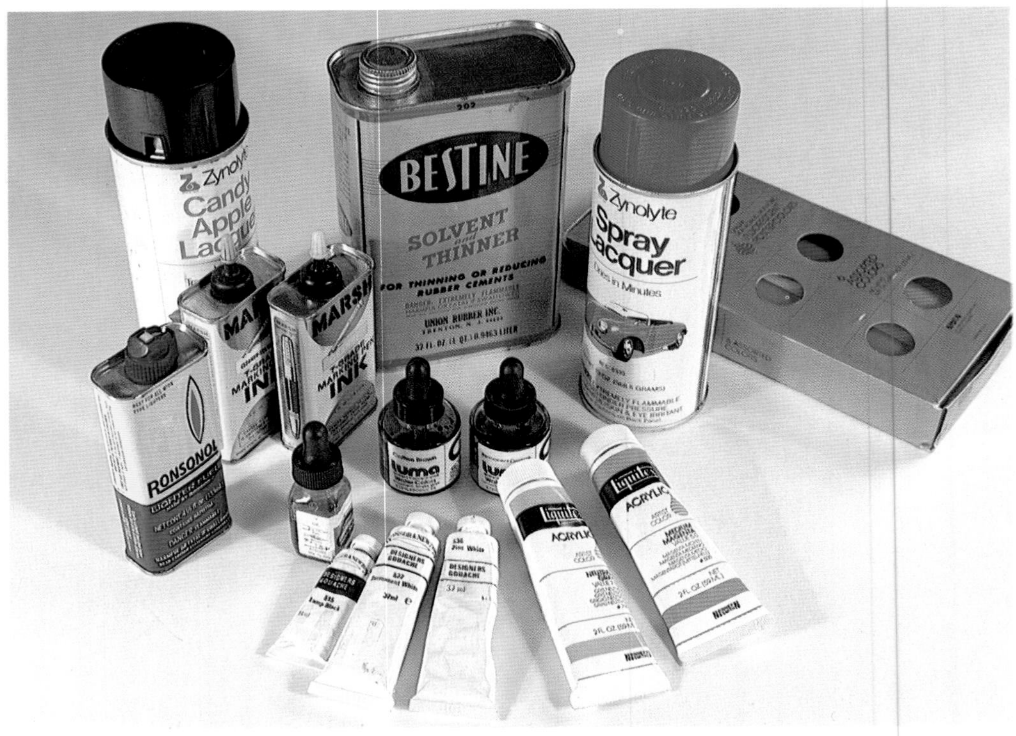

Your mixed-media palette would not be complete without including the wet mediums. Each of these products interacts with one another and with the dry mediums in unique, often unpredictable ways. A chart of compatible interactions can be found on page 38.

Appropriate Background Development

As with all background methods, it is important to maintain a balance between the focus of attention and the visual content around it. With very little effort, wet mediums can produce rather flamboyant results, so you will need to be even more sensitive to this balance when using them.

You need to be aware of your clients' inherent interest in the design process. Are they reviewing the design solution from a marketing or an engineering viewpoint? Will they see a less-than-conservative backdrop as implying a lack of attention to serious engineering details, or will they see it as a dramatic expression of excitement for product potential? These answers should define the appropriateness and limits of your background development.

This background was created by dropping Luma concentrated watercolors onto very wet, hot-press watercolor paper. The results were allowed to dry, and then typical rendering techniques with dry marker and chalk were used.

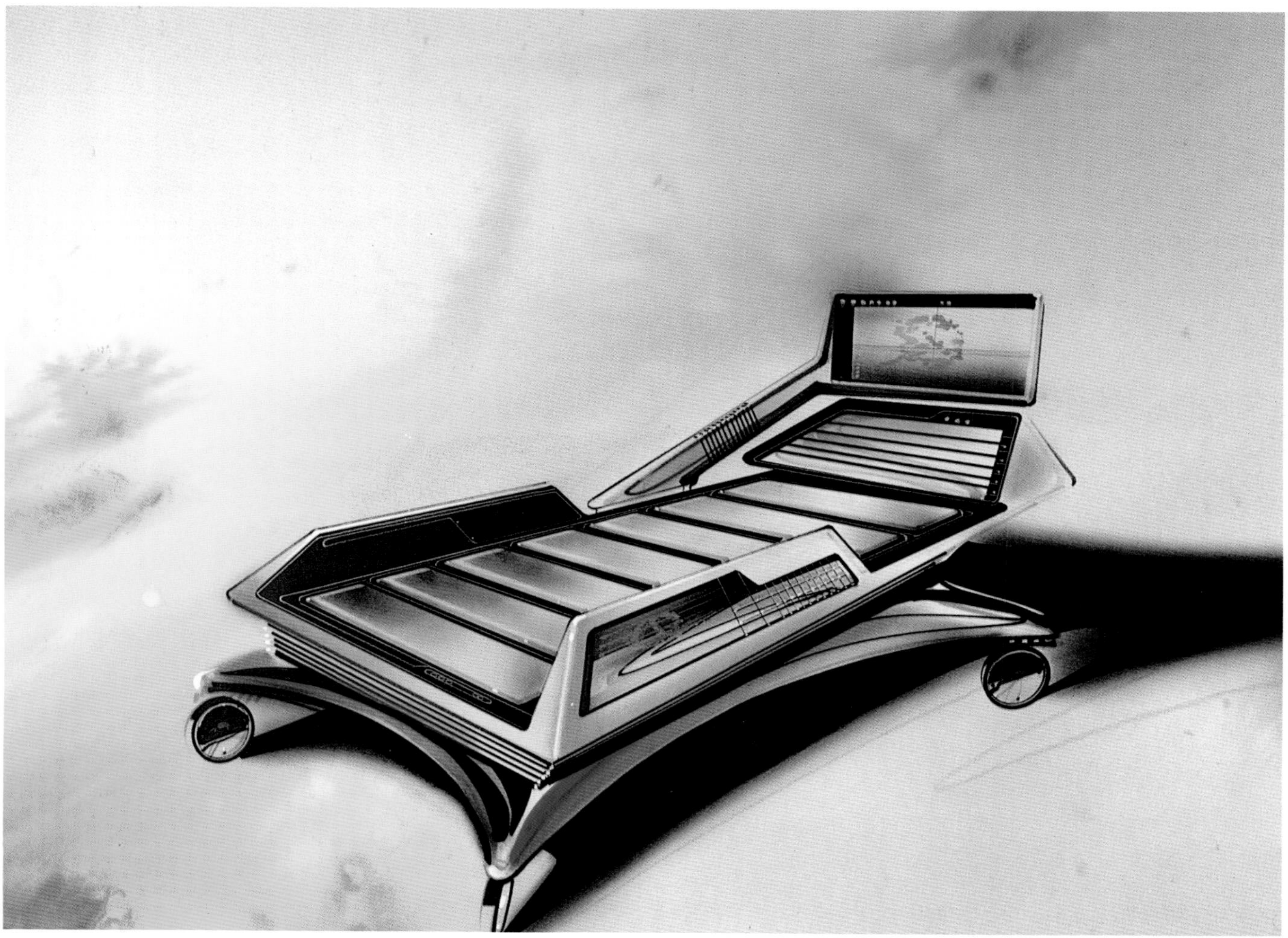

Water-Soluble Dye Concentrates

The dye concentrates, such as Luma Brilliant Concentrated watercolors, are quite intense and lend themselves to a more formal presentation. Since they are water-based, they generally require a longer drying time than petroleum-based products.

I try to capitalize on the unique brilliance of the dyes by using them directly on the drawing surface, with little or no diluting. I use a stretched watercolor paper that can be redampened to receive the dye. As the following illustrations show, the stretching of watercolor paper is a rather simple process.

Use a very smooth board, such as water-resistant plywood or Masonite, as the support and a smooth (hot-press) watercolor paper for the drawing surface. After the stretched paper has dried, dampen the surface and apply the color concentrates. Once the color has dried, which can take up to forty-five minutes, the surface receives dry markers and chalk nicely, and there will be little or no pick up of dye onto the lighter-toned markers.

Demonstration: How to create backgrounds using watercolor concentrates
The selection of watercolor paper is important. You should only use a fine quality hot-press paper such as D'Arches. Thoroughly wet the paper and attach it to a flat, sturdy board, using gummed-back postal tape that will hold when wet. After the paper has dried and shrunk to a nice taut surface, wet it again and apply the concentrates. Tilt the board to allow the inks to flow on the very wet paper.

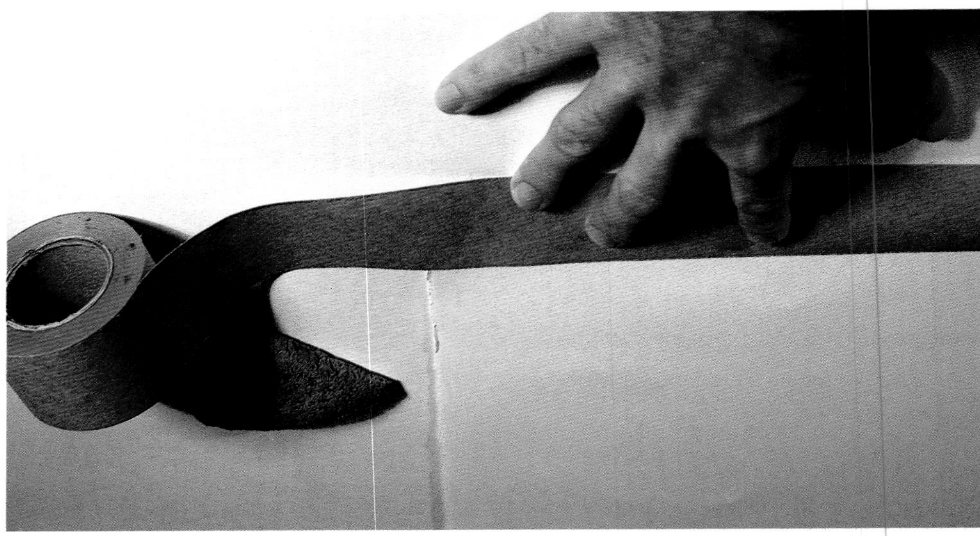

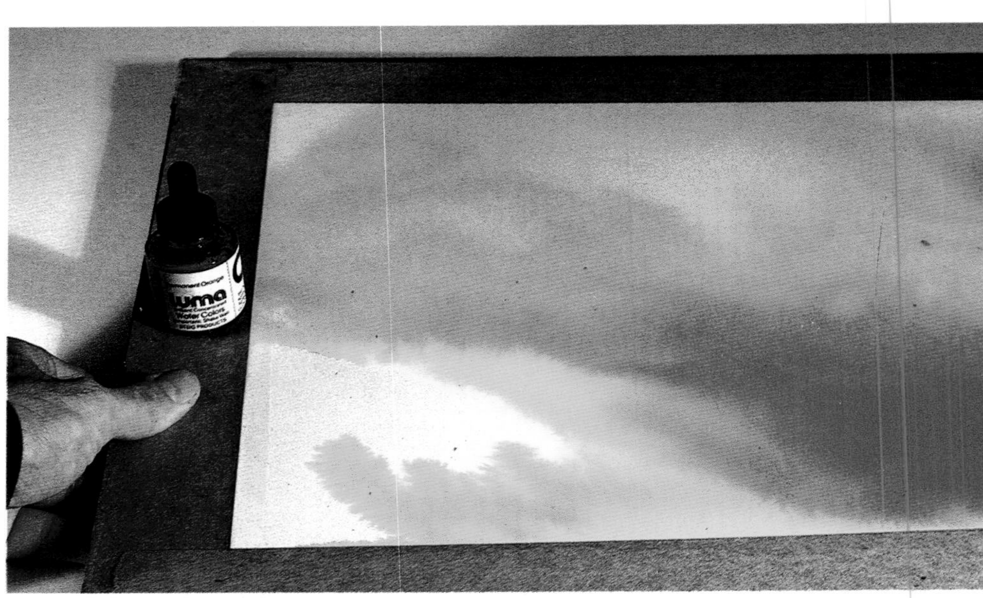

After the concentrate has dried, you can apply dry markers and gouache highlights as if it were a colored-paper background. The completed renderings have a more finished presentation quality to them and can be quite striking.

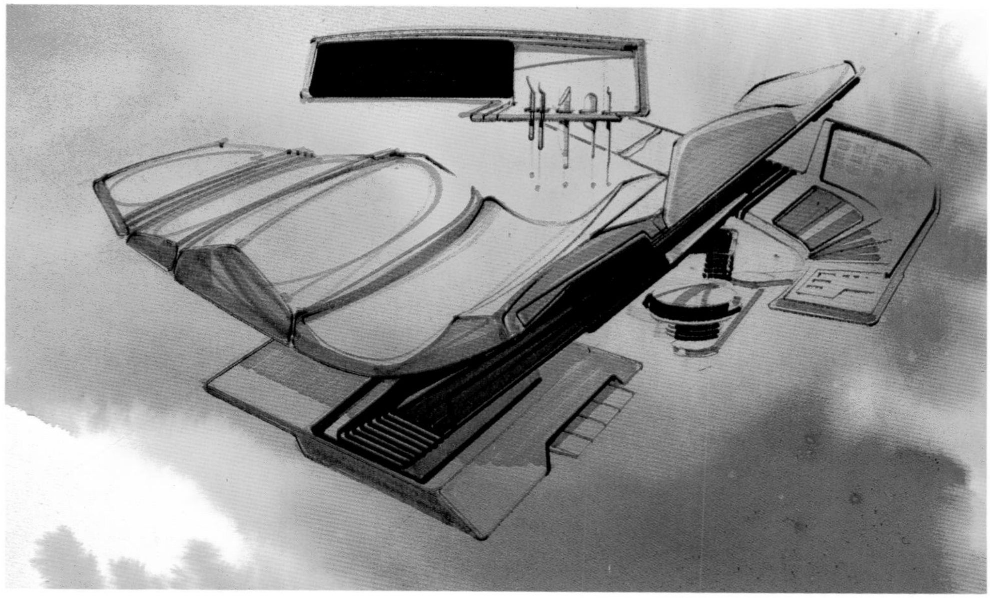

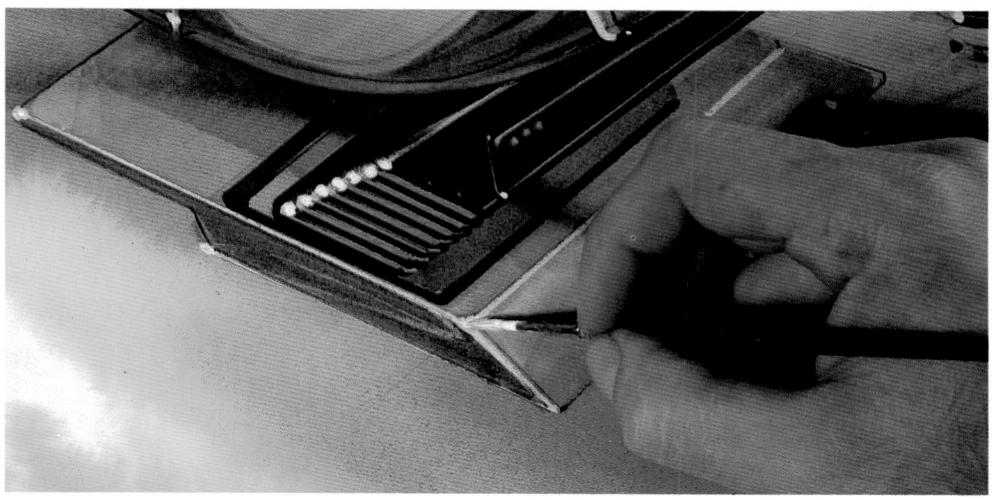

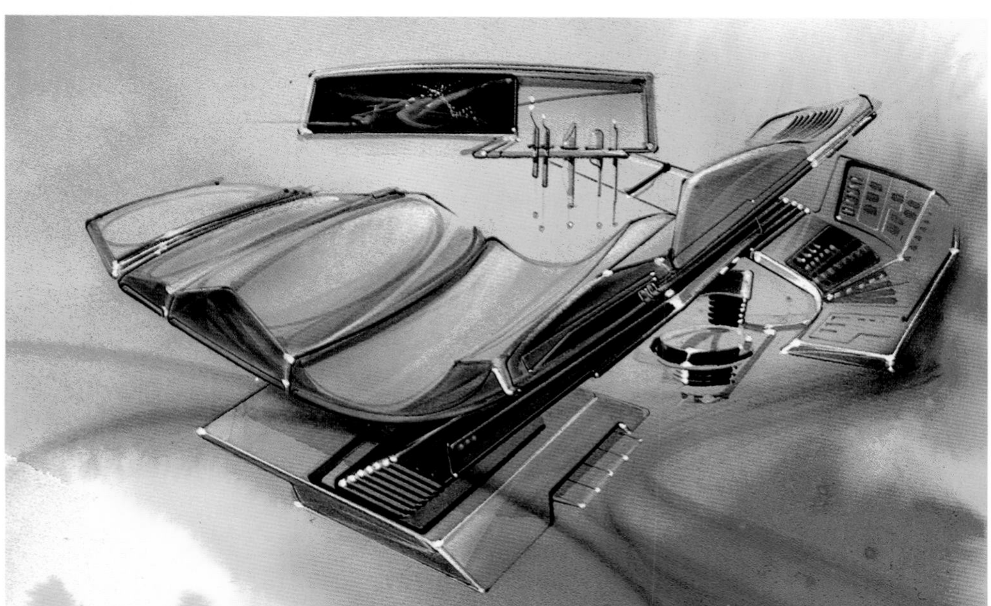

Petroleum-Based Products

Lighter fluid, liquid marker inks, lacquer spray paints, and rubber-cement thinner are all petroleum-based products that can yield interesting results in graphic renderings. (Again, please heed the warning labels regarding the flammability and toxicity of these products.)

With the introduction of a generic lighter fluid as a medium, powdered pastel chalk can be made to "flow" on the drawing surface. Simply take a pastel chalk stick and scrape it with a razor blade; then mix lighter fluid into the resultant powder. Use a sheet of vellum as your palette and a Webril pad as your brush.

Powdered colors can be mixed together, and using the lighter fluid as a carrier works on either marker pad or vellum, with the best results on the latter. You will find that this is a very fast technique for adding large areas of colors and it requires little prep time.

Computer plots that have been copied onto vellum can be effectively rendered over with lighter fluid and chalk. It is usually best to wet the entire area with fluid first, then wash the mixture over it using the Webril pads.

These are several kinds of liquid marker inks, but I recommend using FloMaster or Marsh. These are basically the same inks that are used in dry markers, only in liquid bulk form. When applied with a Webril pad onto a vellum surface, the inks can produce quite an intense area of color. This is an excellent technique for developing large areas of color.

Demonstration: How to mix pastel and lighter fluid
Some very fast effects can be created by using lighter fluid as a medium to carry powdered pastel chalk. Use a razor blade to scrape the chalk stick into a powder form and mix fluid into the chalk until they form a paste. Then apply lighter fluid to a Webril pad, pick up the color with the pad, and transfer the color to paper dampened with lighter fluid. This works best on vellums, since bond paper tends to soak up the lighter fluid too fast.

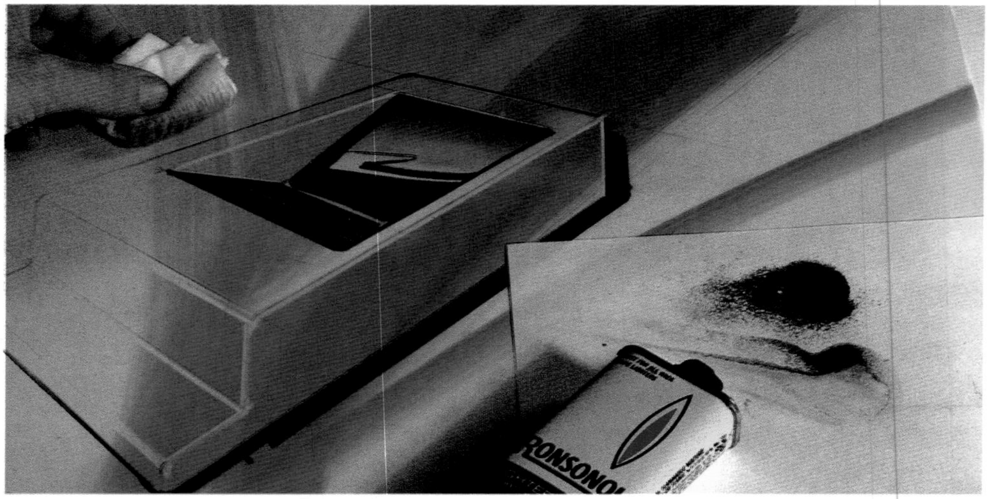

First plotted onto 8½ × 10-inch bond paper and then reproduced on 20 × 30-inch vellum, this rendering of a mobile computer was colored by the lighter-fluid/pastel-chalk method using several colors of chalk.

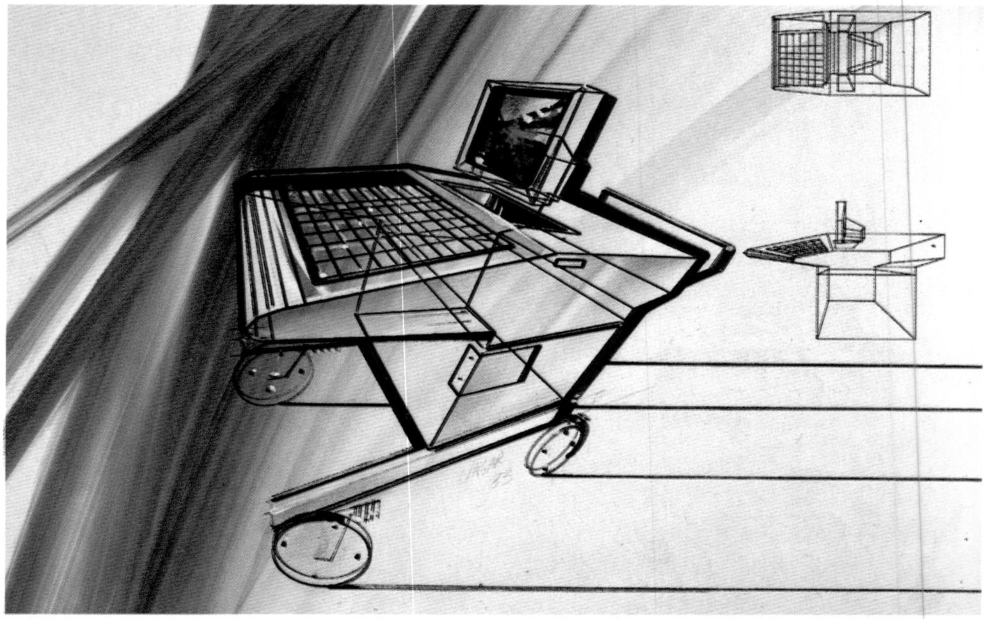

These computer plots were generated onto vellum using Jim Hennessey's Industrial Design Drawing Program from an Apple II computer. The addition of lighter fluid and chalk formalized the plots into renderings that worked well with similar concepts in a presentation to the client.

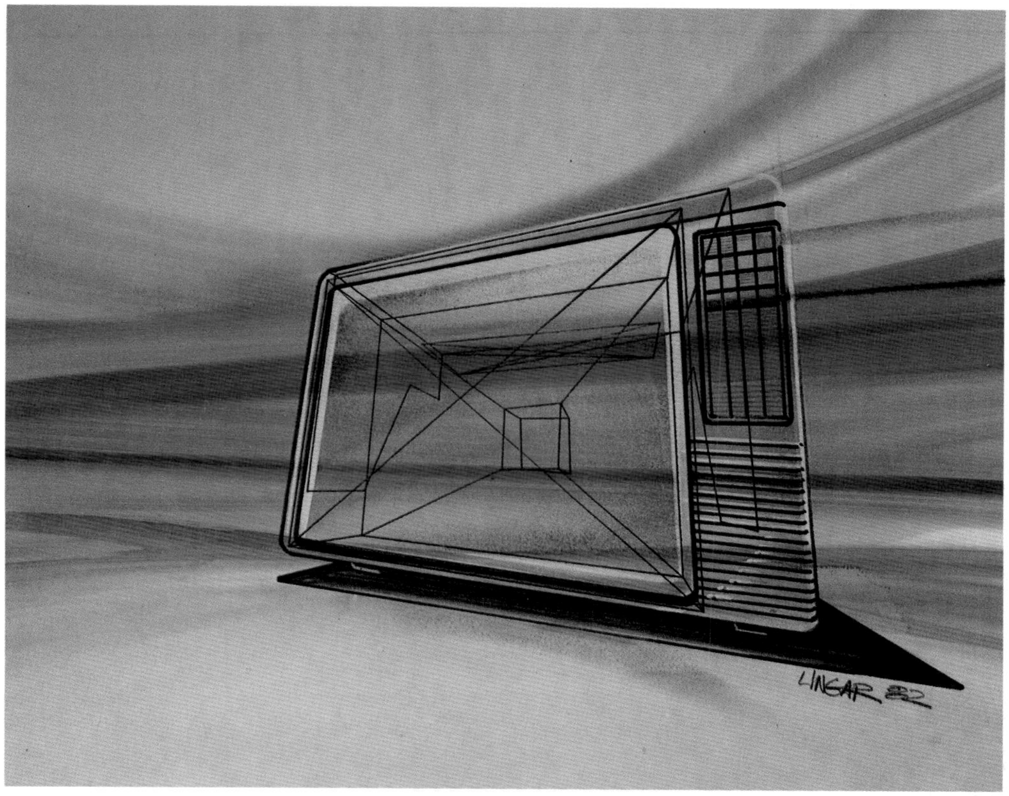

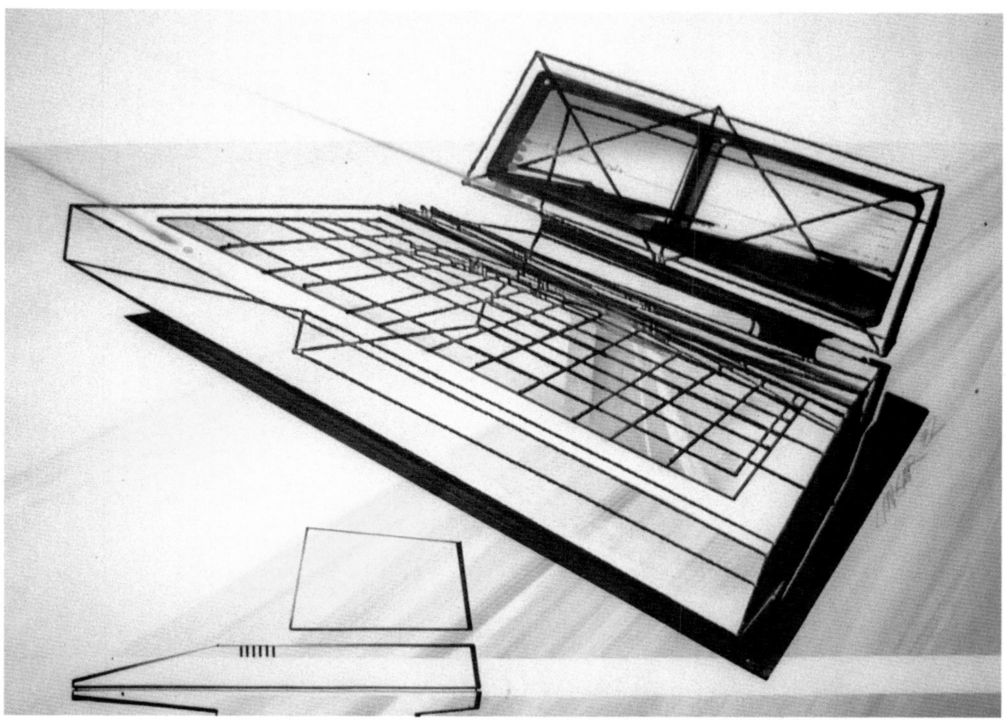

Because these computer plots of desktop calculators were transferred to colored paper too absorbent for lighter fluid, dry markers and marker sprays were used to translate them into finished concepts.

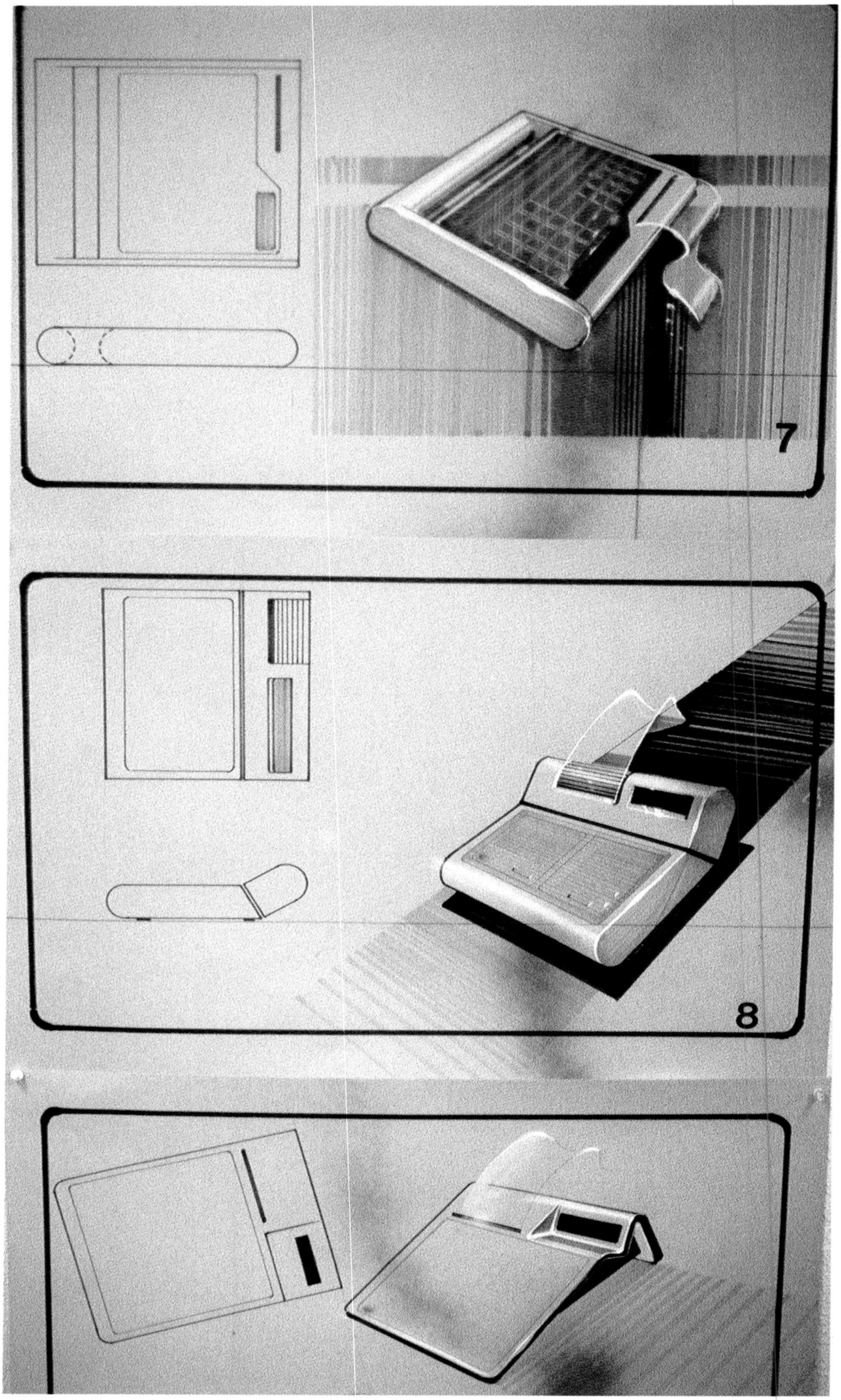

Demonstration: How to use solvent inks as a background medium

The solvent inks work best on vellums, where they can dry without being soaked into the paper. After your layout is drawn onto the vellum, use 3M photographic tape to mask off the product, such as this truck concept, from the background. Other friskets can be used if they have enough tack, but try them out first to evaluate their masking ability with solvent ink on vellum.

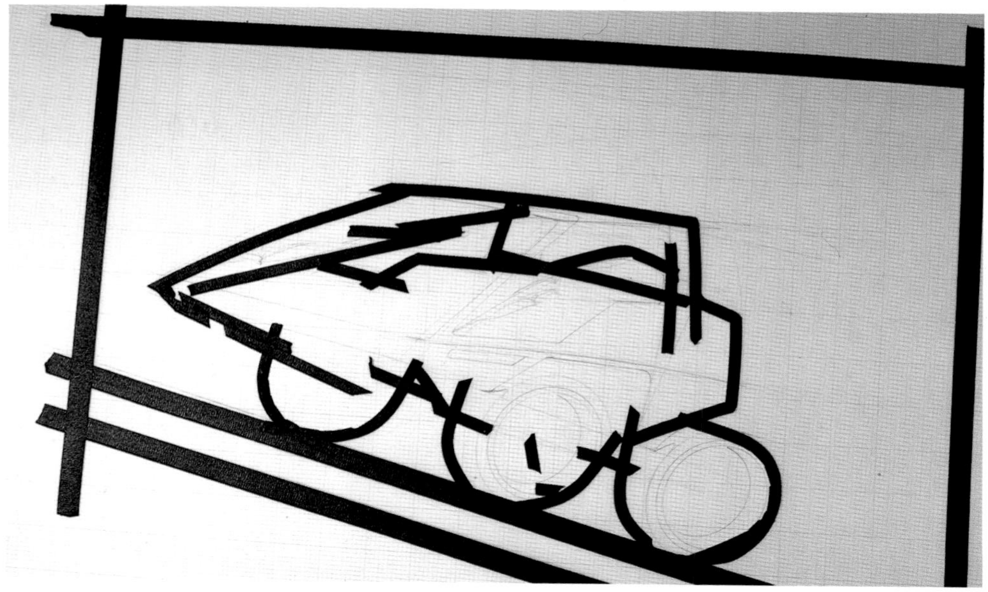

To be sure that no ink will bleed into unwanted areas, you can add additional masking vellum cut to the exact shape of the area to be masked. Use additional 3M photo tape to hold down the mask. When the mask is in place, apply an ink solvent to the entire area that is to be covered with ink.

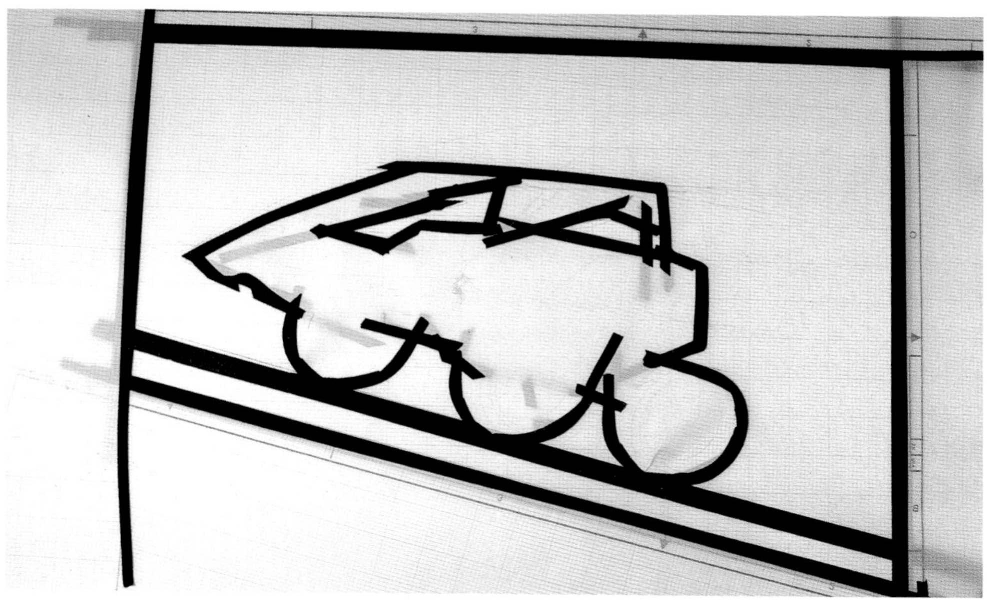

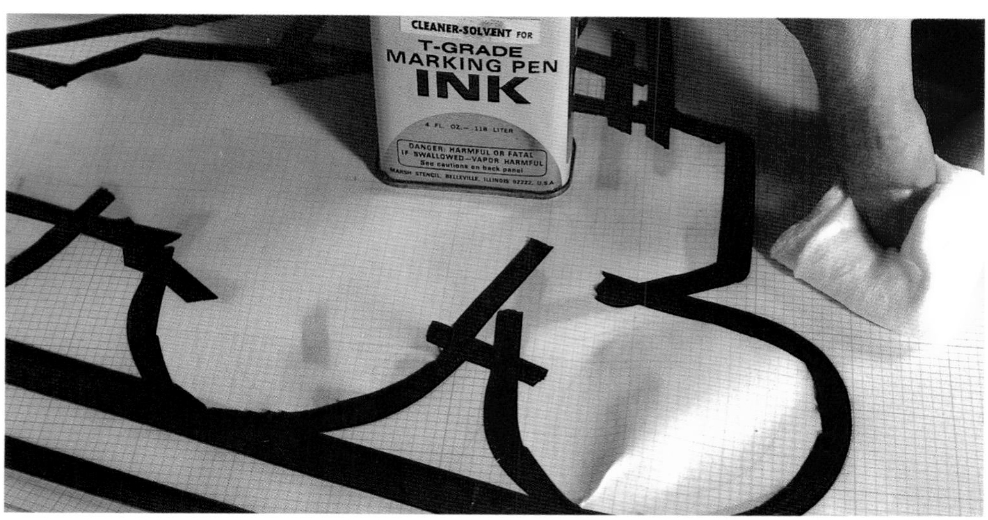

After wetting the area, apply the ink with Webril pads. It helps to hold the pads with a paper clamp. Try to minimize any contact with the ink or its fumes, and be sure to use adequate ventilation. The ink will dry in a few minutes, and you can then remove the masking.

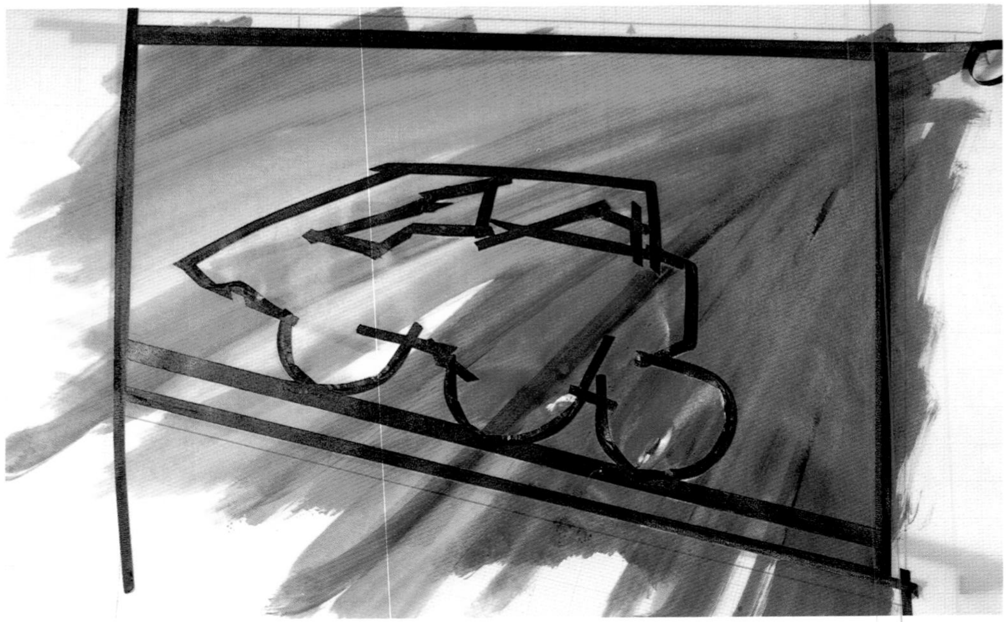

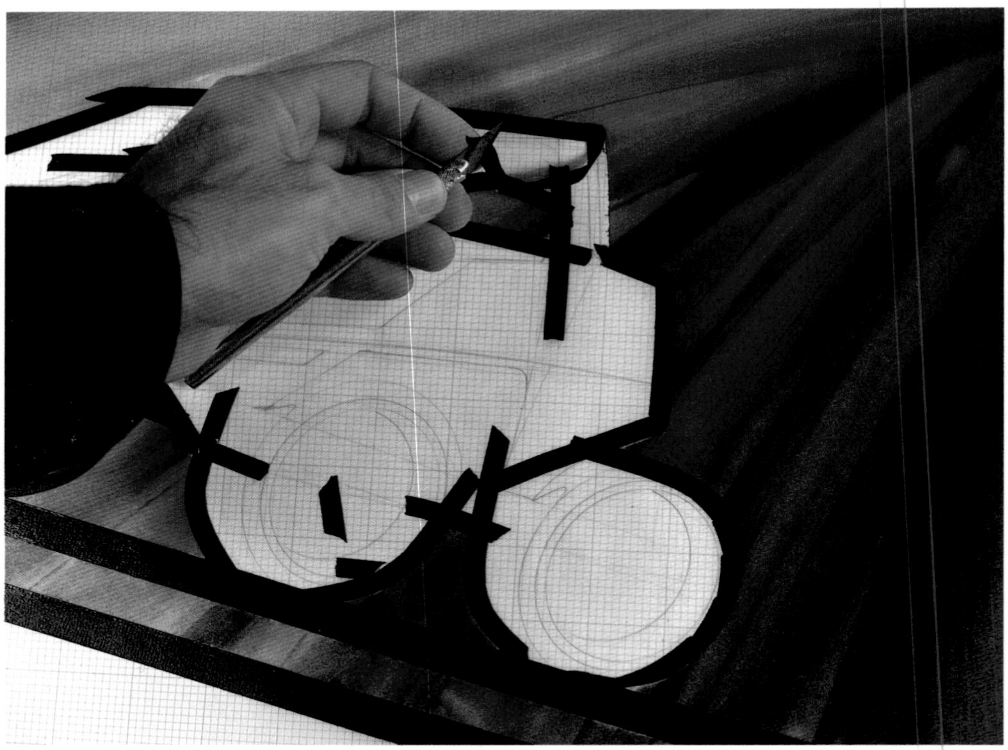

Render the subject by using basic mixed-media techniques. For this truck I wanted a highly reflective surface, so the surface tones of the metal were blended in with orange chalk to play off of the background. The dark reflective areas of the glass allow you to see into the interior, so early planning allowed the background to be seen in those areas.

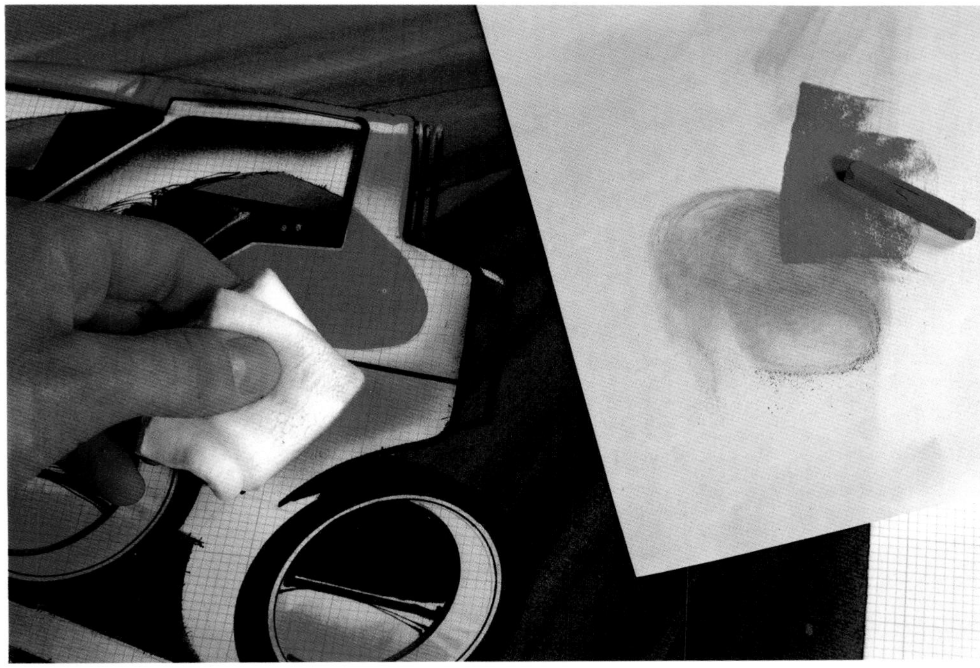

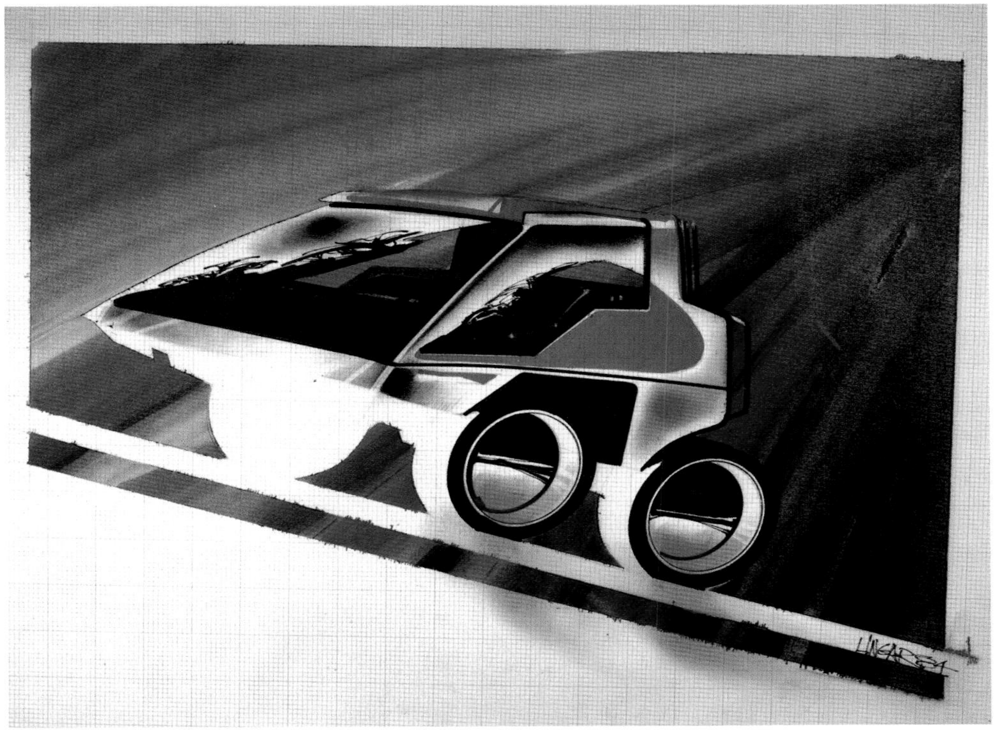

Special Effects with Non-Mixing Media

Many special effects can be created by combining incompatible materials. By applying Krylon lacquer to a surface wet with water, for example, and allowing the two incongruous materials to interact, you can obtain a striking, marbleized effect. This can be done on stretched watercolor paper by simply tilting the wet drawing surface so that the sprayed paint and the water flow together around the prepared paper. Dry media can then be added to render the product against this unusual background.

Another kind of marbleized effect can be created with the introduction of Bestine rubber-cement thinner onto vellum that already has FloMaster ink applied to it. After the ink and thinner have completely dried, the surface can be rendered with chalks and Prismacolor pencils.

I strongly recommend a well-ventilated area for general use of all the petroleum-based media, including the lacquers. Because of potential toxicity, I would also recommend using impervious gloves when handling the inks. You will find that the dramatic results are well worth the prep time.

Demonstration: Mixing water with lacquer paint
One area of the illustration board was masked off and sprayed with automotive lacquer paint. The area next to it is what happens when this same lacquer paint is sprayed onto a wet surface. The incongruous materials do not mix, and by tilting the wet surface, you can create some fairly incredible results.

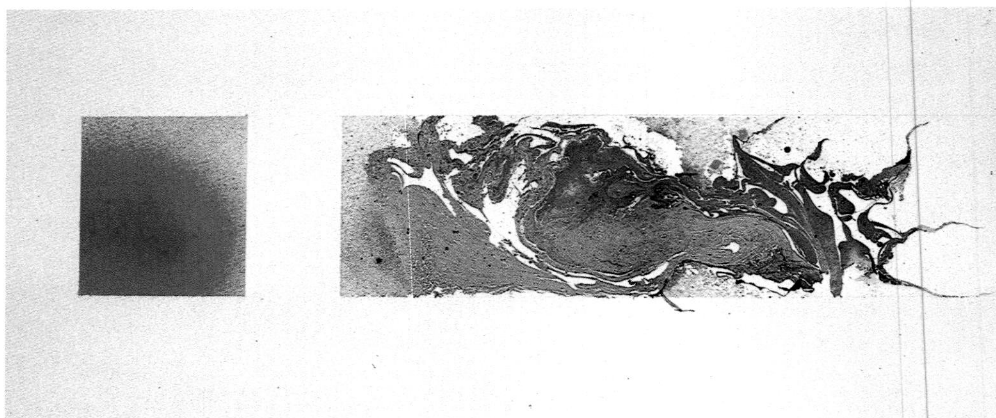

An entire sheet of illustration board was covered with flowing water and then sprayed with red and black lacquer paint. After the board had dried, I selected an area to cut out and use as a dynamic background for a rendering.

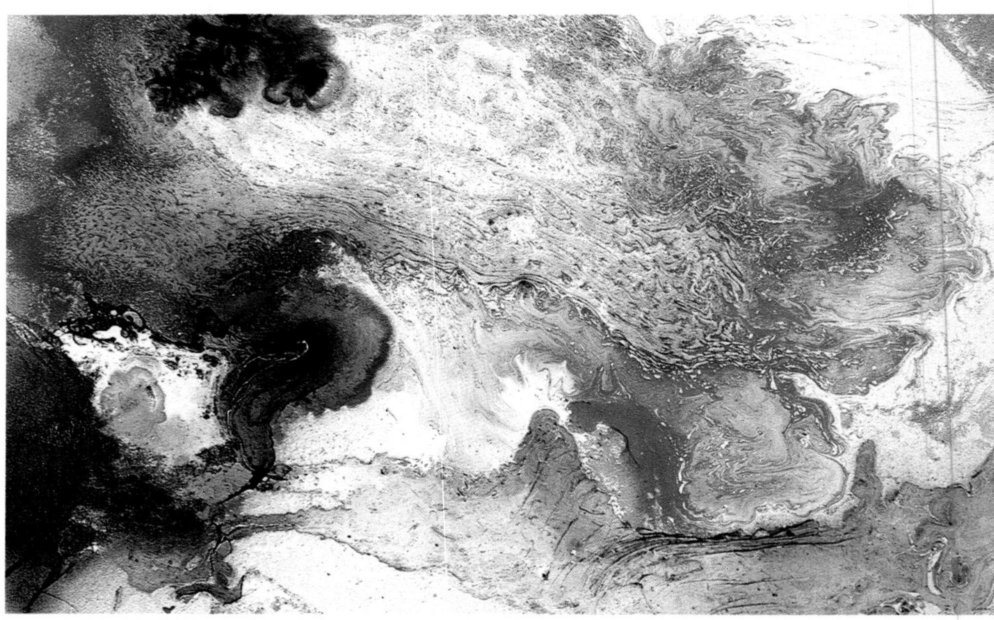

This sketch of an executive desk console was rendered over a selected area from the previous illustration, using pastel chalk, dry marker, and gouache highlights.

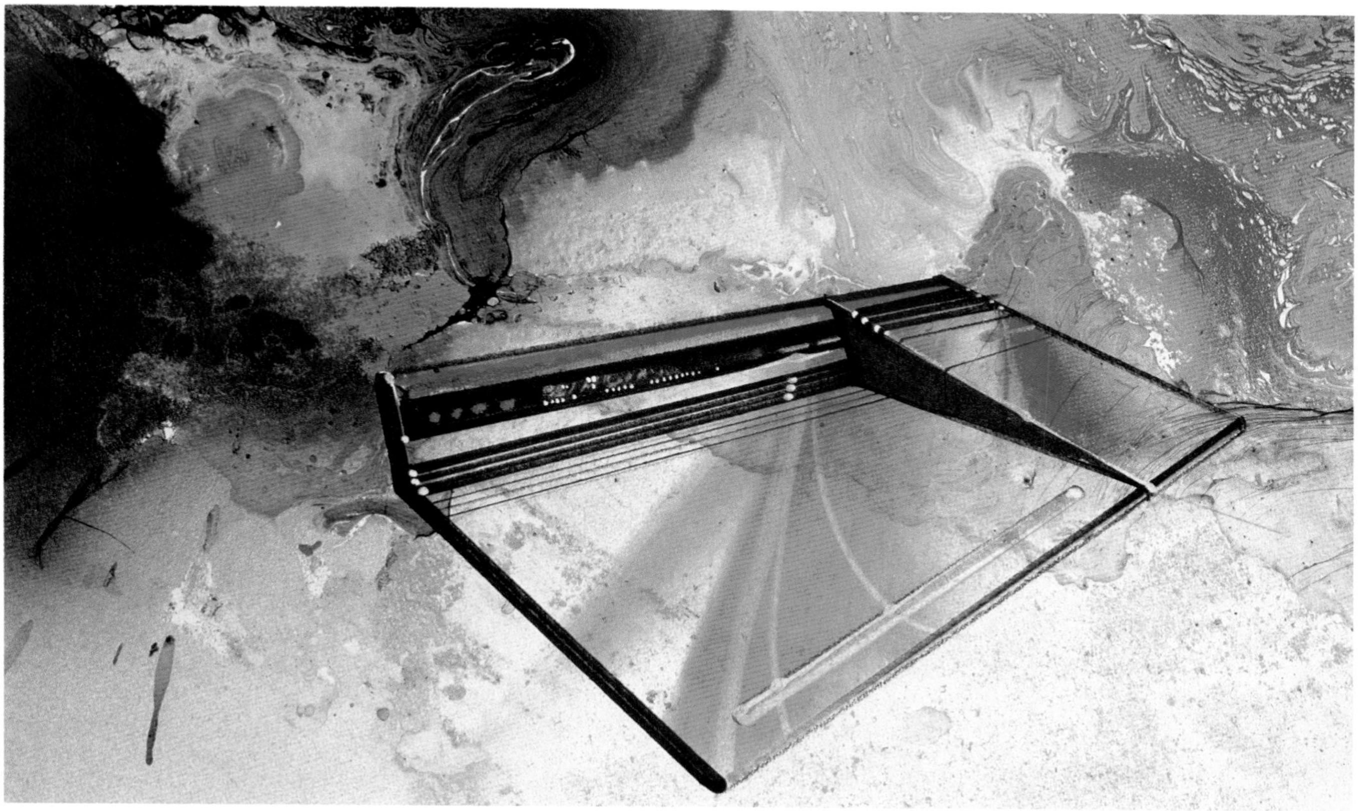

These graphics were simply drawn over a water/lacquer background. Chalk was blended into an area of the background, and the color was picked up in the graphics for effect.

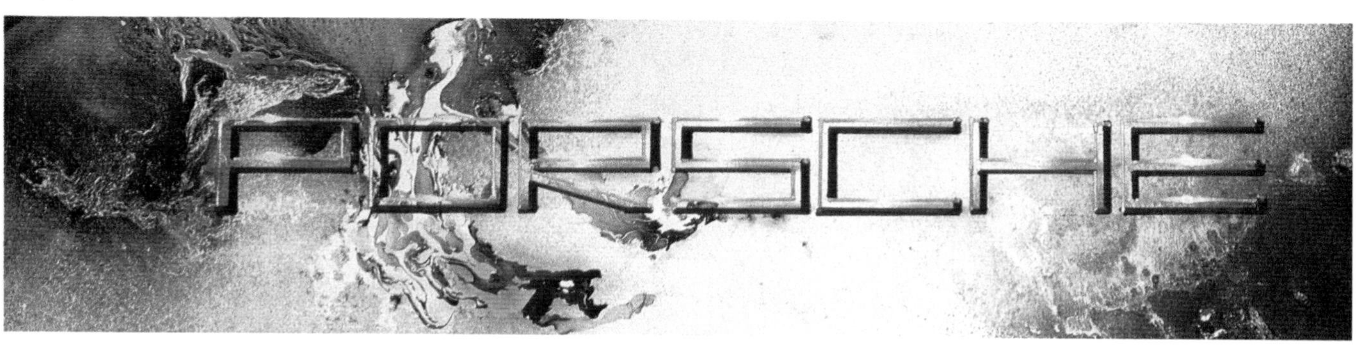

Demonstration: Mixing Bestine with solvent ink
This interesting process is based on the fact that Bestine does not mix with solvent inks, so the results can provide interesting backdrops to renderings. Again this is a process that has best results on vellum. First mask the area with Scotch removable transparent tape or black photo tape. Apply the solvent ink cleaner to the area, and then apply the solvent ink. Allow the ink to almost dry. Just before it is completely dry, add Bestine and allow the patterns to dry.

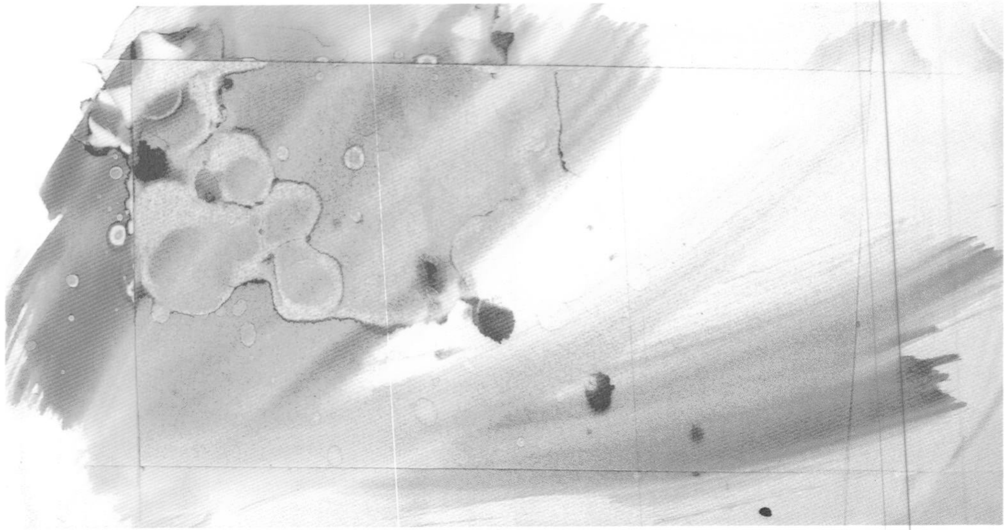

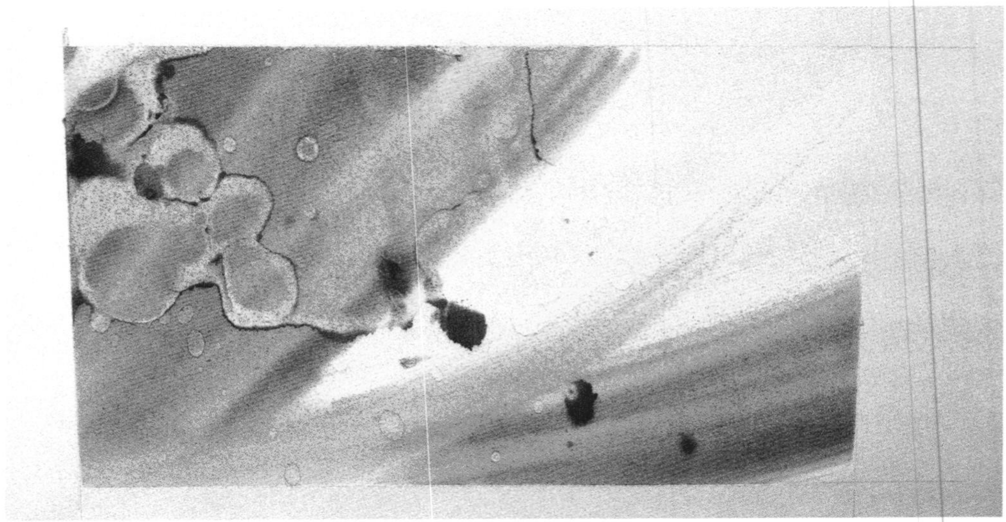

This medical instrument was rendered on a dry-marker pad and then cut out and placed over the dried Bestine/solvent-ink background. You can use this as a fast technique for creating a rather formal-looking drawing without having to spend much time masking.

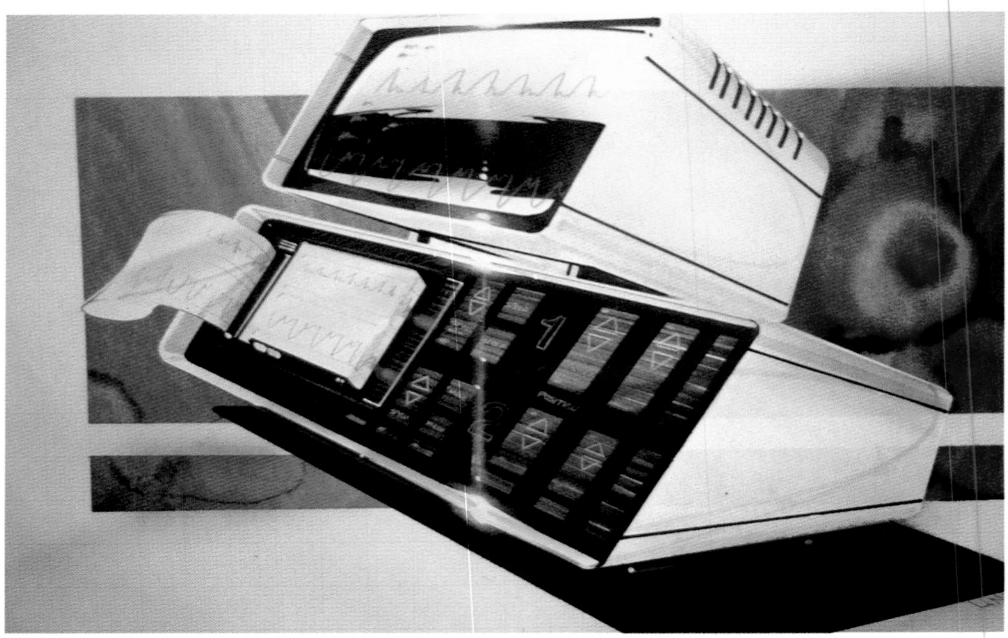

7 PORTFOLIO

The illustrations in this chapter represent a synopsis of recent industrial-design work I have done for a variety of clients. All of the renderings use multimedia techniques as discussed in this book, and I have included the relative drawing times to give you a feeling for the time spent on each concept.

Again, I would like to emphasize that you do not labor on your drawings, but instead let the lines flow quickly and effortlessly from pen to paper. Most of these portfolio pieces were rendered directly onto the background without using the layout-transfer process. This saves much time, and with practice, your level of confidence will allow you to do the same.

Glassware
Media: white gouache, black Prismacolor, pastel chalk; 50 × 70 cm. Drawing time: 3 hr.

It is often effective to emphasize the transparency of glassware, since this is such an important feature of the product material. Drawing glassware can teach you how important it is to observe details such as reflections and refractions of light.

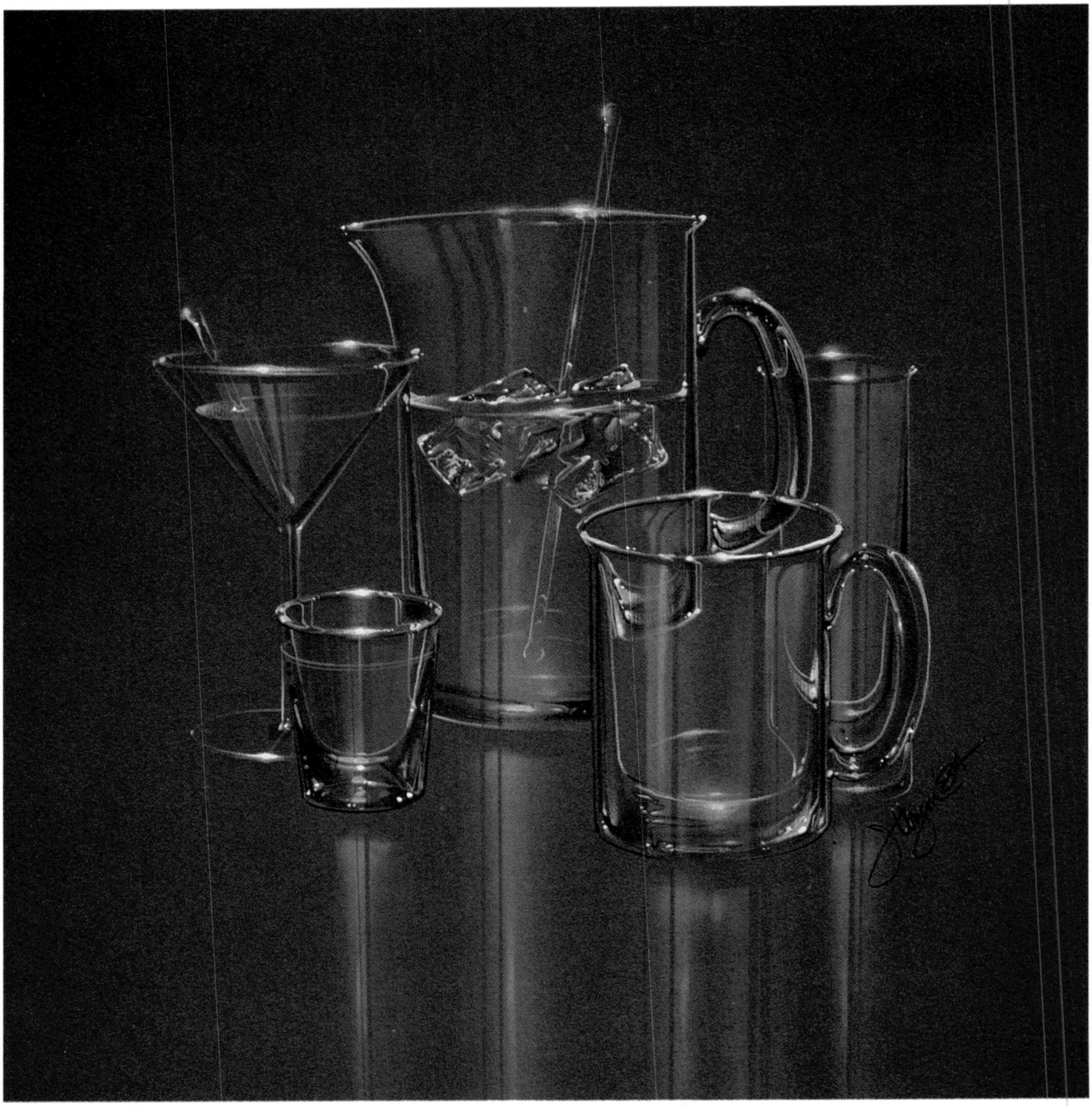

Glassware
Media: gouache, black Prismacolor pencil, pastel, black pen; 36 × 43 cm. Drawing time: 1 hr.

The use of Pantone graduated-tone color paper created a ready-made background such as that often seen in advertisements highlighting the luminous quality of glass. Refractions of lines were essentially guessed at, since the concept was drawn from my imagination. Studying photos or still-life assemblages of glass will increase your confidence in rendering this material.

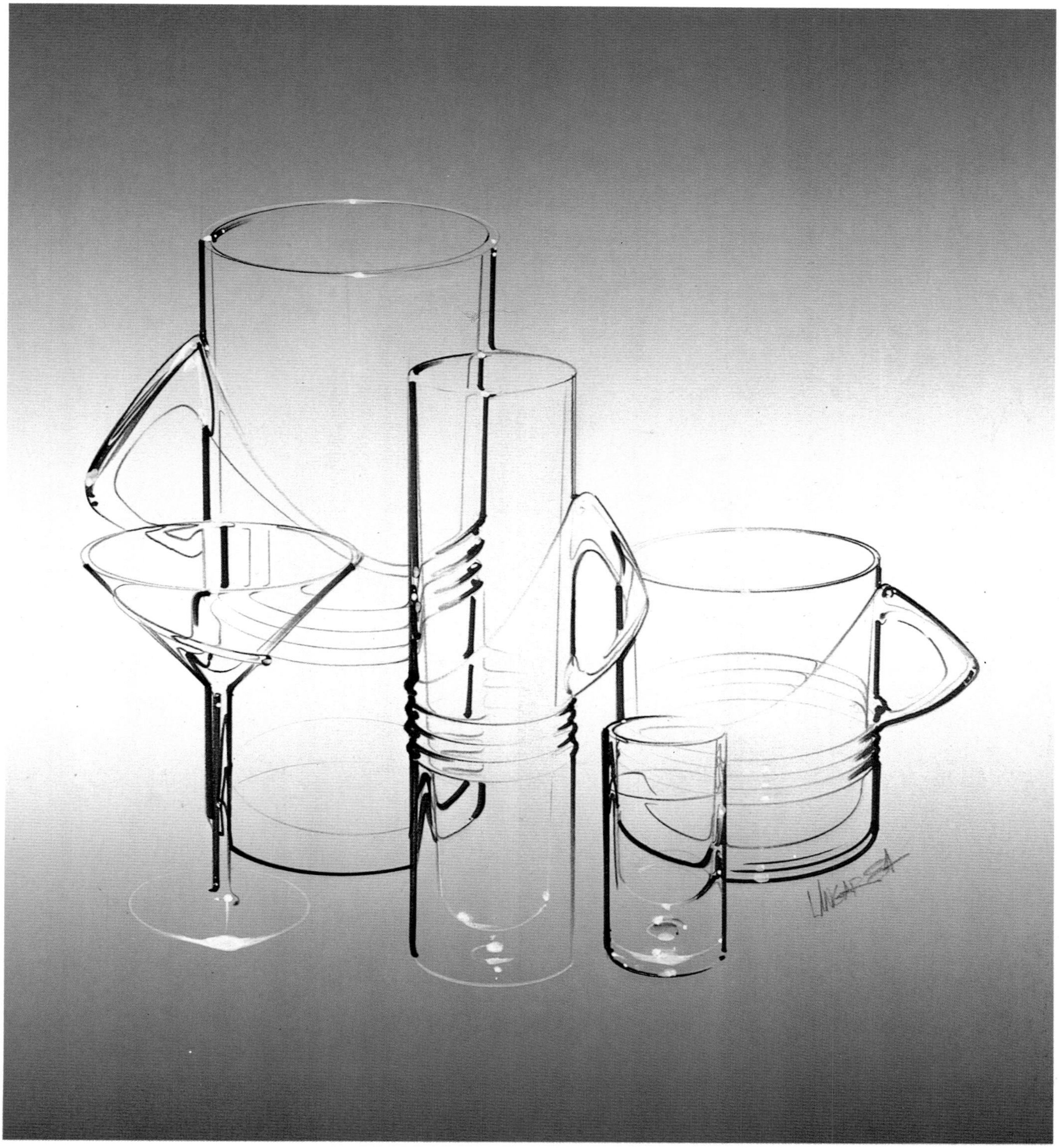

Record disc player
Media: LetraJet, dry marker, gouache, fluorescent paint; 36×43 cm. Drawing time: 1 hr.

A three-view projection allowed the client to visualize the concept clearly. Further line drawings would be done in a similar format, so that referencing between the concept illustration and engineering drawings would be easy.

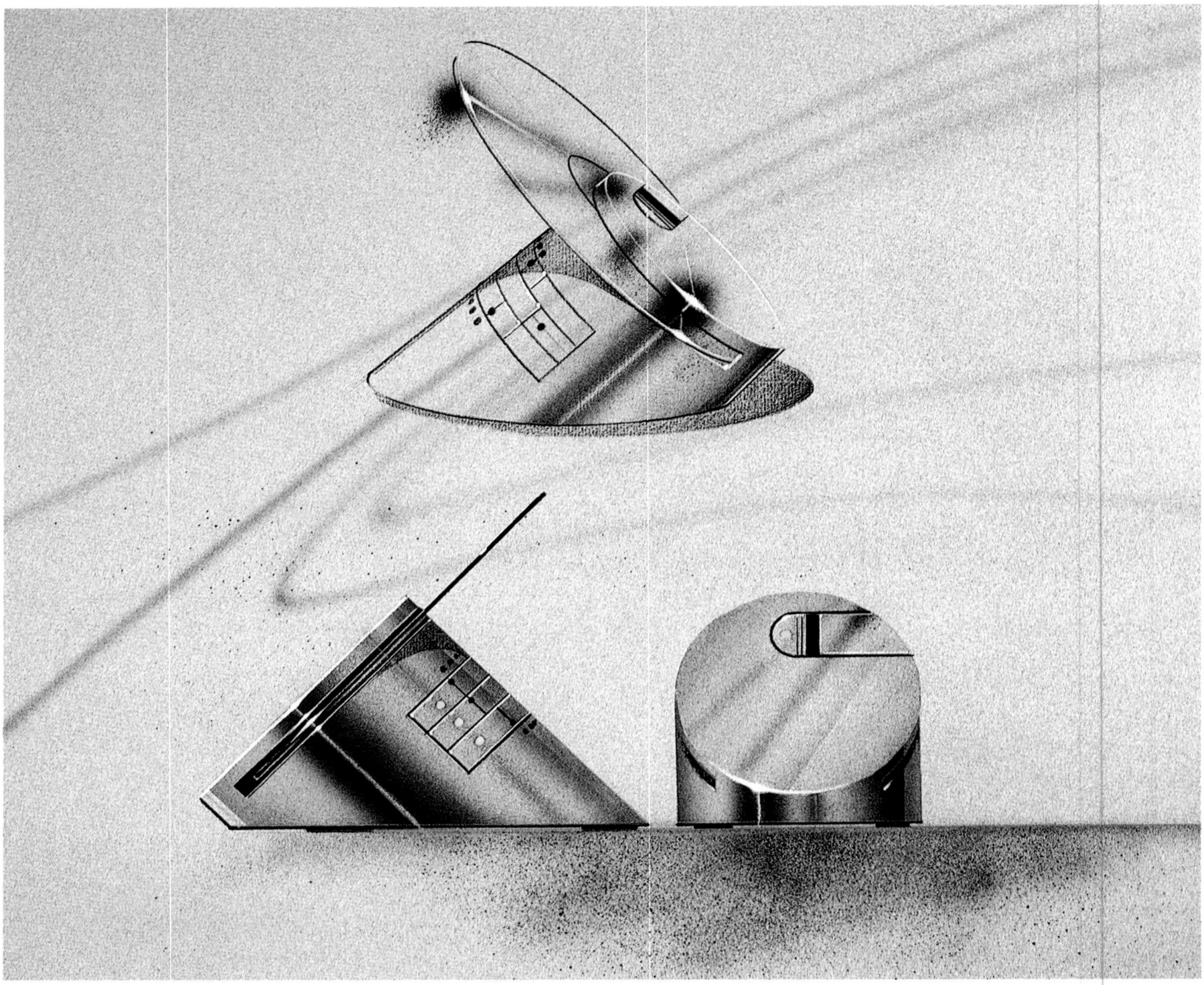

Compact-disc stereo player/tuner
Media: pastel chalk, dry marker, gouache, fluorescent paint; 50 × 70 cm. Drawing time: 2 hr.

By showing dark reflection areas on the product, I was able to bring out details underneath the dust cover on the stereo player. Showing a set of headphones offers a sense of scale to the rendering.

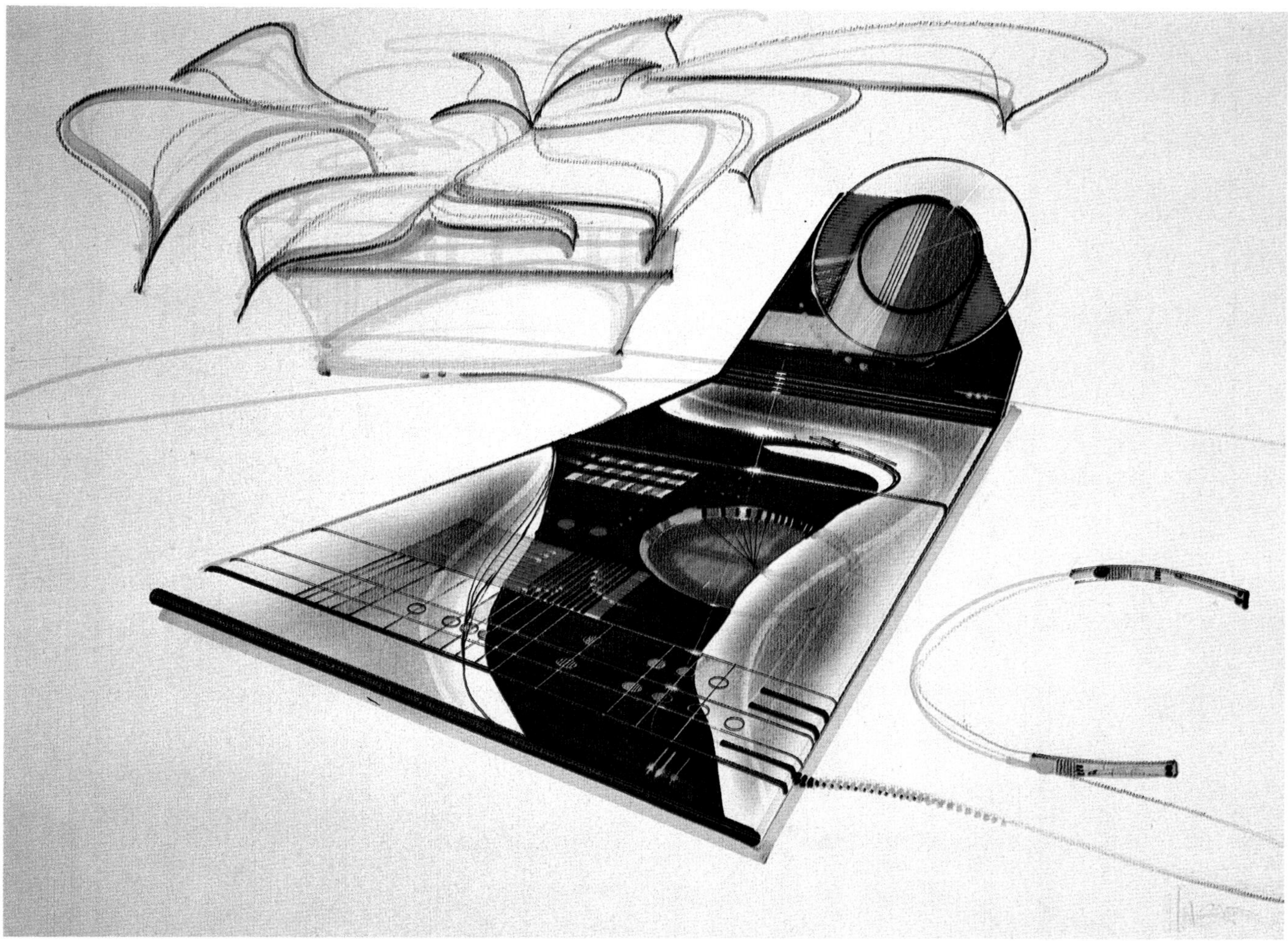

Wall TV/stereo complex
Media: dry marker, pastel chalk, photo montage; 36 × 43 cm. Drawing time: 2 hr.

This home-entertainment system hangs on the wall in a series of modules. The client wanted the design to express a slender profile of compact technology and wanted the product to be seen as no less than a work of art hung on the wall.

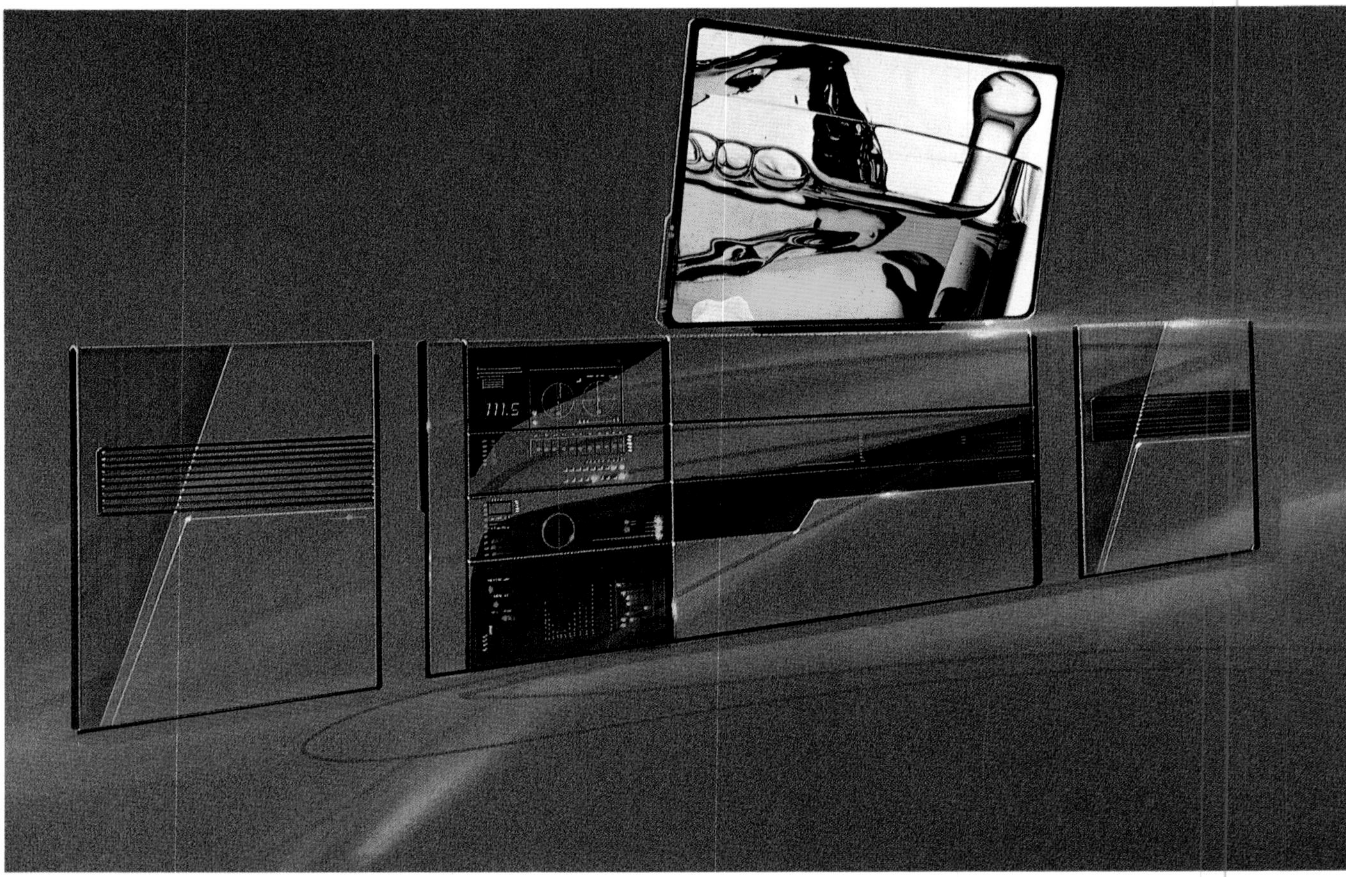

Optical disc player
Media: lacquer/water, pastel chalk, dry marker; 50 × 70 cm.
Drawing time: 1½ hr.

This product shows a possible direction in home-entertainment equipment as technology becomes more compact and controls become more interactive. The client wanted a dynamic background to emphasize product excitement and future directions of the product line.

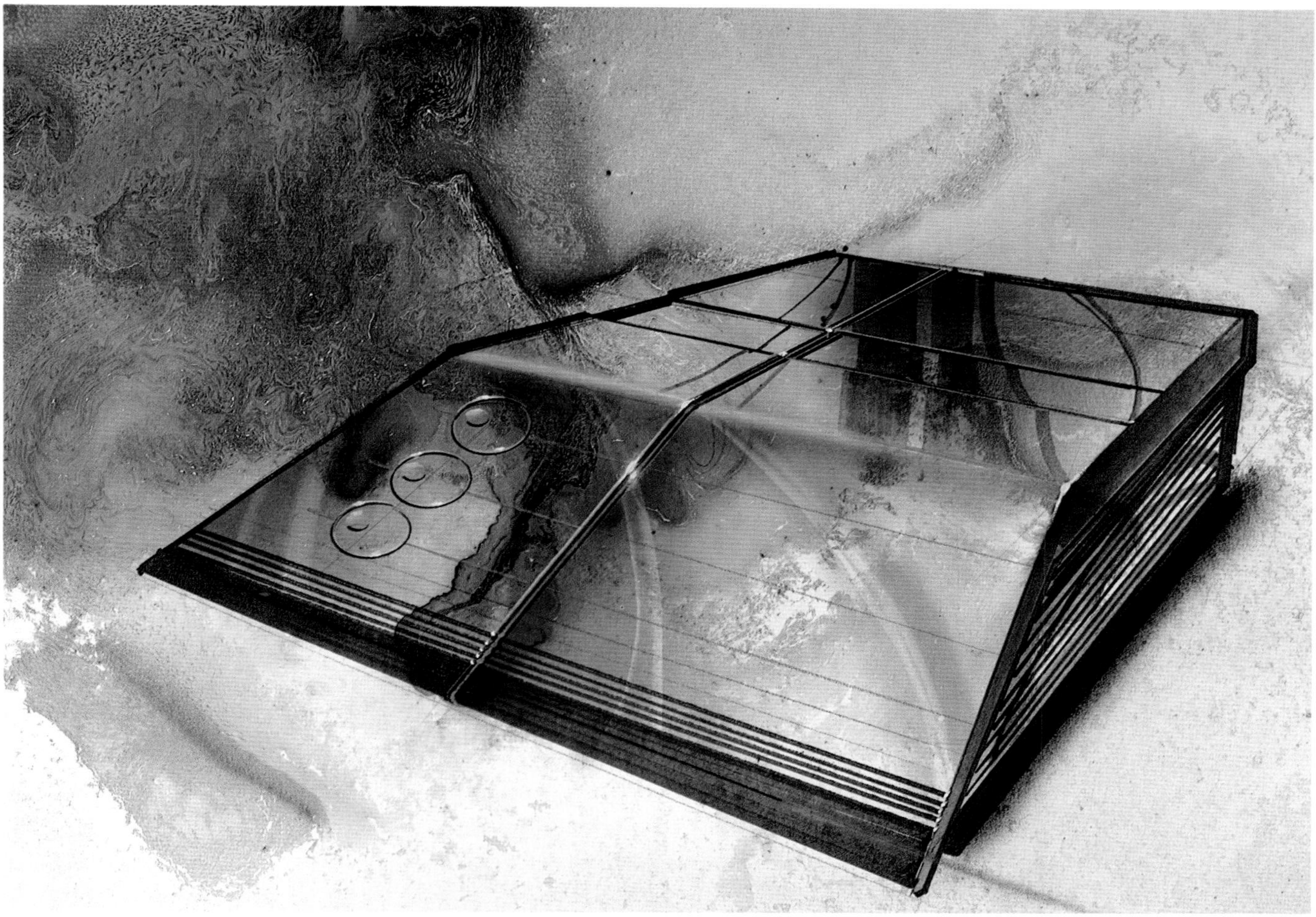

Medical ultrasound computer
Media: Luma watercolor, dry marker, gouache, Prismacolor pencil; 36×43 cm. Drawing time: 2½ hr.

Here the concept was laid out and drawn directly on the concentrated-watercolor background. Allowing the background colors to run through the front panel helped give the product a highly reflective appearance.

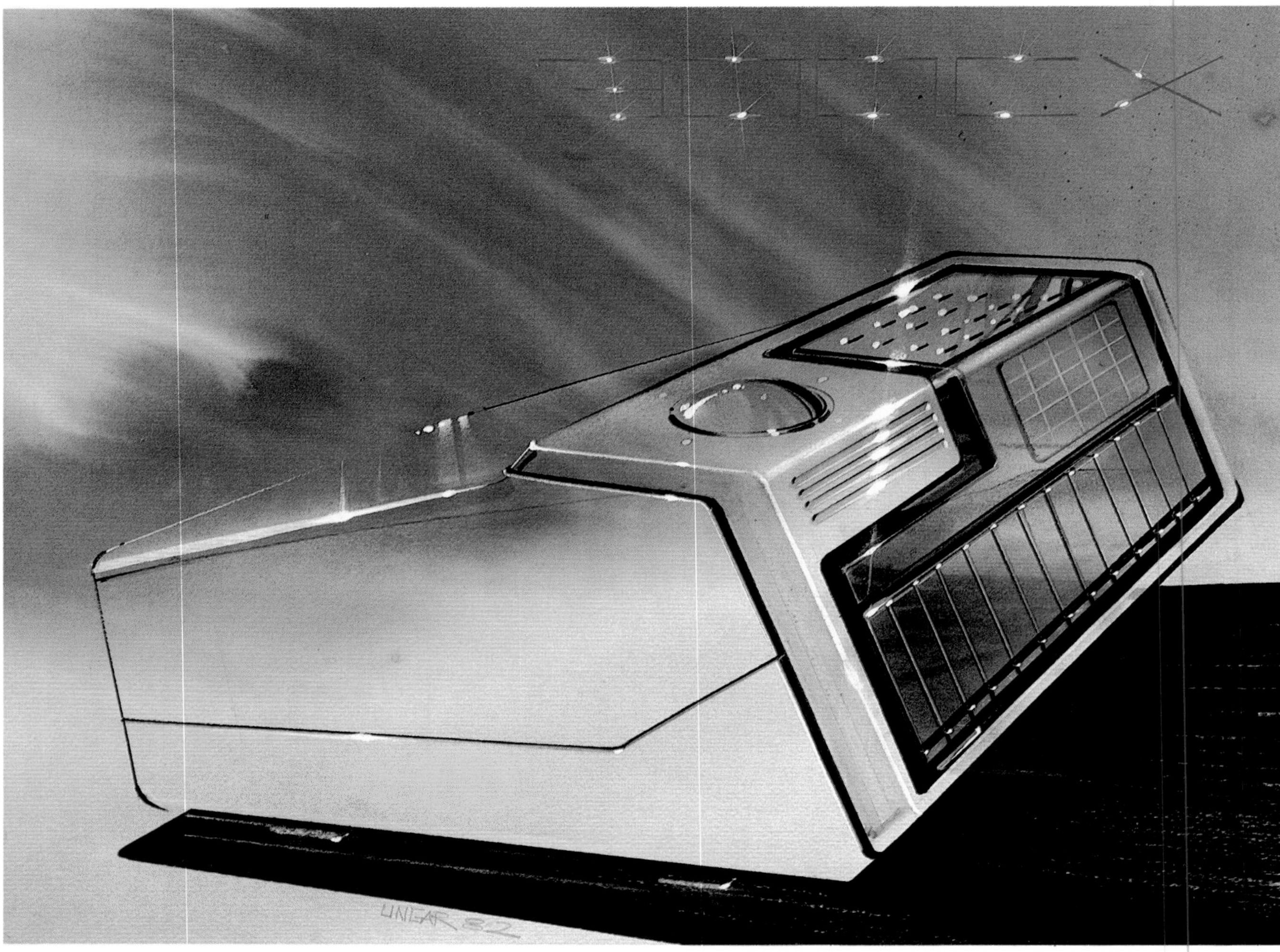

Optical medical-records encoder
Media: Luma watercolor, Prismacolor pencil, dry marker, pastel chalk. Drawing time: 1 hr.

Intense backgrounds can serve to highlight an individual concept and distinguish it from others in a presentation. This concept was an expression of a future computer peripheral for the medical-records industry.

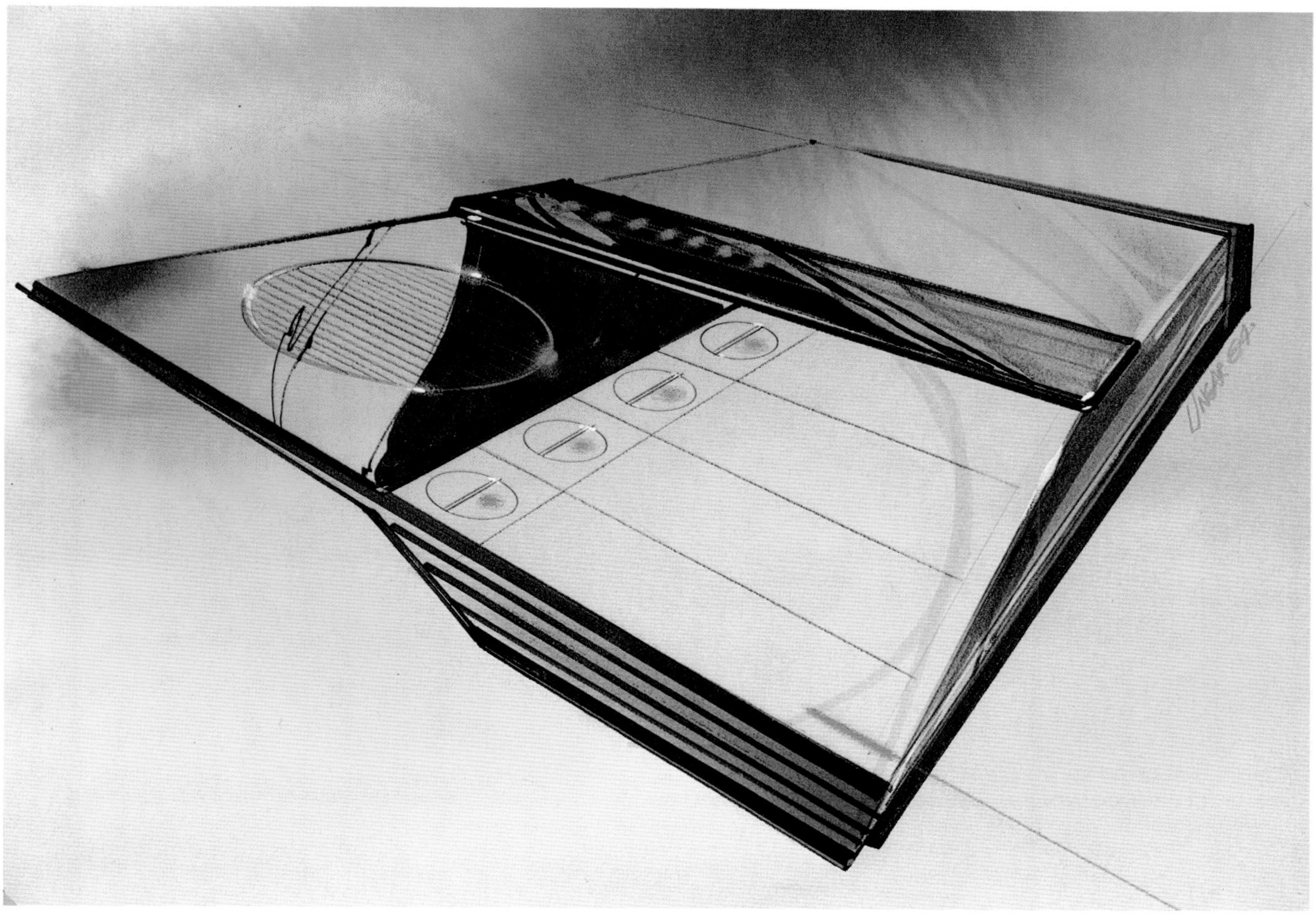

Wall-mount medical computer
Media: Luma watercolor, dry marker, Prismacolor pencil, pastel chalk, gouache; 36 × 43 cm. Drawing time: 3 hr.

Attention is created by the rather flamboyant use of color in the background. Backgrounds such as this are fun, but they must be carefully balanced in order to avoid overshadowing the concept.

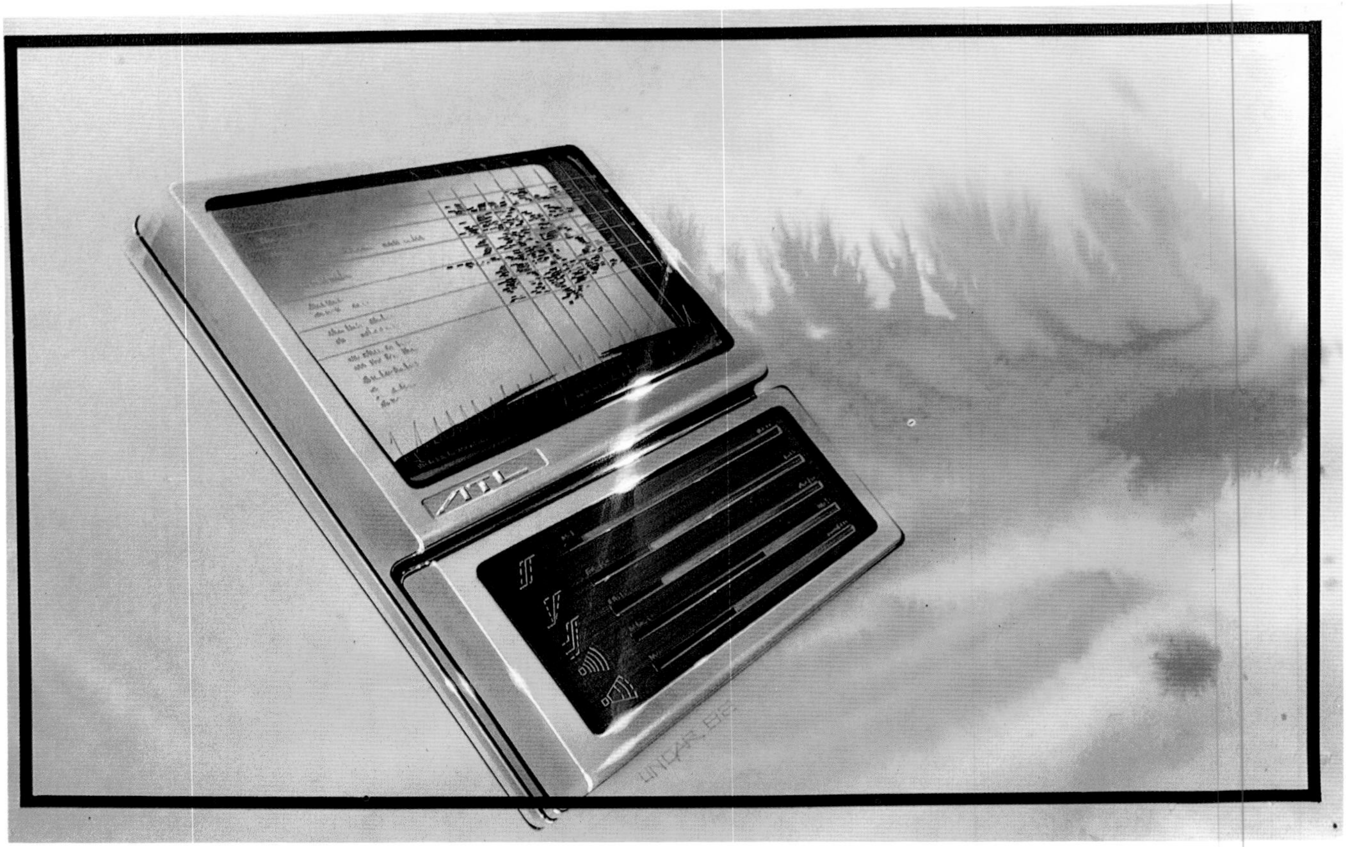

Medical data-acquisition station
Media: Luma watercolor, dry marker, Prismacolor pencil, pastel chalk, gouache, fluorescent paint; 50 × 70 cm. Drawing time: 5 hr.

To express a feeling of warmth, I used warm colors in the background, complemented by the smooth contours of the form. Offsetting the warmth are the fine lines and fluorescent colors of the displays, which portray the advanced, interactive technology.

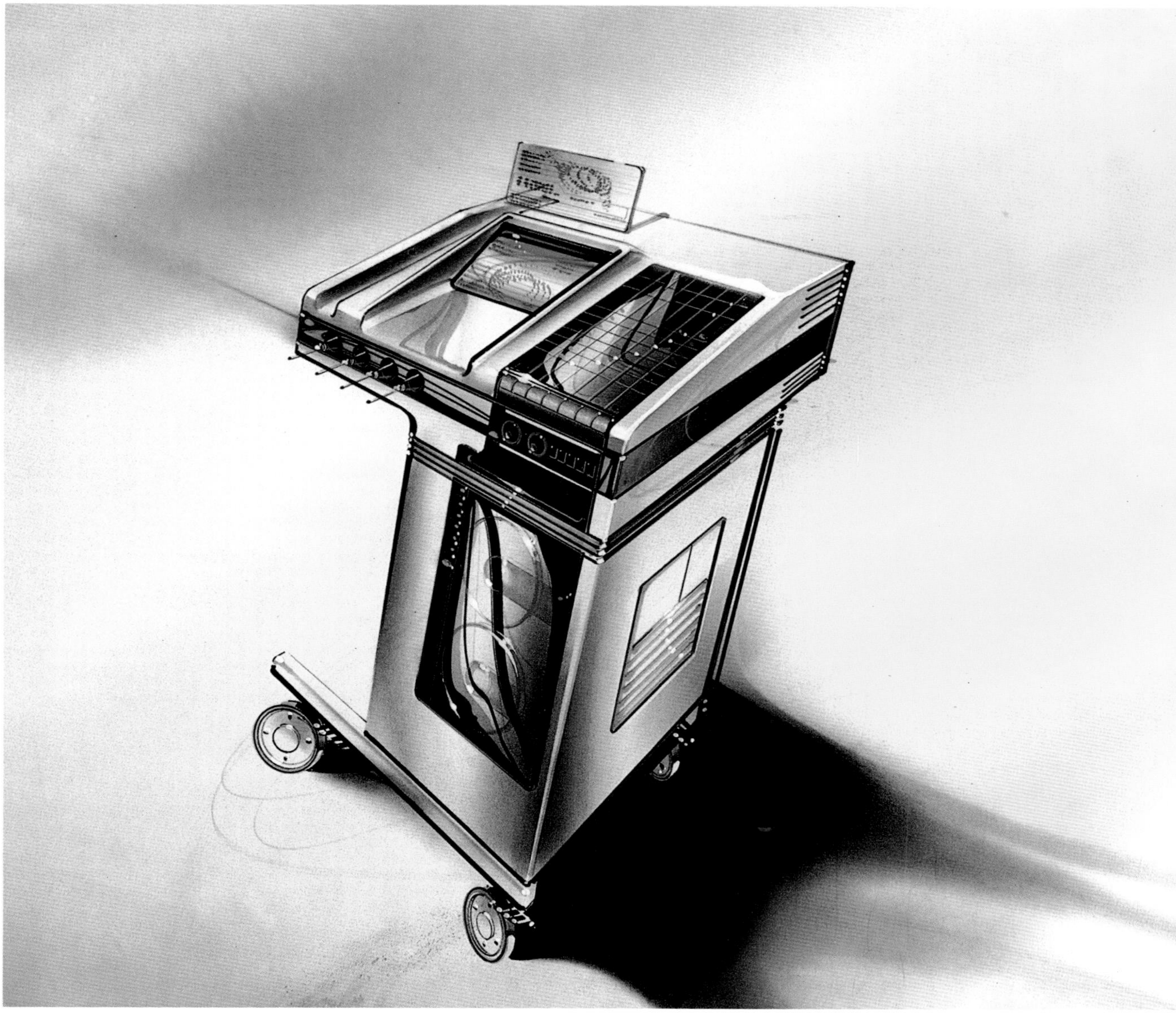

Comfort-zone concept
Media: Lacquer/water, dry marker, Prismacolor pencil, gouache, pastel chalk; 50 × 73 cm. Drawing time: 3 hr.

This concept was done for a client interested in image-projection technology and how it might be used in the home of the future. A high vantage point was used here to encompass the sweeping effect of the wraparound projection screen.

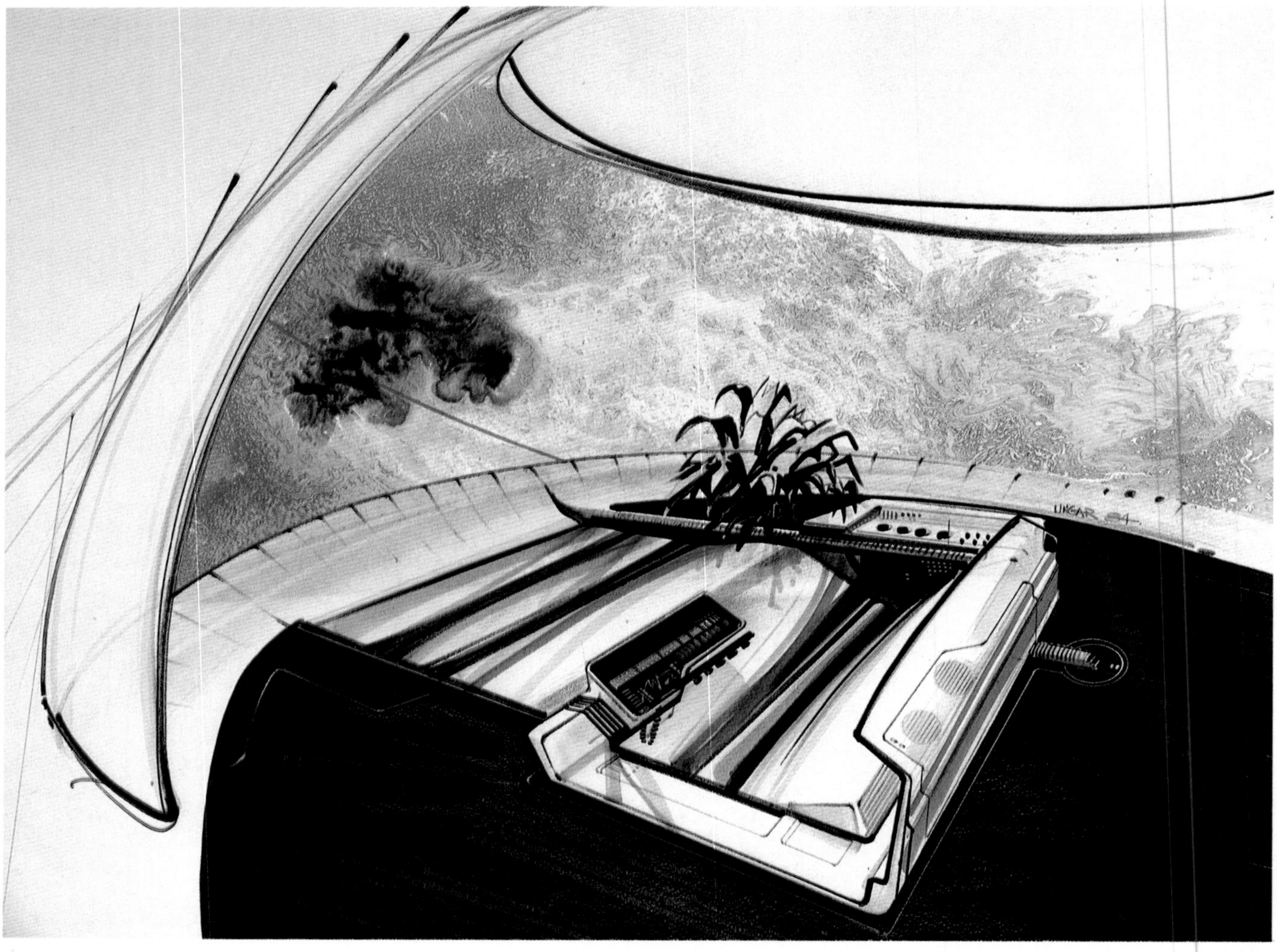

Ski-condo habitat
Media: dry marker, Prismacolor pencil, pastel chalk, fluorescent paint, gouache, photo montage; 50 × 70 cm. Drawing time: 3½ hr.

Current and future television technology is displayed within a playful living space. Rendering the concept on colored paper created a warm middle-tone. Texture plates used under the paper created the carpet effect.

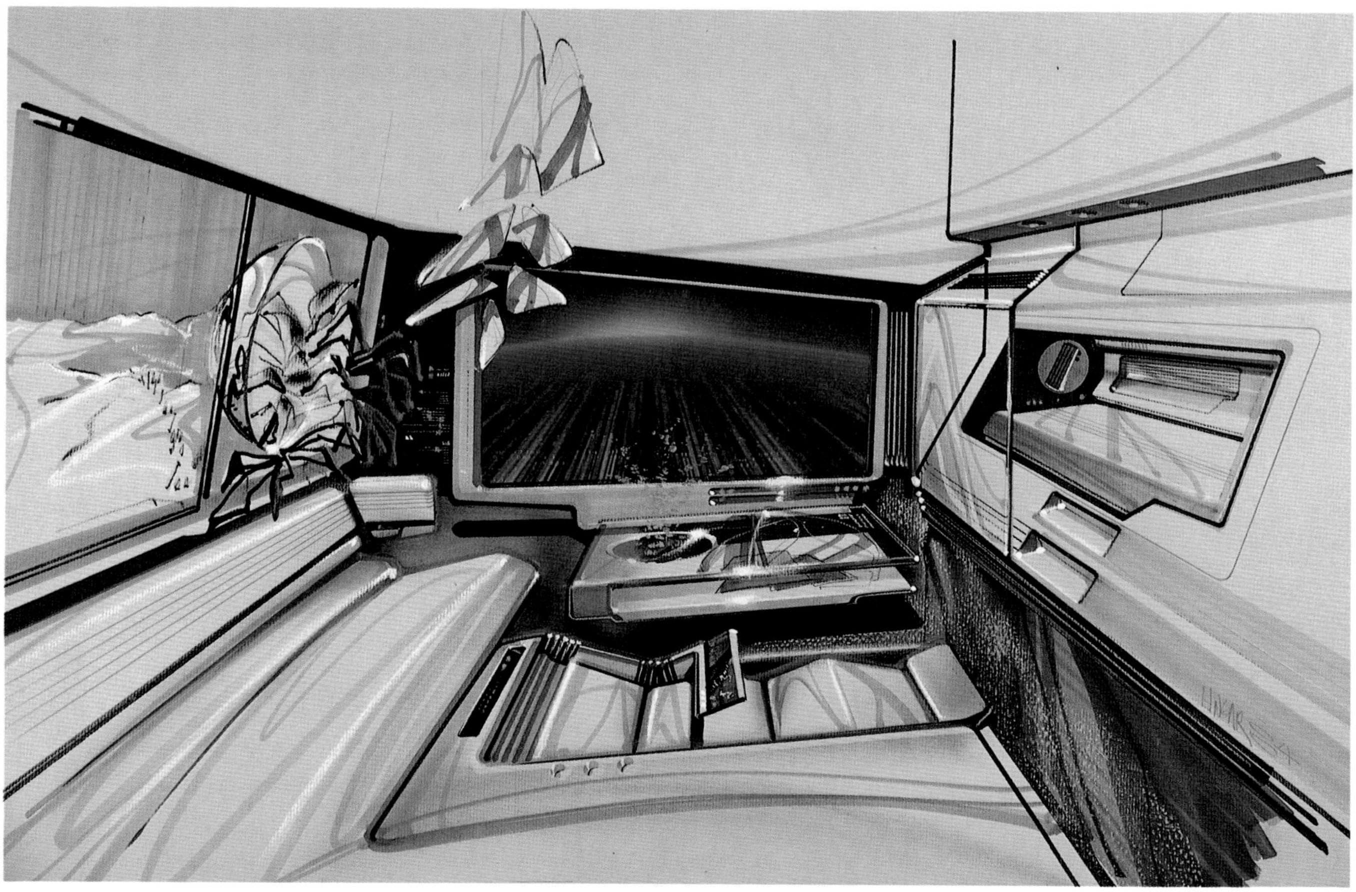

Executive medical-diagnostic station
Media: Luma watercolor, dry marker, pastel chalk, Prismacolor pencil, fluorescent paint; 50 × 70 cm. Drawing time: 3 hr.

This office equipment was rendered in warm dry-marker tones and then gone over with a fine-tipped black pen to achieve a wood grain effect. The hot colors on the displays draw attention to the hidden computer technology in the executive desk.

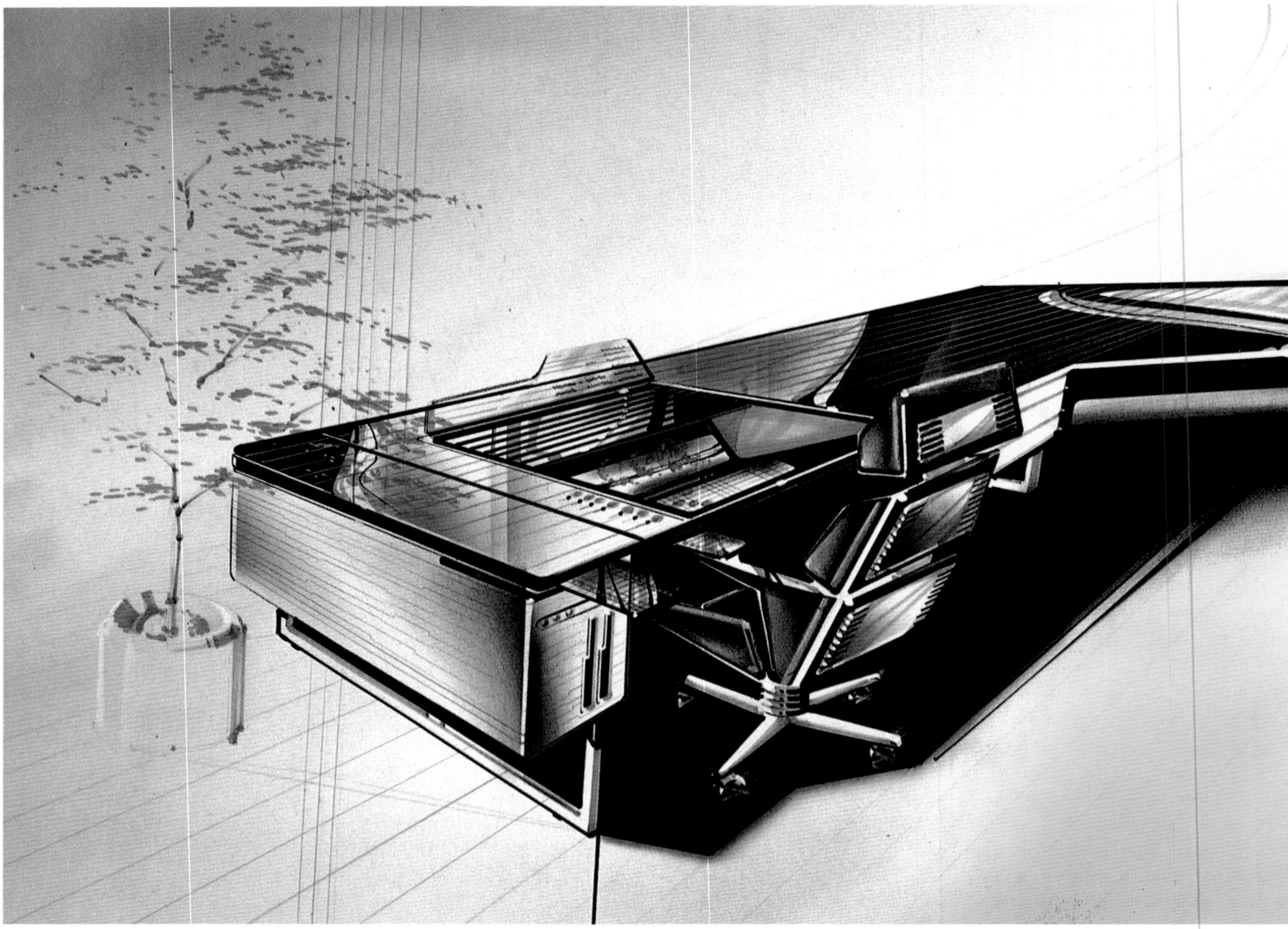

Advanced diagnostic environment
Media: Luma watercolor, pastel chalk, Prismacolor pencil, gouache, dry marker, fluorescent paint; 50 × 70 cm. Drawing time: 4 hr.

A high vantage point was used to better visualize the overall environment that the concept deals with. This illustration expresses a scene of the future based, to a large extent, on technology available today.

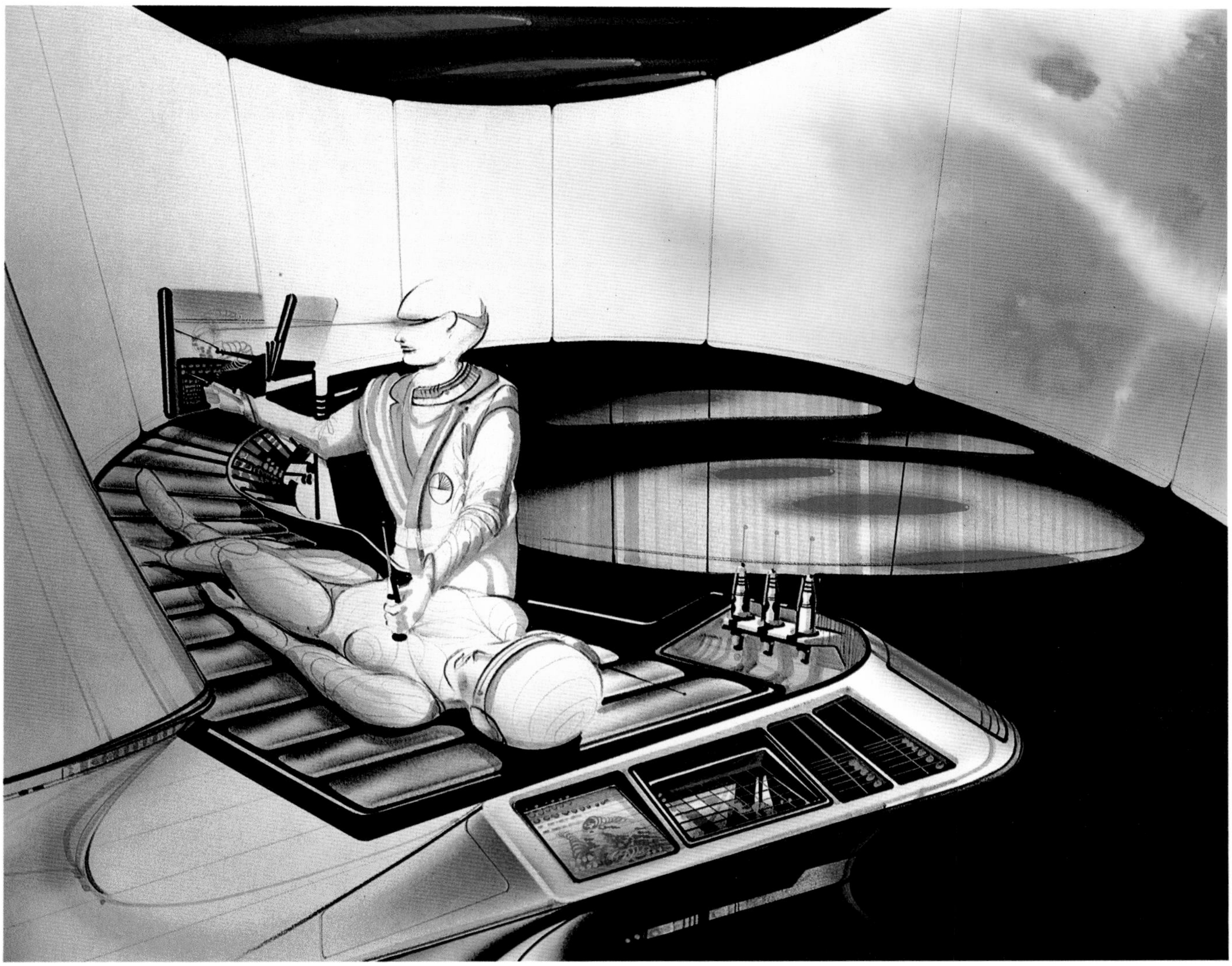

Medical monitor
Media: Luma watercolor, pastel chalk, dry marker, gouache, fluorescent paint; 50 × 70 cm. Drawing time: 3 hr.

An expression of future technology in computer medical-imaging, the concept was rendered directly onto the watercolor background. The imaging device was designed to be friendly, yet technically accurate; hence, warm colors were chosen. Fine brushes were used for expressing detail.

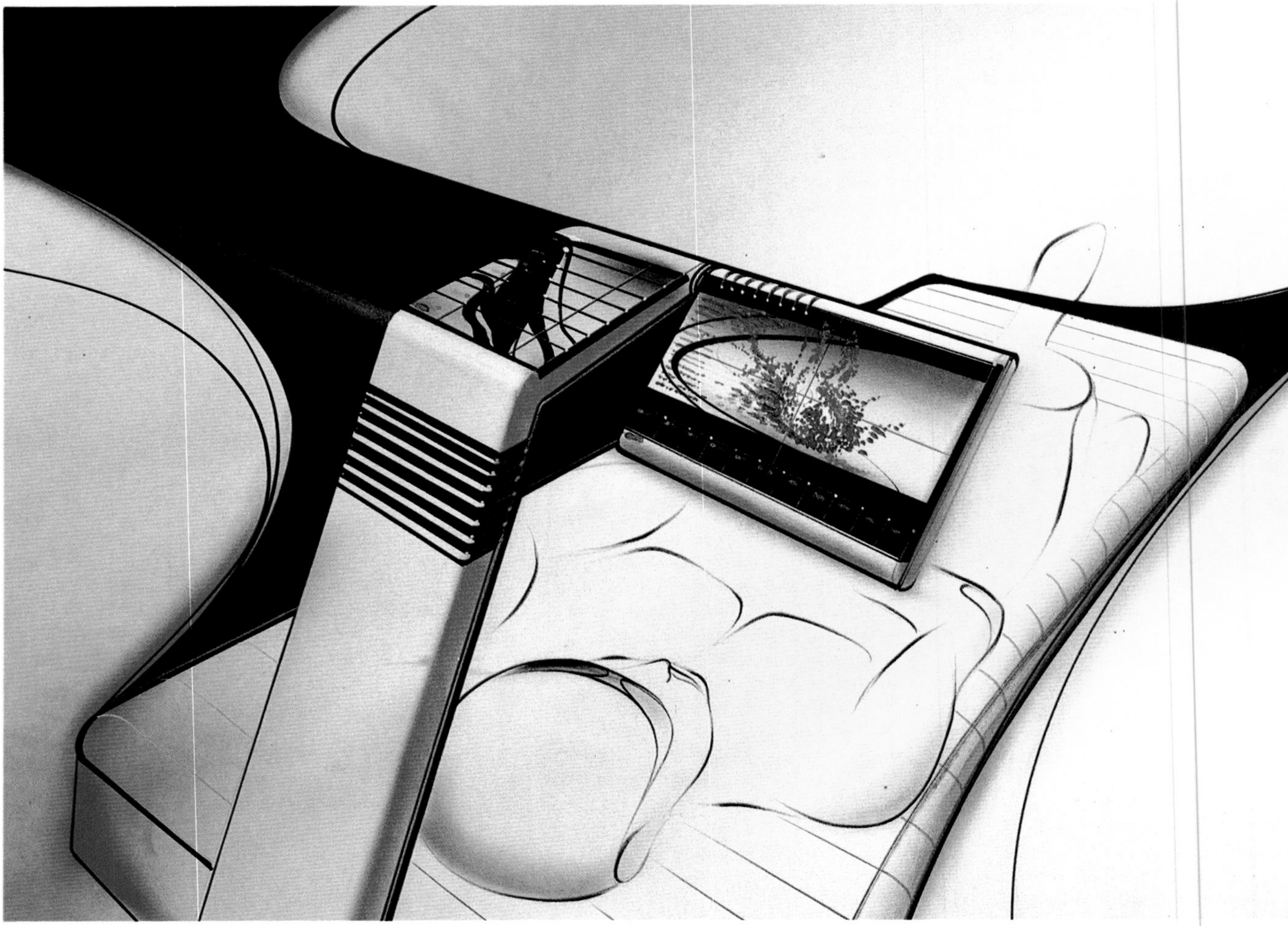

Advanced radiology reading room
Media: dry marker, black Prismacolor pencil, pastel chalk, gouache, fluorescent paint; 22 × 28 cm. Drawing time: 2 hr.

This radiology reading room has a normal viewpoint in an attempt to bring the viewer "into" the rendering. This is an important principle with interior concepts and is very effective.

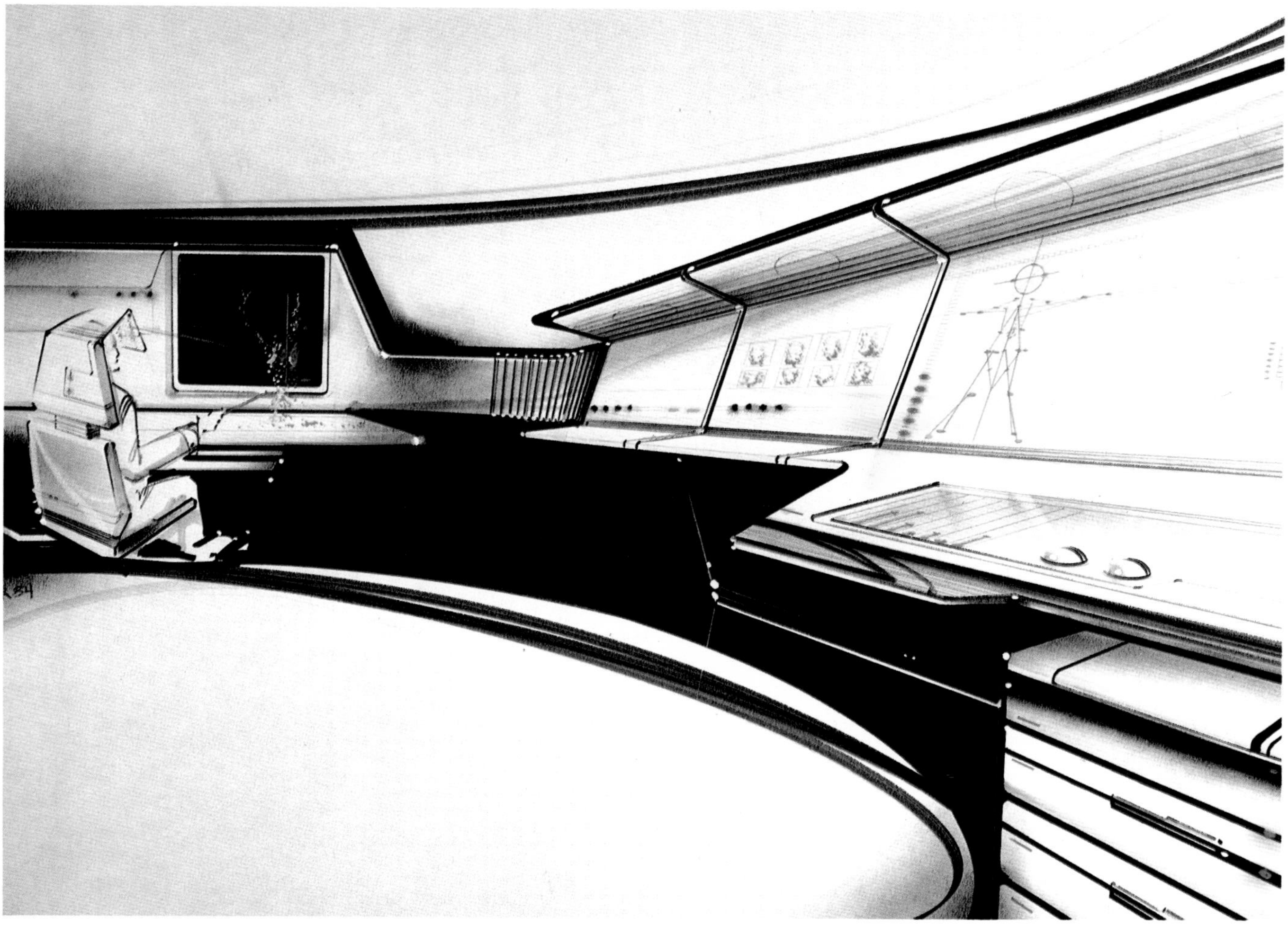

Deep-space habitat
Media: dry marker, gouache, pastel chalk, Prismacolor pencil, fluorescent paint, photo montage; 50 × 70 cm. Drawing time: 3½ hr.

Drawn as a sketch for a science-fiction novel, this habitat interior relies on a normal viewpoint to bring the viewer into the concept. Display technologies are done using fluorescent gouache and fine brushes.

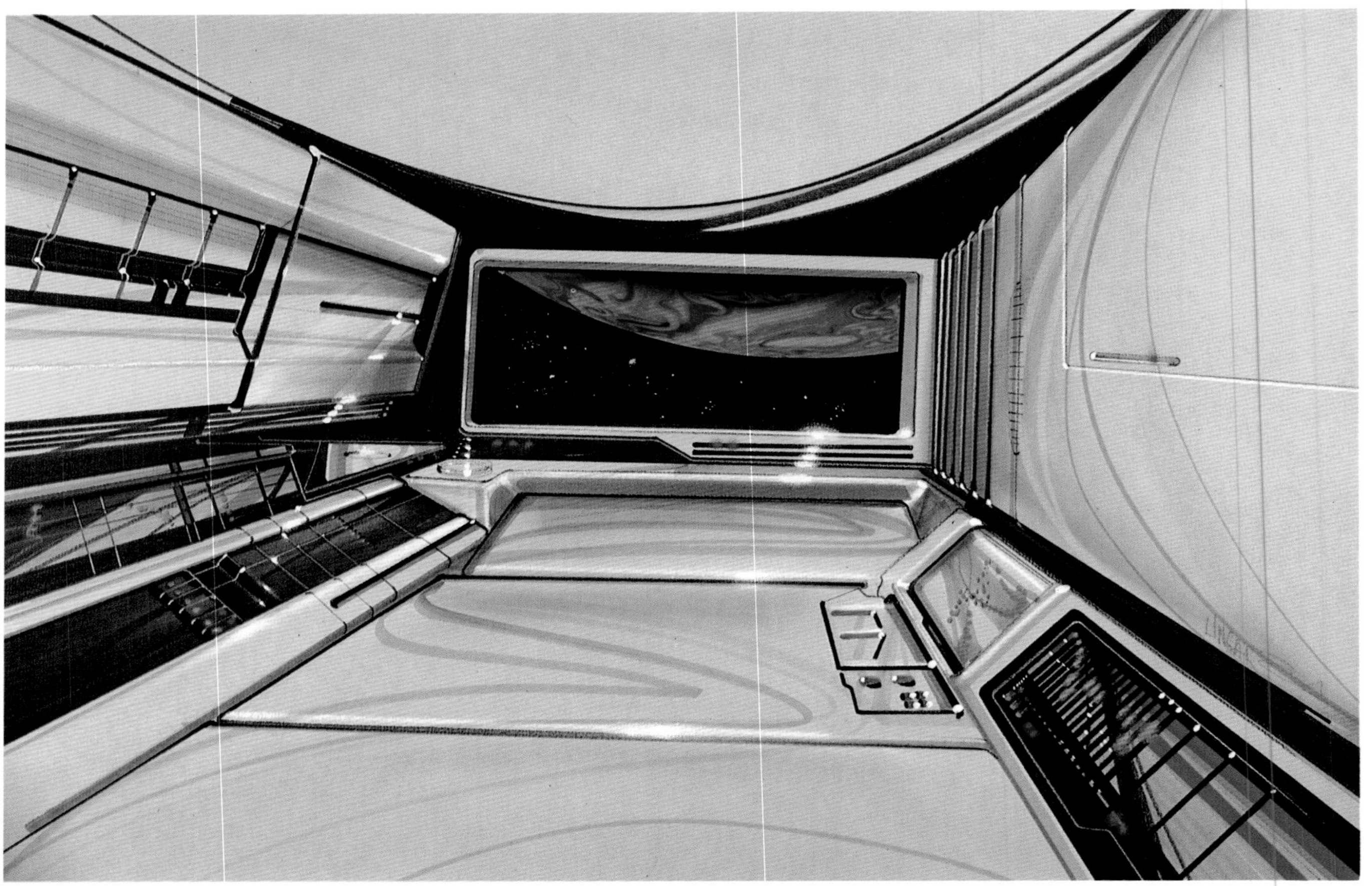

Advanced transportation control-bridge
Media: lacquer/water, dry marker, Prismacolor pencil, gouache , pastel chalk, fluorescent paint; 50 × 70 cm. Drawing time: 4½ hr.

This transportation interior provides a glance at future entertainment and display technologies that may be available when cars are externally driven and controlled by highway computerized monitors. The rendering was first done on dry-marker paper. The concept was then cut out and placed onto a lacquer/water background done separately. A low vantage point allows the viewer to visually be a passenger in the car.

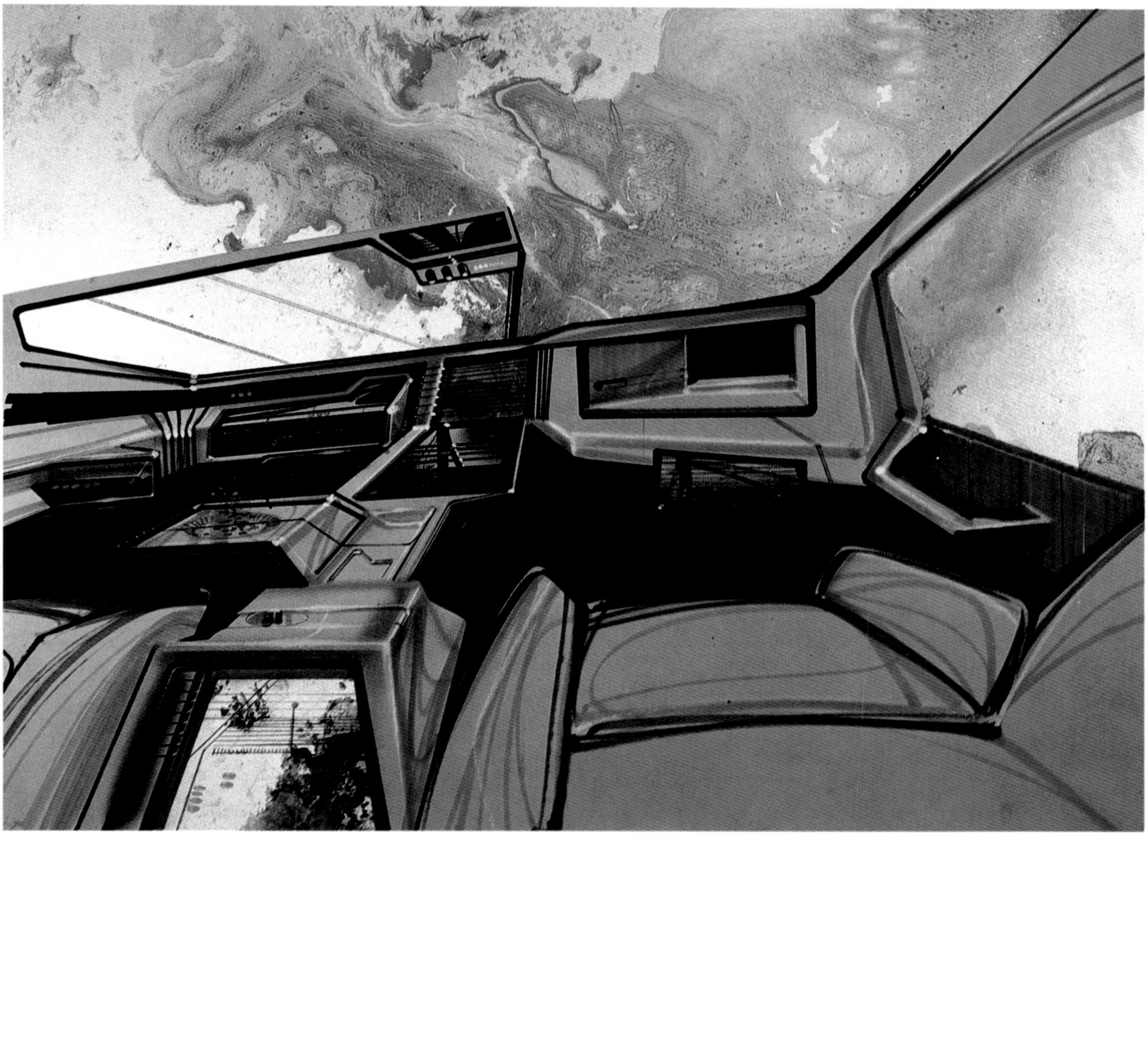

Advanced auto concept
Media: pastel chalk, Winsor & Newton jet black, white gouache, fluorescent paint; 36 × 43 cm. Drawing time: 2 hr.

Using the black-on-black principles discussed in Chapter 5 dramatizes the illustration, and with the careful placement of pastel chalk, the entire concept becomes visually exciting. I merely hinted at displays in the interior so that emphasis would be placed on the exterior form of the car.

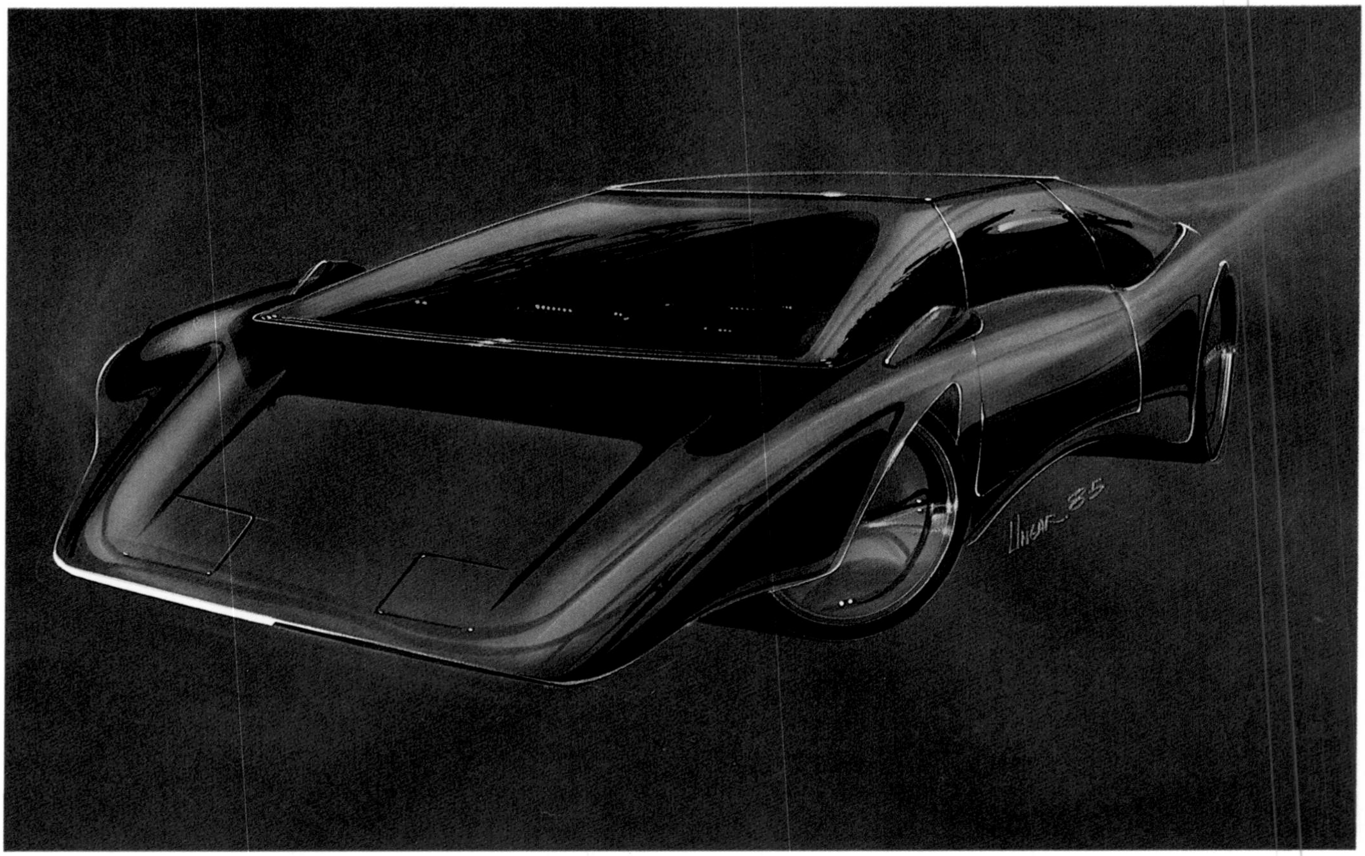

8 SPECIAL RENDERING TECHNIQUES

Subjects that have unique visual characteristics tend to require special attention within a given rendering. These can include such things as reflections on chrome and glass, textural effects like leather grain, glowing electronic displays, and hi-tech computer keyboards. All of these characteristics are treated differently, but effectively, using mixed-media rendering techniques.

In this chapter, I will explain the ease with which these special characteristics can be illustrated. The principles are simple and really only require an attention to detail. The first step is to observe how some of these objects appear to us in their natural environments. Try to see exactly how, for instance, a reflection is seen by your eyes. What makes it read as a reflection? Observe natural highlights and how light plays across a flat or curved shiny surface. It's all there.

A wide variety of materials is depicted in this ski habitat. The transparent glass window at the left reveals the scene outside, while other objects show the reflective qualities of glass and plastic. The large projection display was created by pasting a photo image on the colored-paper background and rendering the surrounding structure in gray markers and black Prismacolor pencil. Texture was added to the carpet areas by using gray Prismacolor pencil and a Mold-Tech plate. Display lights and nuances were added with fluorescent gouache. (See color picture on page 137.)

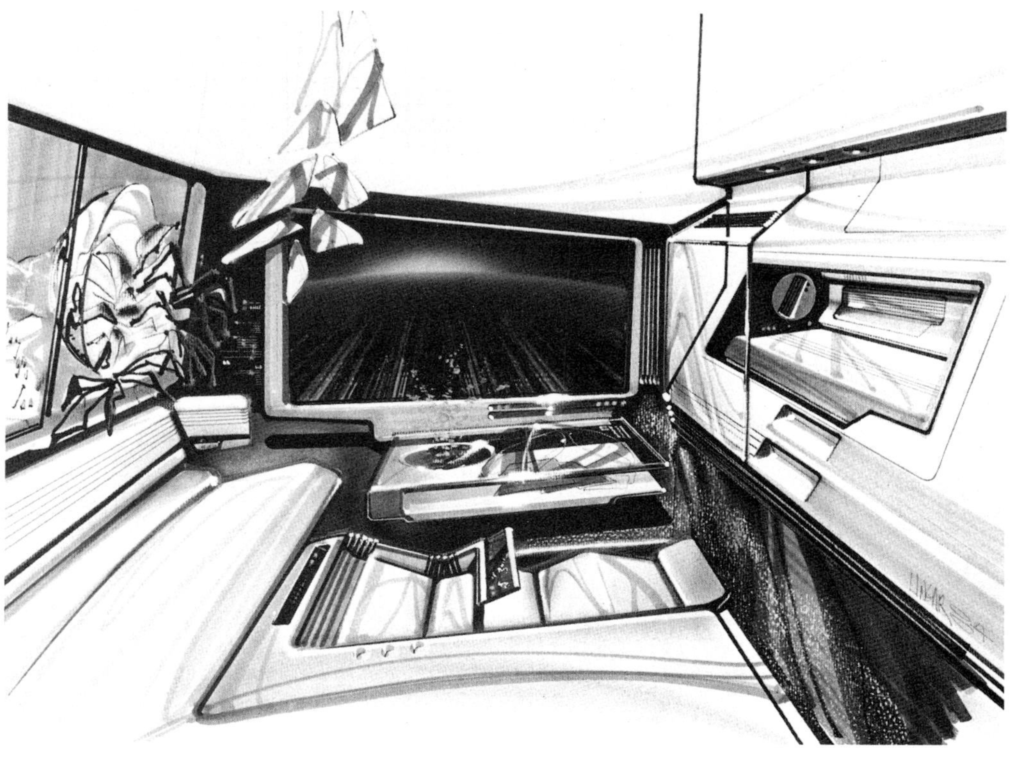

For this holographic digitizing pad, I used dry marker on the reverse side of the paper in order to create subdued reflections on the front. This is basically a working sketch, although, even here, it is important to show graphic strength and confidence.

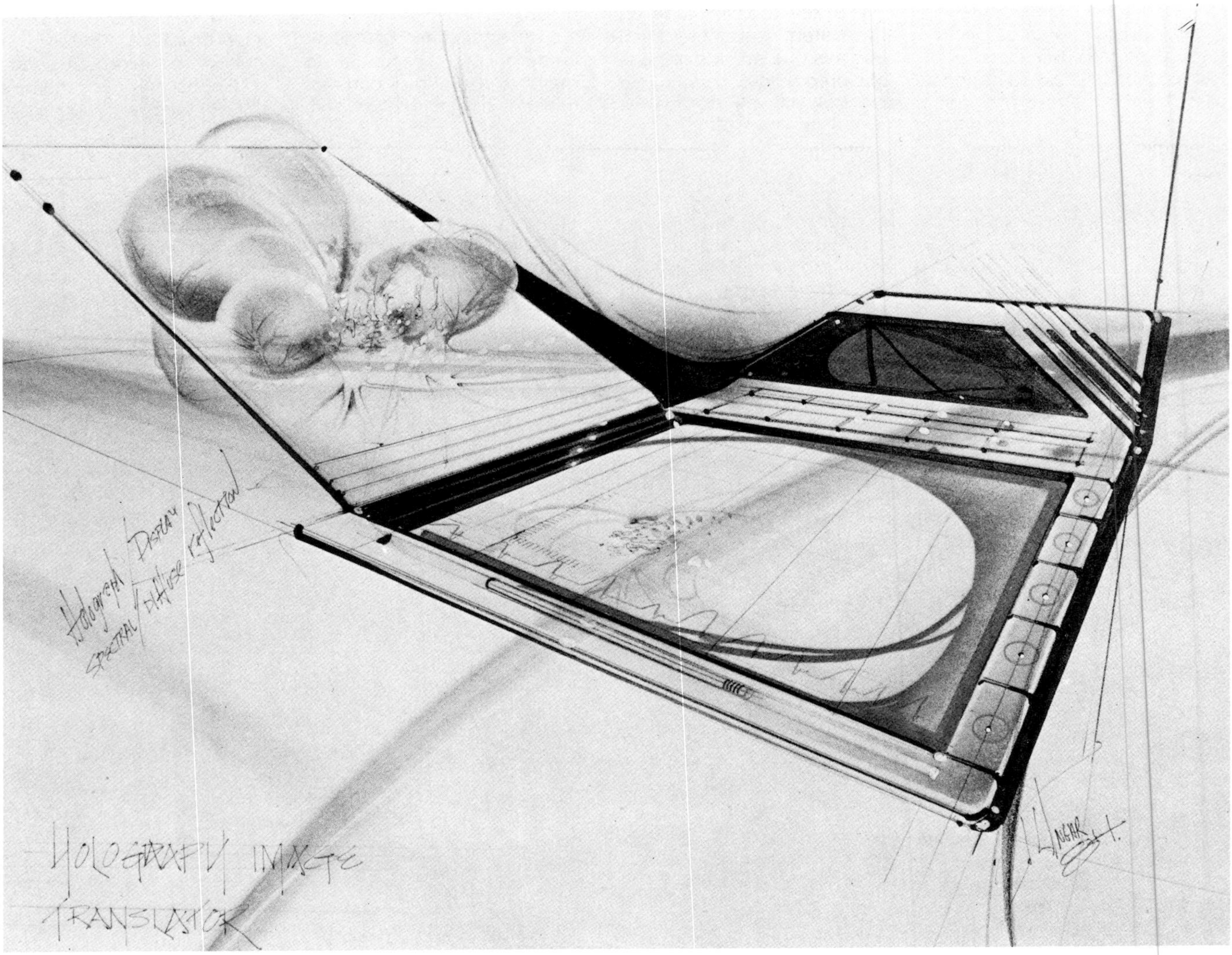

Reflections on Glass, Plastic, and Chrome

Unlike matte surfaces, which reflect light in a soft, diffused way, glossy surfaces yield sharp, brightly defined reflections that are called "spectral." Although surfaces on highly polished glass, metal, ceramic, or similar materials are capable of reflecting precise mirrorlike images, most often these images appear as light and dark areas of reflection. You can illustrate these reflections by stressing the extreme contrast between the sharply defined light areas and dark areas.

The key to reflections on transparent surfaces, such as glass windshields or plastic stereo dust-covers, is that the dark reflections allow us to peer through the glass or plastic into the interior of the product, while the brilliant highlight reflections prevent us from seeing through the material clearly. The interior of the product, therefore, will be represented with very light tones in the semi-opaque highlight areas and very dark tones in the dark, transparent areas.

In illustrating reflections on chrome, it is essential to maintain the abrupt contrast between dark and light areas. Dark areas will be rendered in rich black, and light areas will be rendered in gradated tones of blue or gray fading to pure white. On convex objects, such as hubcaps, viewed out of doors, the classical palette is Prussian blue or an intense gray for the topmost areas of the object, reflecting the sky color, and an earth tone for the bottom or downward areas of the object, reflecting the ground color.

Reflections on complex shapes can really only be approximated. I suggest keeping a photographic file of highly reflective objects. This can be referred to as a resource when rendering unusual reflective surfaces. Photos of highly polished showroom autos can provide a myriad of studies in spectral reflection.

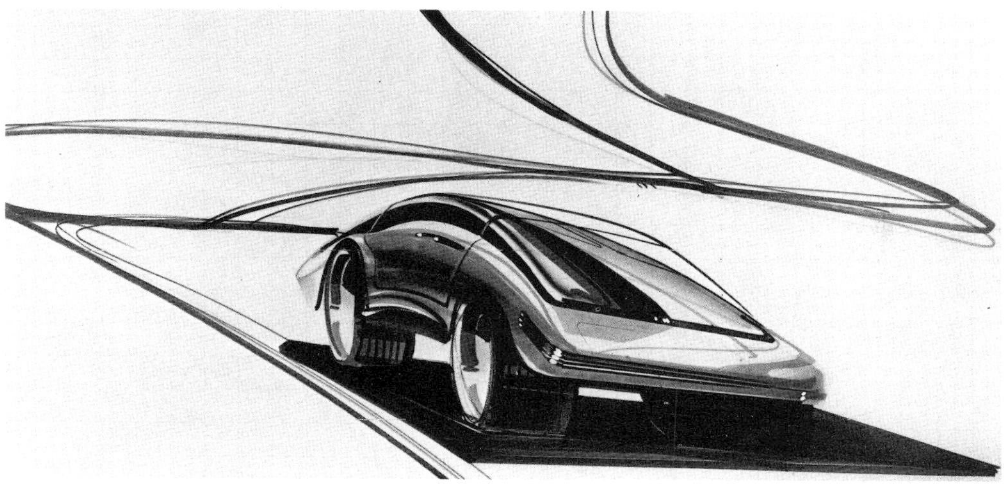

This automobile reads as extremely glossy because the blended pastel chalk used as the reflected light on the glass window contrasts so strongly with the dark reflections. Adjustments in this illusion of reflectivity can be made by reducing the contrast betwen the light and dark tones.

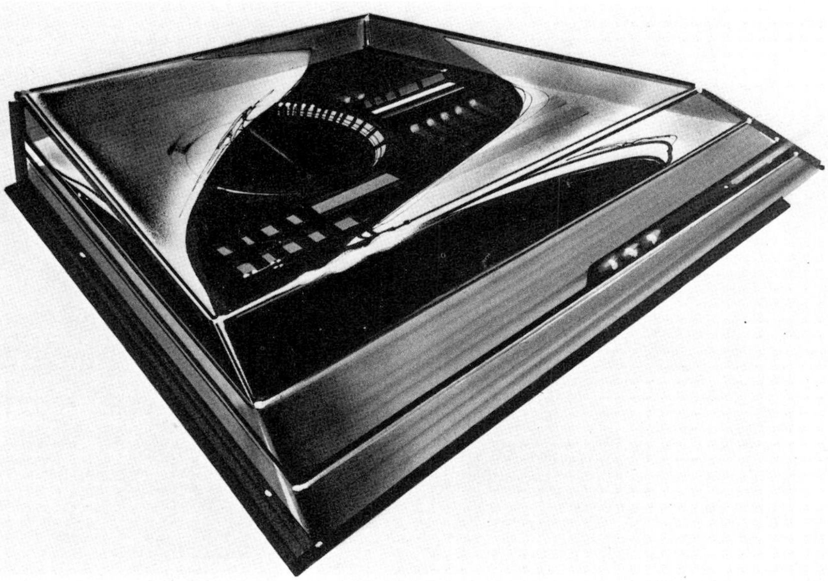

The plastic dust-cover on this stereo shows how you can see into the dark-toned reflective areas, while the light-toned areas remain opaque.

This medical-imaging cart shows a highly reflective monitor and surface. You should render dark areas of reflection as sharply as possible.

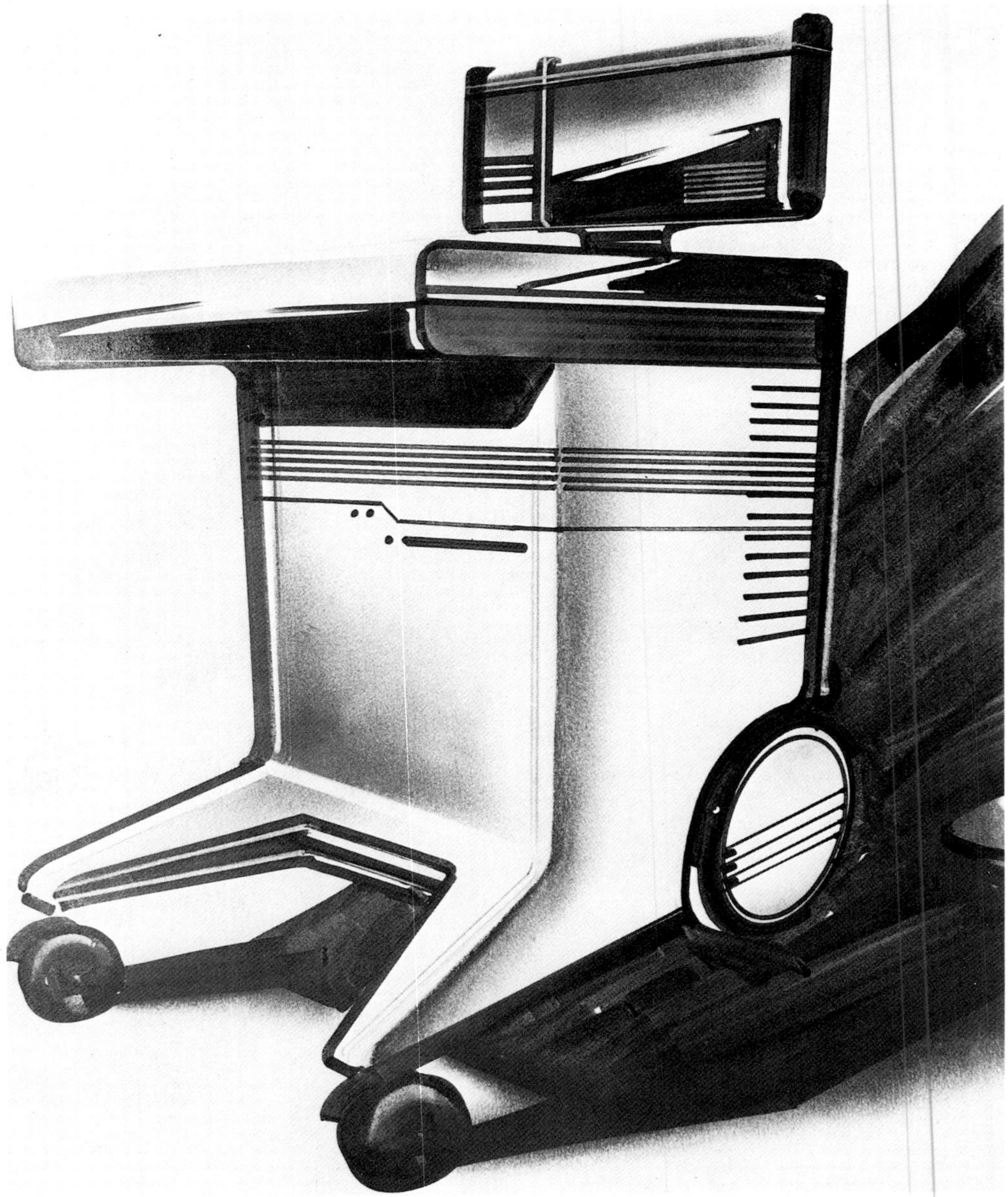

The ability of chrome to reflect mirror images is apparent in this hubcap. Blended pastel chalk used as the sky tone contrasts with the very intense foreground reflection rendered as black. On cylindrical rather than spherical shapes, the black areas are stretched or elongated, providing linear areas of black.

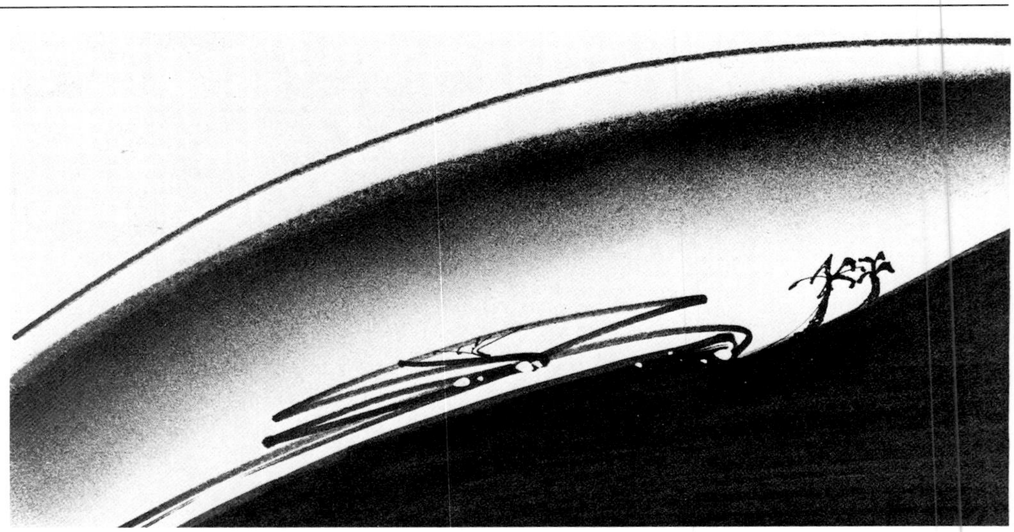

Demonstration:
Rendering chrome

A basic layout of the chrome faucet was first drawn on dry-marker paper. Then a black dry marker was used to render the dark reflections. To obtain the smoothest blending of marker strokes, leave the paper on the marker pad. If the reflections become too sharp for the dry marker, you can finish them off with a Sharpie black pen and then finally a Prismacolor black pencil.

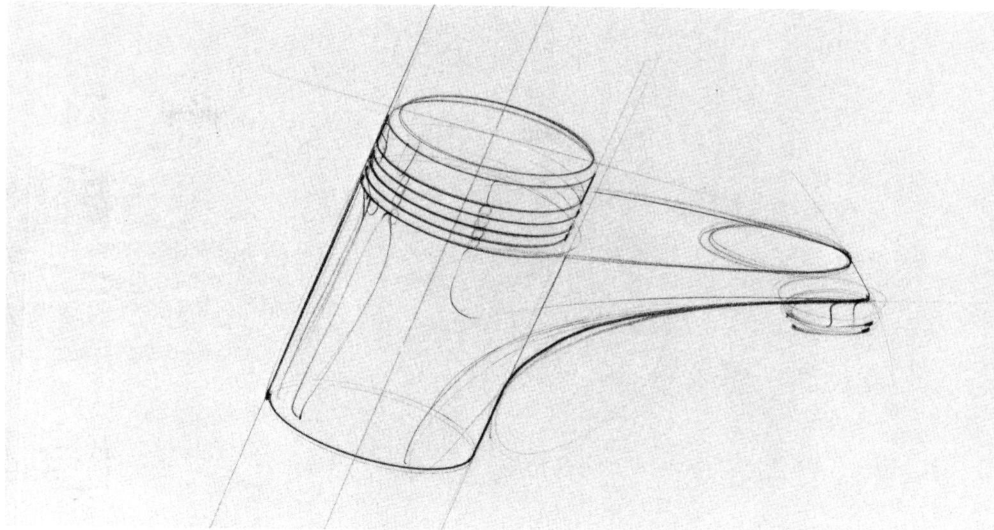

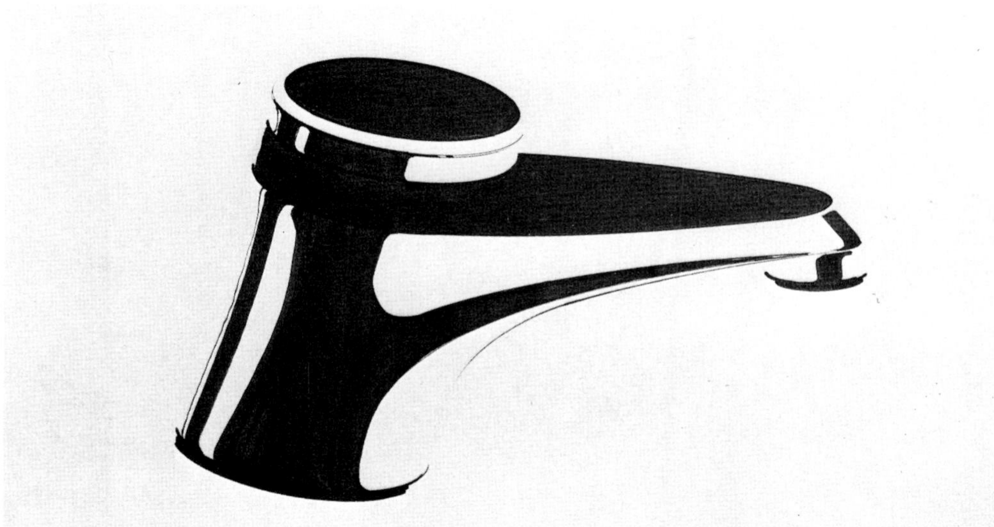

The final illustration adds blended pastel chalk as a gradated tone and a few touches of white gouache for the highlights. Removing some chalk with a sharp eraser can provide realistic nuances to the light tones.

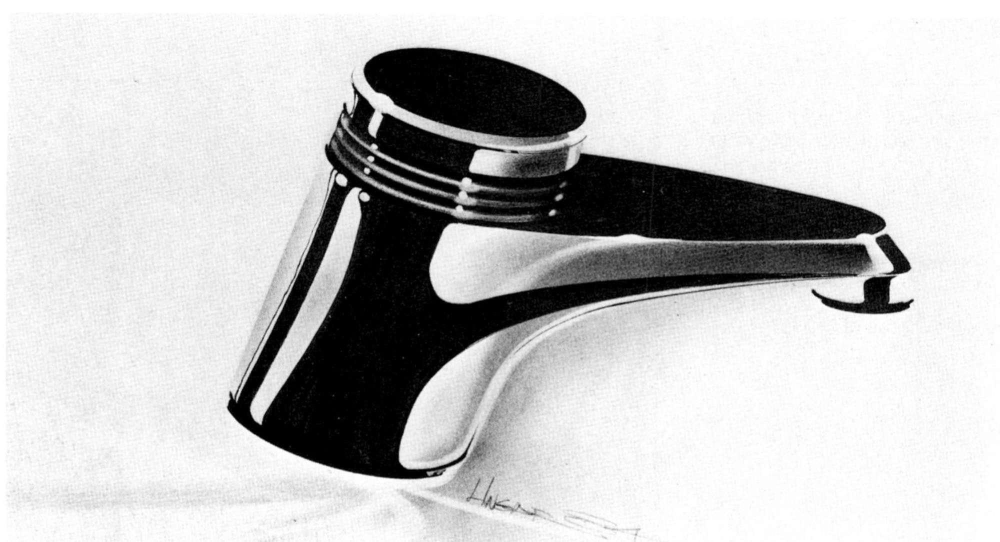

Textures

A very effective method for generating textures is to use Prismacolor pencils and various papers with Mold-Tech texture plates by Standex Company. Apply a blunt Prismacolor pencil to thin marker pad paper, with a texture plate placed underneath. Texture plates are especially effective when used with black and darker colored papers. Black papers require jet-black gouache added for the dark shade areas, and lighter Prismacolor pencil for the textural highlights.

This Mold-Tech texture plate effectively produces various textures. Place the texture plate under your drawing and rub a Prismacolor pencil of the selected color over the drawing's surface. Rubbing the pencil firmly will produce the desired effect if the paper is thin enough.

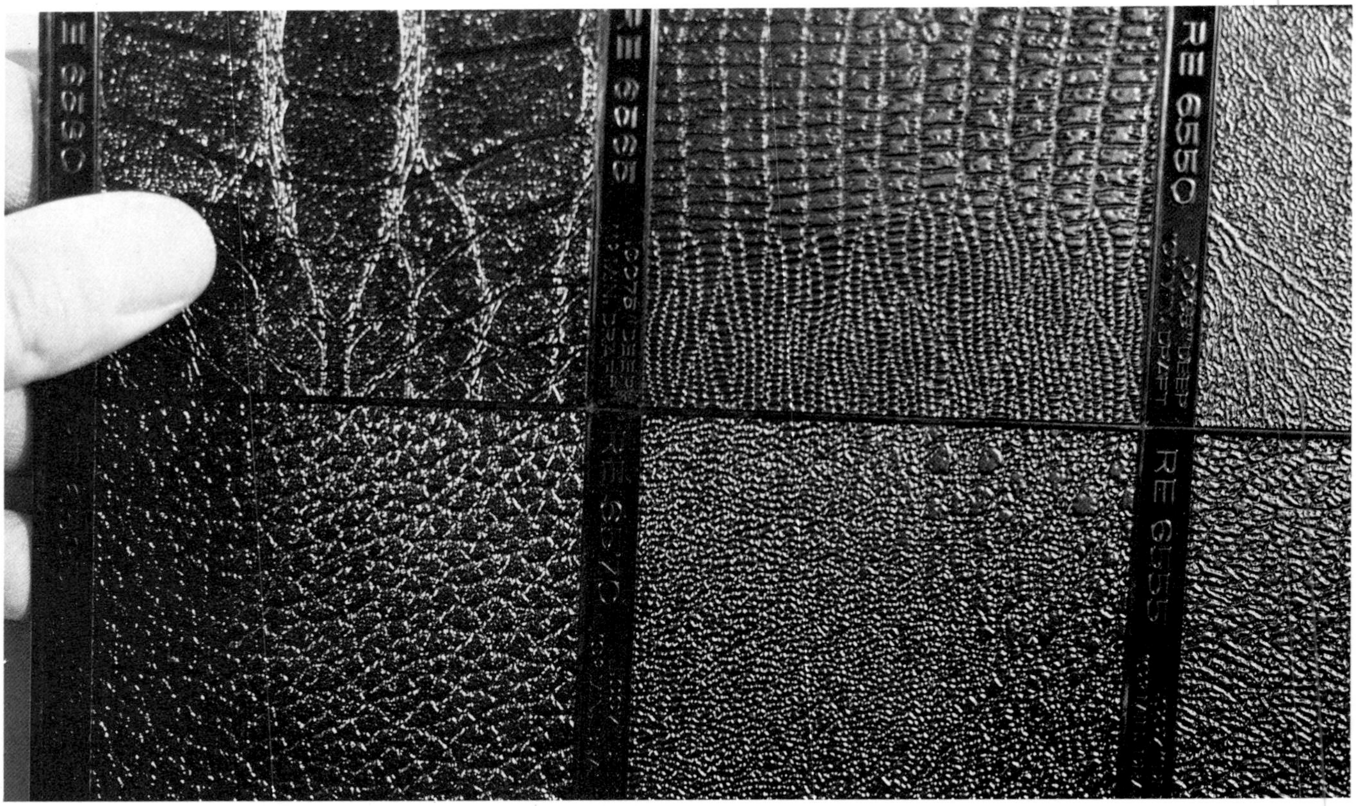

I used black dry marker and gray pastel for the basic rendering of this coffeepot. For the top, I used white and silver Prismacolor pencils rubbed over a Mold-Tech texture sample. Hard-shell briefcases can work as well.

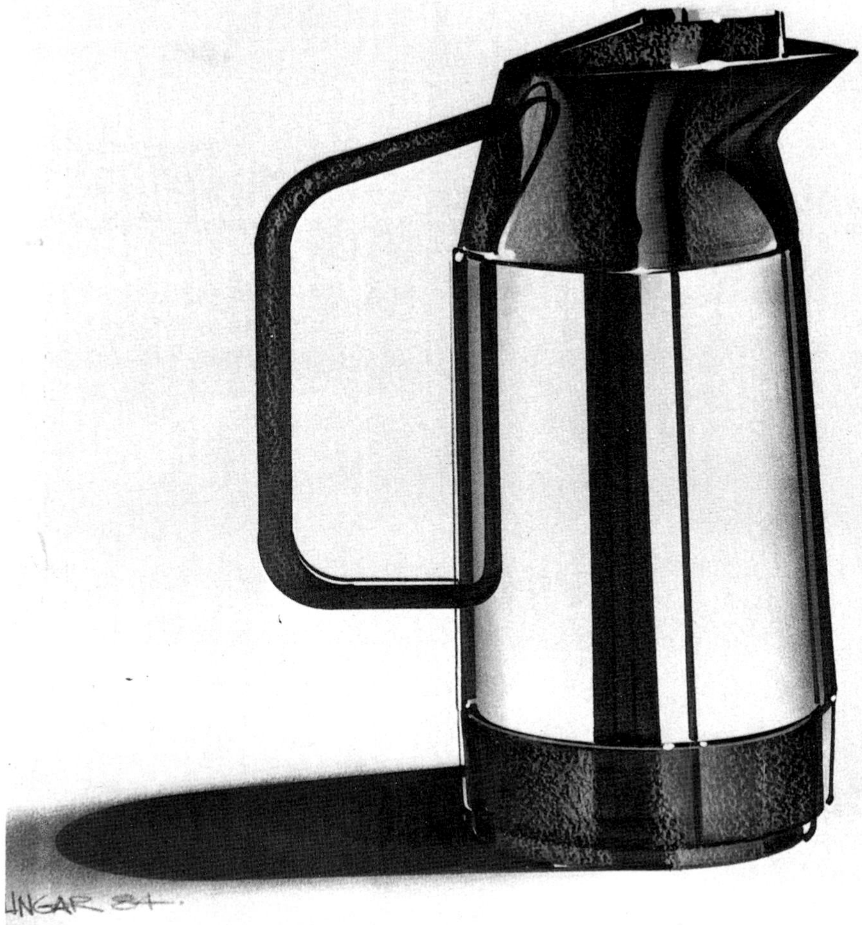

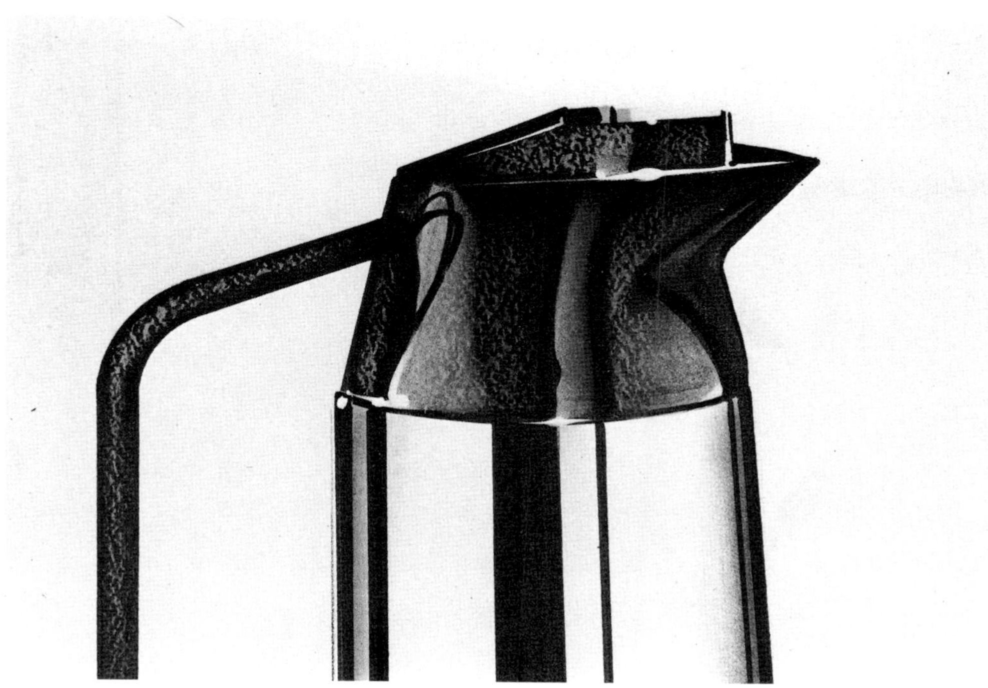

By moving a 2×2-inch texture sample around underneath the paper, I rubbed texture over a large area with black Prismacolor pencil. Note how the absence of texture has been used to create highlight areas on this men's fashion purse. When drawing from your imagination, you will find it helpful to refer to actual examples of textured objects or photographs of such textures.

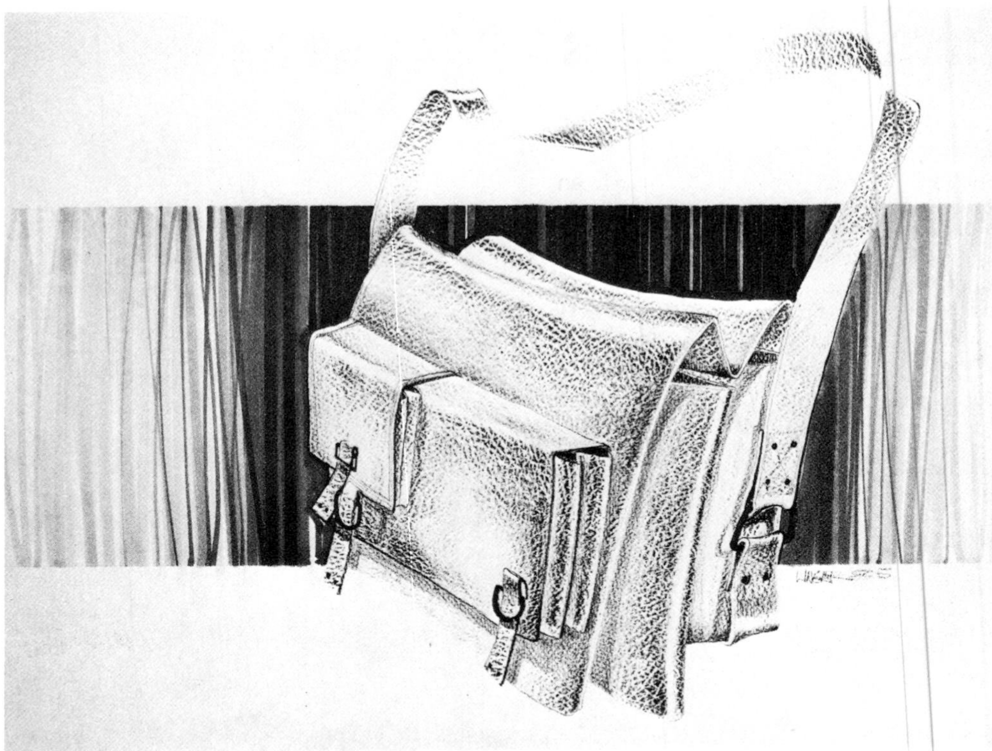

This ladies' shoe was drawn on black Canson paper with white Prismacolor pencil. After the shoe design was complete and all modifications were made, I rubbed on the texture using a texture plate.

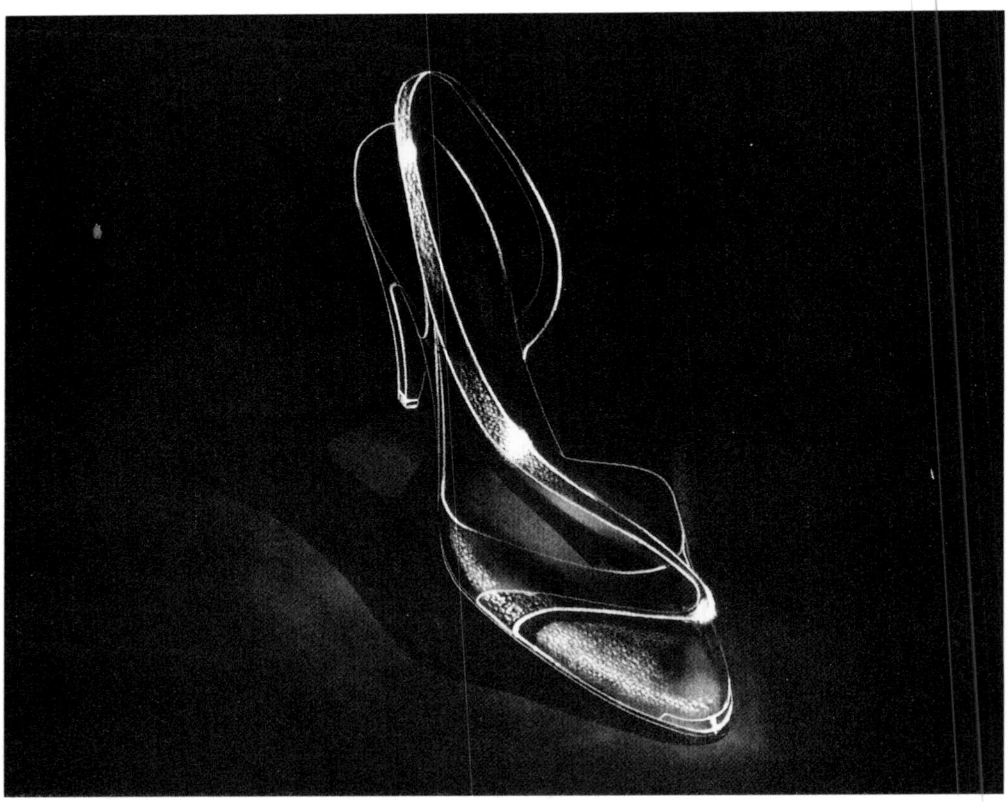

Electronic Displays

Design concepts that suggest electronic technology can be rendered with any of the techniques we have previously examined. With the addition of fluorescent gouache or poster paint, such as Liquitex, the display areas can come alive. (See color pictures on pages 107, 109, and 110.)

These water-based pigments can uniquely approximate glowing display colors, from cathode-ray tubes (CRTs) to dashboard light-emitting diodes (LEDs). Blending the appropriately colored pastel chalk over dots of fluorescent paint can add a fuzzy or glowing aspect to LEDs. Lines of text on a CRT can be approximated by painting the edge of your 30°–60° triangle with green or orange fluorescent paint, and then repeatedly touching your paper with it. The edge of thin cardboard will work also.

The reflective quality of electronic displays can vary depending on the materials they are made from and the technology that they support. This personal computer uses ultra-thin areas for the display and for the control keyboard. For effect, I rendered the two surfaces as if they were highly reflective, although they may not be so in the actual product.

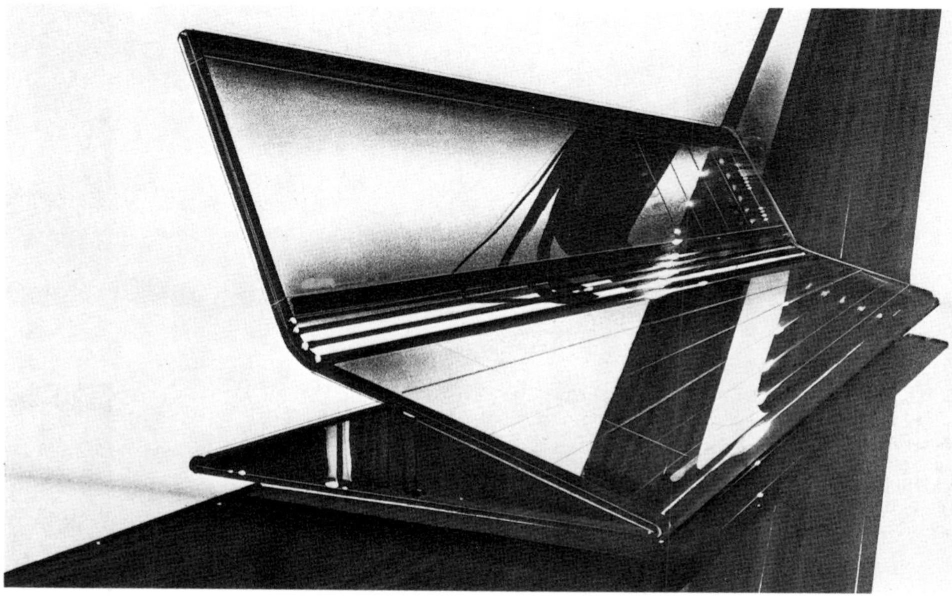

Because this electronic display was based on a semi-transparent technology, I rendered the background through the device. The warm-gray pastel chalk that is blended through the display area helps create the illusion of a non-glare surface.

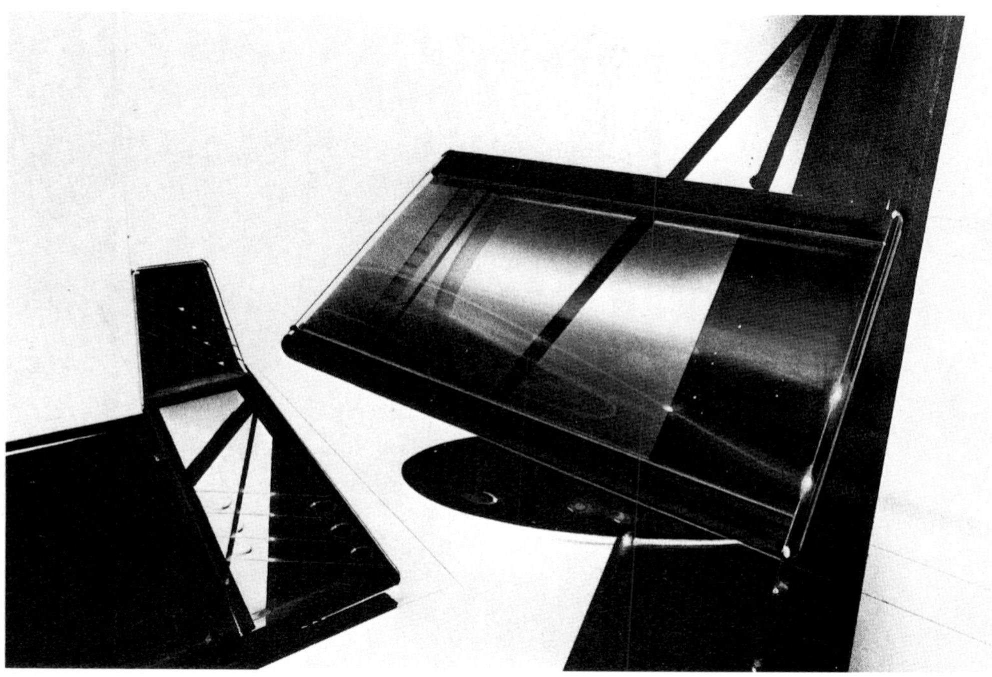

I rendered this particular desktop computer with a somewhat subdued display, using only gray pastel chalk as a diagonal reflection across the area. Prismacolor pencil was used for the graphics.

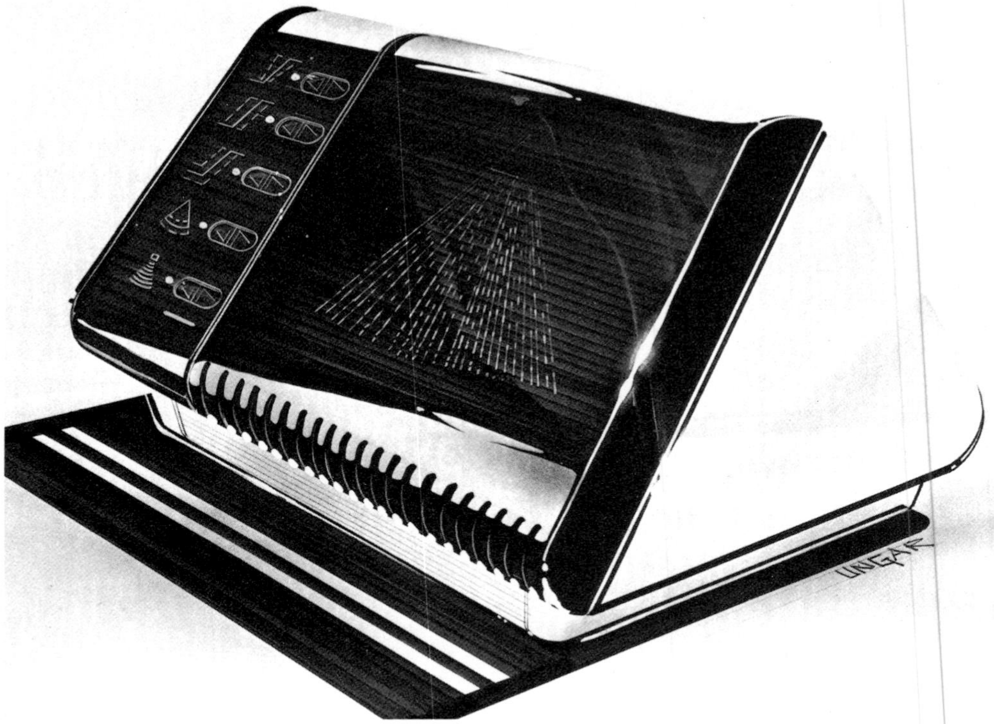

Using both sides of a paper such as Ogilvie Press vellum makes subdued reflections easy to render. Here, dry markers applied in the area of the display were drawn on the reverse side, and hence are automatically muted.

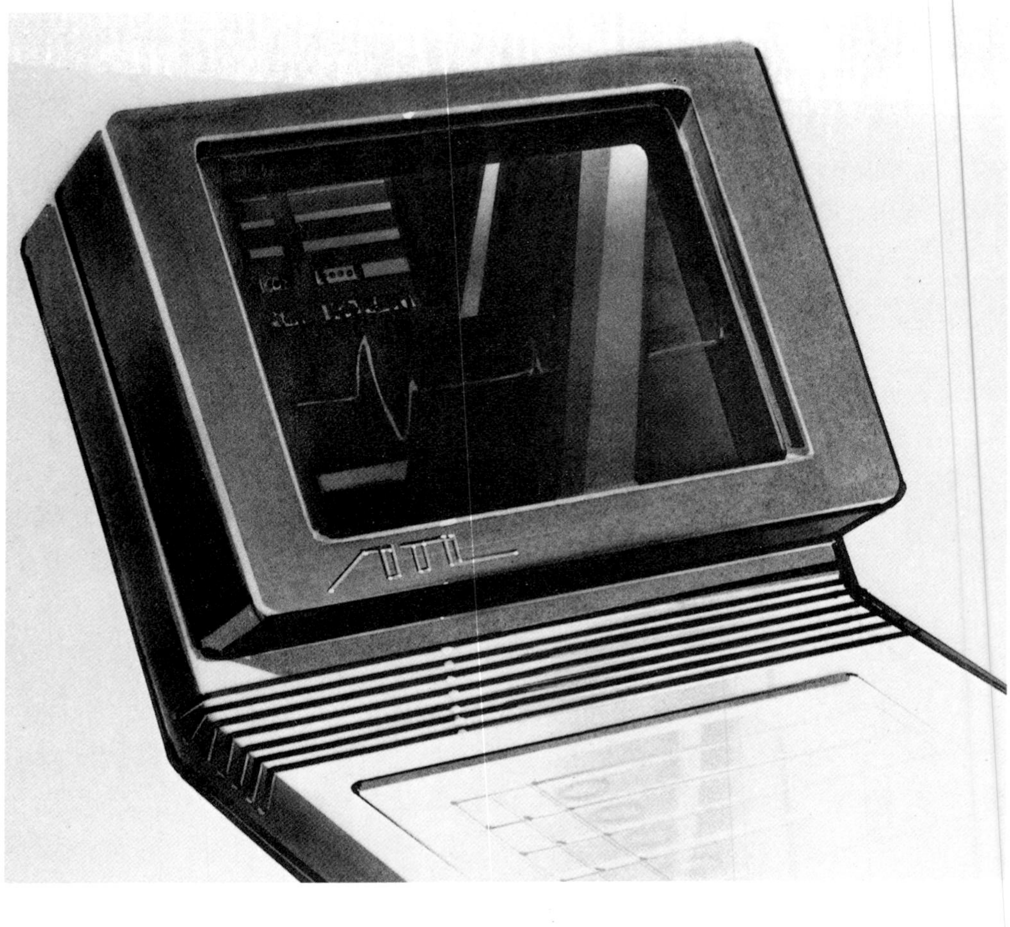

Computer Keyboards

Instead of trying to illustrate the multitude of keys on a keyboard, it is best to render only those that fall in the greatest area of focus. The rest can be suggested by weighted line work only. If the keyboard is a flat panel display type, then render it as though it were a glass panel, with straight reflections. Warm-gray and black dry markers are good for this, with display lights in fluorescent paints.

Demonstration: Flat electronic keyboards
This sequence develops a flat data-entry keyboard that is somewhat reflective. First, you should render the outlines of the panel in dark Prismacolor pencil; then, using dry marker, develop black reflections and a few light-gray reflections. Use a Webril pad to blend warm-gray pastel chalk around the edges of the panel. This will serve as a gradated tone blending from light to dark. Finally, draw in the keytop areas, using silver Prismacolor pencil over the black areas and black pencil or ink over the light areas. A few gouache highlights will finish it up.

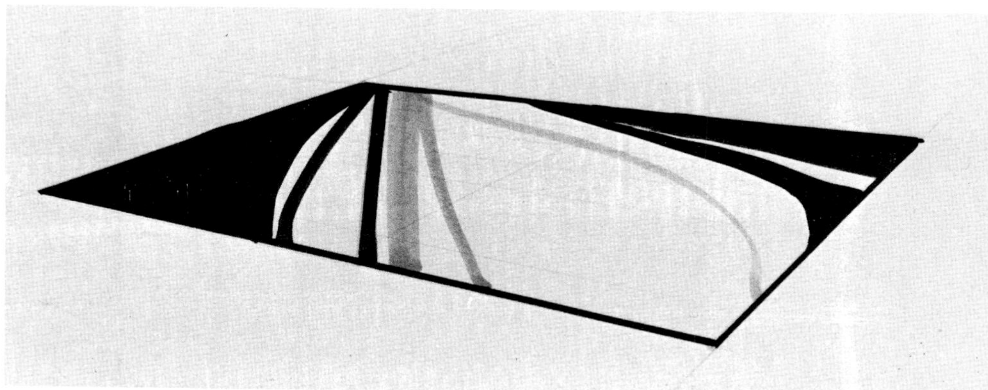

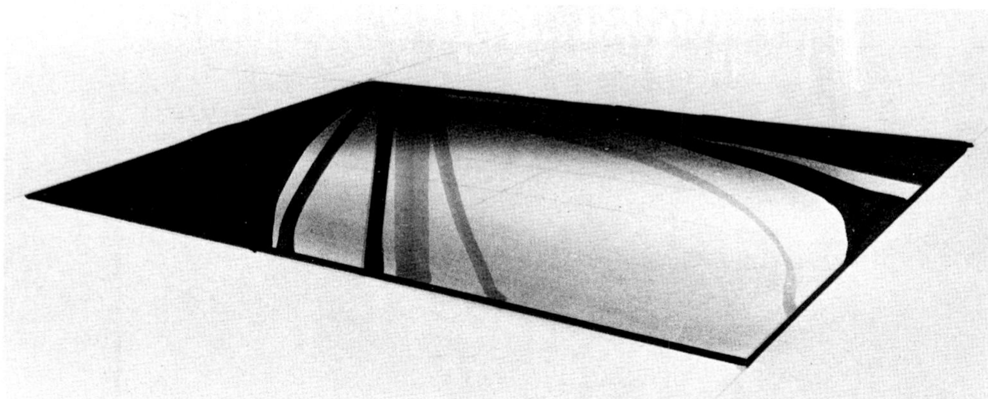

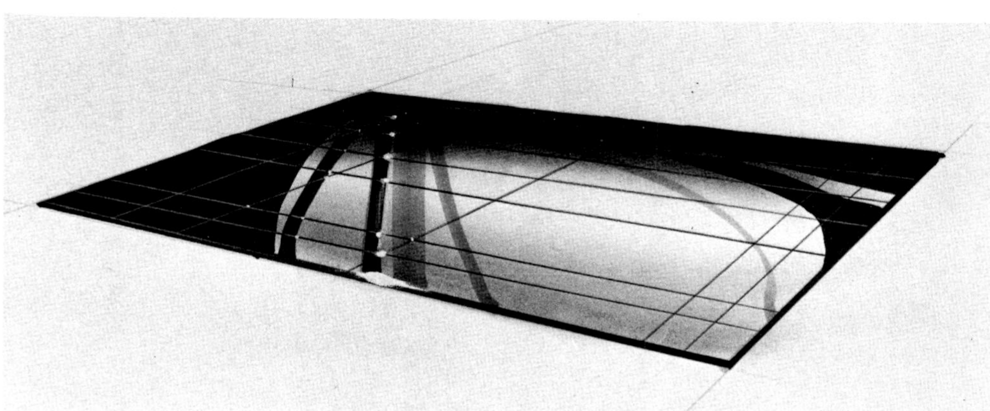

A lightly drawn analysis was done directly over the layout to clarify what the tonal values would be in the final rendering of this computer.

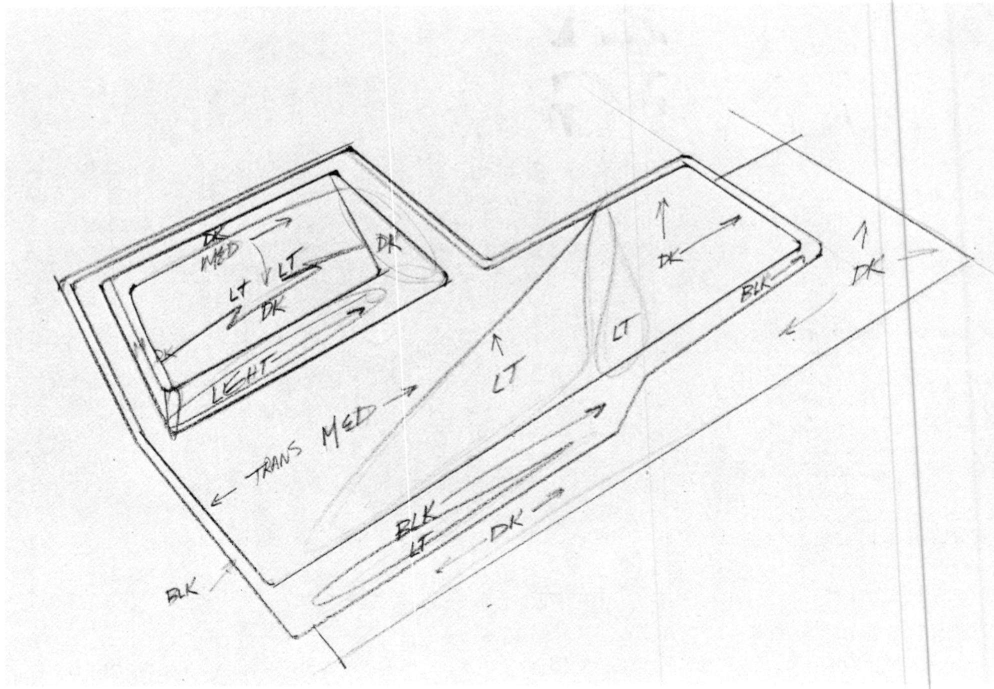

The final quick drawing only slightly develops the keys on the keyboard and just in an area where chalk is blended through. This effect helps create a focal area on the product. Seldom should you have to render all the busy details of keytops unless you are specifically doing it for interest or clarification.

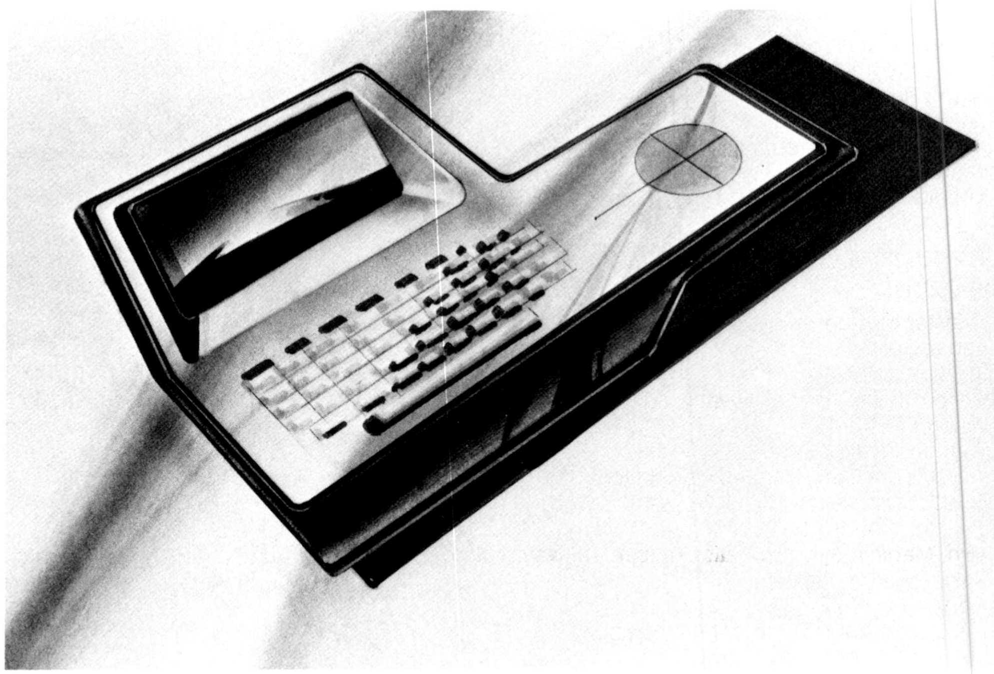

APPENDIX: SOURCE GUIDE

Papers

Copymate 9000 white reproduction paper (8½ × 11)
Western Paper Company
Kent, WA 98031

D'Arches watercolor paper
Seattle Art
Seattle, WA 98109

Clearprint No. 1000 HP-10 vellum
Clearprint Paper Company
Emeryville, CA

Ogilvie Press V-120 engineering sketch pad
Ogilvie Press
Buffalo, NY 14240
Clifton, NJ 07015

Letraset A2 marker pad
Letraset USA Inc.
Paramus, NJ 07652

Bienfang Designer Series marker pads
Hunt/Bienfang
Statesville, NC 28677

Strathmore Ultramarker paper (100% cotton)
Strathmore Paper Company
Westfield, MA 01085

Mediums

FloMaster inks and solvent
Faber-Castell
Newark, NJ 07107

Bestine rubber-cement solvent and thinner
Union Rubber Inc.
Trenton, NJ 08606

Luma Brilliant Concentrated watercolors
Seattle Art
Seattle, WA 98109

Dr. Ph. Martin's Synchromatic Transparent watercolors
Salis International
Hollywood, FL 33020

Prismacolor (Eagle) colored art pencils;
Eagle Verithin pencils
Berol Corporation
Danbury, CT 06810

Col-Erase pencils
Faber-Castell
Newark, NJ 07107

Grumbacher Golden Palette pastels
Grumbacher, Inc.
New York, NY 10001

NuPastel
Eberhard Faber Pen and Pencil Company
New York, NY 10003

Pantone broad-nib markers (warm gray #1 to #10)
Letraset USA Inc.
Paramus, NJ 07652

Design Art markers
Eberhard Faber Pen and Pencil Company
New York, NY 10003

Sharpie (series 3000) permanent fine-point black marker;
Sanford king-size black marker
Sanford, Inc.
Bellwood, IL 60104

Ultra Temp fluorescent poster paint
Palmer Paint Products, Inc.
Troy, MI 48084

Armak black photographic tape
Armak Corporation
Marysville, MI 48040

Software

Bill Budge's 3-D Graphic System
California Pacific Computer Company
Davis, CA 95616

James Hennessey's Industrial Design Drawing Programs
James Hennessey
Seattle, WA 98155

INDEX